ANGLO-NORMAN STUDIES

XVI

PROCEEDINGS OF THE BATTLE CONFERENCE

1993

Edited by Marjorie Chibnall

THE BOYDELL PRESS

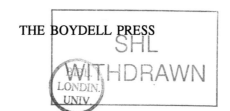

First published 1994
The Boydell Press, Woodbridge

ISBN 0 85115 366 6

ISSN 0954–9927
Anglo-Norman Studies
(Formerly ISSN 0261–9857: Proceedings of the Battle Conference
on Anglo-Norman Studies)

The Boydell Press is an imprint of Boydell & Brewer Ltd
PO Box 9, Woodbridge, Suffolk IP12 3DF, UK
and of Boydell & Brewer Inc.
PO Box 41026, Rochester, NY 14604–4126, USA

British Library Cataloguing-in-Publication Data
A catalogue record for this series is available
from the British Library

Library of Congress Catalog Card Number: 89–646512

This publication is printed on acid-free paper

Printed in Great Britain by
St Edmundsbury Press Ltd, Bury St Edmunds, Suffolk

CONTENTS

ILLUSTRATIONS

Changes in English chant repertories

Figures

Burhgeat and gonfanon

Figures

Judhael of Totnes

Maps

EDITOR'S PREFACE

This volume of *Anglo-Norman Studies* includes all the papers read at the sixteenth Battle Conference, held at Pyke House, Battle, in April 1993, and one paper from the 1992 Palermo Conference. There have been a number of changes since the last Conference held at Battle in 1991. The Education Committee of the East Sussex County Council, which has sponsored the Conference since its inception, generously helped in the establishment of the Allen Brown Memorial Trust as a Registered Charity in 1992; the Trust has now taken over responsibility for the running of the conferences. Happily these can still be held at Pyke House. This year we had finally to say good-bye to Mr Peter Birch, whose tireless care and planning has contributed so much to the success of past conferences. We wished him well in his retirement, and welcomed Mr Danny O'Sullivan MBS, who took up office as Centre Manager at Pyke House in February. With the support of the admirable staff at the Centre he saw that all ran smoothly, in spite of a strike by British Rail on the opening day.

The Outing, planned with the help of Mr Peter Birch, Mr Ian Peirce and Dr Lindy Grant, was to Colchester (where Mr Philip Crummy gave a guided tour of the castle) and to St Michael's and All Saints Church at Copford. Dr Richard Barber and the Directors of the Boydell Press celebrated the publication of the fifteenth volume of *Anglo-Norman Studies* by generously providing lunch for those attending the Conference; this was held at 'Olivers' near Colchester, by courtesy of Mr and Mrs D. Edwards. As always, the present volume owes a very great deal to the skill of Dr Barber and his staff at the Boydell Press.

Marjorie Chibnall
Clare Hall, Cambridge

ABBREVIATIONS

Antiqs Journ.	*The Antiquaries Journal* (Society of Antiquaries of London)
Arch. Journ.	*Archaeological Journal* (Royal Archaeological Institute)
ASC	*Anglo-Saxon Chronicle*, ed. D. Whitelock et al., London 1969
Battle Chronicle	*The Chronicle of Battle Abbey*, ed. Eleanor Searle, Oxford Medieval Texts, 1980
BIHR	*Bulletin of the Institute of Historical Research*
BL	British Library
BN	Bibliothèque Nationale
Cal. Docs France	*Calendar of Documents preserved in France . . .* i, 918–1216, ed. J.H. Round, HMSO, 1899
Carmen	*The Carmen de Hastingae Proelio of Guy bishop of Amiens*, ed. Catherine Morton and Hope Munz, Oxford Medieval Texts, 1972
De gestis pontificum	William of Malmesbury, *De gestis pontificum Anglorum*, ed. N.E.S.A. Hamilton, RS 1870
De gestis regum	William of Malmesbury, *De gestis regum Anglorum*, ed. W. Stubbs, RS 1887
Domesday Book	*Domesday Book, seu liber censualis . . .* , i, ii, ed. A. Farley, 2 vols, 'Record Commission', 1783; iii, iv, ed. H. Ellis, 1816
Dudo	*De moribus et actis primorum Normanniae Ducum auctore Dudone Sancti Quintini Decano*, ed. J. Lair, Société des Antiquaires de Normandie, 1865
Eadmer	*Historia novorum in Anglia*, ed. M. Rule, RS 1884
EHD	*English Historical Documents*, 2nd edn, i, ed. D. Whitelock, London 1979; ii, ed. D.C. Douglas, London 1981
EHR	*English Historical Review*
Fauroux	*Recueil des actes des ducs de Normandie (911–1066)*, ed. M. Fauroux, Mémoires de la Société des Antiquaires de Normandie xxxvi, 1961
GEC	*Complete Peerage of England, Scotland, Ireland, Great Britain and the United Kingdom*, 13 vols in 14, London 1910–59
Gesta Guillelmi	William of Poitiers, *Gesta Guillelmi . . .* , ed. R. Foreville, Paris 1952
Historia Novella	William of Malmesbury, *Historia Novella*, ed. K.R. Potter, Nelson's Medieval Texts, London 1955
HMSO	Her Majesty's Stationery Office, London
Huntingdon	Henry of Huntingdon, *Historia Anglorum*, ed. T. Arnold, RS 1879
Journ. BAA	*Journal of the British Archaeological Association*

Jumièges	William of Jumièges, *Gesta Normannorum Ducum*, ed. J. Marx, Société de l'histoire de Normandie, 1914
Lanfranc's Letters	*The Letters of Lanfranc Archbishop of Canterbury*, ed. H. Clover and M. Gibson, Oxford Medieval Texts, 1979
Med. Arch.	*Medieval Archaeology*
MGH SS	*Monumenta Germaniae Historica, Scriptores*
Monasticon	William Dugdale, *Monasticon Anglicanum*, ed. J. Caley, H. Ellis and B. Bandinel, 6 vols in 8, London 1817–30
ns	new series
Orderic	Ordericus Vitalis, *Historia Ecclesiastica*, ed. M. Chibnall, Oxford Medieval Texts, 1969–80
PRO	Public Record Office
Procs BA	*Proceedings of the British Academy*
Regesta	*Regesta Regum Anglo-Normannorum*, i, ed. H.W.C. Davis, Oxford 1913; ii, ed. C. Johnson, H.A. Cronne, Oxford 1956; iii, ed. H.A. Cronne, R.H.C. Davis, Oxford 1968
RS	Rolls Series, London
ser.	series
Trans.	Transactions
TRHS	*Transactions of the Royal Historical Society*
VCH	*Victoria County History*
Vita Eadwardi	*The Life of Edward the Confessor*, ed. F. Barlow, Oxford Medieval Texts, Oxford 1992
Wace	Wace, *Le Roman de Rou*, ed. A.J. Holden, 3 vols, Société des anciens textes français, Paris 1970–3
Worcester	Florence of Worcester, *Chronicon ex Chronicis*, ed. B. Thorpe, English Historical Society, London 1848–9

ST CUTHBERT, THE SCOTS AND THE NORMANS[1]

W.M. Aird

The Northumbrians presented the greatest challenge to the establishment of the Norman regime in the years following William I's victory over Harold. The revolt in the North of England 1068–1070 was accompanied by the arrival of a Danish expeditionary force. The fact that it provoked such a savage reaction from the Normans emphasised how serious they perceived the threat to be. The devastation of the region by William's troops did not end opposition to the Norman presence in the North. A decade later Bishop Walcher of Durham, who had also assumed responsibility for the governance of the earldom of Northumbria was murdered together with his household at Gateshead on the river Tyne.

The political situation throughout the eleventh century in Northumbria can best be described as volatile. This may be most readily demonstrated by examining the *Historia Regum Anglorum* which is one of the major sources for the North of England in the Anglo-Norman period. The *Historia Regum Anglorum* is a compilation from a number of sources and for the period between the tenth and the early twelfth centuries it relies heavily upon the *Chronicon ex Chronicis* of Florence of Worcester.[2] There are, however, occasional interpolations of original material relating specifically to Northumbria. The annal for 1072, for example, contains an account of the earls of Northumbria from the mid-tenth century until the reign of Henry I.[3]

The main feature of the account of the earls of Northumbria in the *Historia Regum Anglorum* is a series of murders committed by the descendants of earl Uchtred of Bamburgh and those of a certain Thurbrand Hold. The information concerning this feud is also to be found in a tract probably produced at Durham around the beginning of the twelfth century. The tract entitled *De obsessione*

[1] I would like to thank Dr Marjorie Chibnall for inviting me to present this paper to the Battle Conference. In preparing the article for publication I have benefited from the help and advice of Dr Ann Williams, Dr Chris Lewis, Dr David Dumville, Dr David Roffe and the other members of the Conference. My thanks are also due to Prof. Edmund King and my colleagues at Sheffield who were subjected to an earlier version of the paper. Research for the paper was undertaken with the support of the Department of History at the University of Sheffield.
[2] The *Historia Regum Anglorum* is contained in Corpus Christi College, Cambridge MS 139. The manuscript contains a number of items relating to the history of the North of England, M.R. James, *A Descriptive Catalogue of the Manuscripts of Corpus Christi College, Cambridge*, Cambridge 1912, 317–23. The most recent edition is that by T. Arnold, *Symeonis Monachi Opera Omnia*, RS 75, 2 vols 1882–85, vol. ii. The compilation of the *Historia Regum Anglorum* is discussed by P. Hunter Blair, 'Some Observations on the *Historia Regum* of Symeon of Durham', in ed. N.K. Chadwick, *Celt and Saxon: Studies in the Early British Border*, Cambridge 1963, 63–118, and by D. Baker, 'Scissors and Paste: Corpus Christi College Cambridge MS 139, Again', in ed. D. Baker, *Studies in Church History*, ii, 1975, 83–124.
[3] Symeon, *Opera*, ii, 195–200.

Dunelmi et de probitate Ucthredi comitis et de comitibus qui ei successerunt is to be found in Corpus Christi College, Cambridge MS 139, the manuscript which also contains the only copy of the *Historia Regum Anglorum* as well as other material relating to the North of England.[4] Despite its title the tract has little to do with a siege of Durham and concentrates instead on the descent of six estates of the Church of St Cuthbert which were given to earl Uchtred on the occasion of his marriage to Ecgfrida, daughter of Bishop Aldhun of Durham.[5]

The political turmoil described by the *Historia Regum Anglorum* and the *De Obsessione Dunelmi* continued throughout the eleventh century. The instability of the situation was exacerbated by the intervention of the Anglo-Saxon and Danish kings of England and by the periodic invasions of Northumbria by the kings of Scotland. In order to understand the severe problems which William I faced in his attempts to impose his authority on the North of England, it is necessary to examine the political turmoil which preceded the arrival of the Normans.

The term 'Northumbria' itself needs some clarification in this eleventh-century context. Bede was probably responsible for the introduction of this description of the region to the north of the River Humber.[6] Originally Northumbria was an amalgamation of the Anglian kingdoms of Bernicia and Deira together with some smaller Celtic areas which covered most of the North of England and southern Scotland.[7] The Scandinavian invasion and settlement in the period after 867 brought about the desuetude of the term until its revival in the eleventh century by which time Northumbria had acquired dual connotations. In its broad sense it could still refer to a region which stretched from the Humber to the Tweed. The author of the *Historia Regum Anglorum*, for example, noted that 'earl Siward held the earldom of the whole province of the Northumbrians, that is from the Humber to the Tweed'.[8] This acknowledged that the northern part of Bernicia, Lothian, had been lost to the Scots. Later in the same passage the author states that during earl Morkar's period of office, *comitatum ultra Tynam tradidit Osulfo*.[9]. In this, its restricted and, indeed, more usual eleventh-century sense the earldom of North-umbria referred to the area lying to the north of the river Tyne and south of the Tweed. This distinction has its origins in the ancient division between Bernicia and Deira which had been reinforced by the Scandinavian settlement.[10]

The boundary between the Bernicians and the Deirans had been the river Tees. This also marked the limit of the most intensive Scandinavian settlement of the

---

[4] CCCC MS 139, ff. 52r–53v.

[5] The *De obsessione Dunelmi* is translated and discussed at length by C.J. Morris, *Marriage and Murder in eleventh-century Northumbria: a study of 'De Obsessione Dunelmi'*, University of York, Borthwick Institute of Historical Research, Borthwick Paper No. 82, 1992.

[6] Bede experimented with *transhumbrana regio* and *ultrahumbrenses* before deciding upon the less ambiguous *gens Nordanhymbrorum, hoc est ea natio Anglorum quae ad aquilonalem Humbre fluminis plagam habitabat*, *Bede's Ecclesiastical History of the English People*, eds B. Colgrave and R.A.B. Mynors, Oxford 1969, ii, 9, 162.

[7] N.J. Higham, *The Kingdom of Northumbria, AD 350–1100*, Stroud 1993 and B. Yorke, *Kings and Kingdoms in Early Anglo-Saxon England*, 1990, 72–99.

[8] . . . *tocius provincie northanthymbrorum id est ab humbra usque tueda . . .*, Symeon, *Opera*, ii, 198.

[9] Symeon, *Opera*, ii, 198.

[10] P.H. Blair, 'The Boundary between Bernicia and Deira', in *Archaeologia Aeliana*, 4th ser., xxvii, 46–59, reprinted in P.H. Blair, *Anglo-Saxon Northumbria*, Variorum Reprints, 1984.

ninth and tenth centuries.[11] The land between the Tees and the Tyne was granted at the end of the ninth century to the Church of Lindisfarne and formed the heart of the Patrimony of St Cuthbert. Thus, a privileged ecclesiastical franchise was inserted between the Scandinavian kingdom of York and the remnants of Anglian Bernicia which was ruled from the ancient fortress of Bamburgh.[12]

The collapse of Anglian Northumbria drew the attention and fuelled the political ambitions of two emerging kingdoms in the tenth century. The successors of Alfred of Wessex attempted to impose their authority in the North of England and both Athelstan and Edmund are recorded as having made visits to the shrine of St Cuthbert at Chester-le-Street.[13] It is doubtful, however, whether their lordship was as complete as the propaganda of the *Anglo-Saxon Chronicle* suggests. At the same period the kings of Scots were consolidating their power at the expense of the Picts and the Strathclyde Britons. The Scots moved south into Cumbria and by 973 at the latest had detached Lothian and the Merse from Bernicia.[14] Constant Scottish pressure on the North of England during the tenth and eleventh centuries suggests that their long-term aim was to reunite the ancient province of Bernicia and carry Scottish overlordship to the Tyne.[15]

Within Northumbria itself the Anglian and Scandinavian rivalry was open to exploitation by external powers. During the eleventh century Northumbrian politics, that is those of the region between the Humber and the Tweed, were determined largely by ethnic considerations. The Anglians of Bernicia were the natural allies of the West Saxons in their opposition to the Danish kings and their Scandinavian supporters in Yorkshire. Conversely, during the Danish ascendancy, power in the North of England centred on York and the Bernicians of Bamburgh were isolated.[16]

The murders of members of the families of Uchtred of Bamburgh and

---

[11] C.D. Morris, 'Northumbria and the Viking Settlement: the Evidence for Landholding', *Archaeologia Aeliana*, 5th ser., v, 1977, 81–104 and 'Aspects of the Scandinavian Settlement in Northern England: A Review', *Northern History*, xx, 1984, 1–22.

[12] The development of the Patrimony is traced by H.H.E. Craster, 'The Patrimony of St Cuthbert', *EHR*, lxix, 1954, 177–99. See also W.M. Aird, 'The Origins and Development of the Church of St Cuthbert, 635–1153, with special reference to Durham in the period circa 1071–1153', Unpublished Ph.D. thesis, University of Edinburgh, 1991, 24–77.

[13] *Historia de Sancto Cuthberto*, in Symeon, *Opera*, i, 196–214 at 211 [Athelstan] and 212, [Edmund]. For a discussion of the West Saxon patronage of the Church of St Cuthbert, see D. Rollason, 'St Cuthbert and Wessex: the evidence of Cambridge, Corpus Christi College MS 183', in eds G. Bonner, D.W. Rollason, C. Stancliffe, *St Cuthbert, His Cult and Community to AD 1200*, 1989, 413–24 and Luisella Simpson, 'The King Alfred/St Cuthbert episode in the Historia de Sancto Cuthberto', in Bonner, *St Cuthbert*, 397–412.

[14] On the expansion of Scotland, see A.P. Smyth, *Warlords and Holy Men, Scotland AD 80–1000*, Edinburgh 1984, 215–238. There has been much debate over the date of the cession of Lothian, see, for example, B. Meehan, 'The Siege of Durham, the Battle of Carham and the Cession of Lothian', *Scottish History Review*, lv, 1976, 1–19, M.O. Anderson, 'Lothian and the Early Scottish Kings', *Scot. Hist. Rev.*, xxxxix, 1960, 98–112, A.A.M. Duncan, 'The Battle of Carham, 1018', *Scot. Hist. Rev.*, lv, 1976, 20–8 and Smyth, *Warlords*, 232–234.

[15] During the first half of the eleventh century both Malcolm II (in 1006) and his grandson, Duncan I (1039–40) attacked Northumbria, penetrating, in both cases, as far as Durham.

[16] There is evidence to suggest that, at the beginning of the tenth century the Scots and Bernicians were in alliance against the Scandinavians. For example, in 914 and 918 Constantine II of Scotland supported the earls of Bamburgh against Ragnall, king of York; see Smyth, *Warlords*, 229.

Thurbrand Hold have a significant political dimension. They represent a continuing struggle for power in Northumbria. Uchtred's alliance with Æthelred II brought him the earldom of all Northumbria until his murder at Cnut's court.[17] Thereafter the comital house of Bamburgh was restricted to the area to the north of the Tyne. Cnut's appointment of Siward to the earldom of the whole province of the Northumbrians marked a concerted attempt to give the title some practical force. Siward's origins are obscure but he was almost certainly of Scandinavian descent and thus acceptable to the nobility of Yorkshire.[18] His marriage to Aefflaeda, one of earl Uchtred of Bamburgh's grand-daughters probably ensured his acceptance north of the Tyne. His success against the Scots would have done nothing to diminish his standing.[19]

Siward's death in 1055 enabled the House of Godwin to have Tostig installed as earl. The appointment of Tostig and his unpopular regime provoked a violent reaction from both ethnic groupings in Northumbria. Tostig had no natural allies in the North of England but managed to maintain his position there for a decade. There is little evidence as to the nature of his rule and the few notices of his activities suggest that he was intent on maintaining order.[20] His benefactions to the Church of St Cuthbert won him the approbation of the Community and his gifts were well remembered in the early twelfth century.[21] His expulsion from the earldom in 1065 provides a violent prelude to Duke William's attempts to seize the English throne.

The main sources for the history of the North of England in the last decades of the eleventh century were generated by the Community of the Church of St Cuthbert at Durham. The two most substantial works are the *Historia Regum Anglorum*, of which mention has been made, and the *Libellus de exordio atque procursu istius hoc est Dunelmensis ecclesiae*.[22] The latter is a piece of tendentious propaganda probably the work of the Durham monk Symeon who was writing in the first decade of the twelfth century. Information on Symeon himself

---

[17] In 1016 Uchtred and forty of his men were killed at Cnut's order, probably because of the earl's support for Æthelred II and his son Edmund, see *De Obsessione*, in Symeon, *Opera*, i, 218. For these problems with the date of the death of earl Uchtred, see Morris, *Marriage and Murder*, 11.

[18] *A Biographical Dictionary of Dark Age Britain*, eds Ann Williams, A.P. Smyth, D.P. Kirby, sv 'Siward Digera'.

[19] Earl Uchtred's son Ealdred rather unhelpfully named three of his five daughters, Aefflaeda, *De Obsessione*, in Symeon, *Opera*, i, 219. For a discussion of earl Siward's relations with Scotland see W.E. Kapelle, *The Norman Conquest of the North: the region and its transformation, 1000–1135*, London, 1979, 27–49.

[20] Tostig's career as earl of Northumbria is dealt with by Kapelle, *Norman Conquest of the North*, 86–106. A miracle story dating from the late eleventh century records Tostig's capture of a certain outlaw, Aldan-Hamal. The outlaw was imprisoned in Durham but on appealing to St Cuthbert for help his fetters fell away and he managed to gain sanctuary at the church. When Barcwith, one of Tostig's men attempted to enter the church in order to arrest Aldan-Hamal, he was struck down by the saint. *Liber de translationibus et miraculis sancti Cuthberti*, in Symeon, *Opera*, i, 243–5; see B. Colgrave, 'The Post-Bedan Miracles and Translations of St Cuthbert', in eds C. Fox, B. Dickins, *The Early Cultures of North-West Europe: H.M. Chadwick Memorial Studies*), Cambridge 1950, 307–332, at 312, and W.M. Aird, 'The Making of a Medieval Miracle Collection: the Liber de Translationibus et Miraculis Sancti Cuthberti', *Northern History*, xxviii, 1992, 1–24.

[21] Symeon, *Libellus*, in *Opera*, i, 94–95 where Symeon describes a richly decorated crucifix given to the Church of St Cuthbert by Tostig and his wife.

[22] Printed in Symeon, *Opera*, i. The text is sometimes known as the *Historia Dunelmensis Ecclesiae*. An new edition of the Libellus, prepared by Dr David Rollason is forthcoming.

is slight but it suggests that he was the precentor of the Church and an acknowledged expert on the cult of St Cuthbert.[23] Symeon's purpose in writing was twofold. First, he was determined to justify the changes made at Durham in 1083, when the *Congregatio sancti Cuthberti*, an awkwardly constituted body of married priests and monks living according to a monastic rule, was replaced by a Convent of Benedictines. The main purpose of Symeon's work, however, was to reproach Bishop Ranulf Flambard and remind him how the successor to the saintly Bishop-Abbot of Lindisfarne should behave towards his monastic cathedral chapter. Flambard's pontificate (1099–1128), saw a concerted attack on the privileges and property of the monks and Symeon's work may have been part of a propaganda war with the bishop.[24]

Fortunately many of the materials upon which Symeon drew for his *Libellus* are extant and provide a means of verifying Symeon's assertions. The *Historia de Sancto Cuthberto* compiled in the tenth century with some eleventh-century additions is a hybrid source combining miracle accounts and other historical material with a detailed record of the development of the Patrimony of St Cuthbert.[25] The *Chronica monasterii Dunelmensis* composed by a member of the *Congregatio sancti Cuthberti* between 1072 and 1083 and reconstructed by Edmund Craster provides valuable information on the pre-Benedictine Community's relations with the Anglo-Saxon, Danish and Norman kings.[26] There is also a fair amount of historical material interpolated amongst the columns of names in the Durham *Liber Vitae*.[27] Finally, there are shorter pieces such as the *De Obsessione Dunelmi* mentioned above, the *De iniusta vexatione Willelmi episcopi primi*, a tract dealing with the arraignment of Bishop William of Saint-Calais before the king's court in 1088, and the *Liber de translationibus et miraculis sancti Cuthberti*, a collection of the posthumous miracles of St Cuthbert which contains much incidental historical information.[28]

The Durham historical tradition allows us to examine the role of the Church of St Cuthbert in the volatile political events of the last decades of the eleventh century. For the Community at Durham, as for many Anglo-Saxon religious corporations, the period of the Norman conquest was one of great uncertainty.[29]

---

[23] B. Meehan, 'A Reconsideration of the Works Associated with Symeon of Durham', Unpublished Ph.D. thesis, University of Edinburgh 1980. D. Rollason, 'Symeon of Durham and the Community of Durham in the Eleventh Century', in ed. Carola Hicks, *England in the Eleventh Century, Harlaxton Medieval Studies,* II, Stamford 1992, 183–198. The evidence for Symeon's role as local historian and expert on the miraculous comes from H. Farmer, 'The Vision of Orm', *Analecta Bollandiana,* lxxv, 1957, 72–82.

[24] At the end of his life Bishop Ranulf made restitution to the Convent of Durham of some of the property which he had appropriated, see H.S. Offler, *Durham Episcopal Charters, 1071–1152,* Surtees Society, vol. 179, 1968, nos. 24, 25.

[25] Printed Symeon, *Opera,* i, 196–214. And see above, note 12.

[26] H.H.E. Craster, 'The Red Book of Durham', *EHR,* xl, 1925, 504–532.

[27] *Liber Vitae Dunelmensis,* ed. J. Stevenson, Surtees Society, vol. 13, 1841; vol. 128, ed. A. Hamilton Thompson [collotype facsimile]. H.H.E. Craster, 'Some Anglo-Saxon Records of the See of Durham', *Archaeologia Aeliana,* 4th ser., i, 1925, 189–198.

[28] *De iniusta vexatione . . .,* printed in Symeon, *Opera,* i, 17095; and see H.S. Offler, 'The Tractate *De Iniusta Vexatione Willelmi Episcopi Primi*', *EHR,* lxvi, 1951, 32–41 where the tract is assigned to the first quarter of the twelfth century. For the *Liber de translationibus et miraculis sancti Cuthberti* see, Symeon, *Opera,* i, 229–61; ii, 333–62 and note 20 above.

[29] A. Gransden, 'Traditionalism and Continuity during the Last Century of Anglo-Saxon

Yet since its foundation on Lindisfarne in 635 the Church of St Cuthbert had a good track record of surviving the successive political crises which had beset Northumbria. Alone of all the great religious houses of Northumbria, the Church of St Cuthbert had survived. What is more it had managed to build up and retain an extensive agglomeration of landed estates which were the source of considerable wealth and political influence. The Church had relocated several times and had been established at Durham for just seventy years at the time of the Norman Conquest.[30] What role did this powerful institution play in the Northumbrian resistance to the Normans?

The most recent assessment of the progress of the Norman conquest of Northumbria suggests that the Church of St Cuthbert and the *Haliwerfolc*, the inhabitants of the Patrimony, played a key role in the native resistance to William I.[31] The Church of Durham appears as a northern counterpart of the Church of St Etheldreda at Ely. In espousing the cause of the Northumbrians of Bamburgh, the Community of St Cuthbert shared in suffering the consequences of the failure of the rebellion. At first sight the evidence does seem to suggest that the Church of St Cuthbert did play a major part in the opposition to the Norman kings and their representatives in the North of England. There are a number of incidents which have been used as evidence to connect the members of the *Congregatio sancti Cuthberti* with rebellion in the North of England. It is proposed to examine each of these in turn in order to form some opinion of the Community's attitude to royal authority.

The revolt against Tostig in 1065 has been seen as setting the pattern for the Northumbrian resistance to the Normans. It is argued that the leaders of the Church of St Cuthbert sponsored the resistance to Tostig and their actions provided a specific incitement to revolt. In 1069, William I despatched Robert Cumin to assume control of the earldom of Northumbria. However, he and his seven hundred troops were massacred at Durham before they could assume control of the area to the north of the Tyne. Ten years later Bishop Walcher of Durham, who was exercising comital authority after the execution of earl Waltheof, was murdered at Gateshead on the Tyne. An attempt was made in the early twelfth century to suggest that the members of the *Congregatio sancti Cuthberti* had a part in the killing of Bishop Walcher and that this was reason enough for expelling them from Durham in 1083.[32] The case against the Community of St Cuthbert seems compelling, but on closer examination the sources reveal that the reaction of the

---

Monasticism', *Journ. of Ecclesiastical History*, 40, 1989, 159–207, reprinted in *Legends, Traditions and History in Medieval England*, London 1992, 31–79.

[30] The Community of St Cuthbert left Lindisfarne in 875, and, according to Symeon, 'wandered' about Northumbria until 883 when they settled at Chester-le-Street. In 995 the Church of St Cuthbert was relocated to Durham.

[31] Kapelle, *Norman Conquest of the North. Haliwerfolc*, 'the people of the holy man' was the name given to the people who lived on the estates belonging to St Cuthbert and, by association, it came to refer to the land itself.

[32] A forged papal bull of Gregory VII dated 6 January 1083 contains a phrase which suggests that there were political motives behind the expulsion of the members of the *Congregatio*. The bull mentions that the murderers of Bishop Walcher had been punished and then goes on, *verum etiam Dunelmensis clericos maleactionales quosdam etiam eorum tam execrabili sacrilegiorum prosapia oriundos propter vitam suam incorrigibilem auctoritate apostolica inde penitus eliminari*, W. Holtzmann, *Papsturkunden in England*, ii, 2, 132–136 at 134. On the authenticity of this bull see the comments of H.S. Offler 'William of Saint-Calais, First Norman Bishop of Durham', *Trans. of*

Congregatio to Norman authority was less dramatic. Rather than confrontation they sought accommodation and in so doing followed a policy which had served them well throughout their history.

Dr Kapelle has argued that the revolt against Tostig was the result of his harsh regime in Northumbria.[33] The northern historical tradition as represented by the *Historia Regum Anglorum* associates the revolt against Tostig with the murders of three Northumbrian thegns, Gospatric, Gamel, the son of Orm and Ulf, the son of Dolfin.[34] The *Historia Regum Anglorum* adds that the rebellion was also '. . . on account of the huge tribute which he unjustly took from the whole of Northumbria'. The centre of Tostig's power was York where he maintained a substantial force of Danish housecarls and lodged his treasure, consequently the leaders of the rebellion attacked York in early October 1065. Tostig was driven from the earldom and the rebels pushed south to Northampton where they were met by Tostig's brother, earl Harold. Attempts to reconcile Tostig with the Northumbrians at Northampton and later, at Oxford, failed and Tostig was outlawed, together with 'all those who had helped him to establish an unjust law'.[35]

The expulsion of Tostig united the two political factions of Northumbria, the earls of Bamburgh and the nobility of Yorkshire. Kapelle has suggested that what drove these rivals into temporary alliance was an attempt by Tostig to impose a tribute upon the normally fiscally privileged Northumbrians. Tostig's failure to defend the North against attacks by Malcolm III added to Northumbrian grievances. At Durham too, so Kapelle argues, factions developed within the Church of St Cuthbert, centred upon the Bishop, Aethelwin, and the sacrist, Elfred Westou.[36] Aethelwin had come to Durham in the 1020s together with his brother, Aethelric as an adviser to Bishop Edmund. The brothers had come from Peterborough and were seconded to Durham in order to instruct Edmund in monastic observances. They acted as his deputies and eventually Aethelric succeeded Edmund in the episcopal chair.[37] The fact that these monks were recruited from Peterborough to instruct Edmund in the monastic office contradicts Symeon's assertion that from the Community's departure from Lindisfarne in 875 until the introduction of the Benedictine Rule in 1083, there were no monks serving the shrine of St Cuthbert.

The faction at Durham led by Elfred Westou resented the imposition of outsiders and expelled Aethelric in 1045 or 1046. However, the bishop was re-instated by earl Siward and continued to hold the episcopal chair until 1056, the year after Siward's death.[38] Aethelwin succeeded his brother which is a fact

the *Archaeological and Architectural Society of Durham and Northumberland*, x, 1950, 267, n. 29 and 269, n. 36.

[33] Kapelle, 94–99.

[34] Symeon, *Opera*, ii, 178. These individuals are identified as representatives of Tostig's political rivals in Northumbria, Kapelle, 94–95.

[35] *ASC*, CDE, sa 1065. See F. Barlow, *Edward the Confessor*, London 1970, 236–239.

[36] Kapelle, 98.

[37] Symeon, *Opera*, i, 85–87. Symeon, who for the most part is antipathetic towards Aethelric and Aethelwin admits that, Aethelric was skilled in ecclesiastical matters and the monastic office. Symeon, *Opera*, i, 86, [Eadmund] . . . *ab abbate accepit quendam monachum in ecclesiasticis officiis simul et regularis disciplinae observantia excellenter institutum.*

[38] Symeon of Durham accuses Aethelric of plundering the Church of St Cuthbert whereas the author of the *Historia Regum Anglorum* simply says that the bishop retired to Peterborough . . . *ubi nutritus et monachus est factus.* The *Chronica Monasterii Dunelmensis* noted that Aethelric left Durham because he felt that he could not defend the liberty of the church from the *malignorum*

difficult to explain if opposition to the outsiders was as vehement as is suggested. Symeon's view of Aethelwin and Aethelric seems to be at odds with other sources in the Durham historical tradition. This should make us immediately suspicious. Symeon accuses both brothers of absconding with part of the treasure of St Cuthbert. Athelric appropriated valuables discovered at Chester-le-Street during some preparatory excavations for the building of a stone church there.[39] Aethelwin, too, is accused of denuding the Church of St Cuthbert of precious ornaments. According to Symeon's account, Aethelwin denied the charge even after he had been imprisoned at Abingdon. One day, while he was washing his hands an armlet slipped into view and proclaimed his guilt.[40]

In the other sources Aethelric and Aethelwin are portrayed as diligent guardians of the Church of St Cuthbert. Symeon himself shows inconsistency when dealing with the brothers and admits that Aethelwin led the Community to safety after the murder of Robert Cumin in 1069. Of Aethelric's departure from Durham the *Historia Regum Anglorum* states merely that the bishop 'retired to his monastery called Peterborough where he was educated and made a monk and passed twelve years there'. There is no hint of improper behaviour.[41] Symeon's charges against the bishops were probably part of the propaganda war against Ranulf Flambard who busied himself appropriating monastic property in the early twelfth century.

The elevation of St Oswin's relics from their resting place at Tynemouth in 1065, has a special significance for Kapelle in his account of the revolt against Tostig.[42] St Oswin (died 651) was a martyred king of Deira.[43] Elfred Westou's display of Oswin's relics so soon after the death of the Northumbrian noble Cospatric was, it has been argued, 'clearly an attempt by the clerks to incite their flock to revolt'. Cospatric's martyrdom was to be avenged and his murderer expelled.[44]

The elevation of St Oswin's relics probably had little effect on the rebels of 1065. It is very much to be doubted whether the bishop and Community had any wish to incite revolt amongst their flock. Elfred Westou was known to Durham historical tradition as an assiduous relic gatherer. It is difficult to justify this activity as an attempt by the Church of Durham to make up for a lack of relics when the incorrupt body of the greatest saint of Northern England rested at Durham.[45] Elfred's relic gathering probably had a more prosaic purpose to do with advancing the Church of St Cuthbert's claims to the estates of defunct Northumbrian religious houses. When Cuthbert's coffin was opened during the translation of his body from the Anglo-Saxon minster to the Norman cathedral in 1104, it was found to contain not only his incorrupt body, but also a host of other relics

hominum violencia. It is not clear who these enemies of the Church of Durham were, but it seems unlikely that they were members of the Church itself. Symeon, *Opera*, i, 92; ii, 173; Craster, 'Red Book', 528.

[39] Symeon, *Opera*, i, 92.

[40] Symeon, *Opera*, i, 105.

[41] Symeon, *Opera*, ii, 173.

[42] Kapelle, 98.

[43] Williams et al., *Biographical Dictionary*, sv 'Oswine'.

[44] Kapelle, 98.

[45] Kapelle, 98, suggests that the Community of St Cuthbert had to endure abuse from their sophisticated southern bishops concerning the lack of relics in Durham.

including those of Baldred of Tyningham, Aebba of Coldingham and Bede of Jarrow. In these relics the Community of St Cuthbert possessed the title deeds to the estates of these monasteries.[46] St Oswin's association with Tynemouth is important for at the end of the eleventh century the estate there was granted to the monastery of St Albans.[47] The dispute between Durham and St Albans over the ownership of the site continued well into the twelfth century. Thus the elevation of the relics of St Oswin has more to do with the later dispute with the monks of St Albans than with the revolt against Tostig in 1065.

The record of Tostig's benefactions to Durham casts further doubt on the assertion that the Church of St Cuthbert fomented rebellion in 1065. Both Tostig and his lieutenant, Copsig, were remembered as making generous donations to St Cuthbert.[48] Among the gifts which Tostig and his wife presented to the Church of St Cuthbert was a large crucifix adorned with gold, silver and precious stones.[49] Tostig's wife, the Countess Judith, was particularly devoted to the saint and attempted to test his ban on women entering his church. She sent a maid-servant into the church precincts but as soon as she entered she was struck down. The misogyny of St Cuthbert was a later invention of the monks, but it is nevertheless revealing that Tostig's wife should be singled out for her devotion to the saint.[50] The historical tradition preserved at Durham concerning Tostig's treatment of the Church of St Cuthbert seems to argue against the Community's involvement in the rebellion of 1065.

Tostig's replacement was Morkar, brother of the earl of Mercia. Once again the earl's authority seems to have been confined to Yorkshire as the *Historia Regum Anglorum* notes that '. . . Morkar, being burdened with other weighty matters, handed over the earldom beyond the Tyne to the young Osulf, son of the aforementioned earl Eadulf'.[51] Morkar's appointment has been interpreted as a signal that the Northumbrians realised that their best interests were served by uniting with the rest of the Anglo-Saxon polity.[52] As an outsider with no particular allegiances in the North, Morkar would maintain the unity of Northumbria as a whole and commit it to the national interest. Morkar's appointment of Osulf, a representative of the House of Bamburgh effectively granted the Northumbrians living to the north of the Tyne self-determination. It is misleading to attribute nationalist sentiment to the inhabitants of a region which was, at most, a distant province of the Anglo-Saxon kingdom where royal authority was intermittent and probably ineffective.

William I has been criticised for his ill-judged policy towards the Northumbrians.

[46] For a discussion of the proprietorial nature of Elfred Westou's relic gathering see, D. Rollason, 'Undying Landlords', in *Saints and Relics in Anglo-Saxon England*, Oxford 1989, 196–214.

[47] For the grant of Tynemouth to St Albans, see Offler, *Durham Episcopal Charters*, 5–6.

[48] For Tostig's donations see Symeon, *Opera*, i, 94. Copsig granted St Cuthbert the church of St Germanus at Marske in Cleveland and recorded the gift by presenting a silver chalice to the saint, *In cuius donationis signum etiam scyptum argentem obtulit, qui in hac ecclesia servatus aeternam illius facti retinet memoriam*, Symeon, *Opera*, i, 97.

[49] Symeon, *Opera*, i, 95, 101.

[50] Symeon, *Opera*, i, 94–5. Victoria Tudor, 'The Misogyny of St Cuthbert', *Archaeologia Aeliana*, 5th ser., xii, 1984, 157–67.

[51] *Morkarus vero, quoniam alias gravibus negotiis impeditus fueret comitatum ultra Tynam tradidit Osulfo adolescenti filio praefati comitis Eadulfi*, Symeon, *Opera*, ii, 198.

[52] B. Wilkinson, 'Northumbrian Separatism in 1065–66', *Bulletin of the John Rylands Library*, 23, 1939, 504–26.

Kapelle, for example, stated that 'A close study of the northern resistance to William the Conqueror inevitably discloses that he made at least two blunders in dealing with the North and that he rescued himself from the results of these mistakes by committing genocide'.[53] Symeon remarked that *Willelmus autem regnum adeptus Anglorum populos Northanhymbrorum diu rebelles sustinuit.*[54] This may refer to the fact that, until January 1069, the Norman king allowed Northumbrian nobles to retain control of the earldom. It is likely, however, that the earldom of Northumbria in this case was the restricted area to the north of the Tyne. Morkar had capitulated to William before the latter's departure for Normandy at the beginning of 1067 and the earldom was committed to Copsig who had served in Northumbria under Tostig. The *Historia Regum Anglorum* noted that Copsig drove Osulf from the earldom which strongly suggests that he had been given control of the region controlled by the House of Bamburgh.[55] This may indicate that, whilst William I considered Yorkshire an integral part of his newly acquired *regnum* and to be divided up among his followers, his authority in the lands beyond the Tees was more tenuous and could only be exercised through the agency of native officials. If this is the case it is understandable that he should appoint Copsig to the post as someone who had already had experience of government in the North.

Copsig's period as earl lasted barely five weeks before he was assassinated by Osulf at Newburn-on-Tyne.[56] Walbottle close by was an ancient Bernician royal residence and suggests that Copsig had, indeed, ousted Osulf from his position north of the Tyne. At the end of 1067 Osulf met his death while attempting to apprehend an outlaw. His demise offered the opportunity for another member of the House of Bamburgh to assume control north of the Tyne. Cospatric was a grandson of earl Uchtred and offered to purchase the earldom from the king. The fact that William sold the earldom to Cospatric suggests that he did not expect to derive any other revenue from the province. The transaction may also say something about William's attitude to the province. There is no suggestion that Cospatric was to hold Northumbria by any recognised tenure. Whatever the nature of Cospatric's ties to William I, the earl's participation in the first of the northern revolts in 1068 and his subsequent retreat to Scotland in the summer of that year seems to have prompted William I into changing his policy towards the Northumbrians.

In January 1069, William I sent earl Robert Cumin to the Northumbrians on the north side of the Tyne.[57] The seven hundred troops who accompanied the earl seem to have been mercenaries as Symeon noted that Robert paid his men by licensing their plundering.[58] William I may have considered that unleashing a mercenary band on the troublesome outlying province was as effective a means of exercising his claims to lordship as any. The Norman troops got no further than

[53] Kapelle, 3.
[54] Symeon, *Opera*, i, 98.
[55] Symeon, *Opera*, ii, 198.
[56] See F.S. Scott, 'Earl Waltheof of Northumbria', *Archaeologia Aeliana*, 4th ser., xxx, 1952, 172. I am grateful to Professor Geoffrey Barrow for the reference to Walbottle.
[57] *Misit rex Willelmus Northymbris ad aquilonalem plagam Tine comitem Rodbertum cognomento Cumin tertio regni sui anno*, Symeon, *Opera*, ii, 186–187.
[58] Symeon, *Opera*, i, 99.

Durham as they were massacred in the town by the Northumbrians. The flight of the Community of St Cuthbert in the aftermath of this attack has been seen as a sign of collusion in the slaughter. Once more, however, a close reading of the sources suggests that the leaders of the Church of Durham were following a very different strategy in their dealings with the Normans.

At the approach of the Norman force the Northumbrians, and this must mean those living to the north of the Tyne, determined to oppose earl Robert or die in the attempt. Bishop Aethelwin discovered the plot and met the Normans as they approached Durham, informing them of the intended ambush.[59] Bishop Aethelwin had already submitted to William I and undertaken a mission to Malcolm III of Scotland on his behalf so it does not seem unlikely that he would attempt to warn earl Robert of the danger.[60] Details of the account of the massacre reinforce the idea that the Normans were killed by the Northumbrians rather than by the townspeople of Durham. Earl Robert and his men entered the town and were housed in the episcopal palace near the western tower of the cathedral church.[61] During the night of the 27/28 January 1069, the Northumbrians marched to Durham and at dawn burst through the gates and set about the slaughter of the French troops. Earl Robert was trapped in the bishop's house which was burnt down. All but one of his men perished.[62]

The two main sources for the incident, the *Historia Regum Anglorum* and Symeon's *Libellus* agree on the main details. Earl Robert was appointed to govern the inhabitants of the region to the north of the Tyne. The insurgents were from outside Durham. The fact that they marched all night to the town suggests strongly that they had indeed come from beyond the Tyne. Symeon, as is his wont, embroiders his account adding notices of two miracles performed by St Cuthbert on behalf of the *Haliwerfolc*, nevertheless, his account substantially accords with that of the *Historia Regum Anglorum*.[63] It seems likely that Bishop Aethelwin and the members of the Community of St Cuthbert were not participants in the slaughter of earl Robert and his men. There remains, however, the possibility that these sources, both compiled in the twelfth century were seeking to obscure the Church of St Cuthbert's role in these events. Symeon, for example, omits the fact that the house where earl Robert and his men met their deaths was the episcopal palace. This omission is unlikely to have been significant as a far more effective way of exonerating the bishop and Community would have been completely to ignore the episode. If Symeon had wanted to blacken the name of Bishop Aethelwin there would have been no better occasion than this. The hated bishop could have been charged with betraying the earl to his death and bringing destruction and ruin upon the Church in the aftermath. Symeon's account of the incident and its results are, however, very different.

[59] Symeon, *Opera*, i, 99; ii, 187.

[60] Orderic, ii, 218, 219.

[61] The location of the episcopal residence is given by Symeon when he states that the building when set ablaze was close enough to the Church for sparks to threaten to ignite its western tower, *Opera*, i, 99.

[62] Symeon, *Opera*, i, 99–100; ii, 187.

[63] Symeon noted that when the fire threatened to engulf the Church the *Haliwerfolc* prayed to St Cuthbert who conjured up a miraculous east wind which blew back the flames. Later, another metereological miracle created a black mist which persuaded the punitive force sent north by William I to avenge earl Robert's death to turn back at Northallerton, Symeon, *Opera*, i, 99–100.

The murder of Robert Cumin at Durham has been seen as the spark igniting the great rebellion in the North of England of 1069–70, and provoking the savage reprisal by William I. The abandonment of Durham in the aftermath of the murders also seems to indicate that the *Congregatio sancti Cuthberti* feared for their safety following their part in the massacre. The chronology of the revolt of 1069 given in the *Historia Regum Anglorum* suggests that the rebels did not begin their campaign until September. If the murder of earl Robert at Durham was indeed the spark which fired the revolt, the Northumbrians must have been on a very slow-burning fuse. The attack on Durham in mid-winter has all the appearance of an act of desperation, hastily planned and not part of some co-ordinated general uprising. The flight from Durham took place in the aftermath of the failure of the later revolt of September 1069 and did not immediately follow the death of Robert Cumin.

The details of the evacuation of Durham are given, once again, in the *Historia Regum Anglorum* and the *Libellus* of Symeon.[64] Symeon's account is embellished with another miracle story which suggests that earl Cospatric not only persuaded the Community to fly from Durham, but also plundered the town himself. After the failure of the rebellion Cospatric and Waltheof, who was to succeed his kinsman to the earldom, late in 1069, surrendered to William I at a meeting on the Tees, the acknowledged border of the land of the *Haliwerfolc* and England.[65] On his route back to Bamburgh, Cospatric visited Durham and advised Bishop Aethelwin and the Community to abandon the town. Cospatric undoubtedly informed the leaders of the Community of the devastation which William's troops had inflicted on Yorkshire and warned that the Normans were none too scrupulous in distinguishing between the rebels and the innocent. This, at least, is the reason for the flight given in the *Historia Regum Anglorum*.

Durham was evacuated on Friday, 11 December 1069. The Bishop was accompanied by the members of the *Congregatio sancti Cuthberti* and their wives and children.[66] Cuthbert's coffin was removed from the cathedral and carried north to Lindisfarne by way of Jarrow, Bedlington and Tughall, all of which were Cuthbertine possessions. Both Symeon and the author of the *Historia Regum Anglorum* report that, on the Community's arrival on the shore opposite Lindisfarne, the tide receded to allow them to cross and closed behind them as they passed. William's troops entered the Patrimony of St Cuthbert but reportedly found the villages deserted. That some plundering took place is indicated by the burning of the church of St Paul at Jarrow. The church of Durham itself became a refuge for those too sick to flee to Lindisfarne or the woods and high country.[67]

The account of the 'harrying of the North' is so well known that it is something of a surprise to learn that the historical tradition at Durham maintained that the sacking of the church of St Cuthbert was the work of earl Cospatric of Bamburgh

---

[64] Symeon, *Opera*, i, 100–104; ii, 189.

[65] Orderic, ii, 232, 233. Orderic notes that 'There Waltheof and Cospatric submitted to him and took oaths of fealty, Waltheof in person and Cospatric by proxies'. Orderic places this submission after Christmas 1069. Cospatric's absence would agree with the *Historia Regum Anglorum*'s suggestion that he had already made his way north and warned the Community of St Cuthbert to leave Durham by 11 December 1069, *Opera*, ii, 189.

[66] Symeon, *Opera*, i, 100.

[67] Symeon, *Opera*, ii, 189.

and his men rather than William I's troops. Symeon reports that Bishop Aethelwin despatched a certain priest, Earnan, from Lindisfarne to Durham in order to gauge whether or not it was safe to return. En route Earnan stopped to rest and had a dream in which St Cuthbert and St Oswald met him in the church at Durham. They led him to the south side of the town and showed him a valley filled with souls suffering torments for their persecution of the Church of St Cuthbert. Only two of the Church's oppressors are named, Cospatric and a certain Gillomichael whose fate, as revealed to Earnan, was to be continually run through with hay-scythes. When Earnan reported his vision to the earl, Cospatric made a barefoot pilgrimage to Lindisfarne to seek pardon. Gillomichael was found dead by his servants the day after Earnan had his vision.[68]

Although these miracle stories owe a great deal to Symeon's imagination, they are important in that they explode the idea that the Community of St Cuthbert was the natural ally of revolt in Northumbria. Not only did the earl of Bamburgh lead the destruction of the church at Durham but, during the Community's passage from the Tyne to Lindisfarne, it was attacked by the Northumbrian Gillomichael. There may be parallels here with the church of Peterborough which was plundered by Hereward's men in 1070.[69] It was in this year that William I ordered all the monasteries to be plundered of the treasure which the English nobility had lodged in them for safe keeping. It seems unlikely that the stripping of the valuables from Durham was part of this Norman campaign since, when he heard what had happened to the church of St Cuthbert, William ordered the culprits to be arrested and submitted for punishment by the Bishop.[70] The Community returned to Durham in March 1070 and, after liturgically cleansing and re-consecrating the church, restored the body of St Cuthbert to its shrine.[71]

Bishop Aethelwin fled Durham during the spring or summer of 1070 and eventually fetched up at Ely where he was arrested by William I and imprisoned. The bishop's flight and his appearance among Hereward's companions have been cited as evidence of his sympathy with the Northumbrian rebels of 1068–1070. Symeon charged Aethelwin with absconding with part of St Cuthbert's treasure thereby reinforcing the idea that the bishop had little sympathy with the Community over which he presided.[72] The *Historia Regum Anglorum*, on the other hand merely states that Aethelwin's departure was because he saw the parlous state of the English and did not wish to suffer under the harsh regime of foreigners whose customs and language he did not understand.[73] The foreigners have usually been understood to be the Normans. It is possible, however, that it was a reference to the Scots.

Shortly after the Community's return to Durham in 1070, Malcolm III made one of his most ambitious attacks on Northumbria.[74] Malcolm III had inherited his

---

[68] Symeon, *Opera*, i, 102–104. At one point in Earnan's dream St Cuthbert cried out, '*Vae tibi, Cospatrice, vae tibi Cospatrice, ecclesiam meam suis rebus evacuasti et in desertum convertisti*', Symeon, *Opera*, i, 102–103.

[69] *ASC*, E, sa 1070.

[70] Symeon, *Opera*, i, 101.

[71] Symeon, *Opera*, i, 101; ii, 189.

[72] Symeon, *Opera*, i, 105.

[73] Symeon, *Opera*, ii, 190.

[74] Symeon, *Opera*, ii, 190–191. On Malcolm III's reign, see A.A.M. Duncan, *Scotland the Making of the Kingdom, The Edinburgh History of Scotland*, vol. 1, Edinburgh 1975, 117–125; G.W.S.

father's ambition of annexing the rest of Northumbria and adding it to Lothian. In 1070 the Scots attacked from Cumbria in the west plundering Teesdale, Cleveland, and Hartness. They moved up the coast and burnt the church of St Peter at Wearmouth. The defence of the region was left to Cospatric who made a counter-raid into Cumbria which only succeeded in goading Malcolm into further depredations. The Scots' invasion of 1070 coming so soon after the devastation inflicted by the Normans and coupled with the hostile attitude of the Northumbrians of Bamburgh towards the Church of St Cuthbert, may have proved too much for Aethelwin. He first attempted to escape to find a refuge wherever he could which suggests that his intention was not to join the rebels at Ely.[75] Contrary winds drove Aethelwin into Scottish territory where he managed to secure passage south with Siward Barn, one of the rebels of 1069. It is tempting to believe that Bishop Aethelwin was hoping to follow his brother into retirement at Peterborough. The situation which greeted Aethelwin on his arrival at Ely must have dismayed him and brings to mind a much quoted aphorism involving frying pans and fires.

The successful invasion of Northumbria by Malcolm III and the fact that the Scots had been able to penetrate as far as Teesdale on the very border of his kingdom made William I aware of the necessity of controlling Durham. It was the first defensible site beyond the Tees and could be made into the centre of a marcher lordship between Yorkshire, which was already being parcelled out to Frenchmen, and the province of Northumbria beyond the Tyne. William I took the opportunity afforded by Aethelwin's departure to appoint the Lotharingian cleric Walcher to the see of Durham. William's expedition into Scotland in 1072 and the meeting with Malcolm III at Abernethy produced some stability in the North.[76] On his return south William furnished Walcher with a castle at Durham and made his position more secure by depriving Cospatric of the earldom of Northumbria and appointing Waltheof who was not only a scion of the House of Bamburgh but also closely tied to the Norman royal family.[77] Waltheof was the son of earl Siward and Aelfflaed daughter of earl Ealdred of Bamburgh. He was bound to William I by his oath of fealty taken on the banks of the Tees, through his marriage to the king's niece, Judith and by his possession of estates in the south centred upon Northampton.[78]

Walcher and Waltheof seem to have governed Durham and Northumbria with some success until, in 1075, Waltheof's involvement in a plot against William I resulted in his execution.[79] Walcher assumed control of the earldom although his

---

Barrow, *Kingship and Unity: Scotland 1000–1306*, London 1981, 27–31; R.L.G. Ritchie, *The Normans in Scotland*, Edinburgh 1954, 3–83.

[75] Symeon, *Opera*, ii, 190.

[76] On the question of whether or not Malcolm III performed homage to William I see Barrow, *Kingship*, 30, Duncan, *Scotland*, 119–120 and A.O. and M.O. Anderson, 'Anglo-Scottish Relations from Constantine II to William', *Scot. Hist. Rev.*, xlii, 1963, 1–20.

[77] Cospatric was deposed because he had aided those who had murdered earl Robert at Durham, although he had not been present in person, and because he had been part of the rebel army which had attacked York, Symeon, *Opera*, ii, 196.

[78] See Scott, 'Earl Waltheof'.

[79] Walcher was credited by Symeon with the sponsorship of the monastic revival in Northumbria. Despite Walcher's status as a canon, Symeon attempted to claim him for the monastic cause at Durham by saying that, had he lived, he would have become a monk himself, *Opera*, i, 108–118.

regime had to rely upon the co-operation of the House of Bamburgh. Particularly important as the representative of the Northumbrians was Ligulf who, according to the *Historia Regum Anglorum*, had fled north during the disturbances of 1068–70. Ligulf married Ealdgyth, another daughter of earl Ealdred and acquired property interests in Northumbria.[80]

Walcher's regime was founded upon an uneasy alliance between members of his own family and household and the traditional ruling family of Northumbria. There is no evidence to suggest that there was substantial Norman settlement above the Tees as yet and Walcher's position may have been especially vulnerable.[81] In 1079 Malcolm III again launched an attack on Northumbria and the bishop's failure to resist the invasion may point to the fragility of his alliance with the House of Bamburgh. In 1080, rivalries between the bishop's kinsman, Gilbert, his chaplain Leobwin and Ligulf resulted in the death of the latter. It is possible that the plundering of the episcopal troops was at the centre of the dispute.[82] Walcher was held responsible for Ligulf's death and, despite his attempts to distance himself from the incident and offer compensation to the dead man's widow, he was murdered along with his household at Gateshead in May 1080.[83] The inference in the forged bull of Gregory VII that the members of the *Congregatio sancti Cuthberti* were involved in the events at Gateshead seems to be disproved by the fact that the Northumbrians marched south and attacked Durham.[84]

The death of Bishop Walcher brought a punitive expedition north under Odo of Bayeux and Robert Curthose. The Norman army pushed on into Scotland where Robert and Malcolm III renewed the accord of 1072. On his return south Robert constructed the castle at Monkchester on the Tyne. It has been suggested that this *novum castrum* was built against the Scots but it seems more likely that it was constructed to control the Northumbrians and supply a bridgehead into the region if hostilities arose once more.[85] It was at this juncture that William I appointed William of Saint-Calais to the bishopric and Aubrey de Courcy to the earldom. Earl Aubrey later abandoned his commission and returned to Normandy leaving the position open for Robert de Mowbray.[86]

Despite the concerted attempts by historians to involve the Community of St Cuthbert in the resistance to the imposition of Norman authority in Northumbria it

---

[80] For Ligulf's career, see Symeon, *Opera*, ii, 208–209.

[81] There is evidence to suggest that Walcher was short of money, at least on his arrival in the North. Symeon reports that the bishop had to divert to his own purposes part of the money which William I sent to refurbish the Church of St Cuthbert after Cospatric's plundering, Symeon, *Opera*, i, 101.

[82] Symeon, *Opera*, i, 114.

[83] Offler, *Durham Episcopal Charters*, no. 1. Professor Offler argues that there was not enough time between Ligulf's death and that of Walcher for the bishop to make the grant of land described in the memorandum. If Walcher was attempting to avert catastrophe it does not seem unlikely that such a grant could have been expedited.

[84] See above, note 32.

[85] Symeon, *Opera*, ii, 211. For the career of William of Saint-Calais, see H.S. Offler, 'William of Saint-Calais, First Norman Bishop of Durham', *Trans. Architectural and Archaeological Soc. of Durham and Northumberland*, x, 1950, 258–79.

[86] The *Historia Regum Anglorum* states that earl Aubrey was of little use in difficult affairs, *Inde rex dedit illum honorem Albrico. Quo in rebus difficilibus parum valente patriamque reverso . . .*, Symeon, *Opera*, ii, 199.

seems that the members of the church of St Cuthbert made every effort to distance themselves from the rebels. The priority of the *Congregatio sancti Cuthberti* in the late eleventh century, as it had been throughout its history, was survival. Alliances had been made with individuals with sufficient political power to ensure the continuation of the Church of St Cuthbert. During the ninth century the Community moved south from Lindisfarne and took up residence at Chester-le-Street.[87] This move has usually been seen as a response to the threat of attack from the Scandinavians but this thesis seems difficult to support given that the settlement at Chester-le-Street actually brought them closer to the Scandinavians in North Yorkshire. If they were fleeing marauders at all, those marauders were the Scots, who, at the end of the ninth century were beginning to advance southward. At the foundation of the church at Chester-le-Street the Community of St Cuthbert received a grant of land from the Scandinavian leader Guthred. Durham historical tradition maintains that Guthred's rise to power was assisted by the Community and that in his gratitude he granted St Cuthbert the lands between the Tyne and the Wear which were, incidentally, more easily administered from Chester-le-Street than from Lindisfarne.[88]

During the tenth century the church of St Cuthbert received visits from West Saxon kings who made generous gifts to the church and issued confirmations of its possessions and privileges. Renewed Scandinavian threats, especially from the Vikings of the Irish Sea littoral forced the Community to seek protection from the southern kings. The alliance with the House of Bamburgh at the beginning of the eleventh century was probably directed against the double threat of the Scots and the Danes who, under Swegn and his son Cnut were attempting to oust Aethelred II.[89] It is not surprising to discover that Cnut patronised the church of St Cuthbert confirming its privileges and making substantial gifts.[90] The pattern of monarchs visiting the shrine of the greatest of the Northumbrian saints and making benefactions to his church seems to have been well established by the time of Norman arrival in England. The visits to Durham of William I in 1072 and Malcolm III in 1093 suggest that the members of the Community of St Cuthbert were maintaining their policy of forming associations with whichever power might offer them security and survival.

There are two extant accounts of William I's visit to Durham in 1072. The earlier of the two is preserved in the *Chronica Monasterii Dunelmensis*. Symeon also included a description of the king's visit to the shrine but, as ever, the account is witness to the author's penchant for the supernatural and his tendentious approach to the history of his house. According to the *Libellus*, William I's attitude to the Community was hostile.

> [rex Willelmus] . . . diligenter interrogans an corpus beati Cuthberti ibidem requiesceret cunctis vociferantibus et orantibus illud ibi haberi credere no-

---

[87] E. Cambridge, 'Why did the Community of St Cuthbert settle at Chester-le-Street?', in Bonner et al., *St Cuthbert*, 367–86.

[88] *Historia de Sancto Cuthberto*, in Symeon, *Opera*, i, 203.

[89] The marriage between Bishop Aldhun's daughter and earl Uchtred sealed the alliance between the Church of St Cuthbert and Bamburgh, see Morris, *Marriage and Murder*, 12–18.

[90] In a recent study of Cnut's reign Dr M.K. Lawson argues that it was the Danish king's aim to portray himself as the model of a Christian monarch, M.K. Lawson, *Cnut: The Danes in England in the Early Eleventh Century*, London 1993, 119–160.

luit. Decrevit ergo rem visu explorare habens secum episcopos et abbates qui eo iubente id deberent perficere. Iam enim disposuerat ut si sanctum corpus inventum non esset nobiliores et natu maiores universos obtruncari praeciperet.[91]

William's threat to execute the leaders of the Community if the body of St Cuthbert was not found to be at Durham lends support to the notion that the Normans were inimical to the native Anglo-Saxon saints.[92] The involvement of the *Congregatio sancti Cuthberti* in the murder of Robert Cumin and the rebellions against Norman authority in the North of England combined with such religious scepticism would more than account for William's attitude. However, before the king could carry out his threat, St Cuthbert intervened and struck William down with an excessive heat. Fearing for his life William mounted his horse and fled south. Once he had crossed the Tees his affliction disappeared. Symeon's description of the episode prompted the nineteenth-century historian of Durham and Northumberland, James Raine, to suggest that William was the victim of a poisoning plot.[93]

If the Church of St Cuthbert and Durham had been the centre of rebellion, Symeon's account of William's actions in 1072 would not be difficult to understand. However, the earlier of the two accounts, that produced by the members of the *Congregatio sancti Cuthberti* themselves, tells a very different story. According to the *Chronica* William I was made welcome at Durham. He reverently approached the church of St Cuthbert and asked to be told of the saint's life. The elders of the Community explained how Cuthbert had been persuaded to accept the episcopal chair and how, from the earliest times, kings had honoured his church with gifts and had confirmed its liberties and privileges. William took this very large hint and placed a mark of gold and a pallium on the altar promising that,

omnia que mei antecessores huic ecclesie sancte Dei genitricis et sancti Cuthberti confessoris in terris, et legibus et libertate et quietudine contulerunt tanto firmius et stabilius a me meisque heredibus et successoribus servari volo et discerno quanto me meosque heredes et successores omnibus precedentibus regibus dignitate et iusticia precellere cupio; et hec propria manu cum hoc auro et pallio imperpetuum servanda tribuo.[94]

This passage is the written record of the public ceremony conducted at the cathedral altar whereby the Conqueror confirmed the lands, laws and liberties of the Church of St Cuthbert. This ceremony seems to be in keeping with William's need to establish his claim to authority in the North of England. His gifts to the most prestigious religious corporation in Northumbria created a personal bond between the Norman king and the saint and an institutional bond between the

---

[91] Symeon, *Opera*, i, 106.
[92] Susan J. Ridyard, '*Condigna Veneratio*: Post-Conquest Attitudes to The Saints of the Anglo-Saxons', *ante*, ix, 1987, 179–206.
[93] J. Raine, *St Cuthbert*, 1927, 67, . . . 'my reader may perhaps exclaim with Hubert in *King John*, "The king, I fear, is poisoned by a monk".'
[94] Craster, 'Red Book', 528.

Norman monarchy and the Church of St Cuthbert. William's gesture announced that the members of the Community were to consider him their patron. There is a striking similarity between this account of William I's visit to Durham and the earlier oblations performed by Athelstan, Edmund and Cnut at Cuthbert's shrine. When he made his gifts to the Church of St Cuthbert each of these monarchs was attempting to establish his authority in Northumbria. The circumstances of William I's donations were no different. Of course each of these arrangements was reciprocal and the Church of St Cuthbert gained a royal patron and potential defender in return for the saint's recognition of a claim to authority. In this context the account of William I's visit to Durham in 1072 given by the author of the *Chronica Monasterii Dunelmensis* is to be preferred to Symeon's supernatural stage-show.

In 1093 the Church of St Cuthbert had the opportunity of recruiting another royal patron. Throughout his reign, Malcolm III of Scotland had provided ample evidence that he had inherited his father's ambition of re-uniting Lothian and the rest of Northumbria by establishing the limit of his authority at the river Tyne, if not at the Tees. His hopes had been thwarted by the resistance of the earls of Bamburgh and later by the reaction of William I to his invasions of 1070 and 1079. In 1091 Malcolm again attacked Northumbria and managed to penetrate as far as Durham where his army was repulsed by an Anglo-Norman force under William Rufus.[95] The annexation of southern Cumbria and Carlisle by Rufus the following year threatened Malcolm's long-term aims. There is the suggestion that some sort of agreement between the two kings was drawn up and when Rufus failed to honour his part of the bargain Malcolm invaded Northumbria.[96] He met his death on this expedition in 1093 and unwittingly set in motion a series of events which would fundamentally modify the political configuration of the North of England.[97]

On his way south to meet William Rufus at Gloucester in August 1093 Malcolm attended the foundation of the new cathedral church at Durham. It is probable that it was on this occasion that the Church of St Cuthbert drew up a *conventio* on behalf of Malcolm III, his wife Margaret and their children. The monks of St Cuthbert pledged *inter alia* to remember the royal couple, after their deaths in thirty full offices of the dead and, on each day, the *Verba Mea* would be performed on their behalf. The monks would commemorate their anniversary in the same way in which they preserved the memory of King Athelstan, Margaret's illustrious ancestor.[98] The monks were undoubtedly aware of Malcolm's forthcoming meeting with William Rufus and hoped to ensure that, whatever the outcome, the Scots king would join the ranks of the royal patrons of St Cuthbert. Malcolm III's purpose in attending the foundation of the cathedral, and thereby

[95] The relief of Durham coincided with the return of Bishop William of Saint-Calais from exile, *Liber de Translationibus*, in Symeon, *Opera*, ii, 338–341. It is interesting to note that in the miracle account St Cuthbert's intervention causes, not only the disappearance of the Scots, but also that of the Norman relieving force.

[96] For the suggestion that Malcolm III and William Rufus had some bargain relating to Cumbria see Kapelle, 151–52.

[97] Malcolm III's death is described in Symeon, *Opera*, ii, 220.

[98] *Liber Vitae Dunelmensis*, f. 43v.

associating himself with the saint and his church was precisely that of William I and those other kings who had come to Cuthbert's shrine. The King of Scotland was making a general announcement that he had the authority in the region to be able to offer St Cuthbert something in return for the spiritual benefits which were being bestowed upon him. Malcolm's presence betrays his ambition to reunite the ancient kingdom of Bernicia under Scots lordship.

Malcolm III's death brought about a struggle for the Scottish throne which William Rufus was able to exploit. After the failure of Duncan to retain the throne, Rufus ensured the accession of Malcolm's son Edgar in 1097. He was 'clearly the dependent client or vassal of the Norman kings of England'.[99] The removal of the threat of invasion from Scotland created the conditions which allowed French settlement to advance beyond the Tyne. Although there is evidence to suggest that Edgar's successor David I did not entirely relinquish his family's ambition to extend the authority of the Scots kings over Northumbria, 1097 marks the end of a period of political upheaval in the North of England. It is significant that the earliest extant Scottish charters record gifts to the church of St Cuthbert by Duncan and Edgar.[100] The Church of St Cuthbert had survived the crisis and would continue to grow in prestige.

The constitution of the Church of St Cuthbert did not, however, remain unaltered. In 1083 Bishop William of Saint-Calais regularised the Community and with the assistance of Archbishop Lanfranc introduced the Benedictine rule. The married members of the *Congregatio sancti Cuthberti* were forced to give up their wives or leave the church. It is usual to see the events of 1083 as a dramatic break in the continuity of the Church of St Cuthbert; a sign of the triumph of the Normans over the *Haliwerfolc*.[101] The inconsistencies in Symeon's account of the events should arouse our suspicions. The introduction of the Benedictine Rule in 1083 need not have completely eradicated the traditions of the pre-monastic *Congregatio*. Although Symeon says that only one of the monks' predecessors remained behind, the *Libellus* has an abundance of references to aged clerks from whom Symeon gleaned his information.[102]

On a practical level, William of Saint-Calais would have been a reckless man indeed to provoke the *Haliwerfolc* by expelling from the Church of St Cuthbert families whose connections with the surrounding population were deep-rooted.[103] Once the involvement of the members of the Community of St Cuthbert in the Northumbrian resistance to William I is questioned, the perceived threat which they posed to the Norman regime evaporates. In the context of the history of the dealings of the Church of St Cuthbert with outside authority, it seems more likely that the leaders of the Community would seek an accommodation with the

---

[99] Barrow, *Kingship*, 31–32.

[100] A.A.M. Duncan, 'The Earliest Scottish Charters', *Scot. Hist. Rev.*, xxxvii, 1958, 103–35; J.J. Donnelly, 'The Earliest Scottish Charters ?', *Scot. Hist. Rev.*, 1989, 1–21.

[101] A Piper, for example, sees the events of 1083 as bringing about a complete change of personnel, 'The First Generation of Durham Monks and the Cult of St Cuthbert', in Bonner et al., *St Cuthbert*, 437–446. Dr David Rollason in 'Symeon of Durham', has argued that Symeon's account of the events of 1083 disguises a particularly violent upheaval.

[102] For a fuller exposition of this argument, see Aird, 'Origins', 136–192.

[103] Symeon reported that many families around Durham traced their ancestors to the seven porters of the coffin of St Cuthbert during the wanderings of the late ninth century, Symeon, *Opera*, i, 66–68.

Norman kings. Such a policy had proved efficacious in the past and there is no reason to doubt that its success in the late eleventh century was worth the compromise of accepting the operation of the Rule of St Benedict, especially if monastic practices had persisted, albeit in a bastardised form, amongst those who tended the incorrupt body of St Cuthbert.

RHYS AP TEWDWR, KING OF DEHEUBARTH[1]

Robert S. Babcock

In its entry for 1081, the Welsh chronicle *Brut y Tywysogyon* reports that 'William the Bastard, king of the Saxons and the French and the Britons, came on a pilgrimage to Menevia [St Davids] to offer prayers.'[2] As any number of historians have noted, this is unlikely to have been the true reason for William's journey. A well-explored Domesday entry for Herefordshire suggests the more probable reason; in it we are told that *Riset de Wales* owed forty pounds, the same amount that the Cheshire Domesday records that Robert of Rhuddlan paid to hold North Wales for the king. *Riset de Wales* can only be Rhys ap Tewdwr, king of the southwestern Welsh kingdom of Deheubarth, and William's visit must then have been to enforce or secure whatever agreement it was that forced Rhys to pay forty pounds in annual tribute to the Conqueror.[3]

This agreement would prove beneficial to both parties. It would allow William to deal with – and hold responsible – a single ruler in the Southwest of Wales, thus avoiding the potential for troubles that the Welsh had caused him elsewhere. Rhys, however, was able to take advantage of the agreement to reconstruct native rule in the Southwest. To the English, he would become *rex Walliae*, to the Welsh *brenin Deheubarth*, and so great would become his stature that on his death the *Brut* would report that 'thus fell the kingdom of the Britons.'[4]

William the Conqueror's reign and rule have been thoroughly investigated by any number of historians, but those of the other participant at the meeting that may have taken place in 1081 have not. The lack of detailed study of Rhys' reign is perfectly understandable; it has left none of the traces of rule that William's has – no Domesday, no charters, and only terse entries in a troublesome chronicle. To recreate Rhys' reign, as this paper will attempt to do, is to explore the possible, perhaps the probable, but in no way to approach certainty. This *caveat* made, however, much more can be offered about Rhys ap Tewdwr than has previously been attempted. Through careful use of what sources do exist – saints' *vitae*, later genealogies, the corpus of later Welsh laws, the *Brut y Tywysogyon*, and the

[1] I wish to thank the following for their generous support which enabled me to travel to Britain to present this paper: Dr Thomas J. Reeves and Hastings College, Mr and Mrs Robert C. Canfield, and Professor and Mrs Charles L. Babcock. The research for this paper was conducted during a year at Aberystwyth on a Fulbright grant administered by the United States-United Kingdom Educational Commission, and my thanks go out to that organization. My greatest debt, however, is to my host and guide during the year in which this research was conducted, Professor Rees Davies of the University College of Wales, Aberystwyth.
[2] *Brut y Tywysogyon or the Chronicle of the Princes* (*Red Book of Hergest Version*), ed. T. Jones, Cardiff 1955, *sub anno* 1081.
[3] Domesday Book 1, fol. 179b, fol. 269b.
[4] *Brut s.a.* 1093.

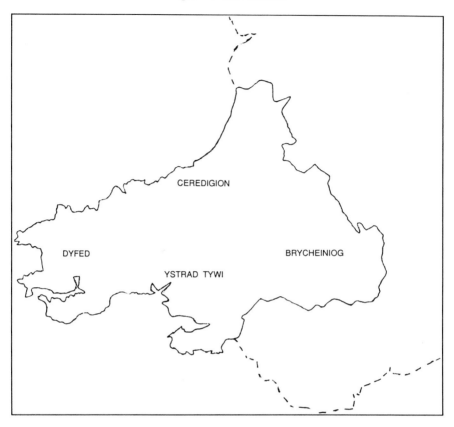

Southwest Wales in the eleventh century (modified from Melville Richards, Welsh Administrative and Territorial Units*)*

fascinating vernacular life of Rhys' counterpart in North Wales, the *Historia Gruffudd vab Kenan* – it can be shown that the meeting with William at St Davids came at a crucial point in Rhys' brief reign, and it can be argued that the agreement that the two men reached was a crucial element in Rhys' ability to reassert royal authority over the free Welsh warriors of the Southwest.

He was Rhys ap Tewdwr ap Cadell ab Einion ab Owain ap Hywel Dda, thus of the lineage of one of the greatest and most legendary kings of all Wales. By the rough calculations of an expert in Welsh genealogies, he would have been in his forties in 1079, when the native chronicler tells us that he 'began to rule.'[5] What he – or for that matter his father or grandfather – had been doing prior to 1079 is unreported. The last of Rhys' direct line to appear in the chronicle before him is his great-grandfather, Einion, whom we find plundering the Gower peninsula in 970 and again in 977, apparently continuing his father Owain ap Hywel's attempts to expand to the southeast. Einion was killed by the men of Gwent in 984, and we

---

[5] *Brut s.a.* 1079. P.C. Bartram, *Welsh Genealogies A.D. 300–1400*, Cardiff 1974, explains his system of calculating his system of 'generations' in his introduction.

know nothing of Rhys' direct ancestors after that.[6] It is likely that Rhys and his forefathers merely lay low in west Wales, serving among the nameless free warriors who made up the armies of prominent rulers like Gruffudd ap Rhydderch or Gruffudd ap Llywelyn. Succession and inheritence in Wales was such that many could claim the right to rule, but what is often lost in the accounts of the deeds and treachery of those who did claim that right is that just as many probably did not claim it. Whether afraid of the consequences of asserting their inheritances or merely satisfied with the way things were, Cadell ab Einion and Tewdwr ap Cadell – and Rhys himself until 1079 – may have chosen to play only supporting roles in the struggles for power in Wales.

If the *Brut* tells us nothing about Rhys before 1079, it is almost as unforthcoming when it tells us that he 'began to rule.' Began to rule what? In its 1088 entry, the *Brut* refers to his kingdom (W. *teyrnas*), and on his death in 1093 the chronicle identifies him as *brenhin Deheubarth*, but we have no way of knowing if these were Rhys' ambitions in 1079.[7] Indeed, the fate – even the existence – of Deheubarth as an independent region may have been difficult to foresee in that year; for the notoriously fluid political geography of eleventh-century Wales had changed once again, and the kingdom of the Southwest appeared in danger of being engulfed in the constructed mega-kingship of Trahaearn ap Caradog, lord of Arwytli.

The political geography of Wales in this period was inextricably linked with personal power. Rule was not so much on the basis of king*dom* as of king*ship*, though it is sometimes difficult to glean from the sources because the identity of regions and localities [W. *gwladoedd*] had been well-established by the eleventh century, but that of political units had not. The names of some kingdoms – Gwent, for instance – were also the names of long-before recognized regions, and tend to be used even if the region had no king or had been absorbed into another kingship at the given time. By the late eleventh century, at least four kingships had demonstrated sufficient durability to seem like permanent fixtures – Gwynedd, Powys, Deheubarth and Gwent – but between these four were smaller regions that could be independent kingships or could be swallowed up by the military successes of a neighboring ruler.

Rhys ap Tewdwr had stepped to the fore of one of the oldest named kingships in Wales. Initially called Dyfed, it had emerged in the Southwest in the early sixth century, but by the ninth it had fallen to a king from the North. The beleaguered, fragmented rulers of the Southwest survived, however, and the region they controlled gradually took on the name Deheubarth. Under Hywell Dda, that name came to refer to territory that included Dyfed, Ystrad Tywi, and Ceredigion. While Hywel did assemble these geographical regions into a single kingship, though, it is misleading to think of the political history of Deheubarth as an unbroken line from Hywel Dda to Rhys ap Tewdwr. The territory of the rulers of the Southwest would break up and reform into new groupings of lands much as it had before, depending upon how successfully kings maintained control over their own and neighboring territory. Deheubarth grew and shrank, waxed and waned, in accordance with the battlefield fortunes of those who claimed to be its kings.

---

[6] *Brut s.a.* 970, 977, 984.
[7] *Brut s.a.* 1088, 1093.

Deheubarth was waning in 1079. Gruffudd ap Llywelyn's death in 1063 had unleashed all the centrifugal forces of Welsh society that he had previously bludgeoned into submission.[8] Maredudd ab Owain ab Edwin had returned to Deheubarth to hold it by 1069, but by 1072 he had been slain on the Rhymney River fighting Caradog ap Gruffudd of Gwent.[9] The site of the battle is so far east that it suggests that Maredudd was either trying to extend his hegemony eastward or was so secure in Deheubarth as to venture far from it on a pillaging raid. In either case, the victor, Caradog, had brought a new ally to the fray. For the first time we read of Normans on Welsh soil, as Caradog had apparently enlisted the aid of England's new rulers against his Welsh enemies.[10] With Maredudd gone, the Normans mounted two forays into Deheubarth, one to Ceredigion and Dyfed in 1073 and another to Ceredigion in 1074. Maredudd's successor, his brother Rhys, must have had his hands full, for Deheubarth in this period was menaced not only by Normans but also by Bleddyn ap Cynfyn, ruler of Gweynedd, who seems to have been expanding his power southward.[11] Even after Bleddyn had been dispatched, Trahaearn ap Caradog continued the pressure. Trahaearn and Rhys ab Owain met in battle in 1078, and Rhys and his war-band were routed. Rhys himself managed to escape, only to be killed later that year by Caradog ap Gruffudd of Gwent. Caradog, buoyed by his Norman allies, seems to have been expanding his power west at Deheubarth's expense just as Trahaearn was expanding south.[12]

This, then, was the situation when Rhys ap Tewdwr began to rule in the late eleventh century. What was left to rule is certainly in question. It is probable that Trahaearn held much if not all of Ceredigion, and likely that Caradog had made inroads into Gower and Ystrad Tywi. Five of Rhys ap Tewdwr's cousins had been slain in the previous five years, all either defending or trying to claim the kingship which fell to him. It is even possible that Rhys did not assert himself in 1079, that the record of such is that of a later scribe who, seeing no other candidate and knowing the eventual outcome of events in the Southwest, assumed that this was the year Rhys stepped forward. We are not told of his actions or his whereabouts in that year, nor in the next, when Scandinavian-Irish raiders pillaged St Davids. It is not until 1081 that we see Rhys taking decisive action towards ruling – perhaps reconstructing is a better term – Deheubarth.

In 1081 the pincers of Caradog ap Gruffudd and Trahaearn ap Caradog's advances finally met; their forces probably combined somewhere in Dyfed. Rhys went to St Davids, perhaps contemplating escape to Ireland, where he would flee successfully when similarly pressed in the future. At St Davids, however, he found the fleet of Gruffudd ap Cynan in the harbor, and an alliance of convenience was born. Gruffudd ap Cynan had earlier made attempts on the kingship of Gwynedd, only to be repelled by the same Trahaearn ap Caradog who was now menacing Dyfed. Since his defeat by Trahaearn sometime after 1075, Gruffudd

---

[8] The apt description is from R.R. Davies, *Conquest, Coexistance and Change: Wales 1063–1415*, Oxford 1987, 24–25.

[9] *Brut s.a.* 1069, 1072.

[10] *Brut s.a.* 1072. For Caradog and the Normans, see Paul Courtney, 'The Norman Invasion of Gwent: a Reassessment,' *Journal of Medieval History* xii, 1986, 297–313, especially 305.

[11] *Brut s.a.* 1073, 1074. J.E. Lloyd, *A History of Wales from the Earliest Times to the Edwardian Conquest*, 3rd edn, London 1939, 377.

[12] *Brut s.a.* 1078.

had been leading the life of a pirate, operating out of Ireland and raiding the coasts of Wales in Scandinavian ships manned by Scandinavian and Irish brigands.[13] Whatever their origins, though, Gruffudd's men were troops which Rhys desperately needed, and the destruction of Trahaearn was in both Rhys' and Gruffudd's interests.

Rhys' brief but momentous association with Gruffudd ap Cynan gives us access to a source beyond the *Brut y Tywysogyon* for the first time. About the climactic battle that followed, the *Brut* is characteristically terse. 'And then there was a battle at Mynydd Carn. And then Trahaearn ap Caradog and Caradog ap Gruffudd [and Meulyr ap Rhiwallon] were slain [by Rhys ap Tewdwr. And Gruffudd] grandson of Iago and Irish along with him [came] to help him.'[14] But Gruffudd ap Cynan is one of the earliest secular figures in the Middle Ages to have had a biography written of him, and while the exaggerated praise of its subject makes some of the content of the *Historia Gruffudd vab Kenan* suspect, the work does include full accounts of the meeting between Rhys and Gruffudd at St Davids and of the battle in Dyfed which followed.

Rhys is in flight, preparing to leave Wales when Gruffudd ap Cynan and a band of followers sail into the harbor. Gruffudd learns of the nearness of their mutual enemy, and Rhys pledges half of his territory in return for aid.

And after they had entered into an alliance in that place, and had received the blessing of the bishop, Gruffudd marched on that selfsame day, with his Danes and Irish and many of the men of Gwynedd to the number of a hundred and sixty, with Cynddelw son of Conus and a few Deheuwyr marched with them, happy in his heart because of the help he was getting.

After they had marched a full day's journey, towards evening they came to a mountain, where lay the camps of the kings mentioned above [Trahaearn and Caradog]. Then Rhys told king Gruffudd: "Lord," said he, "let us postpone the battle till tomorrow, because it is now evening, and the day is spent." "You postpone it," said Gruffudd with a sigh, "if that is what you want. I and my army will rush at them." And so it happened. The kings were however terrified, as they saw the various triumphant forces and the armies of king Gruffudd and his ensigns opposing them, the men of Denmark with their two-edged axes, the Irish with their lances and their sharp-edged iron balls, and the men of Gwynedd armed with spears and shields.

The battle is joined, and because Gruffudd is there his side wins. Trahaearn is killed, but:

After the battle is over, Rhys feared treachery on the part of Gruffudd. He withdrew secretly at dusk from the presence of Gruffudd and his men, and he did not appear to any of them from then on. Because of that Gruffudd sulked, and ordered his men to ravage the territory of Rhys. And so it happened.[15]

[13] *Vitae Sanctorum Britanniae et Genealogiae*, ed. A.W. Wade-Evans, Cardiff 1944, 183–185, describes one of his raids on Gwent.

[14] *Brut s.a.* 1081.

[15] *A Medieval Prince of Wales: The Life of Gruffudd ap Cynan*, ed. D. Simon Evans, Llandysul 1990, 67–68 for translation, 36–37 for original.

Clearly, much of the account may be fiction. Any verbatim dialogue or exact troop numbers in a work written long after the fact must be so categorized. It is a work of propaganda, intended to glorify Gruffudd, his son Owain, and the realm of Gwynedd. As such it glorifies Gruffudd's military prowess, his personality, and his religious piety, and it diminishes all that might detract from that glorification.[16] Rhys' role in the *Historia* must thus be considered carefully; his deeds and behavior may have been described to give maximum credit to Gruffudd, as his submission to Gruffudd, his homage and ceding of territory, was almost certainly included by the author of the *Historia* to support Owain ap Gruffudd's territorial claims and ambitions. Rhys' timidity and the great inferiority of his forces at the battle may be similar inventions to enhance the glory of the northern king.

Yet there might be some grains of truth in the account. Rhys certainly may have been on the run, for the chronicle tells us of nothing but uninterrupted success for Trahaearn and Caradog before Mynydd Carn. If all Rhys had with him was his *teulu*, the band of warriors who owed allegiance to his person rather than those who served him as ruler of Deheubarth (the few *Deheuwyr* of the *Historia*, perhaps), his forces would have been considerably smaller than those of a well-financed sea rover from Ireland. It is quite conceivable that Gruffudd's forces were the deciding factor in the victory at Mynydd Carn.

It is tempting to see Rhys as supreme in Deheubarth after the battle, but there is little actual evidence that he was. The *Brut* merely offers no alternative to that view, having recorded the deaths or exits of all who made claims on Deheubarth previous to Rhys. Yet the successive deaths of those previous claimants, plus the devastation of Trahaearn and Caradog (and of Gruffudd ap Cynan, if the *Historia* is to be believed), must have rendered anything approaching centralizing institutions pretty well non-existent. Good fortune was with Rhys, however, for the previous years had indeed eliminated rivals within his family, and the battle at Mynydd Carn had eliminated Trahaearn and Caradog; and Gruffudd ap Cynan, whom Mynydd Carn had put in a position to compete with Rhys, had, however, angrily, gone north to pursue his ambitions in Gwynedd. Rhys' luck was to hold as well concerning the final potential rival to come to Deheubarth in 1081.

It is now, after the battle, that the *Brut* reports that William came to St Davids. The involvement of Norman warriors in the ambitions of Caradog ap Gruffudd, and perhaps earlier claims that Edward the Confessor had made in South Wales, had drawn the Norman king onto the Welsh scene.[17] William's visit to St Davids was the deepest penetration into Wales yet made by an English king, and the apparent ease with which the visit was made – there is no evidence of any skirmishes or resistance along the way – suggests the near complete submission of the South, due either to the overwhelming force of the Normans or to the complete disorganization of the South. We can only imagine Rhys' feelings when, only months or possibly weeks after finally reversing his fortunes against Trahaearn and Caradog, and having withstood the devastations of Gruffudd ap Cynan, he received word that the Conqueror of England was marching on Deheubarth. It is no wonder that he seems willing to have entered into an accord

[16] *A Medieval Prince of Wales*, 18.
[17] For the English claims to overlordship in Wales, see Davies, *Conquest*, 27. For Edward the Confessor and Wales, especially the posthumous perception of his claims in Wales, see Frank Barlow, *Edward the Confessor*, Los Angeles 1984, 204–212.

with the English king. Beyond the money payment recorded in Domesday, we know nothing of the terms of the agreement which Rhys and William likely reached, but it would seem that Rhys recognized William's right as overlord in Wales, perhaps doing homage for Deheubarth. That there were no further Norman advances into South Wales while the Conqueror lived suggests that in return William made some promise to respect the integrity of Rhys' territory.

The agreement worked in both leaders' interests, but especially in Rhys'. He gained valuable time in which to reconstruct royal authority in Deheubarth unmenaced by his most powerful neighbor. More importantly, William seems to have kept in check the rapacious border lords who were the real threat to Rhys' territory. Freed of that threat, Rhys could turn his attention to the more mundane aspects of rule, forging alliances with powerful local families, sitting in judgment at royal courts, collecting renders and dues. The *Brut* reports nothing of his activities for the next seven years, so it is conjecture to imagine Rhys' actions following his meeting with William, but other sources do reveal the activities associated with rule in Wales in the eleventh century, activities which the authors or editors of the *Brut* show no interest in whatsoever.

Military actions was more to their liking, and it is in a military engagement that we next encounter Rhys ap Tewdwr. In 1088, the sons of Bleddyn ap Cynfyn invaded Deheubarth and forced Rhys to flee to Ireland. Bleddyn had made forays into Deheubarth until his death in 1075, and his cousin was Trahaearn ap Caradog, who had also menaced the Southwest.[18] The invasion by Madog, Cadwgan and Rhiddid ap Bleddyn may have been a continuation of that family's ambitions in the Southwest, or it may have been an act of revenge against the family responsible for the deaths of their father and uncle; whatever its reason, it was initially successful. Rhys escaped to Ireland but returned the same year with a force which the *Brut* describes as being made up of Scots and Irish, probably similar to the mercenaries whom Gruffudd ap Cynan brought to Dyfed in 1081. They killed Madog and Rhiddid in battle and sent Cadwgan in flight back to mid-Wales.[19]

The Scandinavians of the Irish Sea Province could be threats as well as allies, however. In 1089 and again in 1091 sea raiders pillaged St Davids. The next serious threat to Rhys' rule, however, was like the last one, Welsh. This time it came from within Deheubarth itself. Like many polities of eleventh-century Europe, Deheubarth was essentially an amalgam of local aristocracies. Monarchs ruled by obtaining or forcing the consent of these powerful local families. In 1091 Cydifor ap Gollwyn, 'the man who had been supreme lord over the land of Dyfed,' died.[20] Whatever agreement he, as head of a prominent family of one of the regions of Deheubarth, had made or been forced to make with Rhys died with him, for his sons invited Rhys' cousin Maredudd ab Owain to Deheubarth from Herefordshire. The sons presumably wanted Maredudd to replace Rhys as ruler, but Rhys defeated and killed him in battle near St Dogmaels.[21]

William the Conqueror's death reawakened the Norman threat to Deheubarth. William Rufus either advocated or did not restrain Norman advancement along

---

[18] *Brut s.a.* 1075.
[19] *Brut s.a.* 1088.
[20] *Brut s.a.* 1091 on his death, *s.a.* 1116 for the quotation.
[21] *Brut s.a.* 1091.

the March, and the Normans began to establish themselves in Brycheiniog and Morgannwg. Rhys ap Tewdwr seems to have taken the lead in defending these kingdoms, either because of some formal claim to overlordship or because he realized the dangers of further Norman advances into Wales. He was killed in 1093 by 'Normans who were living in Brycheiniog,' most likely in battle, though Gerald of Wales reports long after the fact that he was betrayed by his own troops.[22]

Thus was the reign of Rhys ap Tewdwr, but the sequence of events does little to illuminate his rule, his ability to organize the resources of the Southwest and his ability to make its inhabitants do what he wished of them. As the narrative of his life demonstrates, Rhys faced a number of challenges to that rule; the clearest and most immediate were threats from ambitious neighboring rulers, but the *uchelwyr*, the leading men, of Deheubarth such as the sons of Cydifor ap Gollwyn were also a difficulty. Their rebellion in 1091 also shows that Rhys' extended family, reduced in numbers though it may have been, also could threaten, for Cydifor's sons expressed their rebellion by calling for Rhys' cousin to assume the kingship.

Reaching a conclusion about what resources Rhys had to meet these challenges – even putting forth an argument about it – is difficult because of the nature of the evidence and because of Rhys' questionable status in 1081. It is unclear what resources even a secure ruler might count on in the late eleventh century, and Rhys was hardly that. The fullest evidence for royal resources comes from the lawbooks, but though they purport to depict an ancient tradition, these are nearly all from the late twelfth century, and no manuscript is earlier than the thirteenth. The Blegywryd Redaction, assembled from a Latin text that was probably put together in Deheubarth in the twelfth century, exists in manuscript form only from about 1300.[23]

The picture that emerges from the law books is of a highly organized – if not central – royal administration. The kingdom is divided into administrative units called *cantrefi* [s.*cantref*, frequently rendered in English as 'cantred;'] and *cwmwdau* [s. *cwmwd*, E. commote], the extent of each determined by the number of *maenolydd* [s. *maenol*, E. manor] in it.[24] The king had rights to land in each *cwmwd* and also rights to and responsibility for the oversight of justice there. Both rights were to be exercised in the king's name by local officials called the *maer* and the *cynghellor*. There was a court [W. *llys*] in each *cwmwd*, to which the king travelled to hear sessions and render judgments, and townland called the *maerdref* surrounded each *llys*.[25] Free vills in the *cwmwd* owed *gwestfa*, hospitality, in the form of renders, though these could be commuted into a cash payment called the *twnc* pound.[26] Bond *maenolydd* owed *dawnbwyd*, a food gift, twice a year.[27]

The uniformity of this administrative system is artificial. David Stephenson has shown in some detail that it did not even fully apply to Gwynedd, the state that

---

[22] *Brut s.a.* 1093. Gerald of Wales, *Itinerarium Cambriae*, 1:12.
[23] *The Law of Hywel Dda*, ed. Dafydd Jenkins, Llandysul 1990, xxv–xxvi.
[24] *The Law of Hywel Dda*, 121.
[25] *The Law of Hywel Dda*, 128–9.
[26] *The Law of Hywel Dda*, 128, for *gwesfta*, and 121–22 for the *twnc* pound.
[27] *The Law of Hywel Dda*, 128–29.

produced many of the codes.[28] There were certainly aspects of it that did not apply to eleventh-century Deheubarth; Cantref Mawr in Ystrad Tywi had seven commotes, for instance, rather than the two it should have had according to the law codes.[29] Nonetheless, there is evidence from literature and *Vitae* that date closer to Rhys' reign that seems to suggest that an eleventh-century king could expect certain resources from all of the population that acknowledged him as king, and while the sources are not explicit, they also suggest that the king could expect the rights to some lands in each region of his kingship.

The stories from the *Mabinogion*, for instance, composed perhaps in the mid-eleventh century, show us figures who rule over kingdoms divided into *cantrefi*, who made regular circuits through their territory enjoying the hospitality of their subjects. 'Pwyll Lord of Dyfed' opens with the title character at his principal court [*prif llys idaw*] of Arberth.[30] Such a reference suggests that he had other, lesser courts in his realm. He makes a circuit of his realm, apparently a regular act for a ruler; Math son of Mathownwy, Lord of Gwynedd, was supposed to do the same, but because of events in the story named for him 'he could make no circuit of the land, so his nephews Gilvaethwy son of Don and Gwydyon son of Don – that is, his sister's sons – would go for him, accompanied by his retinue.'[31]

Other sources show that part of the reason for these circuits, whether by the king himself or by his representatives, was to collect what his subjects owed. The *Vita Sancti Cadoci*, compiled around 1100, depicts a king who was owed a yearly render from each region [L. *pagus*] in his realm, and who sent *exactores* to collect it.[32] Further evidence about what a ruler might expect from his subjects on such a circuit through his kingdom comes from the *Vita Sancti Bernachii*, composed in the twelfth century, in which

> . . . the king of Cambria, Maelgwyn, was making a journey not far from the cell of the saint, and sent to him, ordering that he should prepare him a supper. The saint, wishing that he and his *loca* should be free from every suit, asserted that he owed no supper to the king, nor was he willing in any way to obey his unjust command.[33]

Such a story, especially with its reference to a suit, suggests that there were formal relationships in which a king could expect such services from at least some of his subjects, and that such a story would seem credible to a twelfth-century audience suggests that such relationships existed then, too. Similar suggestions may be found in the *Vita Sancti Illtuti*, also from the twelfth century. Its emphasis on the unjust seizure of tribute implies that there was also a just rendering to the king.[34]

---

[28] David Stephenson, *The Governance of Gwynedd*, Cardiff 1984, 64.

[29] Melville Richards, *Welsh Administrative and Territorial Units*, Cardiff 1969, 28.

[30] *Pwyll Pendeuic Dyvet*, ed. R.L. Thomson, Dublin 1986, 1. *The Mabinogion*, trans. Jeffrey Gantz, Harmondsworth 1978, 46.

[31] For Pwyll, *Mabinogion*, 64. For Math, 99.

[32] *Vitae Sanctorum Britanniae*, 137.

[33] *Vitae Sanctorum Britanniae*, 11.

[34] *Vitae Sanctorum Britanniae*, 219. The steward of Merchion, king of Glamorgan, unjustly appropriates many things from Meirchion's subjects in the name of the king. The author of the *Vita* states that the steward 'had wished the holy and most free Illtud to become tributary and to send his tributes to the king's fortresses.'

The political and military chaos of the age, however, may have been so great as to render the effective collection of renders – the enforcement of obligations upon local communities that would constitute recognition of authority – functionally impossible. At the very least, the ever-changing fortunes of the kings of the age, and the resulting changes in political geography that accompanied them, raise serious questions about how any system of governance or rule would have worked. When Rhys ab Owain and Rhydderch ap Caradog held Deheubarth in 1075, for instance, did they share revenues from the entire realm?[35] Did they divide up the realm so that each claimed income from different locales? To which did the bond vills pay *dawnbwyd*? To which did the free vills render *gwestfa*? A year later, Rhydderch was dead and Rhys ab Owain was fighting for his life; who then received the royal income?[36] When Trahaearn routed Rhys ab Owain's forces in battle, did the royal income from the territories he added immediately come to him?[37] The same question must be asked of Caradog ap Gruffudd's conquests in southeastern Deheubarth.[38] Both Trahaearn and Caradog were dead three years after they had made their gains in Deheubarth, three years in which they seem to have been nearly constantly on campaign. Had they had time to establish their authority in any of their new aquisitions?

These kinds of questions will never be answered with the certainty that historians would like, but plausible suggestions may be put forth. The power of the ruler in the commotes and cantrefs of his realm seems to have depended on his relationship with the local nobility of those areas. His income was directly related to their willingness to pay what he claimed was his right or to his ability to force them to render what he demanded. The story of the steward of Meirchion in the *Vita Illtuti* is illustrative of the tensions that existed between the ruler and the ruled in this regard.[39] A just king took only what was his due, but subjects could be forced to pay more than they felt they owed by a strong ruler or his agents; conversely, we may suspect that a weak or uncertain ruler would likely receive as little as his subjects felt that they could get away with paying.

Even if the organized structure of exploitation described in the lawbooks did exist in the eleventh century, a ruler's ability to make it work would still have been determined by his relationship with the *uchelwyr* of his realm. A tantalizing line in the laws suggests what might have been happening in the cantrefs and commotes of Deheubarth at this time: 'it is not right that either *maer* or *cynghellor* be *pencenedl*, but one of the *uchelwyr* of the country.'[40] The *pencenedl* was the 'chief of kindred', and though the title is poorly understood it is a recognized one in the laws and it clearly was an important position in local kin groups. That the later laws prohibit a *pencenedl* from holding office of local administration for the king suggests that at one time such a situation in fact existed, that the offices of *maer* and *cynghellor* were controlled not by the king but by powerful local families. Here again, the tension between 'local' and royal interests would be great; an official with powerful local connections would need to be coerced or

---

35 *Brut s.a.* 1075.
36 *Brut s.a.* 1076.
37 *Brut s.a.* 1978.
38 *Brut s.a.* 1078.
39 See note 34.
40 *The Law of Hywel Dda*, 123.

otherwise obligated to exploit the resources for the king's benefit rather than his own. Given a strong or undisputed king, we may envision local administration working to the ruler's advantage; a weak ruler, however, or one whose legitimacy could be challenged, would not be in as strong a position to demand his dues from an official entrenched in the powerful nobility of the commote. His ability to rule would still depend on his entering into successful relationships with local families.

The *Brut y Tywysogyon* frequently identifies this level of society simply as 'men' [*gwyr*]. Quite often they are the 'men' of a well-defined region, the men of Ystrad Tywi, Gwynedd, Meirionydd or such.[41] The *teulu* can also appear as this faceless collective, as the 'men' of a specific individual such as the 'men of Ifor ap Meurig.'[42] The ways in which the chronicle describes the nobility, then, define them by the bonds which join them to each other or to the higher, royal level of native society. A successful ruler would need to accentuate those vertical bonds between the nobility and himself, perhaps at the expense of the horizontal bonds that joined a noble to the other *uchelwyr* of his locality.

For Rhys ap Tewdwr, having survived at Mynydd Carn and finding himself unchallenged immediately for the rule of Deheubarth, relations with the great local families of his realm would thus have been essential if he were actually to assert the authority that he had just won. Deaths in his own family may have left him considerable lands to exploit, though where these lands were and whether he would have had time to make use of them by 1081 is unclear. He was probably not able to make use of the renders and dues from the commotes in Deheubarth that had been taken by Caradog or Trahearn, and he may not have been able to gain the *dawnbwyd* from those bond vills which were overseen by *meiri* who were important local figures and who may have felt secure enough in their locality to withhold cooperation from an insecure king. This is conjecture, of course, but it would explain why Rhys seems to have had such a disproportionately small force at Mynydd Carn.[43] He would not have had the time and perhaps not the ability to gather a host from Deheubarth, and so was left to fight Trahaearn and Caradog with what may have been only his personal retainers and a few men from the South.

Victory at Mynydd Carn likely placed Rhys in a commanding position in Deheubarth. Enough of his family had perished in the blood-letting of the previous years that there were few alternatives for the nobility of the realm to hang their hats on. His most immediate neighboring Welsh threat, Gruffudd ap Cynan, was occupied in Gwynedd, though subsequent events would show that the line of Bleddyn ap Cynfyn had not forsaken its interests in Deheubarth.[44] Rhys may have seemed in such a strong position that many of the local aristocracies in Deheubarth were prepared to offer him the obligations owed the king of the region, and he may have seemed or actually been so strong that he could coerce those obligations that were not freely given.

We simply do not know the course of events in the Southwest from 1801 to 1088, but the struggles of Gruffudd ap Cynan to assert his authority among the

---

[41] *Brut s.a.* 1047, 1075, 1110.
[42] *Brut s.a.* 1158.
[43] See above p. 25.
[44] See above, p. 27.

local nobilities of Gwynedd may give us some understanding of the kinds of
challenges that faced Rhys. The situations are not exactly parallel, but Gruffudd's
shows clearly the role played by the local families in deciding who will be king
and the importance for any king to coerce, coopt, or conquer the regional nobility
of his kingship if he is to rule successfully.

Gruffudd was in exile in Ireland when he made his first attempt to gain the
kingship of Gwynedd. This was before Mynydd Carn, when Trahaearn ap
Caradog was ruling. Gruffudd first sought out the important nobles on the island
of Anglesey.

> Then Gruffudd sent messengers to the men [*gwyr*] of Anglesey and Arfon,
> and the three sons of Merwydd of Llyn, Asser, Meirion and Gwgon, and
> other leading men [*gwyrda*, an alternative to *uchelwyr*] to ask them to come
> in hast to talk to him. And without delay they came and greeted him and
> told him, 'your coming is welcome.' Then he besought them with all his
> might to help him obtain his patrimony, because he was their rightful lord,
> and in conjunction with him to repel fiercely with arms their usurping lords
> who had come from elsewhere.[45]

From Anglesey, Gruffudd went to Tegeingl, on the English border, which had
fallen to the Norman Robert of Rhuddlan, and he secured Robert's support.
Buttressed by men from Anglesey and Tegeingl, then, Gruffudd defeated and
killed his rival for the kingship of Gwynedd.[46] But defeat of his rival did not lead
to immediate and unchallenged rule; from Llyn, Gruffudd and his followers
moved to subdue Anglesey, Arfon, and Llyn and the cantrefs bordering England,
'and to receive homage from their people.' The *Historia Gruffudd vab Kenan*
reports that 'he proceeded thus and encircled all Gwynedd, his true patrimony.'[47]
After winning his battle with the help of several important local families, then,
Gruffudd moved about in Gwynedd commote by commote, receiving recognition
– and perhaps laying claim to *gwestfa* and *dawnbwyd* owed the king – from the
nobility in each region.

Gruffudd's undoing in his first attempt to rule the kingship of Gwynedd came
from the same people who had been his inroad into Gwynedd, the *uchelwyr* of
Anglesey. Together with the men of Llyn, they revolted against Gruffudd and his
mercenaries. Trahaearn ap Caradog and his allies from Powys took advantage of
this to reinvade Gwynedd, and 'the three sons of Merwydd and the men of Llyn
and Eifionydd . . . betrayed their rightful lord, like perjured faithless men, and
assisted their enemies, serving as guides into the territory.'[48] That situation seems
to parallel that in which Rhys ap Tewdwr found himself in 1091, when the sons of
Cydifor ap Gollwyn expressed their rebellion against him by throwing their support to a rival claimant to the kingship.[49]

Successful claims to rule in late eleventh-century Wales, then, had to be made
with the support or the coerced approval of the local *uchelwyr*. The much vaunted
'treachery' of the nobility of Wales comes from royal or prince-centered sources

---

[45] *A Medieval Prince of Wales*, 59.
[46] *A Medieval Prince of Wales*, 59.
[47] *A Medieval Prince of Wales*, 61.
[48] *A Medieval Prince of Wales*, 62–63.
[49] *Brut s.a.* 1091, and below.

(and often Norman or Normanicized ones at that) which do not explain or understand this dynamic. The *Historia*, for instance, describes the 'treachery of the men of Llyn,' but given the events described above their failure to follow Gruffudd is not treachery so much as a decision to back another candidate in a contested succession.[50] Until 1088, Rhys ap Tewdwr had no clear rivals for rule in Deheubarth, and this may be why we do not read of any treachery on the part of the southern *uchelwyr* after Mynydd Carn. The completely undocumentable factor of personality may be partly responsible for this. The *Historia* draws a sharp contrast between the fierce combative personality of Gruffudd ap Cynan and the considered – it is presented as timidity – demeanor of Rhys.[51] If there is any truth to this portrayal at all, it may be that Rhys, by demanding only what others accepted as his due and by antagonizing no local figure in a position of power, provoked no negative response.

The visit of William the Conqueror to St Davids so soon after Mynydd Carn must also have been a factor in Rhys' apparent ability to assert his rule without incident. One way that Gruffudd ap Cynan was able to gain support from his local nobility upon his return to Gwynedd was that he led them in war against the Normans who had moved out of Rhuddlan to occupy several cantrefs in the North.[52] That Rhys ap Tewdwr apparently met with William, was recognized by him as rightful king of the South, and then made an agreement under which William and the Normans left Deheubarth, may have given Rhys considerable authority among his people. Just as Gruffudd ap Cynan was celebrated as a king who kept the Normans out of Gwynedd, so Rhys may have gained prestige for his role, albeit peaceful, in keeping the Normans out of the Southwest.

Whatever agreement Rhys reached with William seems to have paid off. The years after Mynydd Carn seem so uneventful that the chronicler records little about Rhys and his rule. We may imagine that peace with the Normans and the absence of a native rival freed Rhys to engage in the more mundane and pleasurable aspects of rule, making the circuit of his realm, hearing cases and enjoying the hospitality of his subjects in the same manner hinted at by the law codes and literature. We may imagine as well that he was able to gain access to the renders and dues owed him along with his recognition as rightful king.

The invasion by Bleddyn ap Cynfyn from Powys in 1088 gives us further opportunity to speculate about Rhys' rule in Deheubarth. It is difficult to tell if this was a full-scale invasion, following up on claims, real or imagined, that Bleddyn had made upon Deheubarth, or merely a large pillaging party. Whatever its intent, it was extraordinarily successful, forcing Rhys to flee to Ireland.[53] It is tempting to see Rhys' abrupt setback as evidence of weakness in his rule, to suggest that he was unsuccessful in his defense of his kingship because the local nobility that would have made up his host did not fully support him. If this were the case, it would mean that local bonds, those that tied nobles of a given region, may have been stronger than any vertical bonds that Rhys had been able to forge in the seven years since Mynydd Carn. The evidence to do more than suggest this case is far too flimsy, however, especially as military defeats can take place for all sorts of

---

[50] *A Medieval Prince of Wales*, 62–63.
[51] *A Medieval Prince of Wales*, 66–68.
[52] *A Medieval Prince of Wales*, 72–73.
[53] *Brut s.a.* 1088.

reasons. It is equally possible that the full host of Deheubarth did rally to Rhys and was simply defeated (though the *Brut* is often specific about when a leader fights with a gathered host).

Rhys fled to Ireland, where he assembled a fleet and crews of Scots and Irish, and with them returned to do battle for his kingship. He defeated the sons of Bleddyn, killing two and sending the third to flight. The chronicle takes special care to note that after the battle 'Rhys ap Tewdwr gave immense treasure to the seamen, Scots and Irish, who had come to his aid.'[54] There were many ways that a Welsh warlord might assemble treasure in the eleventh century, but as we have no evidence that Rhys made plundering raids of his own, that he had such wealth to give suggests that he had made the traditional system of renders and hospitality work for the benefit of the king before the 1088 invasion.

There are important parallels between Rhys' experience here and the better documented career of Gruffudd ap Cynan. After regaining Gwynedd following victory at Mydydd Carn, Gruffudd was imprisoned by Hugh d'Avranches, the Norman earl of Chester.[55] When he finally escaped, he made his way to Ireland. From there, he sought aid from the Scandinavian king of the Isles much as Rhys had. Gruffudd returned to Anglesey with ships, supplies and men, 'intending in conjunction with the men of the islands to fight against the castle of the French.'[56] The *Historia* reports, however, that 'the men of the land [*gwyr y wlat*] proved to be too much of an obstacle to them.'[57] Gruffudd, then, did not return to the full support of the local nobles of Gwynedd; indeed, some may even have opposed him. Only after he and his Scandinavian followers have won a battle against the Normans does he receive the submission of the *uchelwyr* of Llyn, Eifionydd, Ardudwy, Rhos and Dyffryn Clwyd. Only then is he 'fortified with a large host,' only then do the men of Gwynedd seem to rally to him against the Normans.[58]

The details do not exist for the historian to know if Rhys faced a similar situation on his return from Ireland with his Irish and Scots force in 1088, but his reliance on that force suggests that he did not have the full support of the nobility of Deheubarth against his enemies in much the same way that Gruffudd may not have initially enjoyed the full support of the men of Gwynedd against the Normans. The *uchelwyr* of both kingships may have waited for the king to prove his power, his ability to defeat his opponent, before making the risky political decision that was entrance into the fray. If this was the case, then neither Rhys ap Tewdwr nor Gruffudd ap Cynan had been able to strengthen vertical bonds of allegiance within their kingdoms enough to make them unquestioned rulers. Local bonds, those horizontal ones of kinship and region, seem to have remained the defining ones.

The threat that such a situation held for Rhys, or for any other ruler who wished to assert his authority throughout the realm he claimed, became clear when Cydifor ap Gollwyn, scion of a great family of Dyfed, died in 1091. The description of Cydifor in the *Brut*, 'supreme lord over all the land of Dyfed' [*penhaf arglwyd ar wlat Dyfet*], suggests that no king could claim authority in

---

54 *Brut s.a.* 1088.
55 *A Medieval Prince of Wales*, 69.
56 *A Medieval Prince of Wales*, 72.
57 *A Medieval Prince of Wales*, 72.
58 *A Medieval Prince of Wales*, 73.

Deheubarth without reaching some accord with him. That there is no record of discord between Cydifor and Rhys ap Tewdwr suggests that they did reach some agreement, though we may only guess at what its terms were. Rhys would have every reason to need such an agreement; not only must Cydifor and his family have held a good deal of territory in Dyfed, so that it would have been from Cydifor that Rhys obtained a fair portion of *gwestfa*, but it may also have been Cydifor or members of his family who had held offices of *maer* of *cynghellor* in the region. Also, according to later genealogies, Cydifor's daughter Ellyw was the wife of Cadwgan ap Bleddyn ap Cynfyn, so there may have been strong ties between Cydifor and the dynasty that had menaced Deheubarth several times over the century.[59] It may have been to counter those ties that Rhydderch ap Tewdwr, Rhys' brother, married his daughter to Cydifor's son Trahaearn, though it is equally likely that Rhydderch was working in his own interest rather than his brother's when the marriage took place.[60]

Whatever the arrangement between Cydifor and Rhys, it did not continue after Cydifor's death. Llywelyn ap Cydifor and his brothers played one of the most common cards available to the *uchelwyr* of the period; they supported a rival candidate to Rhys, calling on his cousin Gruffudd ap Maredudd to come from his exile in Herefordshire to take the kingship. The coup did not succeed; Rhys and his army met Gruffudd, and perhaps the sons of Cydifor as well, at St Dogmaels in Dyfed and defeated the rival force. Gruffudd was killed, though the animosity of Cydifor's sons to Rhys and his family may have continued.[61] One of the sons, Bleddri ap Cydifor, may be the Bleddri who turned to the Normans after they had overrun Deheubarth and served as Henry I's translator.[62]

Rhys did not have long to recover from the insurrection of Llywelyn ap Cydifor and his brothers. William the Conqueror's death had unleashed the forces of Norman expansionism again, and Rhys found himself drawn into the struggles against the Normans on the borders of his realm. He fought them in Brycheiniog, perhaps he recognized the threat that Norman occupation of that region would prove to Cantref Bychan in his own realm, perhaps, because of family connections with important kin groups in Brycheiniog, or perhaps because the men of Brycheiniog had appealed to him as the most powerful native king in the South, one who for whatever reason had been able to send the Normans away from his own realm earlier. On Rhys' death in Brycheiniog, whatever security he had been able to build up in his reign, and whatever central authority or vertical bonds of allegiance he had established, collapsed. The agreement that Rhys ap Tewdwr had made with the Normans in 1081 had been central to his reconstructing the king-ship of Deheubarth. The dissolution of the agreement proved just as central to its destruction.

[59] Bartram, 187.
[60] Bartram, 198.
[61] *Brut s.a.* 1091.
[62] It may be Bleddri who appears as *Blehericus Walensis* in *Pipe Roll 31 Henry I*, holding land in the Carmarthen area, and, as *Bledericus Latemeni*, one of the earliest donors to the Norman priory at Carmarthen. see *Cartularium S. Johannis Bapt. de Carmarthen*, ed. Thomas Philipps, Chelten-ham 1865, charters 32 and 33. As with most genealogical work relating to medieval Wales, of course, the identification of the Bleddri of the charters with Bleddri ap Cydifor relies on the later genealogies used by Bartram. For Bleddri, see Bartram, 187.

'TIME OUT OF MIND': THE KNOWLEDGE AND USE OF THE ELEVENTH- AND TWELFTH-CENTURY PAST IN THIRTEENTH-CENTURY LITIGATION

Paul Brand

In Easter term 1276 William son of Albert of Ramsey brought an action of right against the abbot of Ramsey in the Common Bench at Westminster. He was claiming what he called the manor of 'Uppenhale' in Huntingdonshire.[1] For his title, he went back to the seisin of his ancestor Aylwyn in the reign of 'king Cnut, the king's ancestor' and then traced the descent of the right from Aylwyn through his sister Parnel and six generations of his family to himself. The abbot said that the manor lay within the banlieu of Ramsey and claimed the case for hearing in the banlieu court. Instead of remitting the case to that court, as was the normal practice, the justices simply dismissed it. William had made a claim based on the seisin of his ancestor in the reign of king Cnut. His claim failed, they held, because 'no writ runs from so long a time'.[2]

This case is one of very few recorded on the plea rolls of the thirteenth-century English royal courts in which a claimant did try to go back beyond the Norman Conquest when making a claim to land. The exclusion of lay land claims based on pre-Conquest seisin was probably a well-established phenomenon long before 1200. It is difficult to believe that even in the early twelfth century it would have been possible for a lay claimant to make a claim which implicitly challenged the finality of the land dispositions made in the aftermath of the Norman Conquest. There was, of course, no possible reason for a claimant whose title was ultimately rooted in one of those grants to do so. The real problem only arose with the descendants of pre-Conquest landowners who might, like William, want to re-claim land once in the hands of their family. In the early years of the reign of Henry II we learn of one of the mechanisms preventing this: special recent legislation that barred *Anglici* (but apparently only *Anglici*) from bringing claims based on the seisin of an ancestor at any time more distant than the death of Henry I.[3]

Land claims by religious houses were rather a different matter. Here the exclusion of the Anglo-Saxon past may have been much less clearly established in 1200. In two cases heard in 1199 the bishop of Ely and the abbot of Abingdon traced the beginnings of their church's possession of lands they were claiming to

---

[1]   This is identified by the *VCH* as an otherwise unattested manor of Uphall within Upwood: *VCH Huntingdonshire*, ii, 239.

[2]   PRO, CP 40/14, m. 19.

[3]   *Royal Writs in England from the Conquest to Glanvill*, ed. R.C. Van Caenegem, Selden Soc., lxxvii, 1959, 217, n. 2.

the period before the Conquest.[4] Although both were careful to add to their non-specific allegations of pre-Conquest possession specific claims of more recent seisin and it was perhaps only the more recent seisin that the claimants were committed to proving, neither claimant seems to have thought there was any problem about tracing the root of their title back to the pre-Conquest period.

There are no later examples of claims of this type, but defendants (mainly defendants who were the heads of major religious houses) were still going back to the Anglo-Saxon past much later in the century in making their defences both to land claims and to the king's *quo warranto* claims challenging their right to exercise franchises. In two cases from the 1280s, for example, we find the abbots of Peterborough and Abingdon responding to royal claims based on the alleged seisin of king Richard I with charters of Edward the Confessor granting the manors concerned to their houses and claims to have been seised of the manors concerned ever since, plus, in the Peterborough case, subsequent confirmations from William the Conqueror, Henry II, Richard, John and Henry III.[5] Nor were such pre-Conquest royal charters produced only in response to royal claims. In the 1285 Warwickshire eyre the prior of Coventry answered a claim by Robert de Pinkeny based on the alleged seisin of his ancestor Gerard in the reign of king John by producing what purported to be a grant by earl Leofric in the time of king Edward the Confessor which Edward was said to have confirmed and also mentioned subsequent confirmations by William the Conqueror, Henry II, and Henry III.[6] The point was to delay the litigation while the king was consulted and the prior needed to go back before the Conquest to get to the original grant of which the later royal charters were no more than confirmations.[7]

Franchise-holders went back still further into the real or supposed Anglo-Saxon past in defending their right to exercise franchises in the course of the Edwardian *quo warranto* proceedings. In the 1279–81 Yorkshire eyre we find the bishop of Durham going back to an alleged grant by the seventh-century king of Northumbria Ecgfrith as the basis for the franchises he claimed in the manor of Crayke but not apparently producing any charter of Ecgfrith to prove this.[8] In the 1287 Hertfordshire eyre the abbot of St Alban's claimed extensive franchises on the basis of grants by king Offa, here described as king of England, and by 'his son Atheldred' as well as of kings Henry II and Richard and produced charters or

---

[4] *Curia Regis Rolls*, 17 vols, HMSO, 1923– , i, 93; *Rotuli Curiae Regis*, ed. F. Palgrave, 2 vols, Record Commission 1835, i, 347–8.

[5] *Placita de Quo Warranto*, ed. W. Illingworth and J. Caley, Record Commission 1818, 407, 664.

[6] PRO, JUST 1/958, m. 2d. Leofric's supposed grant of Ufton is part of the forged foundation charter of Coventry priory: P.H. Sawyer, *Anglo-Saxon Charters*, Royal Historical Society 1968, no. 1226. Edward the Confessor's supposed confirmation of this grant is also thought to be spurious: *Anglo-Saxon Charters*, no. 1000. The reference must in fact be to the Gerard de Limesy who died before 1185: I.J. Sanders, *English Baronies*, Oxford 1960, 30.

[7] For other similar cases of the same period in which pre-Conquest royal charters were produced see PRO, CP 40/80, m. 159; JUST 1/622, m. 43d (and for a later stage in the same plea see CP 40/87, m. 106d); JUST 1/544, m. 13d.

[8] He also went back to an alleged grant by the Conqueror (William the Bastard) as the basis for the franchises he claimed in Northallerton and Howdenshire but again did not apparently produce any charter to support this. The only written evidence the bishop did produce was a charter of Henry I restoring these manors to bishop Rannulph as freely as he had held them before being dispossessed: *Placita de Quo Warranto*, 187–8.

supposed charters of all four kings.[9] Continuous seisin since before the Conquest but without the warranty of a royal charter was pleaded by the abbot of Cerne as title to the assize of bread and ale in the 1280 Dorset eyre and a similar title was also pleaded to the same franchise by at least one lay franchise holder in the 1279–81 Yorkshire eyre.[10]

In most of these cases it was a genuine or a forged Anglo-Saxon charter which the litigant produced as evidence that seems to have been the source of his own 'knowledge' of the Anglo-Saxon past. However, it is unlikely that William son of Albert of Ramsey possessed any kind of written evidence of this kind. William probably relied upon a family tradition which linked what had now become a peasant family with their distant and illustrious forebear, the earl Aylwyn who had founded Ramsey and possessed a hall at Upwood.[11]

By 1276 the 'Uppenhale' case had come to be doubly anomalous for it was by then not just the pre-Conquest past that was barred to land claimants in the action of right but also the remainder of the eleventh century and part of the twelfth century as well. Indeed, recently enacted legislation (c. 39 of the statute of Westminster I) barred any claim to land or to advowsons made on the basis of a seisin older than the reign of king Richard I.[12] However, although that statute had been enacted at the Easter parliament of 1275, it had given claimants a period of grace for the initiation of older claims till St John's day (24 June) 1276. When, in 1279, Thomas of Rodborough made a claim based on the seisin of a kinswoman on the day of Henry I's death he argued that the statute allowed 'those who wished to make claims on an older time than the reign of king Richard time to do so till two weeks after the feast of St John the Baptist 1276'.[13] What the statute actually said was that during the period of grace litigants might acquire writs to pursue only those claims that were admissible under the existing limitation rules. These did not in general allow claimants to go back before the beginning of Henry II's reign (1154). Perhaps William son of Albert of Ramsey was acting on a similar misapprehension about the effects of the statute, supposing that it offered a brief window of opportunity during which litigants might lodge claims however old they might be.

But there were also a number of other claims brought by rather better informed litigants at this time. The Common Bench plea rolls show a flurry of actions based on the seisin of ancestors and predecessors during the reign of Henry II in 1276 and over the next three years. I have noted four such claims in 1276; four in 1277; seven in 1278 and no less than eight in 1279. The number then declines to three in 1280 and two in 1281 and there are then no further cases until 1287. The two final cases were heard in 1288 and 1291. Both were brought by Gilbert de Clare, earl of Gloucester to claim property in either Chipping or Broad Campden in Gloucestershire

---

[9] *Placita de Quo Warranto*, 288. For the use of the same charter of king Offa in private litigation in 1293 about woodland in Little Horwood in Buckinghamshire see PRO, CP 40/102, mm. 126–126d.

[10] *Placita de Quo Warranto*, 182–3; *Placita de Quo Warranto*, 188.

[11] The identification with earl Aylwyn is made in *VCH Huntingdonshire*, ii, 239. Aylwyn had, however, died before Cnut came to the throne.

[12] *Statutes of the Realm*, ed. A. Luders and others, 11 vols, Record Commission 1810–1828, i, 36.

[13] PRO, CP 40/30, m. 71d.

and a report of the second case shows that an objection was registered to the claim but the objection overruled 'by favour and against the form of the statute'.[14]

The first general legislation on limitation dates of which a text survives was enacted in February 1237.[15] It allowed claimants to go back to the seisin of an ancestor or predecessor in the reign of Henry II, and it too had allowed claimants a brief period of grace, but only till the following Whitsun, to initiate litigation under the existing limitation rules. These, as the 1237 legislation itself notes, had allowed a claimant in the action of right to go back as far as the seisin of an ancestor or predecessor on the day of Henry I's death (1 December 1135). There was probably a similar rush of litigants attempting to beat this deadline. We can certainly see no less than ten cases where claimants based their title on an 1135 seisin on the Common Bench plea roll for Trinity term 1239. It seems probable that all had been initiated in the brief period of grace between the enactment of the legislation and its coming into effect.[16] Despite the legislation, a small trickle of claims based on the seisin of an ancestor at the death of Henry I continued for the next forty years. I have found at least fifteen such cases during the period between 1240 and 1279 and there were probably others.[17] In three the tenants are not known to have made any objection.[18] More commonly, tenants cited the legislation of 1237 as barring such claims unless brought within the time specified in the legislation.[19] In two cases this led without further recorded argument to the

[14] PRO, CP 40/75, m. 143d; CP 40/91, m. 224d (reported in *Year Books, 21 & 22 Edward I*, ed. A.J. Horwood, RS 1873, 525).

[15] There are texts of this legislation with rather different wording but agreeing in the essentials in *Close Rolls, 1234–1237*, HMSO 1908, 520–1; *Bracton's Note Book*, ed. F.W. Maitland, 3 vols, London 1887, iii, 230; and (as communicated to Ireland) in *Statutes and Ordinances and Acts of the Parliament of Ireland, King John to Henry V*, ed. H.F. Berry, Dublin, 1907, 31–2. It is also summarised in c. 8 of the 'textus receptus' of the so-called statute of Merton of 1236: *Statutes of the Realm*, i, 3.

[16] *Curia Regis Rolls*, xvi, nos. 632, 650, 653, 690, 700, 750, 827, 861, 967. In all of these cases except *Curia Regis Rolls*, xvi, no. 690 (which records the issue put to a grand assize and notes the supplementary question to be put about a predecessor's seisin at Henry I's death) the count as recorded mentioned simply seisin during Henry I's reign but it seems probable that in all cases the count actually mentioned seisin specifically at the death of Henry I. No count is recorded in *Curia Regis Rolls*, xvi, no. 924 but an additional note indicates that a similar count was made and the tenant objected to it on the grounds that the claimant had not brought his case in the county court of Lincolnshire till after Whitsun 1237.

[17] There is also one case heard in the 1240 Suffolk eyre and a second case heard among the foreign pleas of the 1257–8 Suffolk eyre in which the claimants based their title on the seisin of an ancestor in the reign of Henry I. There was no challenge to the first claim but the second case was dismissed for not being based on seisin at Henry I's death: PRO, JUST 1/818, m. 34d; JUST 1/820, m. 33.

[18] No objection is enrolled in the following cases: PRO, KB 26/162, m. 31d (1259); KB 26/169, m. 28d (1260); CP 40/27, m. 71d (1278).

[19] As early as 1244 a tenant making such an objection wrongly cited the legislation as having been made at Merton: PRO, KB 26/133, m. 6 (printed from a parallel roll in *Select Cases in the Court of King's Bench, vol. II*, ed. G.O. Sayles, Selden Society, lvii, 1938, cxxxix). It is also identified as having been made at Merton in a case of 1255: PRO, JUST 1/872, m. 24d. In a case of 1258 the legislation was again said to have been made at Merton but was said to have made an exception 'if any ancestor of the claimant or the claimant himself brought a plea within one year after the enactment of the provision of Merton': PRO, KB 26/160, m. 14. In a case heard in the 1268 Yorkshire eyre the provision was cited as having been made by king John at Runnymede and claimants were now said to have been given a year and a day after the making of the provision to bring their actions: PRO, JUST 1/1050, m. 66d. However, in another plea in the same eyre an

dismissal of the claim.[20] Generally, claimants attempted to show why they were entitled to bring their claim notwithstanding the legislation. The normal justification was that they or one of their ancestors had brought a similar claim prior to the legislation but that this had not led to a final determination. The current litigation was, therefore, no more than a revival or a continuation and so not barred.

The pre-1237 rule had only allowed litigants to go back to the time of Henry I's death: it had not been permissible to bring a claim based on the seisin of an ancestor or predecessor during the intervening period, the reign of king Stephen. The complete absence of cases in which litigants tried and failed to make such claims indicates that the rule barring them had remained well-understood down to 1237. Indeed, only one thirteenth-century litigant is known ever to have brought such a claim. In 1279 Edward I brought a claim to the advowson of a Hampshire church based on the alleged presentation of a clerk to the church by his predecessor, king Stephen.[21] Not surprisingly, the clerk left a blank where the descent of the right from the king's 'ancestor' to himself would normally have been recorded. The case was dismissed when the archbishop of Rouen produced a charter of Henry II granting the church to his predecessor.

Professor Milsom has suggested that the writ of right was itself originally invented specifically to undo the effects of seisins wrongfully acquired during Stephen's reign and that claims based on the seisin of a claimant or his ancestor or predecessor 'on the day that Henry I was alive and dead' were originally the only kind of claim which could be made by this writ. It was only later, he argues, that the remedy was extended to allow litigants to base their claims on more recent seisins.[22] However, *Glanvill*, our main source on the beginnings of the common law, gives two separate specimen counts for the alternative form of the writ of right and the writ of right of advowson where the claimant is basing his claim on seisin in the reign of Henry I. In both places he talks only of an ancestor's seisin 'in the reign of king Henry the First' or 'in the reign of king Henry, the grandfather of king Henry'. There is no reason in either case to suppose that the crucial additional phrase ('on the day the king was alive and dead') has been omitted.[23] It seems therefore to have been perfectly permissible in the final years of Henry II's reign for claimants to make claims based on the seisin of an ancestor at any stage in the reign of Henry I.

This may well have remained the position to c.1200. A legislative change in limitation dates of about that date would explain the vagaries of the title which Roger Waspail is recorded as having made on three successive occasions in litigation against Richard son of Anfrid and then subsequently against Richard's warrantor, the abbess of Shaftesbury. In Trinity term 1200 he is recorded as asserting simply that his grandfather had been seised in the reign of Henry I. In Michaelmas term 1200 he is recorded as claiming on the basis of his grandfather's

almost identical objection was recorded except for the ascription of this legislation to the king's council at Merton: PRO, JUST 1/1050, m. 80d.

[20] PRO, KB 26/172, m. 19; JUST 1/1050, m. 80d. There is also a reference to a case dismissed for this reason some time between 1237 and 1247 in the pleading in a case heard in the 1247 Cambridgeshire eyre: PRO, JUST 1/81, m. 12.

[21] PRO, KB 27/49, m. 25d.

[22] S.F.C. Milsom, *The Legal Framework of English Feudalism*, Cambridge 1976, 183; S.F.C. Milsom, *Historical Foundations of the Common Law*, 2nd edition, London 1981, 128–9.

[23] *Glanvill*, ed. Hall, 23, 46.

seisin both in general during Henry I's reign and more specifically on the day of Henry I's death. In Michaelmas term 1201 he is recorded as claiming on the basis of his grandfather's seisin at the time of Henry I's death alone.[24] It would also explain why it is only in 1201 that we first find a claim being dismissed because it was based on the seisin of an ancestor in Henry I's reign and not specifically on the day of his death.[25] A legislative change in the limitation date in the writ of right c.1200 would also explain why twenty-three of the thirty-six cases in which claimants are recorded as relying on the seisin of their ancestors in the reign of Henry I come from before 1201. There are certainly cases after 1201 where the plea roll enrolment records a claim as made on the seisin of an ancestor in the reign of Henry I but we know from other evidence that the actual claim must have included the additional phrase which made it clear that the seisin alleged was on the day of Henry I's death.[26] Professor Milsom has suggested that all our examples are the result of a similar omission[27] but it seems to me to be rather more likely that the pre-1201 cases really are claims of a kind barred after that date.

In practice, most claims to land and to advowsons in thirteenth-century England rested on recent seisin of the land or advowson concerned. But a significant minority did not. I have noted around ninety cases in which litigants based their claim on the seisin of an ancestor or predecessor at the death of Henry I on the rolls of the king's central courts (Common Bench and King's Bench) during the period between the beginning of the surviving rolls (in 1194) and the enactment of the 1237 legislation. These are mainly claims to land but in at least three cases an advowson was being claimed.[28] There were another ten similar cases between 1237 and 1240 and a further fifteen such cases between 1240 and 1279.[29] To these must be added the thirty-six cases brought before 1237 where claimants are recorded as basing their claims on the seisin of their ancestors or predecessors in the reign of Henry I. All are evidence of claimants going back at least to 1135. Claims based on the seisin of an ancestor or predecessor in the reign of king Henry II remained relatively common right through to about 1280.

These cases are, I think, good evidence for a tenacious memory on the part of plaintiffs and, behind them, of their families or the religious houses to which they belonged that property had once been in the possession of their family or their house. None could quite match the length of recall of William son of Albert of Ramsey but by the time the last cases in which plaintiffs claimed on an 1135 seisin were being heard almost a century and a half had elapsed. Nor was it just a vague and imprecise memory that property had once belonged to the family or the house.

---

[24] *Curia Regis Rolls*, i, 217, 321; *Curia Regis Rolls*, ii, 64.

[25] *Curia Regis Rolls*, ii, 12. A similar judgment was given in a 1228 case: *Curia Regis Rolls*, xiii, no. 507.

[26] For fairly clear examples see *Curia Regis Rolls*, vi, 73 where the additional words are probably concealed by an 'etc.'; and compare *Curia Regis Rolls*, vi, 143 with a second entry in the same litigation at *Curia Regis Rolls*, vi, 279–80. See also *Curia Regis Rolls*, xiv, no. 2013 where the count omits the additional words but the defendant is recorded as proffering half a mark for specific mention of the 'anno et die' in the issue put to the jurors of the grand assize.

[27] Milsom, *Legal Framework of English Feudalism*, 178.

[28] *Curia Regis Rolls*, xi, no. 121; *Curia Regis Rolls*, xi, no. 1573; *Curia Regis Rolls*, xiii, no. 26. As seisin of an advowson was demonstrated only by presentation to a living it would seem probable that in none of these cases are we to take the claim to have been 'seised on the day of Henry I's death' entirely literally.

[29] Above, p. 40.

The count in the writ of right required claimants to assert that a specific named ancestor or predecessor had been seised of the property concerned. The later assumption seems to have been that the ancestor or predecessor named in the claimant's count was always the last to have been in possession of the property. This may well have been the case in most of these instances as well, though the claimant's inability to bring cases based on the seisin of an ancestor during Stephen's reign may mean there are some exceptions.

It was the general thirteenth-century rule that claimants in the action of right were not required, indeed were not able, to go behind the seisin of this last ancestor or predecessor in possession, to show how the property had first come into the possession of the family or house concerned, the root of their title to it. There are, however, a number of late-twelfth and early-thirteenth-century cases where we find claimants doing precisely that. In an 1194 case in which William Brun claimed a Northamptonshire holding on the basis of the seisin of his great-uncle Richard in the reign of Henry I he added that Richard's title was derived from a grant in fee and inheritance by Nigel of Beckhampton. In an 1198 case the abbot of St Mary York claimed four carucates of land in Hook in Yorkshire not just on the basis of the abbey's seisin but also on the basis of a grant by Henry I.[30] We have already noted the two cases heard in 1199 in which the bishop of Ely and the abbot of Abingdon traced the beginnings of their church's possession of the property they were claiming to the period before the Conquest.[31] In seven other cases heard between 1194 and 1219 lay claimants traced the beginning of their family's possession of the property concerned back to the time of the Norman Conquest. In an 1199 case all the claimant said was that his great-grandfather Hervey had been seised of a hide at Hidcote in Gloucestershire 'from the Conquest of England, having come at the Conquest'.[32] In all the other cases, however, claimants also alleged a more recent seisin and it is plain that acquisition of the land at the Conquest and possession since then was being cited as the root of their title to the property.[33] In a similar claim made in 1220 it was the bishop of Lincoln who claimed the manor of Wooburn in Buckinghamshire and one hundred shillings worth of land there on the basis of the seisin of his predecessors since the Conquest of England and specified them as including bishops Remigius, Alexander and bishop Robert de Chesney who had been seised of the land in the reign of Henry II.[34] It is possible that we are seeing in these cases the last examples of what may once have been the normal form of claim in land actions: where claimants showed the root of their title in a grant or in an acquisition of possession at the Conquest and continuous subsequent possession as well as a more recent seisin by the last of their ancestors or predecessors to have been in possession of the property concerned. If this was indeed once the normal form of claim, it must have been the imposition of limitation periods which rendered this form obsolete for they prevented claimants actually proving, or even offering to prove, seisin

[30] *Rotuli Curiae Regis*, i, 59–60; *Memoranda Roll 10 John*, ed. R. Allen Brown, Pipe Roll Society, new series, xxxi, 1956, 106.
[31] Above, pp. 37–8.
[32] *Rotuli Curiae Regis*, i, 358–9.
[33] *Rotuli Curiae Regis*, i, 93; *Rotuli Curiae Regis*, i, 419; *Curia Regis Rolls*, i, 152 and *Curia Regis Rolls*, i, 211; *Curia Regis Rolls*, v, 177; *Curia Regis Rolls*, v, 311; *Curia Regis Rolls*, viii, 123–4 and cf. 130.
[34] *Curia Regis Rolls*, xi, 219. He did not apparently mention bishop Robert Bloet (1094–1123).

going back to the Conquest. On this hypothesis, what had once been an integral part of all land claims survived in these claims as an additional and by now non-functional element in claims that were complete without them.

The normal thirteenth-century practice in the writ of right was for the claimant to say nothing about how the land had been lost by his family or institution. This does not mean that they did not know nor that they did not tell some kind of story about it to the jurors of the grand assize, merely that this was not something which normally entered the official record. There are, however, a number of cases, again mainly from around 1200, where we do learn this from the record. Several sound not at all unlike those stories which thirteenth-century litigants told about the much more recent past. We hear, for example, of property lost after it had been handed over as surety for a loan or on a short-term lease or of property lost during a minority.[35] We do, however, also hear of more distinctively twelfth-century types of loss. In two cases, both heard in 1194, it was alleged that property had been lost to its rightful owners during 'wartime' (here meaning during Stephen's reign).[36] In another we hear of property allegedly lost by the elder of two brothers to his younger brother by the will of the lords of whom it was held and whom the younger brother served and by the elder brother's *impotentia*.[37] We are also told of property originally lost during the Anarchy which was briefly recovered only to be lost again during a minority when it was granted by a lord to his own niece and her husband.[38]

Lay claimants also needed to have detailed knowledge of the family tree which linked them with the ancestor on whose seisin they based their claim. At the time of the earliest plea rolls it seems only to have been necessary to state in general terms how he was related to the ancestor, but after 1208 it became necessary for him to trace how the right to the land had descended to him, step by step.[39] Much of this could be recent history, but it clearly also required a detailed knowledge of the twelfth-century part of their family tree.

It is, of course, much more difficult for us now to know just how accurate the 'knowledge' possessed by thirteenth-century claimants was. The one element in any claim which is perhaps most likely to be true is that the claimant did have an ancestor or predecessor of the name given (or something close to it) and that he was living some time in the twelfth century, quite possibly at the time or in the reign specified by the claimant. Particularly convincing are those claims which went back to twelfth-century ancestors whose names had fallen out of fashion by the thirteenth century but sound not implausible for twelfth-century tenants: for example, the Thurkil allegedly seised of property at Boreham in Essex in 1135 whose heir was a son named Godbold who are mentioned in a 1255 claim.[40] It also seems likely that the claimant's account of his family tree was generally correct or

[35] For property allegedly handed over as surety for a loan or on a short-term lease see *Curia Regis Rolls*, i, 158, 220; *Curia Regis Rolls*, i, 141; *Curia Regis Rolls*, i, 279–80; *Curia Regis Rolls*, ix, 374. For property allegedly lost during a minority see *Curia Regis Rolls*, iv, 129 and *Curia Regis Rolls*, iv, 136.
[36] *Rotuli Curiae Regis*, i, 25–6; *Rotuli Curiae Regis*, i, 93.
[37] *Rotuli Curiae Regis*, i, 360.
[38] *Rotuli Curiae Regis*, i, 419; *Curia Regis Rolls*, ix, 132–8.
[39] Paul Brand, *The Origins of the English Legal Profession*, Oxford 1992, 39.
[40] PRO, JUST 1/872, m. 24d. For other examples see JUST 1/567, m. 2; KB 26/162, m. 31d, KB 26/225, m. 19d and KB 26/172, m. 19; JUST 1/1050, m. 66d.

nearly correct. It took little knowledge of family history for claimants to connect themselves with an ancestor who had allegedly been seised in 1135 in the most commonly occurring type of case, where that ancestor was only the grandfather or grandmother of the current claimant, or in the much smaller number of cases where the last ancestor to have been in possession was the claimant's father or mother.[41] It took rather more knowledge to successfully trace the claimant's relationship to a great-great-grandfather or to a great-great-uncle or (in a 1268 case) for William Malebisse to remember back the seven generations to the Geoffrey Malebisse who had allegedly been seised of three Yorkshire manors in 1135. It seems not implausible, however, that he could do this correctly.[42] It is much less certain whether claimants were generally correct in asserting that their ancestor had been seised as of right of the property concerned. This may well have been true where the tenant did not deny that seisin but asserted that his own title came from a subsequent and valid grant of the property concerned. But where the tenant simply denied both the ancestor's seisin and the claimant's right, we cannot know.

Nor can we say much about how thirteenth-century claimants acquired their knowledge of the eleventh- and twelfth-century past. Even where charters existed they would not normally reveal which ancestors or predecessors were last in seisin of the property. Written genealogies may have been of assistance to lay claimants in tracing their descent from their twelfth-century ancestors. But for the most part claimants must have relied on oral tradition for their knowledge of lands once in their family, knowledge of how and why land was lost and knowledge of their own family tree.

Defendants facing such claims had normally to rely on similar traditions. This was not, of course, necessary if they could find some technical defect in the form of the claim or if they simply offered battle in denial of the claimant's right. But once a defendant had opted for trial by the grand assize he must normally have communicated his own version of the past history of the property justifying his own tenure to the jurors of the grand assize. We see the end results of this process in a jury verdict in a case brought by the king against the prior of Haugham (a dependent prior of the abbey of St Sever) in the 1281–4 Lincolnshire eyre. The king had claimed the manor of Haugham on the basis of Henry II's seisin of it and the prior had simply denied the king's right and the seisin of his ancestor. The jury found that the manor had been the possession of one Hugh son of Thurstin who had come with the Conqueror and been given the manor by William. The manor

---

[41] Thirty-two of these cases are based on the seisin of the claimant's grandfather; six on the seisin of a grandmother. It was also a grandfather's seisin that was alleged in the one customs and services case. Five cases were brought on the seisin of the claimant's father. The latest of these was one heard in 1207: *Curia Regis Rolls*, v, 102. For the one case brought in 1204 on the seisin of the claimant's mother (and her husband) see *Curia Regis Rolls*, iii, 120.

[42] For examples of descent from a great-great-grandfather see *Curia Regis Rolls*, vi, 285–6 and 367; *Curia Regis Rolls*, viii, 252; *Curia Regis Rolls*, x, 108; *Curia Regis Rolls*, xii, no. 2036. In none of these cases was the descent a direct unbroken one in the main male line. For examples of descent from a great-great-uncle see *Curia Regis Rolls*, vi, 259, 335 and *Curia Regis Rolls*, xii, no. 431. For a case of 1204 where a claim was based on the seisin of a great-great-aunt (but no detailed descent traced) see *Curia Regis Rolls*, iii, 201. For the Malebisse case see PRO, JUST 1/1050, m. 80d.

had then been given by Hugh to the abbey of St Sever which had held it ever since. The jurors must have been repeating a story which the prior had told them.[43]

Other defendants made much more informative responses on the record to justify their tenure which provide alternative or supplementary accounts of the eleventh- or twelfth-century past. A good example is the 1199 case where the plaintiff's claim went back to the seisin of his great-grandfather (Bernard le Fraunceys) at the death of Henry I and to how his grandfather had lost the land to his younger brother because of his *impotencia* (his incompetence). The defendant's story was that John had actually acquired this land in return for his service and not by disinheriting his brother, and the proof of this was that it had been John who had held them during the reign of Henry I and in 1135 and thus prior to his father's death.[44] A second example is the 1203 case in which John of Northeye claimed a holding at Barnhorn on the basis of the seisin of his ancestor Engeram during the reign of king Henry I. In answer the abbot proffered a charter of Henry II confirming the land to Battle both on the basis of a prior charter of Henry I and on the basis of the judgment given in favour of abbot Walter of Battle at Clarendon before the king and his barons in litigation against Gilbert de Balliol and John's father Reinger.[45]

Many tenants were able to rely on written documentation: royal charters granting the property; royal charters confirming judgments given in the king's court; final concords made in the king's court and also in seignorial courts; and private charters.[46] But other defences were fairly clearly derived from nothing more than oral tradition. One obvious example is the case of 1199 in which Philip fitzPain claimed a hide at Hidcote in Gloucestershire on the basis of the seisin of his great-grandfather Hervey from the Norman Conquest onwards. The tenant counter-asserted that his mother's grandfather, Roswald or Restwald *miles*, had also come at the Conquest and that he and his heirs had been seised ever since then. Philip did not deny that Roswald had seisin of the land but claimed that he only had it by the 'bail' (as tenant at will) of Hervey who was his elder brother.[47]

Defendants show no signs of being bound by any kind of exclusionary rule which required them only to talk about matters which were within what was later to be called 'the limit of legal memory', the period beyond which claimants could not go in making their own claims to property. As we have seen, Restwald went back to the acquisition of property by his mother's grandfather at the Conquest

---

[43] *Placita de Quo Warranto*, 394. The manor was already held by St Sever at the time Domesday Book was compiled.
[44] *Rotuli Curiae Regis*, i, 360.
[45] *Curia Regis Rolls*, ii, 178–9. The story of the litigation about Barnhorn is, of course, well-known from the Battle abbey chronicle: *The Chronicle of Battle Abbey*, ed. E. Searle, Oxford 1980, 118, 211–21.
[46] For the use of royal charters granting the property see *Rotuli Curiae Regis*, i, 347–8 and *Rotuli Curiae Regis*, i, 93. For the use of royal charters confirming judgments in the king's court see *Curia Regis Rolls*, ii, 178–9; *Curia Regis Rolls*, ii, 64 (and for earlier related litigation see *Curia Regis Rolls*, i, 217, 321); *Curia Regis Rolls*, vi, 176–7; *Curia Regis Rolls*, viii, 43–4. For the use of a final concord made in the king's court see *Curia Regis Rolls*, ix, 284–5. For the use of final concords made in seignorial courts see *Curia Regis Rolls*, v, 181–2; *Rotuli Curiae Regis*, ii, 237–8; *Rotuli Curiae Regis*, i, 440–1. For the use of private charters see *Curia Regis Rolls*, i, 279–80 (but also royal charters); *Curia Regis Rolls*, v, 142–3 (but also a royal charter and a charter of the superior lord of the fee); *Curia Regis Rolls*, xiv, no. 811.
[47] *Rotuli Curiae Regis*, i, 358–9.

though he also alleged continuous seisin since then. In another case of 1206 the bishop of London claimed a soke in Colchester against William the Chaplain on the basis of the seisin of his predecessor, Richard de Belmeis, on the day of Henry I's death.[48] Here the defendant attempted to defend his tenure on the basis of a charter of the same bishop Belmeis confirming his grandfather's tenure of all he had previously held in Colchester and a charter of bishop Gilbert specifically confirming to his father, Benedict son of William, the soke and the schools of Colchester and all he held there, but he was eventually driven to the defence that his ancestors had been tenants of the soke under the bishops of London ever since the Conquest.

Nor was it only in cases where the basis of the plaintiff's claim was the seisin of an ancestor in the twelfth century that defendants went back to the alleged facts of the eleventh- and twelfth-century past or even to the more distant past in making their defences. We have already noted the prior of Coventry's use of a purported grant by earl Leofric in the time of Edward the Confessor in response to a claim in the 1285 Northamptonshire eyre based on seisin in the reign of king John and a number of other cases where defendants produced pre-Conquest charters in answer to claims based on late-twelfth-century or thirteenth-century seisins.[49]

More commonly defendants only went back to the post-Conquest period. In a 1253 case, for example, Richard Harm and John Payn claimed a knight's fee at 'Stokes' in Sussex against William de la Falaise on the basis of the seisin of their kinsman, Richard de Barentyn, at the time of his death in the reign of king John.[50] In his defence William explained how one Edgar had acquired the fee at the Conquest. It had then passed to his son and heir Robert and from Robert to his daughter and heiress Alice. Alice had been under age at the death of her father and king Richard had given her wardship and her marriage to Alexander de Barentyn. After she had been in his wardship for a while she had fled overseas to avoid being given in marriage by him. When Alexander told the king of this the king allowed him to retain her land till she had satisfied him for the value of her marriage. He had then retained the land for life and passed the land on to his son Richard, who also died in possession before the land could be restored. It was only after his death that Alice and her husband (William de la Falaise) had obtained a restoration of the land from king John and the family had held the land ever since.[51]

A second case where the defence takes us back into the late-eleventh- and early-twelfth-century past is one brought by William Fox against Reginald 'de la Rughedone' in the 1262–3 Surrey eyre claiming a holding at Addington in Surrey

---

[48] *Curia Regis Rolls*, iv, 74–5. For earlier related litigation in which what seems to be the same defendant is called William son of Benedict see *Curia Regis Rolls*, iii, 181. Evidently neither party knew that bishop Belmeis could not possibly have been seised in 1135 since he had died in 1127.
[49] Above, p. 38.
[50] PRO, KB 26/148, m. 19.
[51] The jury verdict in the case added to and made some corrections to this story: the original enfeoffment had been by the king's ancestors; the grant of Alice's wardship and marriage had been by Henry II, not Richard, and to a man described as the king's *serviens*; Henry's anger at Alice's disobedience had led to him granting the knight's fee to Alexander on a permanent basis and this grant was subsequently confirmed by king Richard. The jury thus found that Richard had died seised in fee but judgment did not have to be given in his favour because this was also found to have been before the limitation date in this action (king John's return from Ireland to England).

on the basis of the seisin of his grandfather Aylward de la Rughedone at the time of his death some time earlier in the reign of Henry III.[52] Reginald did not simply deny that Aylward had been seised at the time of his death, though this was all that he needed to do. He went on to say that his own ancestors had held the land for two hundred years without Aylward's ancestors ever having had any interest in the land. This may have been a slight exaggeration, but the jury was happy to go back into the early-twelfth-century past (beyond the limitation date even in the writ of right and well beyond the limitation date in this writ) to give a verdict saying not just that Aylward had not died seised and had never had seisin but also that Reginald's ancestors had held the property ever since the reign of Henry I.

Nor was it just in litigation about land and advowsons that thirteenth-century litigants went back into the eleventh and twelfth centuries to find 'facts' to support their claim or to draw 'facts' for their defence.

In a case of 1292, for example, Hugh de la Penne, rector of Stanton Harcourt in Oxfordshire sued his fellow-rector, Hugh de Clifford, parson of Northmoor, for fourteen marks arrears of an annual rent of one mark a year.[53] Hugh cited as his title to this annual rent not just the seisin of all of his predecessors since the time of king Richard I but also an agreement made in the court of Canterbury in the time of archbishop Thomas Becket under which the rent was made payable in perpetuity by the rectors of Northmoor to the rectors of Stanton Harcourt.[54] In a 1284 case John de Audenard, rector of the church of Bledlow in Buckinghamshire, claimed the right to receive two thirds of the crop of every tenth acre of the demesne of Bledlow by virtue of a charter of Robert count of Mortain, former lord of Bledlow, in favour of the Norman abbey of Grestain, the patron of his church, and sued the abbot of Bec for refusing to allow him to take this 'tithe'. He also claimed that two named predecessors had been seised of this 'tithe' in the reign of the present king.[55] The claim was renewed under a different writ in the 1286 Buckinghamshire eyre and the rector now claimed on the basis of the possession of a predecessor in the reign of Henry III. In the course of pleading it again emerged, however, that he was ultimately relying on the grant by Robert count of Mortain. Pleading in the case also makes clear that this due was payable in addition to, rather than in place of, the rector's tithe.[56] The donor must be the Robert count of Mortain who was Domesday lord of extensive English lands including the honour of Berkhamstead, who was tenant of Bledlow at the time of Domesday Book and who had died in 1090.[57]

In an assize of mort d'ancestor brought by Alice Albern in 1261 for a holding at Bishop's Hatfield in Hertfordshire the tenant, John of Bassingbourne, objected

---

[52] PRO, JUST 1/874, m. 11d.

[53] PRO, CP 40/96, m. 114 (and for previous pleading in the same case see CP 40/93, m. 27). The case is reported in BL MS Additional 31826, ff. 55v–56r.

[54] Technically the plaintiff seems to have relied only on the seisin since the time of king Richard as his title. The prior agreement was shown to the court merely *ad evidenciam hujus rei* (to bolster his title). The agreement cited was really one made in the court of Canterbury during the time of archbishop Theobald, not that of Becket. It is dated by Saltman to 1141–8: A. Saltman, *Theobald Archbishop of Canterbury*, London 1956, 433–5. For another case of 1306 in which a plaintiff in a similar annuity case relied on a deed apparently of the mid-1160s see PRO, CP 40/160, m. 269d.

[55] PRO, CP 40/55, m. 50.

[56] PRO, JUST 1/63, m. 7d.

[57] Sanders, *English Baronies*, 14; *VCH Buckinghamshire*, ii, 247.

that she was not entitled to bring the action because her father John had been a villein tenant of his ancestor.[58] John must have been searching around in the family deeds because he now produced as proof of that assertion a writ of Henry II addressed to Nigel bishop of Ely in favour of his ancestor Albert *Anglicus*, confirming his tenure of all his lands as his grandfather had held them in the reign of Henry I and his possession of Aylbert son of Borwace whom he had proved his villein both in the bishop's own court and in the county court of Hertfordshire.[59] John claimed that Aylbert had been Alice Albern's grandfather. Not surprisingly, Alice insisted that whatever might have been the situation in Henry II's reign her father had died seised in fee long afterwards. She also insisted that this Aylbert was not in fact her grandfather. The pleading then shifted on to other matters.

In a 1279 naifty case brought by the prior of Norwich against Richard Ernys of Hemsby the prior started by claiming Richard as his serf on the basis of his predecessor's seisin of his father in the reign of Henry III.[60] It was again the defendant who took the case back into the twelfth-century past by not only claiming that his father was free but also showing why this had been so. His father's grandfather Alfrid had been a foreigner (*alienigena*) born in Normandy. This meant that all descended from him were free. This was denied by the prior. Alfrid had been the villein of his predecessor during Henry II's reign and had been born in Hemsby. He also produced other unfree descendants of his. From this case we get a picture of a rather hazy sense of eleventh- and twelfth-century history on the part not just of the defendant but also of his legal advisers. Alfrid is not the likeliest name for a Norman settler in England and Richard's serjeant, Alexander of Coventry, is reported as saying that Alfrid had come from Normandy 'with the conquerors' ('vynt hors de Normandye ovek les conquerors').

The normal rule of the thirteenth-century common law in cases where what was at stake was wardship of the body and the right of marriage over an heir who held by knight service of more than one lord was that it went to the lord whose ancestor had been the first to grant land to the ancestor of the heir in question.[61] Some litigants went right back to the time of the Norman Conquest or its immediate aftermath in tracing that first feoffment. In 1207 Richard de Umfraville brought an action against Eustace de Vesci for the wardship of the heir of Henry Bataille on the basis of the prior feoffment made by his great-grandfather Robert *cum Barba* to Gilbert Bataille, the great-grandfather of the heir, an enfeoffment made at the Conquest granting Gilbert lands he was to hold for the service of one knight.[62] Eustace did not attempt to set up a prior enfeoffment by his ancestor, clearly the defence anticipated by Richard. Instead he alleged that there had been a previous

---

[58] PRO, JUST 1/1192, m. 8.

[59] The writ is transcribed in full but without any kind of dating clause: 'H. dei gracia etc. Nigello episcopo Elyensi salutem. Precipio quod Aylbertus Anglicus habeat et teneat bene et in pace totam terram et omnia tenementa in bosco etc. sicut umquam avus suus melius et liberius tenuit tempore H. regis avi mei et nominatim Aylbertum filium Borwace villanum suum sicut illum disracionavit in curia tua et in comitatu meo de Hertfford'. On Albert *Anglicus* and his close connexions with bishop Nigel see Edward Miller, *The Abbey and Bishopric of Ely*, Cambridge 1951, 172, 196.

[60] PRO, CP 40/30, m. 28d (reported in Cambridge University Library MS Dd.7.14, f. 387r).

[61] This seems to have been the position already at the time *Glanvill* was written at the end of Henry II's reign: *Glanvill*, 84.

[62] *Curia Regis Rolls*, v, 58–9.

plea about the wardship of the heir's father between his father William de Vescy and Richard's grandfather Odinell in the county court of Northumberland at Warkworth in 2 Henry II initiated by a royal writ which had been settled by an agreement reached through the *amici* of both parties and under which Odinell had quitclaimed the wardship of both Henry and his heirs in perpetuity. Unfortunately for him, he seems to have had no written evidence of this agreement but merely offered to prove it through a champion. Richard denied there had ever been such a plea or such an agreement and denied there could have been. Henry had already been a knight when his father had died three years before this and so was not liable to wardship. Richard recovered the wardship he claimed.

At the very end of the thirteenth century there was beginning to be a problem about such cases. This was that what were being alleged were facts from 'beyond time of memory', facts from beyond the recall of any jury. In a case in the 1299 Cambridgeshire eyre Ralph son of Ralph fitzFulk of Shepreth claimed the wardship of the body of Eleanor the daughter of Bartholomew of Thornton on the grounds that her ancestress had held a messuage and a carucate in Malton in Cambridgeshire of him by the service of a knight's fee.[63] Reginald de Argentein's defence was that her ancestors had held the manor of Meldreth by knight service of his ancestors 'since time out of mind'. The two reports of this case show us that what the plaintiff had wanted to plead in return was that the heiress's ancestors had held the property of her ancestors ever since the Conquest as well as to plead that his own guardian had been seised in his right of the bodies of Agnes and her sister while they were under age. However, the defendant's serjeants objected to this, saying that it was not a proper issue for a jury to decide since it required them to decide on matters 'beyond time of memory'. They tried to get judgment on the grounds that as defendants all they needed to do was to show a title to the wardship by tenure from them since time out of mind.[64] Chief Justice Berwick was not convinced and eventually issue was joined as to whether the feoffment by the ancestors of the plaintiffs was older than that by the defendant's ancestors (as well as on the more recent seisin of the wardship). The plaintiff was then non-suited.

In a replevin case in the 1286 Norfolk eyre Robert of Tattershall sued Roger le Bigod earl of Norfolk for taking two of his greyhounds in what he said was his own free warren at Denton.[65] The earl justified the seizure on the grounds that Henry I had given his ancestor the manor of Earsham and its appurtenant half hundred and free warren within the half hundred both within his own fee and in the fees of others. He had not given Robert permission to hunt and so had seized the dogs as they were hunting there without his permission. Robert did not deny Denton lay within the half hundred but claimed that Henry I had granted his own ancestor (Hugh son of Ives) the manor of Denton with free warren before he granted the half hundred to the earl's ancestor and that they had always hunted freely within the manor since.[66] The court made no attempt to decide on the

---

[63] PRO, JUST 1/96, m. 9.

[64] The reports are in BL MSS Stowe 386, ff. 105v–106r and Additional 31826, ff. 245v–246r.

[65] PRO, JUST 1/578, m. 58d.

[66] Neither charter is recited in the pleadings nor is either to be found in *Regesta*, ii.

priority of these two grants. The issue which went to the jury was whether or not Robert and his ancestors had been seised of hunting freely within the manor.[67]

In a case of 1280 the abbot of Westminster alleged that John Hardel had forcibly recaptured animals which the abbot's bailiff had taken at Wheatley in Rayleigh in Essex. John's defence was that he had been justified in resisting the distraint because the animals had been taken outside the abbot's fee. A jury then found that the animals had been taken within the abbot's fee and judgment was given against John.[68] There is nothing here to suggest any concern with the eleventh- or twelfth-century past. But in 1285 John brought an action of attaint to reverse the verdict in the previous case and in the course of pleading in this second related action it emerged that John's case was that the land where the animals were taken was part of the king's fee and John went back to the twelfth-century past to prove this.[69] The tenement concerned had belonged, he claimed, to Henry of Essex and had been forfeited by him with his other lands. This is the Henry of Essex who was constable to Henry II and lord of the honour of Rayleigh and who forfeited his lands in 1163. It had then been granted, John claimed, to the count of Perche, who had subsequently also forfeited it.[70] It had then passed to Hubert de Burgh and his wife Margaret by the gift of Henry III. John did not explain his own title to the land.[71] The abbot of Westminster likewise went back to early twelfth century facts to show that it belonged to his fee. The tenement where the distraint had been made had once belonged to Swein of Essex (wrongly given the title earl of Essex by the abbot) and he had given it in pure alms to Westminster abbey. This is the Swein of Essex who was Domesday lord of Rayleigh who died in the early twelfth century and who was son of Robert fitz Wimark, staller to Edward the Confessor.[72] The abbey had then regranted it to Swein's son Robert who was liable to pay a rent of sixty shillings a year for it until he assigned them other lands to the value of four pounds a year.[73] This is the Robert who died between 1132 and 1140 and who was succeeded by his son Henry of Essex. The abbey had been seised of the rent ever since and of distraining for any arrears of the rent. The attaint jury found for the king and John recovered his damages.

Litigants knew or thought they knew quite a lot about the eleventh- and twelfth-

---

[67] No verdict is recorded as the two parties later reached an agreement, evidently with the assistance of chief justice Hengham.

[68] PRO, CP 40/36, m. 126.

[69] PRO, CP 40/59, m. 51.

[70] Evidence that Geoffrey count of Perche did indeed have an interest in land here is provided by the charter copied into the Westminster Abbey Domesday which confirmed (with the consent of his wife Maud, grand-daughter of Henry II) Westminster abbey in possession of sixty shillings of rent from Wheatley: *Westminster Abbey Charters, 1066–c.1214*, ed. Emma Mason, Jennifer Bray and Desmond J. Murphy, London Record Society, xxv (1988), no. 465.

[71] This was explained by the abbot in subsequent litigation brought in the 1285 Essex eyre against John Hardel for sixty pounds arrears of the sixty shillings of annual rent. John had been granted the land twenty years previously by John de Burgh (Hubert de Burgh's son): PRO, JUST 1/246, m. 50. But see *Feet of Fines for Essex, vol. II (1272–1326)*, ed. E.F. Kirk, Essex Archaeological Society, 1913–1928, 5.

[72] Sanders, *English Baronies*, 139.

[73] This part of the story could be confirmed from a charter in the Westminster abbey archives. This showed that Wheatley had only been granted by Swein on his death bed and that the grant was completed by Robert and his mother on the day Swein was buried: *Westminster Abbey Charters*, no. 237.

century past. Much of this knowledge was connected with particular property that they possessed or to which they thought they had a claim: remembering that a particular ancestor or predecessor had been the last of their ancestors to be in possession of that property; remembering how the family had lost possession of it; remembering how it was that their family had acquired it or that their title had been confirmed in previous litigation. Claimants also demonstrated, indeed needed to demonstrate, a detailed knowledge of their family history in the eleventh and twelfth centuries as well as in the thirteenth century in order to make their claims. The wardship cases indicate that lords also possessed and might need to possess information about the beginning of their family's seignories over particular tenants and know enough about the tenancies which those tenants held from other lords to argue a convincing case about priority of feoffment.

It is only through this particular lens of individual and family interests that we normally catch glimpses of the events of a much wider world. It is in this context that we find litigants referring to the Norman Conquest. In the late twelfth and early thirteenth centuries we find a number of litigants tracing their title back to the possession of their ancestors since the Conquest. In the later thirteenth century claimants to franchises were still on occasion tracing the roots of their title to those franchises back to the Conquest and continuous exercise of the franchise ever since.[74] When ecclesiastics went back into the pre-Conquest past to make or defend their title to land, they specifically refer to their church's possession before and after the Conquest. We also hear about the events of the Anarchy in the context of specific claims and defences which go back to usurpations during Stephen's reign and subsequent attempts to recover property lost during this period, though we also find at least one litigant generalising about how it had been common for people to usurp property during this period.[75]

The cases which refer to the Anarchy clearly convey a sense that this was a period of war and thus rather different from most of the thirteenth century and the cases which refer to the Conquest clearly also understand that this was an event of major importance in its own right and one which made the pre-Conquest past rather different from the post-Conquest one. How much other evidence is there that thirteenth-century litigants or lawyers were aware that the eleventh and twelfth centuries were different from the thirteenth century: a world of different institutions, different rules and different customs? Chief Justice Hengham in 1285 certainly knew the reason why no really old charters mentioned the franchise of return of writs. This was, he explained, because for a long time after the Conquest 'almost all pleas now pleaded by writ were pleaded by plaint'.[76] Thirteenth-century lawyers also knew that many of the forms of action in use in their day were of comparatively recent invention. In a case of 1292 the serjeant of the prioress of Holywell thought he knew that the action of *quare impedit* had been invented after the reign of king Richard I and that in his reign only the writ of right of advowson and the assize of darrein presentment existed as remedies for those

[74] For examples from the 1280 Nottinghamshire eyre see: PRO, JUST 1/670, mm. 1, 1d. For examples from the 1279–81 Yorkshire eyre see: *Placita de Quo Warranto*, 188, 189, 192. For an example from the 1286 Norfolk eyre see *Placita de Quo Warranto*, 496. For examples from the 1286–7 Suffolk eyre see *Placita de Quo Warranto*, 721–2.
[75] *Curia Regis Rolls*, vi, 176–7.
[76] Paul Brand, *The Making of the Common Law*, London 1992, 441.

claiming advowsons.[77] Although some claimants alleged that their ancestors had been holding pleas of replevin ever since the Conquest the king's serjeant, William of Gisleham, is recorded as asserting in a plea in the 1281 Wiltshire eyre that the plea had only been invented in the reign of king John.[78] Chief justice John of Berwick made the same assertion in the 1302 Cornwall eyre.[79] In the 1285 Essex eyre Gisleham asserted (and this assertion seems to be rather closer to the truth) not that replevin did not exist in the reign of Henry II but that in that reign the plea had only been heard before the chief justiciar and not in the county court or hundred court.[80] Even closer to the real truth seems to be the claim made in a 1236 King's Bench case that it was during the reign of Henry II that the hearing of such cases was first delegated by the king to sheriffs.[81] Thirteenth-century landowners and thirteenth-century lawyers and judges were also well aware – indeed it is difficult to see how they could not have been – that at the time of the Conquest and for some considerable period afterwards it had been the normal practice to transfer land without charter. Thus in the legislation on suit of court which was part of the Provisions of Westminster of 1259 (c.1) we find special rules applying to those 'enfeoffed without a charter from the time of the Conquest or some other ancient feoffment'.[82] Two reports of a speech or speeches by the Common Bench justice, William of Brompton, in a case of 1284 show him (perhaps wrongly) ascribing the invention both of the *murdrum* fine and the frankpledge system to the disorder that followed the Conquest and to English murders of the aliens whom William the Bastard had brought with him.[83]

In these instances we can probably see the role that the collective memory of the legal profession played in preserving a memory of the past and explaining anomalous survivals from that past which still played a part in the thirteenth-century present. Family memory must have been the source for claims like that of William son of Albert of Ramsey and perhaps of other claimants too, though it seems possible that some of these claims go back to some sort of written evidence. Written evidence was certainly available, if not always of a reliable kind, for various grants made in the eleventh and twelfth centuries that supported claims or provided evidence for defences.

From the very beginning of the thirteenth century there were limitations on the uses which could be made of the eleventh- and twelfth-century past. In bringing claims to land and advowsons based on the seisin of an ancestor or predecessor it was permissible to go back to a seisin in 1135 but not to a seisin in the reign of

[77] PRO, CP 40/96, m. 276.
[78] *Placita de Quo Warranto*, 809. For claims to have held such pleas ever since the Conquest see e.g. PRO, JUST 1/238, m. 50 (1254 Essex eyre); JUST 1/132, m. 32 (1278 Cumberland eyre).
[79] *Year Books 30 & 31 Edward I*, ed. A.J. Horwood, RS 1863, 223; cf. John of Mutford's claim in the same eyre that the plea of replevin had been invented 'within time of memory': *Placita de Quo Warranto*, 110.
[80] PRO, JUST 1/246, m. 51. His claim in pleading on a presentment made against Robert fitzRoger in the same eyre was that in Henry II's reign the plea had only been heard before the king or his chief justiciar: PRO, JUST 1/247, m. 9.
[81] See *Curia Regis Rolls*, xv, no. 1968A. cf. *Bracton: on the Laws and Customs of England*, ed. George E. Woodbine and revised by Samuel E. Thorne, 4 vols, Cambridge, Mass., 1968–1977, ii, 439 which talks of a delegation of the hearing of such cases to sheriffs but does not say when it took place.
[82] *Close Rolls, 1259–1261*, HMSO 1934, 146.
[83] BL MSS Harley 493B, ff. 186r–187r and Hargrave 375, f. 80r.

king Stephen. In 1237 and again in 1275 legislation was enacted to exclude claims which went back to a seisin prior to 1154 and then claims which went back to a seisin prior to 1189. The legislation of 1237 and 1275 was framed quite narrowly to apply only to claims, and indeed only to claims to land and advowsons brought by the action of right. It long remained possible to base claims to annuities on agreements made before the limitation date; to ground the obligation to acquit a tenant of services on the basis of acquittal ever since the Conquest; or to undo through the action of *monstraverunt* supposed usurpations of services from the tenants of ancient demesne manors on the basis of assertions about the services which their ancestors had performed while the manor was in the hands of the kings of England before the limitation date.[84] It also long remained possible for defendants to go back to events which had occurred or to royal charters which had been made before the limit of legal memory. It was only shortly before 1300 that we begin to find it being argued that the date of limitation in the writ of right was a more general limit on legal memory.[85] It is only at this point that 1189 really does begin to act as a 'limit of legal memory' in a more general sense and almost all of the eleventh and twelfth centuries becomes excluded from the functioning and usable legal past, to begin to be treated as truly 'time out of mind'.

[84] Above, pp. 39–41. For examples of claims to acquittal on such a basis see PRO, JUST 1/319, m. 12d; JUST 1/275, m. 4d; CP 40/54, m. 60. For an assertion about the services done by tenants of an ancient demesne manor while it was in the hands of Henry I see CP 40/33, m. 69d; for an assertion about the services done by tenants of an ancient demesne manor while it was in the hands of Henry II see CP 40/42, m. 41.

[85] Above, p. 50. See also PRO, CP 40/91, m. 287d (reported in *Year Books 21 & 22 Edward I*, ed. A.J. Horwood, RS 1866, pp. 499–505); CP 40/91, m. 126.

THE *ADELAE COMITISSAE* OF BAUDRI OF BOURGEUIL AND THE BAYEUX TAPESTRY

Shirley Ann Brown and Michael W. Herren*

One of the ongoing issues in Bayeux Tapestry studies is the relationship between the embroidery and the 'Adelae Comitissae', a poem written by Baudri of Bourgeuil. Baudri is one of those literary figures bridging the eleventh and twelfth centuries whose writings have remained fairly inaccessible except to scholars of medieval Latin literature.[1] The available information about Baudri comes largely from his own writings, namely his poems and *Itinerarium*.[2] There are also

* This article was co-authored in the truest sense. The authors are listed in alphabetical order.

[1] Léopold Delisle, 'Notes sur les poésies de Baudri, abbé de Bourgeuil', *Romania* 1, 1872, 23–50; Henri Pasquier, *Un poète latin à la fin du XIe siècle: Baudri, abbé de Bourgeuil, archevêque de Dol*, Paris 1878; Max Manitius, *Geschichte der lateinischen Literatur des Mittelalters*, Munich 1931, iii, 885–96; Otto Schumann, 'Baudri von Bourgeuil als Dichter', *Studien zur Lateinischen Dichtung des Mittelalters. Ehrengabe für Karl Strecker zum 4 September 1931*, Dresden 1939 (repr. K. Langosch, *Mittellateinische Dichtung*, Darmstadt 1969, 330–42); Phyllis Abrahams, *Les Oeuvres poétiques de Baudri de Bourgeuil (1046–1130)*, Paris 1926; F.J.E. Raby, *A History of Secular Latin Poetry in the Middle Ages*, 2nd edn, Oxford 1957, i, 337–48; Karl Forstner, 'Das Traumgedicht Baudris von Bourgeuil (Carmen 37)', *Mittellateinisches Jahrbuch* 6, 1970, 45–57; N. Bartolomucci, 'Note lessicali al Carme CXCVI di Baldrico di Bourgeuil', *Giornale italiano di filologia* 7, 1976, 192–96; Sabine Schuelper, 'Ovid aus der Sicht des Balderich von Bourgeuil, dargestellt anhand des Briefwechsels Florus-Ovid', *Mittellateinisches Jahrbuch* 14, 1979, 93–118; Jean-Yves Tilliette, 'Culture classique et humanisme monastique: Les Poèmes de Baudri de Bourgeuil', *La Littérature angevine médiévale: Actes du Colloque de samedi 22 mars 1980*, Angers 1981, 77–88; Jean-Yves Tilliette, *Rhétorique et poétique chez les poètes latins médiévaux: recherches sur Baudri de Bourgeuil* (Thèse de 3ème cycle dactylographiée) Université de Paris IV, 1981; Jean-Yves Tilliette, 'La Chambre de la Comtesse Adèle: Savoir scientifique et technique littéraire dans le C. CXCVI de Baudri de Bourgeuil', *Romania* 102, 1981, 145–71; Peter Dronke, 'Personal Poetry by Women: The Eleventh and Twelfth Centuries', in Dronke, *Women Writers in the Middle Ages: A Critical Study of Texts from Perpetua (†203) to Marguerite Porete (†1310)*, Cambridge 1984, 84–106; Gerald Bond, ' "Iocus Amoris": The Poetry of Baudri of Bourgeuil and the Formation of the Ovidian Subculture', *Traditio* 42, 1986, 143–93.

[2] The poems were collected into a manuscript of 152 leaves probably by the mid-twelfth century. In the seventeenth century this manuscript appeared in the collection of Alexandre Petau from which André Duschesne transcribed a selection, several of which were published in 1641 in *Historiae Francorum scriptores coaetanei*, iv, 251–77. The published poems were reprinted in Migne, *Patrologia Latina*, clxvi, cols 1181–1208; the other copies are in the Bibliothèque nationale, Collection Duschesne, nos. 20 and 49. In 1650 the manuscript was among those sold by Petau to Queen Christina of Sweden, who gave it to the Vatican. The manuscript was sent, upon demand, to Paris in 1797 but was returned to the Vatican in 1815 where it resumed its position as MS Vat reg 1351 in the collection of the Queen of Sweden. For a discussion of a newly-discovered fragment (saec. XIV) see Patrick Gauthier Dalché and Jean-Yves Tilliette, 'Un nouveau document sur la tradition du poème de Baudri de Bourgeuil à la comtesse Adèle', *Bibliothèque de l'École des Chartes* 144, 1986, 241–57. The *Itinerarium* was published in Migne, *PL*, clxvi, cols 1173–1182.

scattered references to him by contemporary writers such as Orderic Vitalis and Hildebert of Lavardin, bishop of Le Mans, then archbishop of Tours.[3] A number of letters written to him as well as some charters dealing with his administration of the monastery of Bourgeuil have survived.[4]

Baudri was born in 1046 at Meung and studied in nearby Orléans, then possibly at Angers and Cluny. He entered the Benedictine monastery at Bourgeuil at an unknown date and became its abbot in 1078. He failed in his candidacy for the bishopric of Orléans in 1096, but was appointed to the newly created arch-bishopric of Dol in Brittany in 1107. It would appear that Baudri was a less-than-distinguished ecclesiastic, spending much of his time away from his See. In his *Itinerarium* he reveals his disdain for the Bretons – a condition that drove him to travel in England and Normandy. He journeyed on at least three occasions to Rome. Baudri died at a ripe old age in 1130 and was buried at Préaux.[5]

Baudri, perhaps, enjoyed more success as a writer. He left a fairly large collection of occasional poems, several saints' lives, an account of the translation of the head of St Valentine martyr, a history of the First Crusade entitled *Hieroslymitae historiae*, the *Itinerarium*, written in the form of a letter to the monks of Fécamp outlining his travels through England and Normandy, and a treatise entitled *De scuto et gladio S.Michaelis*. Apart from the poems, Baudri's work has scarcely been studied. Only the poems have been critically edited, while the other writings remain buried in the *Patrologia Latina*. One of the saints' lives, the *Life of St Samson*, and the *De scuto* remain unpublished.[6] It is noteworthy that very little has been written on Baudri's treatment of the First Crusade, especially in view of the fact that he was a contemporary of the event and came from the region where it was launched.

If historians have largely neglected Baudri's prose, medieval Latinists have certainly made a good beginning in the study of his poetical writings. There are three modern editions of the poems: the first, by Phyllis Abrahams appeared in 1926; a second, relatively little-known edition of 1936 by M.T. Razzoli; a third by Karlheinz Hilbert, completed in 1979.[7]

The first of two poems which Baudri addressed to Adèle, Countess of Blois, and daughter of William the Conqueror, is best known for the rather lengthy section which purports to describe a tapestry in her possesssion which depicts the events culminating in her father's being crowned King of England on Christmas Day, 1066.[8] What has heightened interest in Baudri's poem is not so much that he

---

[3] Orderic, x, 20 (Chibnall, v, 324–25); Epistolae Hildeberti Cenomanensis Ecclesiae Episcopi, II.xxxv (19), Migne, *PL*, clxxi, cols. 258D–259A.

[4] See Manitius, iii, 883f; Abrahams, xx–xxii.

[5] For summaries of Baudri's life see Manitius, iii, 883–98; Abrahams, xx–xxii; but most recently, Bond, 145–49.

[6] See Michael Lapidge and Richard Sharpe, *A Bibliography of Celtic-Latin Literature*, Dublin 1985, 234–36.

[7] Abrahams, 'Les oeuvres poétiques'; M.T. Razzoli, *Le epistole metriche di Baldericus Burguliensis*, Milan 1936; Karlheinz Hilbert (ed.), *Baldricus Burgulianus: Carmina*, Heidelberg 1979. There is general agreement that Phyllis Abraham's edition was highly unsatisfactory: it is marred by errors of transcription and the failure to correct even the most obvious errors in the principal manuscript, Vat. reg. lat. 1351. Nonetheless, Abraham's Introduction and Notes to the Text are very valuable, and her work must still be used, as Hilbert's improved Latin text offers the reader nothing in the way of helps.

[8] The poem was first published in its entirety in Léopold Delisle, 'Poème adressé à Adèle, fille de

incorporated a Battle of Hastings narrative into it, as the fact that he says he is describing a pictorial wall hanging decorated with these scenes. Historians and art historians alike have leapt upon Baudri's words, in the hope that they have cast some light on the early history of the Bayeux Tapestry, one of the most famous works of art of the Middle Ages. This textile depicts episodes from the story of the Norman invasion of England and has been considered as an historical source for the Norman Conquest.[9]

The reason for this scholarly interest is evident when it is remembered that the first trustworthy, documented reference to the Bayeux Tapestry occurs in the 1476 Inventory of the Treasure of Bayeux Cathedral, Item 262. Since scholars now generally agree that the Bayeux Tapestry was produced during the 1070s or 1080s, this leaves an uncomfortable 400-year gap in the record of its known whereabouts.[10]

Baudri's poem has been attributed to the years between 1099 and 1102.[11] It has been used by some historians as evidence that the Bayeux Tapestry was in existence by the time the poem was composed and it also has been suggested that Baudri was using the embroidery as one of his sources.[12] Others, particularly literary scholars, have argued that Baudri's highly developed literary style and

Guillaume le Conquérant par Baudri, abbé de Bourgeuil', *Mémoires de la Société des Antiquaires de Normandie*, 3rd series, 8, 1871, 187–224. The poem appears as No. CXCVI in Abrahams, 196–253, and as no. 134 in Hilbert, 154–64. There is a separate edition of the poem in N. Bartolomuccci, 'L'epistola CXCVI di Balderico di Bourgeuil. Testo critico', *Annali della Facoltà di lettere e filosofia, Bari* 22, 1979, 5–52. There is a partial translation of no. CXCVI (134) by Michael W. Herren in Shirley Ann Brown, *The Bayeux Tapestry: History and Bibliography*, Woodbridge 1988, 167–77. A full translation of this poem by M. Herren is forthcoming in *The Journal of Medieval Latin*, v, 1995. Poem CXCVII (135 in Hilbert) is a follow-up to the longer poem and reminds Adèle of Baudri's request for compensation.

[9] Since many of the articles have been written in response to published suggestions, the following list has been arranged chronologically: Delisle, 'Notes sur les poésies', 41–42; Albert Marignan, *La Tapisserie de Bayeux. Étude archéologique et critique*, Paris 1902, xiv–xxi; M. Lanore, 'La Tapisserie de Bayeux', *Bibliothèque de l'École des Chartes* 64, 1903, 83–93, especially 88; Johannes Steenstrup, *Die Bayeux-Tapete: ein Leitfaden für Besucher des nationalhistorischen Museums im Schlosse Frederiksborg*, Copenhagen 1905, 443–44; Philippe Lauer, 'Le Poème de Baudri de Bourgeuil adressé à Adèle, fille de Guillaume le Conquérant, et la date de la Tapisserie de Bayeux', *Mélanges d'Histoire offerts à M.Charles Bemont*, Paris 1913, 43–58; Henri Prentout, 'La Conquête de l'Angleterre par les Normands – Les Sources – La Tapisserie de Bayeux', *Revue bimensuelle des cours et conférences*, 2nd series, vol. 23, no. 2, 1921–22, 16–29, 193–200, 302–12, especially 311–12; Abrahams, 244–47; Suzanne Turgis, *La Reine Mathilde et la Tapisserie de Bayeux*, Paris and Caen 1928, 88; Eric Maclagan, *The Bayeux Tapestry*, London and New York 1943, 18; Charles H. Gibbs-Smith, 'The Death of Harold at the Battle of Hastings', *History Today* 10, 1960, 188–91; Richard Drogereit, 'Bemerkungen zum Bayeux-Teppich' *Mitteilungen des Instituts für Österreichische Geschichtsforschung* 70, 1962, 257–93, especially 293; Simone Bertrand, *La Tapisserie de Bayeux et la manière de vivre au onzième siècle*, La Pierre-qui-Vire 1966, 40–46; Otto K. Werkmeister, 'The Political Ideology of the Bayeux Tapestry', *Studi Medievali* 17, no. 2, 1976, 535–95, especially 554–63; Nicholas P. Brooks and H.E. Walker, 'The authority and interpretation of the Bayeux Tapestry', *ante*, i, 1978, 1–34, especially 26–28; Michel Parisse, *The Bayeux Tapestry*, Paris 1983, 36–40; David J. Bernstein, *The Mystery of the Bayeux Tapestry*, Chicago and London 1986, 90.

[10] For the controversy over the dating of the Bayeux Tapestry see S.A. Brown, 'Bayeux Tapestry', 26–31. See also S.A. Brown, 'The Bayeux Tapestry: Why Eustace, Odo and William?', *ante*, xii, 1989, 8–28.

[11] Abrahams, 232.

[12] Lauer, 57–8; Gibbs-Smith, 188; Werkmeister, 561; Parisse, 40, among others.

ironic technique leave many of his factual assertions open to doubt and have concluded that the poem is of limited value in Bayeux Tapestry studies.[13]

There are really two questions that interest the historian and the art historian: (1) Did Baudri himself have direct experience of the Bayeux Tapestry? (2) If so, did he see it in the chamber of Adèle, Countess of Blois?

To answer the first question, it will be necessary to determine if elements of Baudri's account of Adèle's Conquest hanging can be explained *only* by reference to the Bayeux Tapestry, assuming, independently of Baudri's poem, that this work of art already existed and was theoretically available to him. In this attempt to answer the question as definitively as possible, Baudri's words will be compared closely to parallel scenes in the Bayeux Tapestry and also to the accompanying tituli. The similarities of individual scenes as well as the ordering of the scenes will be taken into account.[14] It will be necessary to examine other parts of Baudri's poem as well as what is known of Baudri's methods and poetical techniques.

The section of the *Adelae Comitissae* which purports to describe what is usually referred to as a tapestry depicting the Norman Conquest comprises 337 lines (vv. 235–572) of the total of 1367. Baudri constantly uses the word *uelum* to refer to his object, a word which refers to a wall hanging of any material and technique and does not necessarily have to be understood as a tapestry. Baudri claims that Adèle's hanging is made of precious materials: gold, silver, and silk (vv. 211–12), studded here and there with bright gems and pearls (vv. 229–30), the whole exhibiting a technique unsurpassed even by the mythical skills of Pallas and Arachne (vv. 217–28). This should alert the reader immediately that Baudri is not providing a factual description of the Bayeux Tapestry with its much humbler materials. As is well known, the so-called Bayeux Tapestry is actually an embroidery of wool on a linen carrier. Baudri has signalled that the hanging which he is describing is part of a very luxurious interior and reflects the courtly love of gold and glitter.

Baudri then proceeds to describe the 'new and true stories' which were depicted on the hanging, saying that they were all accompanied by titles (vv. 233–34).[15] Tituli indeed play an important role in the Bayeux Tapestry, for although cursory, they are essential for an identification of people and places, and for an understanding of what is being depicted. On the embroidery, people and places are identified by single epithets, such as *Willelmus, Harold, Turold, Ecclesia, Bagias*; actions are introduced by *Hic*, while *Ubi* introduces actions associated with a particular location just mentioned.[16]

Baudri launches into his narrative about William of Normandy, starting with a short reference to the difficulties the young Duke overcame while establishing, and then maintaining, his control over the duchy (vv. 235–42). He continues with a lengthy description of the comet of Spring 1066 and the people's dumbfounded

---

[13] Marignan, xxi; Prentout, 311–12; Abrahams, 247; Bernstein, 90; Bond, 181; Tilliette, 'La Chambre d'Adèle', 153, among others.

[14] Although several scholars have compared the poem's account of Adèle's textile with the Bayeux Tapestry, none so far has published a full analysis in which the sequence and details of the embroidery's scenes are compared to Baudri's version.

[15] Porro recenseres titulorum scripta legendo

    In uelo ueras historiasque nouas. (Hilbert, 155)

[16] *Pace* Parisse, 53–54 and 138, who thinks *Hic* and *Ubi* are merely undifferentiated 'bardic signals' to the Tapestry's observer.

reaction to it (vv. 243–59). The real narrative gets underway with a council called by William, where, in the first of several great speeches, William explains why his allies have been gathered and what he expects from them – support for his invasion of England (vv. 260–328).

By inserting full-fledged speeches into his narrative, Baudri has moved away very quickly from describing a visual narrative depicted on an art object to writing in a literary mode. The speeches pull the reader into the story in a manner very different from the less dramatic effects of medieval pictorial narrative which must rely on depicted gesture and disposition of figures. Baudri takes advantage of the emotion-heightening possibilities inherent in reported speech.

When Baudri returns to the description of Adèle's wall hanging, the building of William's fleet follows, with emphasis on the all-out effort put into the enterprise which results in 3000 ships, all filled quickly with cavalry and horses (vv. 329–56).[17] The cross-Channel sailing is immediate and uneventful, although in the poem, much is made of the grief and wailing issuing from the families and friends who remained at home in Normandy (vv. 357–86). In Baudri's narrative, the Duke, upon reaching England's shore, promises to rescue the country from the hands of the usurping perjurer (vv. 387–94). Contrary to the delays indicated in the Bayeux Tapestry, in the poem the fighting between the Anglo-Saxons and the French begins almost immediately. The first clash occurs when the invaders encounter the famous Anglo-Saxon shield wall. In the poetical battle, the feigned flight which drew off English stragglers to the slaughter is quickly passed over, so that much more attention can be paid to a more central issue – the rout of the Normans. To counteract this potential disaster, William removes his helmet and takes the opportunity to harangue his fleeing men. The fighting resumes with Duke William at its head, Harold is killed by an arrow, and the demoralized, leaderless English flee (vv. 395–494). Baudri's poem continues, describing the continuation of the Norman campaign until the capitulation of the city, probably London, and William's acceptance by the inhabitants as their king (vv. 495–556).

Let us now closely compare Baudri's poetical images and the visual images on the Bayeux Tapestry, starting with the first correspondence, the appearance of the comet. The Bayeux Tapestry incorporates a comet with a red tail in the upper border, to which a group of men are pointing in agitated surprise or wonder. The caption reads: 'Isti mirant stellam'. (Plate 1) In Baudri's Latin text, the comet is described as a *stella* (v. 245) as well as *cometes* (v. 243), and *miratur* (v. 251) is also used. Baudri then proceeds at some length to represent popular astonishment (vv. 251–58). At vv. 255–56 he says:

> A younger generation seeks answers from its elders,
> and inquisitive boys hang on the lips of old men.[18]

---

[17] This of course may be poetical exaggeration. The ship list written c.1070 indicated 776 ships were given by the magnates, but in the second section it indicates the total number was 1000; it was apparently augmented by many more ships given by men according to their means. William of Jumièges placed the number at 3000. See Elisabeth van Houts, 'The Ship List of William the Conqueror', *ante*, x, 1987, 159–83, especially 169–70.

[18] A patribus responsa petit sibi iunior etas
Atque rogando senis pendet ab ore puer. (Hilbert, 155–56)

Plate 1. Bayeux Tapestry: Comet and Onlookers

On the Bayeux Tapestry, the small figure in the group, who has established eye-contact with the solitary tall figure, looks as if he is seeking instruction. Even though the 1066 appearance of Halley's Comet occurs in other sources, the correspondence between Baudri's words and the Bayeux Tapestry's images explains Baudri's comet passage much better than any literary source. The closest written source is the *Carmen de Hastingae proelio* at vv. 125–26: 'And blazing from heaven the streaming hair of a comet proclaimed to the English foreordained destruction'.[19] But its author has transposed the appearance of the comet to the landing in England and does not mention popular reaction. William of Jumièges (VII,13) mentions the comet as a star with three tails; William of Poitiers doesn't mention the comet.

Baudri appears, at first, to omit the next section shown on the Bayeux Tapestry for he proceeds immediately to describe William's war council at vv. 261–62:

> William himself, sitting in an exalted place,
> orders the court to sit, as was proper according to custom.[20]

In the corresponding Tapestry scene we see William seated in the middle on a double lion throne; to the right and slightly behind is his half-brother, Bishop Odo of Bayeux, also seated; to the left is a standing figure who appears to be an excited messenger; to the right of Odo is another standing figure with a tool in his hand. The setting seems to be a palace. The titulus reads: *Hic Willelm Dux iussit naves edificare.* (Plate 2)

In Baudri's text, William launches into a long speech in which he outlines his

---

[19] '*Carmen*', trans. by Morton and Muntz, 19.
[20] Ipse loco residens Guillelmus in ediciori
    Quo decuit proceres more sedere iubet. (Hilbert, 156)

Plate 2. Bayeux Tapestry: Duke William and Odo of Bayeux at War Council

claims to England, based doubly upon consanguinity and the promise of the English King Edward brought by his legates. He then says at vv. 281–82:

> A certain perjurer was also sent to us
> to usurp the crown that is our due.[21]

This desire to justify the decision to invade England is in line with the accepted interpretation of the first third of the Bayeux Tapestry which depicts the voyage of Harold Godwinsson to Normandy in 1064, culminating in his swearing to support William's claim to the English throne. William then calls on his legates who have just returned from England to speak, and these confirm what William has said. At the end of the speech William's court immediately ratifies the decision to build ships. In lines 335–39 the summoning of craftsmen is reported.

This entire passage in Baudri is best explained with reference to the sections of the Bayeux Tapestry immediately preceeding the council scene which depict the crowning of Harold and the voyage of an English ship to Normandy, presumably to relay the message of Harold's coronation. The Tapestry depicts a legate excitedly relaying the news to William at the war council, where Odo represents the councillors, and the decision is taken to build ships, as reported in the caption. A craftsman stands waiting to execute the royal command. The chain of events represented by Baudri and the speed with which things occur reflect exactly the same chain of events seen in the Tapestry. Indeed, the Tapestry is the only known source, pictorial or literary, that can explain precisely the concatenation of events in Baudri's poem.

---

[21] Quidam periurus quod nos diadema deceret
Vsurpat nobis missus et ipse fuit. (Hilbert, 156)

Plate 3. Bayeux Tapestry: Boat building

Baudri next describes the building and the fitting of the ships in some detail in vv. 341–46:

> Bilge-holds, oars, sailyards, cross-banks, yardropes,
> and other items of use are fitted by everyone.
> Forests are cut down – the ash, the oak, and the ilex fall;
> the pine is uprooted by the trunk.
> The aged fir is hauled down from the steep mountains;
> labour gives value to all trees.[22]

The Bayeux Tapestry also depicts the building and outfitting of the ships in some considerable detail. We see the chopping down of trees, the lopping of branches and a figure who is planing a stripped log that has been wedged into the 'V' of a tree. Next we see groups of craftsmen working on the interior of two boats, possibly installing benches. (Plate 3)

Although the correspondences between poem and artifact are not precise – Baudri gives more details – both agree in relating the cutting of trees and the building of the ships. Again, no other source can explain the appearance of this section in Baudri. The actual building of the ships is not described in the *Carmen*. William of Jumièges (VII,14) and William of Poitiers (II,2) likewise pass over the construction of the ships, saying only that a fleet was prepared.

One detail of the sailing raises the question of whether Baudri employed the Tapestry or the *'Carmen' de Hastingae Proelio* as his source. Baudri writes at vv. 353–54:

> Moreover, there were separate ships for the infantry;
> some ships carried the cavalry; others, the horses.[23]

[22] Sentinas, remos, antemnas, transtra, cherucos
Et reliquos usus omnis adaptat homo.
Ceduntur silue cadit ornus, quercus et ilex
Deque suo pinus stipite diripitur
Aduehiturque senex abies a montibus altis
Cunctis arboribus fecit opus precium. (Hilbert, 158)
[23] Has preter turbe fuerat sua cimba pedestri
Altera fert dominos, altera nauis equos. (Hilbert, 158)

Plate 4a. Bayeux Tapestry: Ships sailing to England

Plate 4b. Bayeux Tapestry: Ships sailing to England

In the *Carmen* at vv. 84–85 we find:

> . . . the most part forced the knights' horses aboard
> the ships, the rest hurried to stow their arms.

In the large section on the sailing, the Bayeux Tapestry depicts three classes of ships: large ones carrying a mixture of horses and men, other large ones carrying only men and their arms (represented by the shields), and small ones in the background carrying only men. At the end of the scene in the Tapestry there is the titulus *Hic exeunt caballi*. (Plates 4a and 4b)

A possible – and we think plausible – reading of the Tapestry here is that the horses and men in some of the large ships are the war horses and their grooms; the men's status as grooms is shown in the final scene of the crossing, where a horse is led off by the bridle, not ridden by a knight. The men with shields in the other large ships are the cavalry; the men in the small boats might well be the infantry, specifically the archers, who are depicted later on; the smaller boats would represent their lower status, rather than being an attempt at perspective or functioning as mere space fillers, as is the usual suggestion. At all events, the Tapestry presents a tripartite division of ships, corresponding to Baudri's tripartite division. The *'Carmen'* poet, on the other hand, refers only to the stowing of arms and the boarding of the horses; there is no mention of separate ships with different functions. Again, it seems virtually certain that Baudri's depiction of the crossing can be ascribed to a reading of the Bayeux Tapestry.

One final scene of the crossing demands our attention: the landing itself. Baudri writes at vv. 381–84:

> And now the steersman watches the winds and the stars,
>   and the men immediately fall to their tasks.
> Turning the folds of their sails, they veer into the wind.
>   At length their oars fall silent and they gain the shore.[24]

Surely these lines can be based on a plausible reading of the Tapestry. Sailyards are being turned, and it looks as though the sails are at a wide angle to the path of the ships. The lookouts are looking out intently, and there is a great flurry of activity. No literary source available to Baudri described the landing in this way.

At the end of the section on the crossing (vv. 385–86), Baudri's Latin text says:

> Naves et proceres procerumque uocabula uelum
> Illud habet, uelum si tamen illud erat.

In our first translation, we were misled by the word *uelum*, taking it for a synonym of *carbasa* in line 383, hence a word for 'sail'. It is much more plausible, however, that Baudri is once again talking about the wall hanging, for which *uelum* is his usual word. What the line therefore means is this:

> This hanging contains ships and leaders and names of
> leaders, if however this hanging existed.[25]

For the moment we shall leave aside the problem of the 'if'-clause and concentrate on the main statement. It is impossible to identify the leaders of individual ships in the Bayeux Tapestry. Each crew consists of a helmsman to manage the rudder, some of whom also manoeuvre the sail-yard, while at the opposite end of the boat there is a lookout. But the word *proceres* implies more than nautical captains; it would mean something like the commanders of a body of men. The tituli of the Bayeux Tapestry frequently identify the leaders and important men on both sides of the conflict, men like Odo of Bayeux, Robert of Mortain, Eustace of Boulogne, Harold Godwinsson and his brothers Leofwine and Gyrth, among others. Once more we seem to have a correspondence between Baudri and the Bayeux Tapestry.

In Baudri's poem, as in William of Jumièges, there is no preamble between the landing of the French in England and the onset of the fighting. In the other sources – the *'Carmen'*, William of Poitiers and the Bayeux Tapestry – there are descriptions of messengers, spies, meals, and fortification building.

In the battle section of the poem, Baudri refers specifically to three events which had been depicted on the Bayeux Tapestry: the attack on the English shield wall (vv. 405–16), William's lifting his helmet to prove to his troops that he is still alive (vv. 429–32), and the death of Harold (vv. 463–64). The first two events are mentioned in too many of the sources to allow for a nexus solely between the Tapestry and Baudri's poem. In fact, there are very close correspondences between

---

[24] Iamque gubernator uentos et sidera spectat
   Incumbuntque suo iugiter officio.
  Obliquando sinus in uentos carbasa uertunt
   Tandem tranquillo remige littus habent. (Hilbert, 159)

[25] The previous translation was:
  Commanders and orders hold ships and sails in check
   that is, if the ships really had sails. (M.W.H.)

Plate 5. Bayeux Tapestry: Anglo-Saxon Shield Wall

Baudri's version of the initial encounter between the French and the English and that found in the *Carmen*, such as the statement in both that the Anglo-Saxon defenders stood so tightly packed that the dead could not fall (*Carmen*, vv. 415–16). The Bayeux Tapestry image gives the same impression. (Plate 5)

The incident of the Norman rout and William baring his face is found in all the Norman sources as well as the Bayeux Tapestry, but there are noticeable differences in the personages involved. (Plate 6) In the Tapestry, Odo of Bayeux and Eustace of Boulogne are given important roles in this incident, probably for reasons having to do with the purpose for which the Bayeux Tapestry was created.[26] In Baudri's version, William is the sole hero and the poet takes the opportunity to put a rousing speech into his mouth (vv. 433–48). The Duke asserts that he is still alive and well and that victory is almost within reach. They should remember past Norman victories and the possibility of gain. Besides, where would they flee, for the ships are far from shore and there is neither refuge nor escape for them. They must all fight or perish! This closely echoes the parallel speech written by the author of the *Carmen de Hastingae Proelio* (vv. 444–64).

According to Baudri's vision, the fighting resumed with an increased viciousness and both sides suffered terrible losses. At lines 459–60 he wrote:

Plate 6. Bayeux Tapestry: Odo, William and Eustace and the French Rout

---

26 Brown, 'Eustace, Odo and William'.

Plate 7. Bayeux Tapestry: Slaughter in Battle

> Victory without injury is granted to neither side,
>   and the dry earth runs with the blood of the slain.[27]

The analagous Bayeux Tapestry caption reads *Hic ceciderunt simul Angli et Franci in proelio*, as the carnage spreads into the borders of the fabric. (Plate 7) This is a common theme in the various versions of the battle.

However, it can be argued that Baudri used the Bayeux Tapestry *and no other source* for his description of Harold's death. (Plate 8) Baudri writes (vv. 463–64):

> A shaft pierces Harold with deadly doom;
>   he is the end of the war: he was also its cause.[28]

Baudri was the first writer to describe the death of Harold in this way. Both William of Jumièges and William of Poitiers stated merely that Harold was killed near the end of the day. The author of the *Carmen* (vv. 533–50) depicts Harold's slaughter in close combat at the hands of four knights, including William. In fact, the Tapestry can be read as being in agreement with this version.[29] However, the presence of the caption *Haroldus Rex interfectus est* with *Haroldus* written directly over a foot soldier with an arrow in his face undoubtedly gave rise to the long and popular tradition, initiated by Baudri, that Harold was killed by an arrow.[30] More probably, Harold is the figure whose leg is being hewn off by a mounted knight. In any event, a misreading of the Tapestry scene and the caption is the only explanation – apart from oral tradition that cannot be confirmed – why Baudri describes the death of Harold in the manner he does.

This is where the Bayeux Tapestry now ends, but the poem continues. Baudri describes in lengthy and gory detail how the blood-roused Normans pursue and slaughter the hapless English, so that future war will be avoided. Only nightfall mercifully puts an end to the carnage and allows the vanquished to crawl away into hiding or to die. At daybreak, William presses his fighters forward with

[27] Indemnis neutri cedet uictoria parti
    Arida cesorum gleba cruore fluit. (Hilbert, 161)
[28] Perforat Hairaldum casu letalis arundo
    Is belli finis, is quoque causa fuit. (Hilbert, 161)
[29] Brown, 'Eustace, Odo and William', 17–18.
[30] The further embellishment that the arrow pierced Harold's eye first appeared in William of Malmesbury's *Gesta Regum*, c.1125. C. Gibbs-Smith was incorrect when he claimed that Baudri was the first to say that Harold had been killed by an arrow in the eye. Gibbs-Smith, 188.

Plate 8. Bayeux Tapestry: Harold's Death

another speech, in which he indicates they had best strike while the English were still disorganized and the cities and towns vulnerable. It was their only chance for a quick victory and the establishment of peace. The fighting progresses to the city walls – presumably London – for which the English had rallied the only people left within – girls, old men and boys. In a moment of magnanimity to allow the inhabitants to save face, William offers terms of peace, which are immediately accepted and the gates are opened to him with rejoicing. William is proclaimed King, as had been announced by the Star trailing blood.

Baudri ends this section of the poem by taking his reader out of the mode of battle poetry and returning to his claim that he had seen all this indicated on the hanging in Adèle's chamber. He wrote (vv. 561–64):

> The wealth of the king, his glory, his wars and triumphs –
>   each could be seen and read on the tapestry.
> I would believe that the figures were real and alive,
>   if flesh and sensation were not wanting in the images.[31]

He reiterates the reference to the tituli that he had made in lines 233–34 when he began to describe the hanging. He now says (vv. 565–66):

> Letters pointed out the events and each of the figures in such a way
>   that whoever sees them can read them, if he knows how.[32]

This is an intriguing statement for it would seem to indicate that Baudri was indeed familar with the format of the Bayeux Tapestry and the functioning of the text it contains.

Perhaps to tease the baited reader further, Baudri then includes the following (vv. 567–68):

> If you could believe that this weaving really existed,
>   you would read true things on it, O writing paper.[33]

---

[31] Regis diuitie, sua gloria, bella, triumphi
   In uelo poterant singula uisa legi.
   Veras crediderim uiuasque fuisse figuras,
   Ni caro, ni sensus deesset imaginibus. (Hilbert, 164)
[32] Littera signabat sic res et quasque figuras,
   Vt quisquis uideat, si sapit, ipsa legat. (Hilbert, 164)
[33] Hec quoque, si credas, hec uere uela fuisse
   In uelis uere, cartula nostra, legas. (Hilbert, 164)

And so Baudri casts doubt upon the veracity of his own words. What can be made of this, almost 900 years later?

It is now possible to summarize the evidence that would indicate that Baudri had had direct contact with the Bayeux Tapestry:

1. The poet describes a wall hanging of the Norman Conquest that is supplied with tituli that point out events and the leading individuals, even though he himself does not name them.

2. Baudri's account of the events in his tapestry follows the exact order found on the Bayeux Tapestry, allowing for items omitted and the section at the end of the poem, which the lost portion of the Tapestry might be expected to have contained in some abbreviated fashion.

3. Baudri's narrative includes details of the Conquest known only from the Bayeux Tapestry. Especially close are the details of the appearance of the comet and the reaction of the people; William's council of war; the cutting of the forest and building of the ships; the tripartite classification of the ships; the actions of the crew during the landing; and the death of Harold.

This evidence supports the notion that Baudri had studied with particular care the scenes of the Tapestry from the appearance of the comet to the landing in England.

The contradictory evidence should also be set out:

1. Baudri describes a tapestry made of gold, silver, and silk threads and studded with gems and pearls. The Bayeux Tapestry is made of wool on a linen base and contains no gems or pearls.

2. Baudri's described artifact mentions only William and Harold by name. The Bayeux Tapestry names numerous individuals on both sides of the conflict.

3. Baudri undercuts his claims with remarks such as (v. 386): 'If however this hanging existed'; or (v. 567): 'If you believe that this weaving really existed'.

These objections can be disposed of:

1. Baudri's description of a luxury tapestry can be explained by two factors: (1) his desire to enhance his description of the chamber of his would-be patron and his claim to describe objects worthy of her beauty (vv. 567–72); (2) his reliance on a literary source. Baudri borrows his description from Ovid, *Metamorphoses* 6, which depicts a tapestry with gold and silver threads and also portrays the weaving contest of Pallas and Arachne, a theme which finds a reverberation in Baudri's poem in vv. 217–27.

2. In reading the 337 lines which Baudri dedicated to his description of the Conquest Tapestry in Adèle's bedchamber, we can quickly see that he has set out deliberately to create a panegyric to her father in the form of a narrative. William is the sole hero of the story, and its true focus. Baudri's intent seems to be to draw a portrait of William as a legitimate ruler of England and Normandy. It was not his primary concern to recreate events which had occurred some thirty-five years earlier, shortly before Adèle herself was born, and when Baudri was twenty years old.

3. Baudri casts doubt on the tapestry he depicts precisely because it is an imaginary tapestry – one that is very like, yet also different from, the Bayeux Tapestry. Baudri expects that Adèle, his ideal reader, has a close acquaintance with

the details of the Bayeux Tapestry and would be amused by his literary tapestry which, while embellishing and editing the real object, remains strikingly like the original.

An answer to the question of whether or not Baudri had seen the Bayeux Tapestry can now be advanced. Evidence indicates that Baudri had indeed seen that embroidery and had studied it carefully. He edits its narrative to make it focus on William, the father of Adèle, to whom he is offering a lengthy panegyric. He fills out the narrative of the Conquest with borrowings from other accounts, particularly the *Carmen de Hastingae Proelio* and William of Poitiers. However, references to the narrative and format of the Bayeux Tapestry are unmistakeable, and only a hypothesis allowing for Baudri's close knowledge of the famous artifact can account for the structure and details of this section of his poem.

It is here that we would ask our readers to consult their own experiences of viewing the Bayeux Tapestry *in situ* rather than through a reproduction. We believe that all would agree that because the Tapestry is very long and exception-ally detailed, viewer fatigue sets in at some stage before everything is seen. It is also impossible to devote the same level of attention to all parts of the visual narrative. If one wishes to retain visual details, then one must study a portion of the Tapestry on one day, and return on another to take up a new section. It seems to us that Baudri studied two sections of the Bayeux Tapestry in detail: from the appearance of the comet to the landing at Pevensey, and from the first battle encounter to the death of Harold. He was at least generally familar with the rest.

The second question – Did Baudri see the Bayeux Tapestry in Adèle's chamber? – can be disposed of somewhat more easily. The poet begins this section of the poem by telling us that he is going to describe a wonderful hanging that surrounds Adèle's bed. The actual Bayeux Tapestry, which is incomplete at the right end, still measures an impressive seventy metres in length. The suggestion that it was used as a bed hanging can be disposed of without controversy. The Bayeux Tapestry is a very large object, suitable for a Great Hall, and far too big for a private chamber, especially one which, according to Baudri's account, was already crowded with other tapestries. One could invoke the theory that Adèle had com-missioned a miniature of the actual Bayeux Tapestry, perhaps ordering up a luxury copy.[34] But there is no evidence to support this idea and there is no indication that it was a practice in this period to commission copies of secular-subject em-broideries.

If Baudri's poem cannot be used as a witness to the exact location of the Bayeux Tapestry at the time the poem was written, it can be used as proof that the embroidery was in existence by then. The dating of the poem becomes crucial at this point. Baudri makes a reference to Adèle's married state which implies that her husband is absent, but living, in vv. 61–66:

> Her probity and chaste heart adorn her,
>> So too her noble offspring and the love of her husband.
> There are many men, whose manners and character
>> and good looks would commend them to girls,

[34] Parisse, 37.

> Who might have tempted her; but what would it profit to try?
> She keeps inviolable the bond of her marriage bed.[35]

Stephen of Blois joined the First Crusade and was in the Holy Land between 1096 and 1099. After a short stay at home, he returned to the East in 1101 and was killed there in 1102. Abrahams favoured a date of c.1100 for the composition of the poem.

Since the Bayeux Tapestry is not referred to in any other sources found so far, it must be assumed that it was not available to a general public and probably not exhibited in Bayeux Cathedral at this early date, as is commonly held today. There is no hard evidence that the embroidery was originally meant for Bayeux Cathedral even though its connection with Odo, Bishop of Bayeux, is no longer disputed, since he seems so inextricably interwoven into the narrative it relates. Nobody has uncovered any evidence that it was ever in the actual possession of either William the Conqueror or his wife Matilda, although this may have been its intended destination.[36]

If the Tapestry was designed, sewn and stitched in England, as internal evidence would indicate, then it obviously found its way across the Channel sometime before 1476, possibly shortly after it was completed. For Baudri to have seen it before composing the *Adelae Comitissae*, it would have had to be on the continent before 1100, for there is no indication that Baudri visited England before that.[37] One possibility is that the Tapestry may have come back with Odo of Bayeux, the man who probably was responsible for its creation, when he was finally expelled from England in 1088 by William Rufus. It is possible that the Bayeux Tapestry remained in Odo's possession until his death during the winter of 1096–97. Baudri may have seen the Tapestry somewhere in Bayeux, which is not too far from Bourgueil. But there is no evidence in his written works that he was in contact with Odo of Bayeux. There are several persons named Odo addressed or mentioned by Baudri in his poems, but none of these, apparently, is the Bishop of Bayeux.[38] It can be hazarded that if he were familiar with so powerful a man, Baudri would have either written to him or at least mentioned him.

Wherever it was in northern France, and however it was exhibited, Baudri had enjoyed leisurely access to the Bayeux Tapestry and was able to use it as a source when he composed his long poem to William's daughter Adèle. In light of Baudri's writing, we cannot disregard the possibility that by 1100 the Bayeux Tapestry had found its way into Adèle's possession, although certainly not into her bedroom.

---

[35] Hanc morum probitas, hanc castum pectus honestat,
  Nobilis hanc soboles ornat amorque uiri.
 Sunt tamen et multi, quos commendare puellis
  Et decus et probitas et sua forma queat,
 Hanc qui temptassent sed quid temptasse iuuaret?
  Seruat pacta sui non uiolanda thori. (Hilbert 150–51)

[36] Its size and long, narrow format made the Bayeux Tapestry an awkward object to exhibit or trundle from one place to another. The amazingly intact condition of the embroidery today attests to the fact that it has not been exposed to handling and exhibition conditions during most of its existence.

[37] Baudri did visit England, but it was after he became Archbishop of Dol in 1107, as attested in his *Itinerarium*.

[38] See Abrahams' index, 386.

The plain fact which emerges from the poem is that it is very unlikely that Baudry had ever met Adèle in person, much less visited her in her chamber. He tells us as much in lines 83–86:

> Scarcely did I see her, yet I recall having seen her,
>   just as I remember the dreams I have seen.
> In the same way I often recall having seen a new moon:
>   either I just caught a glimpse of it or believe that I did.[39]

It appears that Baudri, unprompted, sent his panegyric to Adèle with a plea for patronage: he asks for a *cappa* or *tunica* as a sign of her favour (v. 1358). At the very end of the poem (vv. 1367–68) he tells Adèle that he has sent a messenger to recite his *libellum*, but is prepared to come in person, if only she would bid him.

The plea for patronage and a private audience caps a long panegyric that praises the daughter of William by praising her surroundings, namely the objects in her chamber. Everything in her room, mentioned by Baudri, reflects her learning, her piety, and her connection to her father. The walls are covered with tapestries with scenes from the Bible and from pagan mythology. The central tapestry, of course, is the one portraying her father's conquest. The ceiling is bedecked with the signs of the zodiac and other constellations as well as the planets – all purporting to demonstrate her avid interest in astronomy. The floor contains a map of the known world – oceans, rivers, mountains, nations and races – all claiming to prove Adèle's deep knowledge of geography. On the bedposts are carved Philosophy – at the head – and the seven liberal arts – at the foot. It would seem that there is no science or art that Adèle has not mastered. Behind the hyperbole and poetic license hides an honest rogue. Baudri tells us in several places that he has invented much in the pursuit of patronage. At the end of the section on the Conquest Tapestry, Baudri says frankly (vv. 567–72):

> If you could believe that this weaving really existed
>   you would read true things on it, O writing paper.
> But you might also say: 'What he wrote ought to have been;
>   a subject like this was becoming to this goddess.
> He wrote by arranging matters which behoved
>   the beauty of his Lady – and they are worthy of her'.[40]

And near the very end of the poem (vv. 1353–54) the same sentiment is repeated:

---

[39] Vix ideo uidi uidisse tamen reminiscor,
    Vt reminiscor ego somnia uisa michi.
  Sic me sepe nouam lunam uidisse recordor
    Vel, cum uix uideo, meue uidere puto. (Hilbert, 151)
[40] Hec quoque, si credas, hec uere uela fuisse
    In uelis uere, cartula nostra, legas
  Sin autem, dicas 'quod scripsit, debuit esse
    Hanc diuam talis materies decuit.
  Ipse coaptando, que conueniant speciei
    Istius domine, scripsit et ista decent'. (Hilbert, 164)

> Verily so great a chamber befits so great a countess,
> but I sang of more than what was, as was fitting.[41]

And finally, an open admission of his jesting character (vv. 1343–47):

> While I labour over these matters, Adèle, I trifle;
> With my verses I have painted a lovely chamber for you.
> As for you, requite us with something worthy of our fable;
> consider how much our fable is worth.[42]

In another poem, Baudri stresses the fictional quality of his poems: 'I utter words in many roles and describe myself now as rejoicing, now as sorrowing; and speaking like a young man, "I hate" or "I love something or other" . . . but it's not true, I make it all up'.[43]

Thus, Baudri probably never saw Adèle, he certainly was never in her chamber, and therefore he did not see a tapestry of any kind in that location. His poem is largely a skilful fiction designed to gain him an introduction to Adèle. That he failed in this attempt is shown by the poem immediately following in the collection, where Baudri repeats his plea. But Baudri *had* seen the Bayeux Tapestry. The imagined tapestry in his poem is, we believe, demonstrably based upon first-hand knowledge of the famous artifact. The pleasure to be derived from Baudri's poem by sophisticated contemporaries, including Adèle, was, in large part, the pleasure of recognition.

The idea of recognition leads to a literary matter, namely the question of the poem's genre. It is perfectly apparent that the *Adelae Comitissae* is a panegyric. There are several examples of medieval panegyric that achieve their aim by reference to works of art or buildings associated with the ruler or magnate addressed. Among these are Ermoldus Nigellus' poem to Louis the Pious that describes a series of frescoes in the emperor's palace and church at Ingelheim.[44] Another example is Walahfrid Strabo's poem to the same emperor on the statue of Theodoric placed in a courtyard before the palace.[45] A third is John Scottus' poem

---

[41] Nempe decet talem talis thalamus comitissam
   At plus, quod decuit, quam quod erat, cecini. (Hilbert, 184)

[42] Dum tibi desudo, dum sudans, Adela, nugor,
   Depinxi pulchrum carminibus thalamum.
   Tu uero nostre fabelle digna repende
   Et pensa, quanti fabula constiterit. (Hilbert, 184)

[43] See Abrahams, Poem CXLVII vv. 35–39; Hilbert, Poem 85; trans. Bond, 177, fn. 101. The Latin text is as follows:
   Quod uero tanquam de certis scriptito rebus
   Et quod personis impono uocabula multis
   Et modo gaudentem, modo me describo dolentem
   Aut puerile loquens uel amo uel quidlibet odi,
   Crede michi: non uera loquor magis omnia fingo. (Hilbert, 89)

[44] 'In Honorem Hludowici Liber IV', vv. 179–282, ed. Ernst Dümmler, *Monumenta Germaniae Historica: Poetae Latini Aevi Carolini*, ii, Berlin 1884, 63–66. See also, Walther Lammers, 'Ein karolingisches Bildprogramm in der Aula regia von Ingelheim', *Vestigia mediaevalia ausgewählte zur mittelalterlichen Historiographie, Landes-und Kirchengeschichte*, Wiesbaden 1979 (Frankfurter Historische Adhandlungen 19), 219–83.

[45] Michael W. Herren, 'The "De imagine Tetrici" of Walahfrid Strabo: Edition and Translation', *The Journal of Medieval Latin* 1, 1991, 118–39; earlier edition by E. Dümmler, *Poetae Latini*, ii, 370–78.

to Charles the Bald on the church of St Mary built by Charles at Compiègne to serve as a royal chapel.[46]

In all three cases there is documentary or archaeological-cum-art historical evidence to show that the objects or buildings described actually existed. This fact seems to indicate that poets did not strain their patrons' credulity by referring to an object or building associated with the patron which was imaginary. Baudri, therefore, adopted the conventions of earlier Latin panegyric *in large part*. Adèle, who is described by Baudri as a reader of books and patroness of poets, would have seen through Baudri's hyperbole and recognized the reference to an object bearing her family's history as factually based.

Recently, literary scholars have made much of the innovative qualities of Baudri's poetry, especially his 'courtliness', and the ironic character of his poetry cast in the Ovidian mould.[47] However, in writing a major panegyric work with its plea for patronage, Baudri remains steadfastly in the Carolingian tradition of objectivity when dealing with an artifact that held close and powerful associations for the potential patron. We must therefore disagree with the conclusion of Jean-Yves Tilliette in his otherwise important and perceptive study of Baudri's poem:

> Il est donc vain de chercher dans ce poème la moindre indication archéologique précise; c'est une oeuvre littéraire, faite de mots, et qui doit d'abord être etudiée comme telle.[48]

The case is more complicated.

Postcript. After our paper had gone to press, we became aware of the important new book by Christine Ratkowitsch, *Descriptio Picturae: Die literarische Funktion der Beschreibung von Kunstwerken in der lateinischen Grossdichtung des 12. Jahrhunderts* (Vienna, 1991), which devotes more than 100 pages to an interpretation of Baudri's poem (pp. 17–127). This work should certainly be consulted for its literary insights, chiefly those regarding the poem's overall structure and purpose. However, Ratkowitsch did not undertake the close comparison of image and text that we have presented here, and we do not believe that there is anything in her work that would challenge or weaken our conclusion. (M.W.H.)

---

[46] 'Aulae Sidereae', ed. and trans. by M.W. Herren in *Iohannis Scotti Eriugenae Carmina*, Dublin 1993 (Scriptores Latini Hiberniae 12), 116–21; earlier edition by L. Traube, *Poetae Latini*, iii, Berlin 1896, 550–52.

[47] Dronke, 'Personal Poetry'; Bond, 'Iocus Amoris'.

[48] Tilliette, 'La Chambre de la Contesse Adèle', 153.

GIUSEPPE DEL RE'S 'CRITICAL' EDITION OF FALCO OF BENEVENTO'S CHRONICLE*

Edoardo D'Angelo

Falco of Benevento's *Chronicon* is – as everyone knows – one of the most important sources for the history, not only of Benevento, but also of all South Italy in the first half of the twelfth century.

His historiographical significance, however, has not found support in the attention that scholars have devoted to the text from the strictly philological viewpoint. On the contrary, the *status* of the tradition of the *Chronicon* is really disastrous.

In my paper, which anticipates the study of Falco's tradition on which I am engaged, I have chosen to speak about Giuseppe Del Re's edition of the text[1] (so this paper is a quasi-recension that is one century and a half late!), for a definite reason: even if Del Re is not the first and only person responsible for the numerous errors present in the text (if an editor can *not* be responsible for the quality of the text he publishes), but inherits them from former editions, his *Cronisti e scrittori sincroni* surely represents the *vulgata* of Falco's text; nearly all the scholars, historiographers and philologists, that is, have read, and are reading the *Chronicon* in Del Re's edition (because it can be found more easily than others). It may, therefore, be helpful to indicate in advance in this paper some of the peculiarities of this text, as they have emerged from my studies.

The first press edition of Falco of Benevento's chronicle was published at Naples in 1626, *'opera ac studio'* of the Reverend Father Antonio Caracciolo;[2] this edition has been followed by all other publications of the text; so, none of the later editions has added anything new as regards the *editio princeps*, of which they merely – at best – reproduce the text exactly. As far as Caracciolo's edition is concerned, it is vitiated by numerous, often serious, imperfections. They are due to two basic reasons: (a) Caracciolo probably used a manuscript (today lost), that may have been in a worse condition than the manuscripts that we can use at this moment; (b) Caracciolo behaved in a very 'free' way as regards the manuscript that he submitted for publication.[3] The same is true of Ludovico Antonio Muratori, who in the fifth volume of his *Rerum Italicarum Scriptores*, published in 1723, reprinted the work of the Beneventan notary as edited by the Neapolitan Father,[4] by adding the *'Castigationes'*, a series of footnotes, in part also textual,

---

* This paper is a part of my work on Falco's text ('Studi sulla tradizione del testo di Falcone Beneventano') that will be published, next year, in the first number of *Filologia Mediolatina*. I want to thank Dr Marjorie Chibnall, who has been so kind as to help me with the English translation of the text for this conference.

1   G. Del Re, *Cronisti e scrittori sincroni*, Naples, Stamperia dell'Iride, 1845, vol. 1, 160–276.
2   A. Caracciolo, *Antiqui chronologi quatuor*, Naples 1626, 178–343.
3   For a specific analysis of Caracciolo's edition, see above, n. *, 'Studi sulla tradizione'.
4   L.A. Muratori, *Rerum Italicarum Scriptores*, Milan 1724, vol. 5, 82–123.

that the learned Camillo Pellegrini had added, in his *Historia Principum Lango-bardorum*, to Caracciolo's text.[5] Muratori's text presents some deviations – prob-ably misprints –, from Caracciolo's text, that are again copied by Del Re.

In 1753 appeared the fourth volume of the new edition of Pellegrini's *Historia Principum Langobardorum*, edited by the Capuan canon Francesco Maria Pratilli, that includes a reprint of the Falconian chronicle.[6] Since this particular scholar's skill as a forger of other texts in his collection has already been unmasked (some whole chronicles were entirely forged by him!), I have brought to light Pratilli's lies about Falco's chronicle as well: Pratilli, pretending to be in possession of some other manuscripts of the chronicle, intervenes over and over again, totally arbitrarily, in the text established by Caracciolo, sometimes giving information in a footnote, sometimes without any information. This results in significant alter-ations of the text.[7]

In 1845 appeared the *Cronisti e scrittori sincroni*, published by Del Re in collaboration with several scholars; Stanislao Gatti collaborated in the Italian translation, and Michelangelo Naldi in some footnotes to Falco's text. Del Re adds to the text and translation some of his own footnotes, Pellegrino's '*Castigationes*' (translated into Italian), and Pratilli's footnotes. In the 'Proemio', Del Re explains on what 'philological criterion' his edition is based: the edition will be based 'on Muratori's edition compared with Pratilli's edition; there are only a few small discrepancies between these two texts'.[8] These words immediately reveal the scientific level of Del Re's edition, especially the indefinite and vague verb *raffrontare*, 'to compare'; moreover, he *raffronta*, – he compares (whatever that may mean) – two editions that are already themselves very bad. The philological *status* of Del Re's text is, therefore, this:

Caracciolo's errors and 'freedoms'

+

Muratori's misprints

+

Pratilli's frauds (and misprints)

+

Del Re's own misprints

I want here to give some examples of each type of deviation (comparing Del Re's text with the text restored by me). In particular, Del Re's text is very bad

[5] C. Pellegrini, *Historia Principum Langobardorum*, Naples 1644, vol. 2, 145–184. Pellegrini didn't use other manuscripts: he made his emendations only *ope ingenii*, and on the ground of Cesare Baronio's partial edition of the text (*Annales Ecclesiastici*, Rome 1607, vol. 12, passim) that, as just showed E. Gervasio, 'Falcone Beneventano e la sua Cronaca', *Bull. Ist. stor. Ital.*, liv, 1939, 83–92.
[6] F.M. Pratilli, *Historia Principum Langobardorum*, Naples 1749–54, vol. iv, 143–313.
[7] About this 'new' fraud of Pratilli, see my 'Imposture pratilliane in margine al testo di Falcone Beneventano', that will be published in the *Atti dell'Accademia Peloritana dei Pericolanti. Classe di Lettere, Filosofia e Belle Arti*, of Messina.
[8] Del Re, 160. Il testo nella versione italiana suona così: 'sull'edizione del Muratori *raffrontan-dola* con quella del Pratilli, tra le quali sono poche e leggiere discordanze'.

from the typographical viewpoint.[9] Then, there is a very long sequence of misprints in it. Here are some examples:[10]

Del Re's edition	Chronicon
164,30 *illius . . . Normandis . . . abeuntibus*	*illis . . . Normandis . . . abeuntibus*
165, 4 *Dominus Castelli Ceppaluni*	*dominus castelli Ceppalunis*
165,41 *prout melius potuisset, faceret*	*prout melius potuissent, facerent*
168,27 *securitate accepto*	*securitate accepta*
168,43 *honori solitu reddidisset*	*honori solito reddidisset*
177,35 *et alter . . . converti non posse aspicientes*	*et aliter . . . converti non posse aspicientes*
178,32 *indignius ego osculatus sum*	*indignus ego osculatus sum*
182,6 *qui amici . . . Apostolicum precatur*	*qui amici . . . Apostolicum precantur*
183,27 *Monasterium illud*	*monasterium istud*
183,53 *et multis alii viris . . . aspicientibus*	*et multis aliis viris . . . aspicientibus*
190,19 *sex etenim mentium spatio*	*sex etenim mensium spatio*
191,13 *ante altare te prosternite*	*ante altare te prosternito*
202, 1 *anno igitur pro*	*anno igitur ipso*
214,20 *vasorum aureorum abundantiam, et vestimentorum infinitas varietates*	*vasorum aureorum abundantiam, vestimentorum infinitas varietates*
220,15 *ut mulieres, et eorum infantes vinculis destinavit*	*et mulieres, et eorum infantes vinculis destinavit*
220,19 *cum uxoribus et filii*	*cum uxoribus et filiis*
226,23 *quid longius moror ?*	*quid longius morer ?*
233,5 *obsederunt eam*	*obsederunt*
237,12 *Rossemannus Antistes*	*Rossemannus Beneventanus antistes*
243,21 *et his decussis*	*et his decursis*
251,24 *acto romesinas valentem*	*octo romesinas valentem*

But we could add still more examples.

Then, two ample lacunae in the continuity of the text are present:

Del Re's edition	Chronicon
189,11 *et coram omnibus, Sanctorum reliquiae*	*et coram omnibus episcoporum solacio illud confregit, et altare fracto sanctorum reliquiae*

and

---

[9] We should also speak about the orthographic choices, today maybe unacceptable; there is a total 'classicization' of the orthography; the use of the letter -j-, some 'iperclassical' graphies like *lachryma*, and *quotidie*, an improper use of the capital letters, etc.
[10] The two numbers of the quotation refer, respectively, to the number of page and line in Del Re's edition. Some of the following of Del Re's readings could also not be misprints, as in the case of 178,32; 183,24; 214,20; 233,5.

228,32 *ad eamdem civitatem venit, et cursu celeri Pisas revertitur*	*ad eamdem civitatem venit, et imperatoris adventum firmiter propalavit, et cursu celeri Pisas revertitur*

Since those two omissions are respectively of 52 and 44 characters, it's very probable that they represent two lines missed in the preparation of the lead for the pagination (the average number of characters per line in the Latin text of Del Re's edition is just 50).

Del Re inherits moreover from Caracciolo (through Muratori) three other ample lacunae:

Del Re's edition	***Chronicon***
178,51 *jussa . . . executi sunt, et laudibus innumeris*	*iussa . . . executi sunt, continuo portarum singularum sacerdotes in unum congregati sunt, et laudibus innumeris*
221,47 *vindemias dimisimus famis quidem penuriam, et sitis*	*vindemias dimisimus, et predicti regis nefandis petitionibus ullo modo favere noluimus; famis quidem penuriam, et sitis*
231,54 *constantiam justitiae inter vos*; *civitatem vero*	*constantiam iustitiae inter vos; nam vita comite dignam vobis retributionem impendemus; civitatem vero*

It isn't possible to say for certain if those lacunae are Caracciolo's (probably unintentional) omissions, or errors that the Theatine inherits from his *antigraphus* (I hypothesize he used a *codex deperditus*). However, we can say that the first two lacunae are probably due to the fall of a line at the time of printing: in fact, both consist of 63 characters; furthermore, the lacuna of 178,51 is preceded by the same word it ends with (*sunt*), while the lacuna of 221,47 is preceded by the word *dimisimus*, and ends by a word in homoeoteleuton, *noluimus*. On the contrary, there are 51 characters in the lacuna of 231,54. Those omissions have repercussions on Gatti's Italian translation.

Another lacuna, even if less ample, Del Re inherits from Caracciolo (but this is a very important omission for the reconstruction of the *stemma codicum* of the falconian tradition): the lacuna in question is the name of the fourth judge who, in the year 1120, in Benevento, together with his colleagues *Ioannes*, *Persicus* and *Landulphus*, escorted pope Paschal II from the bishop's residence to the *Sacrum Palatium Beneventanum* (181,60); the name – and the person – in question is the judge *Guisliccio*, named also another time in the *Chronicon*, 200,33.[11]

The third type of deviation that's present in Del Re's edition is due to the lection that Del Re thought read well in Muratori's and Pratilli's texts. From the first, he inherits the following deviations:

[11] For this problem, see always E. D'Angelo, 'Studi sulla tradizione', above, n. *.

Del Re's edition	Chronicon
162,34 *civitatem intrinsecis conspirationibus . . . turbavissent*	*civitatem intrinsecus conspirationibus . . . turbavissent*
231,33 *Falco judex, et Falco*	*Falco iudex, et Roffridus iudex, et Falco*
239,58 *consilio habito, illud dimisit*	*consilio habito, castellum illud dimisit*

From both, because in the following two cases Pratilli's interventions coincide with two – maybe due to misprints – of Muratori's deviations:[12]

Del Re's edition	Chronicon
162,45 *quid agendum esset . . . sciscitatus est*	*quod agendum esset . . . sciscitatus est*
169,49 *mense octobri*	*mense octubro*

In practice, Del Re follows Pratilli in every case that the Capuan canon deviates from Caracciolo's text. Here are some exemples:

Del Re's/Pratilli's edition	Caracciolo's edition
165,47 *misit . . . ut, consulens necessitati, comestabiliam deponeret*	*misit . . . ut, condolens necessitati, comestabiliam deponeret*
166,17 *alia quidem die surgens pars Archiepiscopi*	*alia quidem die surgente pars Archiepiscopi*
171,35 *claves . . . qui eas retinent, fidelem omnino confitemur*	*claves . . . qui eas retinet, fidelem tuum omnino confitemur*
174,6 *properarunt*	*properaverunt*
174,10 *secunda die*	*secundo die*
174,33 *quae a praedicto Pontifice audierat Regi renunciaverunt*	*quae a praedicto Pontifice audierant Regi renunciaverunt*
174,47 *quorum mens fixa manebant*	*quorum mens fixa manebat*
175,44 *et Romana Sedes*	*Romana Sedes*
175,62 *ad Pontificalem infulam promoverunt*	*ad Pontificalem infulam promovetur*
176,25 *Episcopi clericos . . . fecit vocari*	*Episcopii clericos . . . fecit vocari*
176,52 *Suffraganei circiter viginti et monasteriorum Abbates sex affuere*	*Suffraganei circiter viginti, Monasteriorum abbates sex affuere*
177,11 *aratris . . . evolvi . . . praecepit*	*aratris . . . volvi . . . praecepit*
177,47 *tum . . . Landulphus . . . tenderet*	*dum . . . Landulphus . . . tenderet*
178,22 *Sanctorum . . . Dori, Potiti, Prosperi*	*Sanctorum . . . Dori, Potiti et Prosperi*
179,29 *ibi stolii manus operantes videres*	*ibi studii manus operantes videres*
179,61 *qui triginta et tres annos . . . in Episcopatu advixit*	*qui triginta et tres annos . . . in Episcopatum advixit*
180,34 *illud circumeunt . . . machinis . . . utuntur*	*illud circumeunt et . . . machinis utuntur*
181,40 *aliique Monachorum sapientes*	*aliique Monachorum sapientum*
182,35 *personam . . . dignam fore clamavere*	*personam . . . dignam fore dignam clamavere*

[12] About the hypothesis that Pratilli also used Muratori's text (together with Caracciolo's text) for his edition, see my 'Imposture pratilliane', above, n. 7.

183,10	*festivitas Sancti Januarii celebratur,* *quae erat XIX. die mensis Septembris*	*festivitas Sancti Januarii celebratur*
192,57	*lachrymas precesque effudit*	*lacrimas preces effudit*
197,14	*haec . . . Pontifice Honorio* *. . . predicandae*	*haec . . . Pontifice Honorio* *. . . predicante*
198,62	*solidos illos elargitus est*	*solidos illos largitus est*
200,62	*quos de civitate ejicerant revocarent*	*quos de civitate ejicerant in civitatem* *revocarent*
201, 29	*Leo Frangepanem*	*Leo Frangens panem*
201,38	*mense Martii*	*mense Martio*
206,56	*civium Barensium traditione* *manifesta*	*civium Barensium traditione* *manifestata*
207,21	*uxor charissima et filius sic* *ablati fuissent*	*uxor charissima et filius sic* *ablata fuisset*
208,31	*Tancredum vero de Conversano*	*Tancredum vero*
208,33	*in transmarinas partes eum* *destinavit*	*transmarinas partes eum destinavit*
209,53	*Cardinalis haec audiens*	*Cardinalis exaudiens*
211,27	*fortuna volatili animo defecit*	*fortuna volatili animo defeci*
211,43	*amoverunt*	*amovere*
214,33	*super auditis occisionibus*	*super inauditis occisionibus*
217,52	*homicidii finem poneret*	*homicidii magnitudini finem poneret*
219,62	*civitatis Clerum omnem, et* *Monachos . . . convocans*	*civitatis Clerum omnem, civitatis et* *Monachos . . . convocans*
220,45	*qualiter autem cum Pisanis egerit* *. . . ad nostram pervenit notitiam*	*qualiter autem cum Pisanis egerit . . .* *ad nostram perventum est notitiam*
222,56	*quosdam . . . muneribus, quosdam* *autem pollicitationibus*	*quosdam . . . muneribus, quosdam* *pollicitationibus*
224,30	*et vidimus, et audivimus*	*vidimus et audivimus*
226,11	*et nos crinibus solutis*	*et crinibus solutis*
227,3	*Comitem Rainulphum*	*Comitem illum Rainulphum*
228,38	*civitas . . . Neapolis*	*civitas . . . Neapolitana*
228,42	*qui libertati invigilabant, quippe* *. . . sequebantur honestatem*	*qui libertati invigilabant, quique* *. . . sequebantur honestatem*
229,3	*qui obviam Imperatori . . . exierant* *. . . literas suas . . . delegarunt*	*qui obviam Imperatori . . . exierant* *. . . literas suas . . . delegavit*
230,5	*Malfridum de Grimaldo Abbatem*	*Malfridum de Grimaldo Abbate*
230,12	*putantes eis timorem inducere* *aut eos in fuga sectari*	*putantes eis timorem inducere* *et eos in fuga sectari*
230,51	*usque ad Portam Ruffini*	*usque Portam Ruffini*
232,34	*cumque castellum . . . comprehensum* *esset*	*cumque castellum . . . comprehensum* *est*
233,10	*Siculorum multi captivi ducti sunt*	*Siculorum captivi ducti sunt*
234,14	*patres, avi et proavi*	*patres, avi, proavi*
236,3	*super Nuceriam veniens, illam* *suae obtinuit potestati*	*super Nucerium veniens, suae* *illud obtinuit potestati*

237,28	*Rogerius Dei gratia Siciliae et Italiae Rex*	*Rogerius Dei gratia Siciliae Italiae Rex*
239,50	*sicut statutum erat*	*sicut satutum est*
240,8	*mortem ipsius Anacleti scilicet significando*	*mortem ipsius Anacleti significando*
242,15	*in finibus festinavit Benafri, civitates illas suae submittere volens potestati*	*in finibus festinavit Benafri, civitates illas suae submittere potestati*
244,29	*literas omnibus suis . . . direxit, ut . . . ad eum conveniat*	*literas omnibus suis . . . direxit, ut . . . ad eum conveniant*
246,26	*o quantus luctus, et moeroris abundantiam . . . quae si radicitus describere vellem*	*o quantus luctus, et moeroris abundantiam . . . quod si radicitus describere vellem*
247,9	*S. Bartholomei*	*Bartholomei*
247,14	*civitate exivit*	*civitatem exivit*
250,2	*primo gallorum cantu*	*primo pullorum cantu*
252,44	*super . . . execrandis actionibus mirabatur*	*super execrandis actibus mirabatur*

Summing up this short paper, it is possible to say, on the whole, that Del Re's edition of Falco of Benevento's chronicle is worse than Caracciolo's edition and many others; but, because it is the most recent[13] and, in many countries, the most easily accessible, it is more used by scholars than all the others. This is a confirmation (don't forget that the text in hand is a printed text of the first half of the nineteenth century!), a confirmation, I said, of the equation, of lachmannian memory, between 'more recent' and 'worse' manuscripts. I hope, on the contrary, by my next edition of the *Chronicon*, to assign a point to Giorgio Pasquali's motto 'recentiores non deteriores'.[14]

---

[13] There is only one other reprint of the Caracciolo's text in the *Patrologia Latina*, clxxiii, cols 1151–1262, published in 1895.

[14] These words are the title of a chapter (pp. 41–8) of his *Storia della tradizione e critica del testo*, Florence 1988[2].

ANGLO-SAXON BOOKS:
TREASURE IN NORMAN HANDS?

David N. Dumville

The movable wealth of an Anglo-Saxon church was often in danger of travelling in the wrong direction – away from that church's possession, whether in the hands of predators or up in smoke because of a fire (however begun). At no time was this risk more acute than in the course of invasion, for churches could not expect to be immune from the rapaciousness of an invading army, be it pagan or christian, Anglo-Saxon or foreign. Destruction was an ever-present threat. Warfare, however, brought a range of added hazards, one or all of which could combine and lead to a significant diminution in a church's ownership of property, whether real or movable. Straightforward plundering was only one of the ways, albeit the most direct, in which a church might be affected by warfare. When an external ruler in a commanding military position demanded tribute, churches – often wealthy corporations – had to pay their share: if sufficient liquidity were not available, a church would have to raise money by a transaction of more or less commercial nature. This could involve the sale of assets for cash or instead the pledging of such against repayment. We have examples of each of these phenomena attested from the Viking Ages. Indeed, in scholars' minds this sort of process has come to be particularly associated with the viking period.[1]

There is no *a priori* reason why such events should not be seen in connexion with that much more successful military conquest of England which occurred in 1066. We have to ask ourselves about the nature of the spoils of conquest after 1066. Historians' attention has tended to be focussed on the political and tenurial results, on office- and landholding, while students of manuscripts have concentrated on the changes in book-production and library-organisation wrought by Norman takeover.[2] Only art-historians, it seems, have had their eyes fixed firmly on the issue of the movable spoils of war and on the attitudes of the conquerors as triumphant victors.[3]

---

[1] In 872 the bishop of Worcester had to lease land to obtain money to pay the tribute to the Danes: P.H. Sawyer, *Anglo-Saxon Charters. An Annotated List and Bibliography*, London 1968, no. 1278; cf. *English Historical Documents, c. 500–1042*, transl. Dorothy Whitelock, 2nd edn, London 1979, 532 (no. 94). On the reign of Æthelred the Unready, see M.K. Lawson, 'The Collection of Danegeld and Heregeld in the Reigns of Aethelred II and Cnut', *EHR*, xcix, 1984, 721–38. For periodisation, see P.H. Sawyer et al., 'The Two Viking Ages of Britain. A Discussion', *Mediaeval Scandinavia* ii, 1969, 163–207.

[2] For the standard account, see N.R. Ker, *English Manuscripts in the Century after the Norman Conquest*, Oxford 1960. For provocative discussion, see R.M. Thomson, 'The Norman Conquest and English Libraries', in *The Role of the Book in Medieval Culture*, ed. Peter Ganz, 2 vols, Turnhout 1986, ii.27–40.

[3] The best discussions are by C.R. Dodwell, 'Losses of Anglo-Saxon Art in the Middle Ages',

English Channel

BELGIUM

GERMANY

22 •

LUXEM-
BOURG

• 20

• 10

• 4   9   F
2   5   7

C   • 16

B   E   • 11

8   D • 3

G   17
15 • • 19

6 1   A

• 13

• 14

F R A N C E

12

18 •

21 •

NORMAN ECCLESIASTICAL DIOCESES OF 11th and 12th CENTURIES	LOCATIONS IN NORMANDY	LOCATIONS ELSEWHERE IN FRANCE	LOCATION IN GERMANY
A Avranches	1 Avranches	10 Arras	22 Köln
B Bayeux	2 Cherbourg	11 Beauvais	
C Coutances	3 Evreux	12 Berry	
D Evreux	4 Fécamp	13 Bonneval	
E Lisieux	5 Jumièges	14 Fleury	
F Rouen	6 Mont Saint~Michel	15 Jouarre	
G Sées	7 Rouen	16 Laon	
	8 Saint~Evroul	17 Paris	
	9 Saint~Wandrille	18 Saint~Claude	
		19 Saint~Maur~des~Fossés	
		20 Saint~Omer	
		21 Seyssel	

The Dispersal of Anglo-Saxon MSS after 1066

At the purely political level, we may allow that King William needed to show not merely that his gamble for the English throne had succeeded but that there were rich pickings which would be distributed far and wide among those who supported him and among those whom he chose or needed to impress. A well known page of William of Poitiers is hyperbolic in tone but offers some clear indications of what happened.[4] He tells us that, in England,

> treasures, great in their number, their kind and their workmanship, had been amassed, destined either to be kept for the empty pleasure of avarice or to be used shamefully in English luxury. Some of these he generously bestowed on those who had helped in the war now concluded: most of them, and these the most precious, he distributed among the needy monasteries of various provinces. He sent to the Roman church of St. Peter more abundant wealth in gold and silver than would be believed if we told it, and sent into the possession of Pope Alexander ornaments which Byzantium would hold very dear. We might specially mention the banner of King Harold, which had the figure of an armed man woven in it in purest gold: with this booty he made return for the gift which had been sent to him through the kindness of this Apostle. . . . In a thousand churches in France, Aquitaine, Burgundy and Auvergne and other regions, the memory of King William will be celebrated in perpetuity. The ever-present greatness of his benefaction will not allow the memory of the benefactor to die. Some received gold crucifixes of great size remarkably adorned with jewels, many were given pounds of gold or vessels made of the same metal, several received vestments or other precious gifts. The least of the gifts with which he gladdened a small monastery would splendidly adorn a metropolitan basilica. . . . But, the most pleasurable gifts were sent to Normandy . . . where they were found more acceptable than any gift of beauty or delight which Arabia might have made.

William of Poitiers also tells us of William's parading his captives and spoils in Normandy[5] – as C.R. Dodwell has put it, 'William was compared by his biographer to a Roman general and he did not deny himself his own form of Roman triumph'. William remarked that the Normans gawped at the wealth of gold and silver vessels brought from conquered England, the description of whose 'number and beauty would strain credulity'.[6]

The attitudes of those who came to own or govern English churches would necessarily have been more complex. It is not likely that the religious accoutrements of the English aristocracy were spared from seizure where these families were supplanted by Normans. Private chapels and estate-churches would have been obvious targets. But where a Norman-appointed abbot or bishop took control of a major institution he might find that the church had already suffered considerable losses before his appointment; he could choose to defend the interests of his

Bulletin of the John Rylands University Library of Manchester lvi, 1973/4, 74–92, and *Anglo-Saxon Art. A New Perspective*, Manchester 1982, 216–34 and 320–31.
[4] *Guillaume de Poitiers: Histoire de Guillaume le Conquérant*, ed. Raymonde Foreville, Paris 1952, 224. The translation which follows is, with minor alteration, that of Dodwell, 'Losses', 85.
[5] *Guillaume*, ed. Foreville, 260–2.
[6] Dodwell, *Anglo-Saxon Art*, 217, and 'Losses', 85, drawing from *Guillaume*, ed. Foreville, 256.

new church with full vigour; or he might remember his loyalty to his former house, sending gifts of precious ecclesiastical objects to adorn that church in honour of its patron-saint. No doubt all these possibilities were realised, as well as other permutations of response to circumstance and loyalty.

I have already observed that it is art-historians who have emphasised the material effects of the Norman conquest of England in terms of ecclesiastical treasures' migrations. The literary accounts stress, as would perhaps be expected, the scale and wondrous quality of what changed ownership. But, as Dodwell has pointed out, such statements give us no sense of what was *not* plundered and we can hear of both great and successive losses from the same church.[7] Before our natural, rising scepticism causes us to discount such notices altogether we must remember that physical evidence does in fact survive across the European continent to document losses incurred by English owners in the aftermath of the battle of Hastings. The extent to which England was plundered – and quite naturally so – after the Conquest is not a theme to which many modern historians have warmed, and perhaps for two reasons. The predisposition to find continuity, which is such a strong impulse among many historians, does not favour this topic. Likewise, the marked disinclination now so often shown by historians to dwell on the unpleasant effects of hostile activity is a factor which leads to a minimising approach to a subject such as ours.

Curiously, given art-historians' willingness directly to address this issue, manuscripts have not proved to be a prominent class of testimony. Metalwork in particular has loomed very large, inevitably (no doubt) in view of what was considered particularly precious in both secular and ecclesiastical society.[8] The point at which – for our purpose – metalwork and manuscripts intersect is in the bindings of books, whose boards might be adorned with metalwork-fittings which could in turn bear precious jewels or delicately carved ivory-panels;[9] alternatively or additionally, a book might be kept in a case or shrine of precious metal, comparably adorned. Our knowledge of the extent to which bejewelled and gilded bookbindings extended across the range of high-status book-production is circumscribed on the one hand by survival and on the other by literary or documentary accounts.[10] Survival has been attenuated by the value of the adornments. Literary accounts suggest that, when a binding was despoiled of its ornament, the binding as a whole was a casualty and the book, if it survived, would need to be repaired and rebound.

All accounts of treasure tend to have a compulsory reference to one richly ornamented gospel-book or more: it seems to be a convention, a topos, of this kind of description.[11] We know, then, that observers counted such books among treasure – and, indeed, they often occur in mediaeval inventories of church-furnishings, along with church-plate and ecclesiastical vestments, rather than with

---

[7] Dodwell, 'Losses'.

[8] See n. 3, above.

[9] See Paul Needham, *Twelve Centuries of Bookbindings 400–1600*, New York 1979, 33–5 (no. 8), for an example of an immediately pre-Conquest gilt silver and jewelled bookcover (on New York, Pierpont Morgan Library, MS. M.708).

[10] For accounts of bindings, see Edith Diehl, *Bookbinding: its Background and Technique*, 2 vols, New York 1946; Needham, *Twelve Centuries*.

[11] See the range of examples quoted by Dodwell (as n. 3, above).

books in library-lists or catalogues.[12] While bindings and cases or shrines constituted the immediate source of visible wealth, the visual display which the manuscript itself might offer should not be underestimated as an attraction.

Books which were typically given such grand bindings might include gospelbooks and psalters (and some other biblical manuscripts), as well as more narrowly liturgical service-books. The immediately holy associations of such books gave them an automatic degree of status which could invite honorific decoration. Such holiness might, however, be perceived as greatly augmented if a particular book's previous owner had been exceptionally saintly.[13] Among the ornament which a binding might carry could be small reliquaries: it is a nice question whether the presence of saintly relics was a further response to the holy associations of a book or itself a factor tending to augment a book's holiness – or both.[14] It is similarly a question whether the presence of such relics would increase the general attraction of the object as a whole or rather give it some protection from abstraction or simply render it desirable to a more specialist kind of plunderer.

What is particularly unclear is whether other types of high-status books – as defined by their internal decoration and the quality of parchment and script – would attract ornamentation of their bindings in even remotely comparable ways. For example, the Christian Latin poetry of Prudentius was often accompanied by a cycle of illustrations which seems likely to have endowed the manuscripts with considerable status.[15] But would such a book ever have borne a heavily ornamented binding? Furthermore, in England in the second quarter of the eleventh century, we know of the production of high-status vernacular illustrated manuscripts, whether of biblical texts or of literary miscellanies.[16] Would these have attracted such binding and encrustation with displays of wealth? I know of no English evidence which would answer the question satisfactorily. This conclusion must limit the ways in which my argument develops henceforth.

One of the subgroups within the corpus of pre-Conquest English manuscripts offers, if properly displayed, eloquent testimony on this subject. For a significant quantity of late Anglo-Saxon books is known from Continental collections; many of these bear evidence for early Continental provenance.[17] I shall turn in due

---

[12] See the discussions by F. Wormald, 'The Monastic Library', in *The English Library before 1700. Studies in its History*, edd. Francis Wormald and C.E. Wright, London 1958, 15–31 (with plates 4–6), and D.N. Dumville, 'English Libraries before 1066: Use and Abuse of the Manuscript Evidence', in *Anglo-Saxon Manuscripts: Basic Readings*, ed. Mary P. Richards, New York 1994.

[13] One may suspect that this was the case with the pontifical of Archbishop Dunstan (no. 22 in the Appendix, below) which passed first to his disciple, Wulfsige: on its history see David N. Dumville, *Liturgy and the Ecclesiastical History of Late Anglo-Saxon England: Four Studies*, Woodbridge 1992, 82–4.

[14] Cf. A. Frolow, *Les Reliquaires de la Vraie Croix*, Paris 1965.

[15] Richard Stettiner, *Die illustrierten Prudentiushandschriften*, 2 vols, Berlin 1895/1905.

[16] For facsimiles see *The Old English Illustrated Hexateuch. British Museum Cotton Claudius B.IV*, edd. C.R. Dodwell and P. Clemoes, Copenhagen 1974; *An Eleventh-Century Anglo-Saxon Illustrated Miscellany. British Library Cotton Tiberius B.V Part 1 together with Leaves from British Library Cotton Nero D.II*, edd. P. McGurk et al., Copenhagen 1983.

[17] A list is given in the Appendix, below. Several such books can be shown to have travelled to the Continent before 1066. For accounts of these, see M. Harrsen, 'The Countess Judith of Flanders and the Library of Weingarten Abbey', *Papers of the Bibliographical Society of America* xxiv, 1930, 1–13 (with plates I–VIII); W.M. Hinkle, 'The Gift of an Anglo-Saxon Gospel Book to the Abbey of Saint-Remi, Reims', *Journal of the British Archaeological Association*, 3rd series, xxxiii, 1970, 21–35 (with plates VII–IX); D. Gremont and L. Donnat, 'Fleury, Le Mont Saint-

course to a consideration of the possible reasons for their export: for the moment, I wish merely to establish the basic facts and introduce the manuscripts themselves.

Somewhat in excess of forty surviving top-grade late Anglo-Saxon manuscripts can be deduced to have travelled to the Continent in the late eleventh or the twelfth century.[18] Mostly these exist more or less entire, but in some instances we are dependent on highly fragmentary survival – a couple of pages of a liturgical kalendar, for example,[19] or a document cut out of a gospel-book bringing some of the biblical text and evidence for the format of the volume from which it survives.[20] The overwhelming quantity of this testimony to export of high-status English manuscripts is of course – almost by definition – provided by liturgical books, but decorated copies of the works of Boethius, Prudentius, and Vergil should be noted too. Late Anglo-Saxon manuscripts of lesser status are also attested from Continental locations, but the bulk of these can be shown to have travelled thither at times beyond the scope of this paper, for example in the sixteenth and seventeenth centuries.[21] It is, therefore, the liturgical books which loom largest and seem to form the most coherent block.

Analysing their contents more precisely, we find that gospel-books – ranging in scale from an imported pocket-size volume of royal association to the grandest-size format – form a very substantial part of this corpus: other types of book, as defined by content, are fairly evenly divided. The largest group is provided by four *libelli* of individual saints, usually a single or double *uita*, occasionally with some additional *liturgica* attached – small manuscripts, that is, when measured in terms of the number of leaves.[22] The hagiographical *libellus* may typically have stood on an altar dedicated to the saint whose *uita* occupied that manuscript:[23] therefore, it too would be a candidate for rich external decoration in that saint's honour. Next come psalters, of which four are known from relevant Continental locations: the early tenth-century Junius Psalter, the Bury St Edmunds Psalter at the Vatican, and another of the eleventh century at Rouen, as well as the bilingual psalter of unusual format now in Paris.[24]

Michel et l'Angleterre à la fin du Xe et au début du XIe siècle à propos du manuscrit d'Orléans No. 127 (105)', in *Millénaire monastique du Mont Saint-Michel*, edd. Jean Laporte et al., 4 vols, Paris 1967, i.751–93 (cf. Dumville, *Liturgy*, 80–1); *The Missal of Robert of Jumièges*, ed. H.A. Wilson, London 1896. With the exception of Orléans, Bibliothèque municipale, MS. 127 (105), all these books can be shown to have emigrated in the years immediately before the Conquest.

[18] In the Appendix, below, I have listed fifty specimens, but some of these are of lesser status (fine parchment and execution but decorated only with initials) and for others the evidence for their date of departure from England is not wholly satisfactory. The standard account of illustrated manuscripts of the period is by Elżbieta Temple, *Anglo-Saxon Manuscripts, 900–1066*, London 1976.

[19] Appendix, no. 30. Cf. David N. Dumville, *English Caroline Script and Monastic History: Studies in Benedictinism, A.D. 950–1030*, Woodbridge 1993, 108, 115 n. 23, 124 n. 67.

[20] Appendix, no. 13; cf. Dumville, *Liturgy*, 121 and 146, n. 366.

[21] For example, the codex now divided between Antwerpen, Museum Plantijn-Moretus, MSS. 47 and 190, and Bruxelles, Bibliothèque royale, MS. 1650 (1520): see N.R. Ker, *Catalogue of Manuscripts containing Anglo-Saxon*, Oxford 1957, 1–3 and 6–7 (nos. 2, 3, 8).

[22] Appendix, nos. 10, 18, 24, 39 (cf. Dumville, *Liturgy*, 108–10, 139–41).

[23] Cf. Dumville, *Liturgy*, 108, for this suggestion.

[24] Appendix, nos. 19, 38, 44, and 28, respectively. It is not evident that the Normans reacted adversely to *bilingual* English-Latin manuscripts.

Next in line are three groups of three manuscripts each. Among the gospel-lectionaries are one in the famous hand attributed to Eadwig Basan, monk of Canterbury from at least c.1020,[25] and the spectacular illustrated fragments once at Damme, now in the Getty Museum at Malibu.[26] The two other categories of this group are both episcopal books – benedictionals and pontificals.[27] In this group are numbered one of the treasures of late Anglo-Saxon art, the so-called 'Benedictional of Archbishop Robert', the so-called 'Ramsey Benedictional', and an almost unknown fragment, now part of a famous Saint-Evroul codex at Alençon, which Jonathan Alexander attempted to draw to scholarly attention in 1970. The pontificals are the Dunstan or Sherborne Pontifical, the Ecgberht Pontifical (both of these now in Paris), and the Lanalet Pontifical at Rouen.[28]

In the liturgical or paraliturgical context, customaries must not be overlooked – for example, a Commentary on the Rule, of Fécamp provenance, and a copy of other texts relating to the Rule, of Jumièges provenance.[29] After these we are down to single items: a manuscript of homilies with *Martinellus*, now at Avranches; a missal of New Minster, Winchester, use, but now at Le Havre; a fragmentary kalendar – one bifolium – of Canterbury Cathedral use but subsequently at Saint-Evroul, a liturgical commonplace-book; and a mystery service-book early at Avranches but of uncertain identity (to which I shall return).[30]

Among these books the liturgical variety is therefore very great. The picture may, however, be expanded still further. Although the most striking distribution is that of late Anglo-Saxon books in Normandy and its environs,[31] this is not the whole story; for we may identify also a small number of English manuscripts of pre-Viking-Age date which seem to correspond, in terms of provenance, to the geographical spread represented by the later books. Two eighth-century manuscripts and two of the ninth deserve to be mentioned in this regard. A large-format gospel-book in English Uncial script of the later eighth century is now divided between two Paris codices but has a mediaeval Fécamp provenance.[32] Likewise, the Barberini Gospels in the Vatican, of similar date but Insular script, seem likely to owe their transmission to this context rather than to any of the other major recognised channels.[33] From Canterbury, an early ninth-century passional made its way to Normandy by the twelfth century.[34] And already by the end of the eleventh

---

[25] Appendix, no. 7. Cf. Dumville, *English Caroline Script*, 117, 119–20, 139–40, and plate XII.

[26] Appendix, no. 14. Cf. A. Boutemy, 'Les Feuillets de Damme', *Scriptorium* xx, 1966, 60–5 (with plates 7b–10), and Dumville, *English Caroline Script*, 58, n. 259.

[27] For discussion of these as a group, see Dumville, *Liturgy*, 66–95.

[28] Appendix, nos. 46, 23, and 1, respectively, for the benedictionals. On the last, see J.J. G. Alexander, *Norman Illumination at Mont St Michel, 966–1100*, Oxford 1970, 238, n. 1 (cf. Dumville, *Liturgy*, 95, n. 174, for the first subsequent reference). For the pontificals, see Appendix, nos. 22, 31, 43.

[29] Appendix, nos. 25 and 45.

[30] Appendix, nos. 2, 11, 30 (cf. n. 19, above), 40 (cf. Dumville, *Liturgy*, 86, 136–7), and 41. On no. 2 see Geneviève Nortier, *Les Bibliothèques médiévales des abbayes bénédictines de Normandie*, Paris 1971, 63–4, 84. On no. 41 see below, p. 96.

[31] See the map which accompanies this paper (p. 84).

[32] Appendix, no. 21. Cf. J.J.G. Alexander, *Insular Manuscripts, 6th to the 9th Century*, London 1978, 60 (no. 34) and plates 166–168.

[33] Appendix, no. 37. Cf. Alexander, *Insular Manuscripts*, 61–2 (no. 36) and plates 169–178.

[34] Appendix, no. 32. See M.P. Brown, 'Paris, Bibliothèque Nationale, lat. 10861 and the Scriptorium of Christ Church, Canterbury', *Anglo-Saxon England* xv, 1986, 119–37 (with plates I–IV).

century the Bern pocket-gospelbook had reached France, a ninth-century Welsh or Cornish manuscript which had come probably into royal hands in Wessex by soon after 900 and certainly into the possession of the royal minster at Bedwyn (Wiltshire) by the 920s.[35] It is possible that the Stockholm Golden Gospels should be added to this list, seen therefore as having left Canterbury in the aftermath of the Norman takeover; other Uncial manuscripts which may have been taken from England at this time include the St Petersburg Anglo-Saxon gospel-books and the Paris Gregory.[36]

We must briefly place the travels of these manuscripts, of various sorts, within the total context of the movements of Anglo-Saxon manuscripts outside England. While any individual manuscript might in principle be taken abroad at any time, there are nevertheless three broad movements or connexions which seem to have caused the export of the bulk of those Anglo-Saxon books which left England before 1066. The first is on the whole an eighth-century phenomenon, although it began in the late seventh and no doubt continued in some measure in the first half of the ninth: the presence of English missions to the heathen Frisians and Germans (and of English ecclesiastics on related business in Francia) led to the export – including, in some (no doubt numerous) cases, the writing for export – of many books; among these, I might add, was a good number which had previously been imported from the Continent in the founding era of English christianity.[37] A connexion of a rather different nature – which ran through much of the pre-Conquest period – was that with the abbey of Saint-Bertin at Saint-Omer in the Pas de Calais. A high point was perhaps reached in the abbacy of Odbert c. A.D. 1000 when – it is clear – English books were important models in the Saint-Bertin scriptorium and English artists and perhaps scribes worked in the scriptorial atelier.[38] Third and last, we come to another English missionary effort, that in Scandinavia, which seems to have begun in the late tenth century and continued well beyond the Norman conquest. English sources for the period know effectively nothing about this historic movement. The usually deployed evidence, such as it is, comes from a variety of Scandinavian sources of very varying quality. There exists, however, a significant and growing body of manuscript material which until very recently has been known only to Scandinavian liturgists and palaeographers. All of it has been recovered from the sixteenth- and seventeenth-century bindings of early modern papers and printed books, principally in Norway and Sweden. Some few manuscripts have almost reached the point where they have been recovered entire, albeit folio by folio. By this process of recovery we are enabled to see something of the volume of export of pre-Conquest English liturgical manuscripts in the last century of the Anglo-Saxon state (and perhaps

---

[35] Appendix, no. 3. For discussion of its history see David N. Dumville, *Wessex and England from Alfred to Edgar*, Woodbridge 1992, 79–82, 94, 110–11 (cf. *Liturgy*, 111, 117 on the dating, 119–23).

[36] Appendix, nos. 50, 48–49, and 29, respectively. On these see E.A. Lowe, *Codices Latini Antiquiores*, 11 vols and supplement, Oxford 1934–71, xi, no. 1642; xi, no. 1605; vi, no. 730; v, no. 590.

[37] I have discussed this process in a forthcoming paper, 'The Importation of Mediterranean Books into Theodore's England'.

[38] Cf. Dumville, *English Caroline Script*, 131–2, and the references given there.

even beyond the Conquest) and the nature of the institutional links implied. Here truly is a new frontier in English manuscript studies and ecclesiastical history.[39]

These processes are at once attested by and testimony to the export of books from England in the periods indicated. There is little evidence for the travels of Anglo-Saxon manuscripts outside the country other than as a part of these three movements – save, that is, for what I am discussing here. In the history and distribution of Anglo-Saxon manuscripts, the only other such movement of any significance occurred in the sixteenth and seventeenth centuries when books were exported for a variety of reasons, including scrap.[40]

The one other control which needs to be applied to this material concerns what remained at home in England. In so far as high-status books of Anglo-Saxon date did survive in the possession of ecclesiastical houses until the Dissolution, there is no question of arguing that all such treasures were rounded up and sent off to the Continent after the Norman conquest. A considerable number of fine, or once fine, gospel-books remained in the country, a fair quantity of pontificals (though by no means the most heavily decorated ones), and a modest group of benedictionals and sacramentaries.[41] The gospel-books are testimony to, as much as anything else, what must once have been the very great quantity of these manuscripts in existence – more than one, no doubt, at every major church in the land by 1066 (and who can imagine how many others at minor churches and in private hands?). As far as I can see, the situation (except perhaps with regard to gospel-books) is that high-status books comparable with those exported after 1066 did survive the middle ages in England, but that the most attractive or most highly decorated specimens underwent Continental exile in the aftermath of the Norman conquest and are now mostly in foreign collections.

One noteworthy category of manuscript does, however, have an exclusively English distribution of mediaeval provenances. This is the English vernacular illustrated book. It may be recognised in the record from the beginning of the tenth century – starting with the Tanner Bede[42] – but it reached a level of significant elaboration before the Conquest (particularly in the products of the Canterbury scriptoria in the second quarter of the eleventh century).[43] We have no evidence for export of such volumes. This by itself must indicate that, if high-status books' export had anything to do with their contents, intelligibility was then an important consideration.

A further point emerges immediately from comparison between what stayed at home and what travelled to the Continent after 1066. One of the largest collections

---

[39] Lesley Abrams, Alicia Corrêa, and I have work in hand on these manuscripts and the contexts of their execution, export, and Scandinavian reception. For the moment, see Dumville, *English Caroline Script*, 64, n. 278, and *Liturgy*, 67–9, 81, 88.

[40] For an example of export at that date, see above, n. 21. On the trade in parchment for scrap, see the eloquent indignation of John Bale, writing in 1560: H.R. Luard, 'A Letter from Bishop Bale to Archbishop Parker', *Cambridge Antiquarian Communications* iii, 1864–76, 157–73, at p. 157.

[41] For such stay-at-home high-grade *liturgica*, see H. Gneuss, 'A Preliminary List of Manuscripts written or owned in England up to 1100', *Anglo-Saxon England* ix, 1981, 1–60: nos. 39, 111, 585 (sacramentaries); nos. 40, 46, 51, 155, 302, 314, 363 (pontificals); nos. 259, 301, 429 (benedictionals); nos. 381, 754, 862 (psalters); nos. 28, 432 (prayerbooks); not to mention numerous gospel-books.

[42] Oxford, Bodleian Library, MS. Tanner 10 (*S.C.* 9830); see the discussion by R. Gameson, 'The Decoration of the Tanner Bede', *Anglo-Saxon England* xxi, 1992, 115–59.

[43] See above, n. 16.

of liturgical books (and perhaps, indeed, of books in general) assembled in late Anglo-Saxon England was that brought together by Bishop Leofric at Exeter between 1050 and 1072. The only identifiable escapee from among the books which were at Exeter in the eleventh century is a gospel-book now in the Bibliothèque nationale, Paris (MS. latin 14782), but which may not even have been written before 1072. Otherwise the Anglo-Saxon collection seems to be more or less intact.[44] Likewise – albeit on a very different scale – it has not proved possible to identify Anglo-Saxon books from Durham among those exported after the Conquest. On the other hand, the corpus of exported manuscripts includes items from Canterbury, Winchester, Sherborne.[45] One is bound to wonder whether the absence of a strong and credible bishop in possession in the immediate, post-Conquest years was a major factor leading to alienation of Church-treasure, as of land. The implication, if a positive rather than a negative conclusion be drawn, is that a strong head of a church could hope to guard a church's movable property, or at least its books, if minded so to do: there was no protection to be had, of course, if such a leader decided to send her or his church's books as gifts to Continental houses. There is nothing particularly surprising about either of these conclusions when they are seen in general context, but again they have not been discussed with reference to the history of manuscripts.

It may be worthwhile at this point to halt to consider the relationship of lay aristocracy, scribes, Latin books, vernacular books, and churches in the last century of Anglo-Saxon England. A crucial text in that regard, and one which has been much discussed lately, derives from the Colloquy of Ælfric Bata who wrote at Canterbury in the early eleventh century.[46]

> CUSTOMER: You, scribe, good sweet boy, I ask you humbly to write for me a sample (of your work) on a sheet or charter or a parchment-scrap or in a diptych.
>
> SCRIBE: Only if you wish to pay me.
>
> CUSTOMER: Write me first a psalter or a hymnal or an epistolary or a troper or a missal or a travel-book or a capitulary all properly laid out and arranged and accurately written and corrected, and I shall pay you a good price, or I shall purchase from you straightaway all these books and pay their price, either in gold or in silver or in horses or mares or cows or sheep or pigs or goats or clothing or in wine or honey or grain or vegetable-produce.

[44] On Leofric, cf. Dumville, *Liturgy*, 90 and n. 144; Patrick W. Conner, *Anglo-Saxon Exeter: a Tenth-Century Cultural History*, Woodbridge 1993, 1–20. For the Paris gospel-book see C.M. Kauffmann, *Romanesque Manuscripts, 1066–1190*, London 1975, 54 (no. 2).

[45] Appendix, nos. 6–8 (Canterbury), 11 (Winchester), 12 (Canterbury), 16 (Canterbury), 19 (Canterbury/Winchester, disputed), 22 (last English provenance Sherborne), 23 (last English provenance Canterbury), 26–27 (Canterbury), 30 (Canterbury), 39 (Canterbury), 46 (Winchester), 50 (last English provenance Canterbury). This list could be extended to include Bury St Edmunds and Worcester, among others, but the pattern would be different from that deduced here.

[46] For the Latin original, see *Early Scholastic Colloquies*, ed. W.H. Stevenson, Oxford 1929, pp. 50–1. I have adapted the translation from that of M. Lapidge, 'Artistic and Literary Patronage in Anglo-Saxon England', *Settimane di Studio del Centro italiano di studi sull'alto medioevo* xxxix, 1991, 137–98, at pp. 143–5. On Ælfric Bata, see further D.N. Dumville, 'Beowulf come lately. Some Notes on the Palaeography of the Nowell Codex', *Archiv für das Studium der neueren Sprachen und Literaturen* ccxxv, 1988, 49–63, at p. 60 and n. 58 (cf. David N. Dumville, *Britons and Anglo-Saxons in the Early Middle Ages*, Aldershot 1993, ch. vii).

SCRIBE: Nothing is more dear to me, than that you give me cash, since whoever has cash can acquire whatever he wants.

CUSTOMER: You're already very wise.

SCRIBE: You're much smarter than me, who am a simple man.

CUSTOMER: Let's stop bantering like this. How much cash must I give you for one missal?

SCRIBE: You need to give me two pounds of pure silver if you wish to have it; if you don't want it, someone else will buy it. It costs a lot; but someone else would have to pay even more than you.

CUSTOMER: Someone else may wish to be that stupid, but I don't; I wish to be cautious and to buy your book at a fair price; and since my friends may tell me how much it's worth, let that be its price.

SCRIBE: How much do you wish to pay me?

CUSTOMER: Not as much as you said.

SCRIBE: Then how much *do* you want to pay, or how many silver pennies, or how many mancusses?

CUSTOMER: Believe me, I don't dare to give you more, or to pay too dearly for it. Take this, if you wish; it's worth no more. I wish to give you twelve mancusses [viz, 1½ pounds of silver] and count them out into your hand . . .

SCRIBE: Count out the coins here, so that I may see what they're worth, and whether they're made of pure silver . . .

A similar situation seems to be envisaged in a ninth-century Continental commentary (attributed to Hildemar) on the Benedictine Rule.[47] We should not therefore be surprised if we find evidence which implies that scribes accepted external (and no doubt often lay) commissions (under whatever conditions imposed by the head of the church in question). One possible type of book which might have derived from such a relationship is the 'Claudius Hexateuch', an elaborately illustrated Old English version of the first six books of the Old Testament.[48] For our immediate purpose, however, the relevant type of manuscript is probably the gospel-book. In eleventh-century England these existed in two principal forms, vernacular and Latin. While examining the corpus for another purpose, I tried to find evidence that the vernacular form was considered less holy than its Latin counterpart. I failed. At Bath and Malmesbury Abbeys and at Exeter Cathedral in the eleventh and twelfth centuries, English-language gospel-books were in use in church and serving at least some of the functions of Latin equivalents.[49]

Either kind of gospel-book might conceivably be commissioned by a lay aristocrat: if he or she wanted the book for private reading, one might suppose that there would be a preference for the vernacular; but otherwise we have no reason to make such a supposition. The following text, from the chronicle of Waltham Abbey, which C.R. Dodwell in particular drew to scholars' attention in this regard, suggests that a principal motive when a layperson went to a scribe with a

---

[47] Noted by Bernhard Bischoff, *Latin Palaeography: Antiquity and the Middle Ages*, Cambridge 1990, 207, n. 43.
[48] See above, n. 16.
[49] Dumville, *Liturgy*, 122–3.

commission was to gain specialist help in making a pious benefaction to a church.[50] The next stop after the scribe (and perhaps an illuminator) would perhaps be a specialist or specialists who would supply the manuscript with an ornamented binding. It would be possible to imagine some churches groaning under the burden of such donations and this very point subsequently acting as an argument, however disreputable, in favour of liquidation of such accumulated assets.

The Waltham chronicler recorded William II's depredations of the abbey: 'on one occasion alone, he removed from the church – in the form of gold and silver caskets, crucifixes, gospel-books, and other gold and silver – works of art estimated at 6,666 pounds'. The churches of Caen, we are told, 'rejoice even today in the spoils thus acquired, and there are inscribed in these very caskets and gospel-books the names of the nobles who presented them to the church at Waltham with the witness of Archbishop Cynesige'.[51] If sequestration or disinvestment was a process which saw significant numbers of gospel-books being lost by churches to which laypeople were devoted, we might imagine that estate-churches and private chapels might the more be denuded of such treasures in the aftermath of the Conquest.

The distribution-map which can be created from the mediaeval provenances of these late Anglo-Saxon liturgical manuscripts is rather revealing. It shows churches in all parts of Normandy receiving such books, as well as a ring of locations in metropolitan France. Avranches, Cherbourg, Evreux, Fécamp, Jumièges, Mont Saint-Michel, Rouen, Saint-Evroul, Saint-Wandrille are Norman examples. Beyond the Norman frontiers, Arras, Berry, Bonneval, Jouarre, Paris, Saint-Claude, Saint-Omer, and Savoie are all examples of places or areas where late Anglo-Saxon *liturgica* found a later mediaeval home.[52] The implications would appear to be quite straightforward. Whoever exported the books from England, whether laypersons or ecclesiastics, were collectively devotees of or politically connected with churches in the various parts of Normandy. As for the French locations beyond Normandy, we can begin by remembering the words of William of Poitiers on the subject as providing the simplest explanation.[53]

What survives is, if William of Poitiers is in any measure to be credited, but a modest percentage of what was exported after the Conquest.[54] I have observed that a natural reason for such export would reside in the wealth associated with the ornamented bindings of high-grade liturgical or paraliturgical books. That would perhaps particularly apply where laypeople were involved, but it would be naïve to overlook this as a motive inspiring ecclesiastics also.[55] We should not, however, ignore the appeal of a handsomely illuminated manuscript, or one which was beautifully written in large, formal script, or one which had exquisitely unsullied

---

[50] Dodwell, 'Losses', 86.

[51] Archbishop of York, 1051–1060. A new edition of the Waltham Chronicle, ed. and transl. L. Watkiss and M. Chibnall, is forthcoming in Oxford Medieval Texts.

[52] See the Appendix, below.

[53] Cf. n. 4, above.

[54] For discussion of various sources, each with its own particular interest, see n. 3, above. It is also worth remembering that items ended up in places in the Empire: see Appendix, nos. 8, 9?, 15, 16 (Köln).

[55] In other words, we could see seizure of such books as an example of 'holy theft': Patrick J. Geary, *Furta Sacra. Thefts of Relics in the Central Middle Ages*, Princeton 1978.

white parchment. Aesthetic response to the appearance of the *inside* of a book should not therefore be ruled out! It would also, of course, be foolish to overlook the attraction of a useful manuscript, particularly if it were also a good-looking one. It is in the nature of a liturgical book, however, that it is unlikely to be entirely suitable for immediate use in another church without extensive revision to bring it into line with the usage of that host-institution.[56]

This leads us on to the question of such a book's function after export, the answer to which in any given case might offer more evidence for the reason for its travels. Other factors, beside the material and the aesthetic, which could have led to the relocation of a high-status book, include two of a quite different sort. First, we must consider the holy associations which a book might have, not because of a relic-fragment embedded in its decorated binding but as a result of previous ownership: we might, for example, think the 'Dunstan Pontifical' (or 'Sherborne Pontifical') to have had such associations.[57] However, it is a curious fact that, if such ever was the motive, no record of previous English individual possession has been preserved by Continental owners of these books. This stands in stark contrast to the case of seculars who made grants of such high-status books to Continental churches before the Conquest. Whether this is chance, or means that previous ownership was deliberately overlooked or that it was simply of no interest, is an open issue. One other possibility worth mentioning arises from change in liturgical fashion. Liturgical books, particularly if not heavily decorated or ornamented, were likely to be treated as scrap. To export such a book, if it proved attractive to someone, was perhaps a way of discarding it without destroying it and all that it might have represented. And there were many reasons why English liturgical books would be under threat of cannibalisation after 1066.

Examination of the evidence for the use to which exported liturgical books were put in their new locations offers some surprises but also some useful critical criteria. Here I give merely a few examples. Most of these books – I think it fair to say – in their current condition show no evidence for further mediaeval use, although rebinding will often have deprived us of useful information. There is little to suggest that they continued in liturgical use – and where we do find such evidence it is perhaps in the most unexpected of places.[58] The one manuscript (out of the many exported) which shows unmistakable evidence of continued liturgical use might appear to be among the least likely to be treated thus, for it is one of the relatively few among those known to have been sent abroad which is written in Insular script – English Square minuscule of c. A.D. 1000. This is the so-called 'Ecgberht Pontifical', perhaps written at Worcester, which was in use at Evreux before it was a century old.[59] The script one might have thought to be sufficiently exotic there to prevent use – could the bishop of Evreux have been in desperate need of a pontifical? Or was Insular minuscule less of a problem for readers of

---

[56] For a wholly English example, see Dumville, *Liturgy*, 72–3 (the 'Samson Pontifical').

[57] Dumville, *Liturgy*, 82–4, 88–95, and 'John Bale, Owner of St Dunstan's Benedictional', *Notes and Queries* ccxxxix, 1994.

[58] Dumville, *Liturgy*, 94–5.

[59] Dumville, *Liturgy*, 85–6, and references given there. For its origin, compare Sawyer, *Anglo-Saxon Charters*, no. 1326, written at Worcester in A.D. 969, whose script (see Wolfgang Keller, *Angelsächsische Palaeographie*, 2 vols, Berlin 1906, ii, no. 5) shows an earlier version of the same scriptorium-style. See further D.N. Dumville, 'Scriptorium, Muniments, and Library at Worcester Cathedral in the Era of St Oswald', in *St Oswald*, ed. N.P. Brooks, London 1994.

Caroline script than one is usually led to suppose, not least by the reaction of Norman ecclesiastics in England? Among the indications that this might be so is the Cottonian fragment of a Square-minuscule gospel-book whose last folio survives, bearing the foundation-charter of Duke William and his wife Matilda for a house of St Mary at Cherbourg.[60] This leads to the further observation that at least two other books in Insular script – one of them in often very difficult small ninth-century minuscules – also attracted additions of a paraliturgical nature at unidentified locations in France at the end of the eleventh century.[61] Is it a reasonable assumption that liturgical books receiving quasi-liturgical additions (such as charters) were still in liturgical use? I know not, but if so then the numbers seen as continuing to function can be increased. Another case where it is clear that use continued is the fragment of an eleventh-century Canterbury kalendar which had been adapted for use at Saint-Evroul not later than the early twelfth century.[62] The kalendar-fragment was probably part of a larger book, whether a psalter or a sacramentary or whatever, which presumptively therefore also continued in use. On the other hand, a psalter with kalendar which seems unlikely to have maintained a liturgical function in exile is the 'Junius Psalter': additions were made to its sparse kalendar in the twelfth century, but these were computistical, not liturgical, and the beginning of the psalter itself was erased to receive computistical literature.[63]

Consideration of the ways in which liturgical books were used has allowed further probable identification of exported Anglo-Saxon high-status books. Perhaps the most remarkable example comprises five stray folios in a miscellaneous manuscript in the Vatican Library: MS. Reg. lat. 946, fos 72-76, has luxury quality and layout but bears no liturgical text. One suspects that the leaves were saved, or seized, by someone with historical interests. The sole item of English interest is an Old English text of a lawcode of King Æthelred the Unready (75v). The only other pages on which writing is found bear an account (apparently unpublished) of the duties owed by the abbots of the monasteries in the diocese of Avranches, and some notice of the obligations of the see of Avranches to Rouen.[64] Closely similar types of fragment from English liturgical books are found in purely English circumstances – lawcodes, charters, surveys, etc. –; sometimes these occur in full gospel-books (or other liturgical manuscripts), thus establishing their natural context beyond doubt.[65]

It should not be pretended that the only way in which Anglo-Saxon books travelled or could travel abroad was as loot. Some manuscripts we know to have moved east in the pre-Conquest years, whether accompanying their owners or as gifts to Continental churches – such as the memorial donation of a gospel-book to Saint-Remi a couple of years before the Conquest.[66] We have to hypothesise from

---

[60] Appendix, no. 13; cf. n. 20, above.

[61] Appendix, nos. 3 and 22.

[62] Appendix, no. 30; cf. n. 19, above.

[63] Appendix, no. 19; cf. Dumville, *Liturgy*, 2.

[64] Appendix, no. 41; cf. Dumville, *Liturgy*, 127 and n. 236. I am indebted to Simon Keynes and Donald Bullough for help with this item. The only published description is that of Ker, *Catalogue*, 459 (no. 392). For similar fragmentary survivals, see Dumville, *Liturgy*, 127.

[65] As, for example, in York, Minster Library, MS. Add. 1: for the type, see Dumville, *Liturgy*, 119–27.

[66] For details, see n. 17, above.

the script of pre-Conquest Norman books and documents that Anglo-Saxon models made a profound impact in the duchy.[67] This has been studied in the book-production of the abbey of Mont Saint-Michel whose English connexions were developed and intensified after the Conquest.[68]

In the immediate aftermath of the events of 1066, various ecclesiastics and aristocratic laypeople fled England. For our purpose, one of the most significant was Sæwold, abbot of Bath, who a few years later is found bequeathing more than thirty books (some of which can still be identified) to the abbey of Saint-Vaast at Arras.[69] A glossed psalter which long survived at Brugge may have left England at much the same time in the possession of a royal lady.[70] We should suppose that this was a more general pattern.

Some members of the Anglo-Saxon aristocracy would have found themselves in what might be called genteel captivity in the years after 1066, particularly – for obvious reasons of colonial security – in Normandy. Given what seems to have been the widespread diffusion of gospels and devotional books among that class in the last Anglo-Saxon century, it would not be surprising if this had provided a route for some high-status books into the possession of Norman churches.

After the Conquest the links between English and Continental churches were vastly multiplied, greatly intensified, and significantly diversified. Continental houses became the owners of English churches. Confraternity-agreements were developed. Personnel moved between houses over wide areas. Scholarly contacts were created between members of churches at opposite ends of the Norman realm, and beyond. The resulting movements of books could in some instances be characterised as plunder, but in many cases they must simply have represented normal, but now greatly increased, intellectual and religious traffic. Exchange is not to be underrated as a mechanism for bringing English books to the Continent: although the dictates of intellectual fashion ensured that the ecclesiastical colonists needed to import currently popular texts into English collections (and we know that many Continental manuscripts came to England in the post-Conquest generations), some unusual texts, attractively written volumes, or elaborate gospel-books might have found themselves offered in exchange for specimens of the new learning.[71]

All these possibilities exist and are documented in general, but particular cases remain much harder to establish. We must remember that books have always been objects of value which could be exchanged (not necessarily for other books), bought and sold, and offered freely as gifts. But, by the same criterion, they could

---

[67] Dumville, *English Caroline Script*, 137, n. 108, and 150.

[68] Alexander, *Norman Illumination*.

[69] M. Lapidge, 'Surviving Booklists from Anglo-Saxon England', in *Learning and Literature in Anglo-Saxon England. Studies presented to Peter Clemoes*, edd. Michael Lapidge and H. Gneuss, Cambridge 1985, 33–89, at pp. 58–62 (no. VIII); cf. P. Grierson, 'Les Livres de l'abbé Seiwold de Bath', *Revue bénédictine* lii, 1940, 96–116.

[70] Ker, *Catalogue*, 469 (no. 403); his identification of Gunhild, the lady in question, has been challenged by Lapidge, 'Surviving Booklists', 92–3, but eleventh-century Gunhilds are too numerous for convenience, as may be seen from Ann Williams et al., *A Biographical Dictionary of Dark Age Britain: England, Scotland and Wales, c. 500–c. 1050*, London 1991, 147.

[71] For the ecclesiastical developments of this period, see Frank Barlow, *The English Church, 1066–1154*, London 1979; on books see Ker, *English Manuscripts*; for an important study of the first-generation colonial Church, see Margaret Gibson, *Lanfranc of Bec*, Oxford 1978.

be seized or extorted, not least when their value was increased by richness of binding. It is certain that in the immediate aftermath of invasion many books were taken as treasure and carried off thus to the Continent. The conquest of England was not, however, the work of a few years: the colonisation of both secular and ecclesiastical society continued for some generations. Measured as an identifiable and significant cultural movement, the outflow of Anglo-Saxon manuscripts to the Continent can be seen to have continued through the first half of the twelfth century. That it then largely ceased is no doubt to be accounted for partly by the increasing antiquity of pre-Conquest books, but the simplest explanation would be that the process of conquest had run its course: the travels of English manuscripts to the Continent could then fall back into a more traditional pattern of ecclesiastical, intellectual, and commercial traffic. What seems clear is that, for almost a century, the normal history of English book-ownership had been interrupted by a sudden outflow from the country, a process which might be thought best explained in general as a product of conquest.[72]

APPENDIX

List of High-status Manuscripts Exported from England after 1066

Location and Shelf-mark	Date	Content	Continental Provenance
1. Alençon, B.M., 14, fos 91–114	xi^1	Benedictional	Saint-Evroul
2. Avranches, B.M., 29	x/xi	Homilies & *uita*	Mont Saint-Michel
3. Bern, Burgerbibliothek, 671	$ix^2(B)–x^1$	Pocket gospels	France (xi/xii)
4. Besançon, B.M., 14	x *ex.*	Gospels	Saint-Claude (Jura)
5. Boulogne-sur-mer, B.M., 10	x^1	Gospels	Arras
6. 189	x/xi	Prudentius	Saint-Omer
7. Firenze, Bibl. Medicea Laurenziana, Plut. xvii.20	$xi^{2/4}$	Gospel-lectionary	Continent (xi)
8. Hannover, Kestner-Museum, W.M. xxia, 36	$xi^{2/4}$	Gospels	Germany (xi)
9. København, K.B., G.K.S. 10.2°	x *ex.*	Gospels	
10. G.K.S. 2034.4°	x/xi	*Vita*	Paris
11. Le Havre, B.M., 330	xi^2	Missal	Saint-Wandrille
12. Leiden, U.B., Scaliger 69	x^2	Ethicus Ister	
13. London, B.L., Cotton Tiberius A.xv, fo 174	x	Gospel(s)	Cherbourg
14. Malibu, Getty Museum, 9	xi *in.*	Gospel-lectionary	
15. München, Bayerische Staatsbibliothek, Clm 29031[b]	xi *in.*	Prudentius	Germany (xv)
16. New York, Pierpont Morgan Library, M.869	x *ex.*	Gospels	Köln
17. New York, Public Library, 115	ix/x(C)	Gospels	
18. Orléans, B.M., 342 (290)	x/xi	*Vita*	Fleury
19. Oxford, B.L., Junius 27 (*S.C.* 5139)	x^1	Psalter	Continent (xii^2)

[72] I should like to record my gratitude to the members of the Battle Conference for a lively, informative, and stimulating discussion of my paper, which has greatly helped me in preparing it for publication. I am also specially indebted to Simon Keynes for his assistance.

Location and Shelf-mark	Date	Content	Continental Provenance
20. Paris, B.N., latin 272	x^2	Gospels	
21. latin 281 & 298	viii *ex.*	Gospels	Fécamp
22. latin 943	x^2–xi *in.*	Pontifical	France (xi *ex.*)
23. latin 987	x^2–xi *med.*	Benedictional	
24. latin 2825, fos 57–81	x *ex.*	*Vita*	
25. latin 4210	x/xi	Customary	Fécamp
26. latin 6401A	x *ex.*	Boethius	Seyssel (Savoie)
27. latin 7585	ix^1(C)–xi^1	Isidorus	
28. latin 8824	xi *med.*	Psalter	Berry
29. latin 9561	viii	Gregorius	Saint-Omer
30. latin 10062, fos 162–163	xi^1	Kalendar	Saint-Evroul
31. latin 10575	x/xi	Pontifical	Evreux
32. latin 10861	ix^1	Passional	Beauvais
33. latin 14380, part i	x *ex.*	Boethius	
34. latin 14782	xi^2	Gospels	Paris
35. latin 17814	x *ex.*	Boethius	
36. Paris, Bibliothèque Sainte-Geneviève, 2410	xi *in.*	Poetry	Laon
37. Roma, B.A.V., Barberini lat. 570	viii^2	Gospels	
38. Reg. lat. 12	$xi^{2/4}$	Psalter	Jouarre (dioc. Meaux)
39. Reg. lat. 204	xi *in.*	*Vita*	Bonneval (nr Chartres)
40. Reg. lat. 338, fos 64–126	x(C)–xi^1	*Misc. liturg.*	
41. Reg. lat. 946, fos 72–76	xi^1	? (documents)	Avranches
42. Reg. lat. 1671	x^2	Vergil	
43. Rouen, B.M., A.27 (368)	xi *in.*	Pontifical	Jumièges
44. A.44 (231)	xi *ex.*	Psalter	Jumièges
45. U.107 (1385), fos 20–26	x/xi	Customary	Jumièges
46. Y.7 (369)	x^2–xi *med.*	Benedictional	Rouen
47. Saint-Lô, B.M., 1	xi^2	Gospels	
48. St Petersburg, Public Library, F.v.I.8	viii *ex.*	Gospels	Saint-Maur-des-Fossés
49. O.v.I.1 + Avranches, B.M., 48 + 66 + 71 (flyleaves)	viii^1	Gospels	Mont Saint-Michel
50. Stockholm, K.B., A.135	viii *ex.*	Gospels	Spain (xvi)

GEOFFREY OF CHAUMONT, THIBAUD OF BLOIS AND WILLIAM THE CONQUEROR

Jean Dunbabin

'O happy man, on whom God deigned to confer the grace of so many and so great virtues!' Thus the author of the *Gesta Ambaziensium dominorum*[1] lauds Geoffrey of Chaumont when describing his participation in the Norman conquest of England. A source written about a century after the conquest by an author who shared the standard predilection for transforming historical figures into epic heroes[2] does not usually inspire much confidence. In this case, scepticism as to the veracity of the portrait is increased when the reader realises that the author paints the sagacious Geoffrey in glowing colours as a counterpoint to his picture of Supplicius II of Amboise, Geoffrey's great-great-nephew, whose errors he deplores. He is writing didactic literature, packaged with the standard 'handle with care' notice.

As has recently been pointed out, the historical Geoffrey can be found witnessing certain Anglo-Norman royal charters.[3] In fact, he has also left his traces on quite a large number of documents, particularly those connected with the monastery of Marmoutier. I set out to discover as much as I could about him, with the intention of establishing just how far the author of the *Gesta* had romanticised him. My initial aim was to contribute to the understanding of twelfth-century historiography.

My results, however, were unsatisfactory for an investigation of that sort. I found no evidence that disproved anything the author said about Geoffrey's life, much that seemed to confirm it, and only one worrying blank where confirmation might reasonably be expected. Nor did the author's perspective on Geoffrey look seriously distorted. I concluded that scepticism about the historical value of medieval narrative sources can sometimes be taken too far. But in coming to this conclusion I found my interest had been awakened in Geoffrey himself. The *Gesta*, which concentrates on Supplicius of Amboise, Geoffrey's nephew by marriage, and his descendants, leaves intriguing gaps in its account of Geoffrey of Chaumont's life. As I thought about these gaps, an hypothesis about his political significance slowly emerged in my mind. This paper is therefore an attempt to place Geoffrey as a main character in a play about the relations between Blois and Normandy in the decades before and after the Norman conquest of England. In

---

[1] *Chroniques des comtes d'Anjou et des seigneurs d'Amboise*, ed. Louis Halphen and René Poupardin, Paris 1913, 74–132.
[2] On this see Jean Dunbabin, 'Discovering a past for the French aristocracy', in ed. Paul Magdalino, *The Perception of the Past in Twelfth-century Europe*, London and Rio Grande 1992, 8–12.
[3] Elizabeth Van Houts, 'Latin poetry and the Anglo-Norman court 1066–1135: the *Carmen de Hastingae Proelio*', *Journal of Medieval History* 15, 1989, 48, first correctly identified Geoffrey.

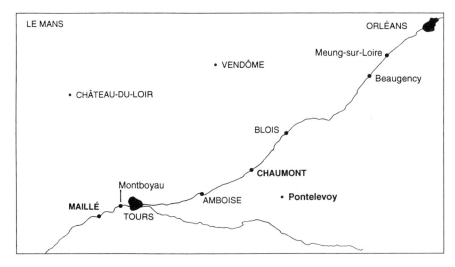

Chaumont and its environs

describing events I have tried, as far as possible, to use sources other than the *Gesta*, in order to substantiate its testimony.

Geoffrey of Chaumont's early life was lived against the background of the ferocious struggle between the houses of Blois and Anjou for control of the Loire valley. He was the son of Gelduin of Saumur, the man whom Fulk Nerra, count of Anjou, referred to as 'the devil of Saumur', and whose ferocity others explained in terms of his Danish extraction.[4] Born some time in the early 1020s, Geoffrey was the heir to a very substantial lordship in the Touraine, the origins of which went back at least two generations, and perhaps even to the end of the ninth century when the lords of Blois first established their *fideles* in the area.[5] But its apparent solidity was shattered by Fulk Nerra's attack a decade after his unexpected defeat of Eudes II of Blois at the battle of Pontelevoy in 1016.

In 1017 the count of Anjou had built a fortification at Montboyau which threatened Eudes's hold on the Thouet valley. Eudes's other preoccupations (which were many) prevented him from responding to the challenge until 1026, when he brought up his army, including Gelduin, to besiege Montboyau. Perhaps consciousness of his tardiness in coming made Eudes determined not to be diverted from the destruction of the castle. He certainly failed to respond until too late to Fulk Nerra's clever diversionary tactic, the siege of Saumur. In the absence of Gelduin, its lord, that ancient town which controlled the easiest crossing of the Loire fell to the Angevin.[6] The chief centre of Eudes's authority between Angers

---

[4] *Historia Sancti Florentii Salmurensis* in *Chroniques des églises d'Anjou*, ed. Paul Marchegay and Emile Mabille, Paris 1869, 275; and *Gesta ambaziensium dominorum*, 78.

[5] *Cartulaire de Marmoutier pour le Dunois*, ed. Emile Mabille, Chateaudun 1874, xix–xx; *Historia Sancti Florentii*, 275 refers to his father, *Gelduinus senior*, and 277 says of him that he was *longo baronum et equitum agmine constipatus*.

[6] *Fragmentum veteris historiae Sancti Florentii*, 212 and *Historia Sancti Florentii*, 276, both in *Chroniques des églises d'Anjou*. Cf. the account in *Chronique de Saint-Maixent*, ed. Jean Verdon, Paris 1979, 110.

and Tours was gone for good; Tours itself lay exposed to Angevin aggression. The assistance of Henry, son of King Robert II, in the following year was insufficient to reverse the disaster.[7] And although Fulk in 1027 undertook to destroy Montboyau, it was small compensation for what Eudes had lost.[8]

His lord's loss was felt yet more acutely by Gelduin, who was deprived of the linchpin of his territorial lordship and of the town with which he was popularly identified. Eudes, following the precepts of princely generosity, offered him lands in Brie or Champagne where he would be sheltered from the Angevin menace. These Gelduin declined in favour of Chaumont-sur-Loire,[9] a dominant rocky fortification on the river bank that was completely exposed to attack from neighbouring Angevin Amboise, and which in turn sheltered Blois from the enemy. Gelduin's deliberate choice of so exposed and dangerous a place is the clearest insight we have into his character.

It was therefore at Chaumont that Geoffrey spent much of his childhood. There he must have learned to fear Lisois of Maine, who controlled Fulk Nerra's bastion in nearby Amboise, and also Supplicius, treasurer of St Martin of Tours and *fidelis* of Fulk, who had built in Amboise a tower so tall it was rumoured he could see Tours from it.[10] Though fighting was sporadic, the threat of attack always loomed from the west. But in the other direction lay Blois, where Gelduin's brother was viscount, whence help might easily be summoned, and where strategies might be laid for defending what remained of Eudes's once extensive power base on the Loire.[11] Eudes himself was less than dedicated to this cause; the lure of domination in Lotharingia absorbed him for the last decade of his life. But his southern vassals fought his fight with the determination born of desperation. The survival of Tours, Blois and Chaumont in Eudes's hands was the only guarantee of their own independence.

Gelduin accepted the irreversibility of 1026 fairly soon, as is apparent in his establishment in 1034 or 1035 of a family mausoleum at Pontelevoy, near Chaumont.[12] Pontelevoy, unlike Chaumont, had belonged to his ancestors, and he had a fortified dwelling there.[13] He now called a group of monks from St Florent of Saumur to inhabit his new foundation. He and his family were in death to be prayed for by an offshoot of that monastic body with which they had long been associated. The endowment of Pontelevoy gave shape and character to his new and much smaller lordship.

Then came the task of securing this hazardous territory by opening and holding a route to Chartres, which lay at the heart of count Eudes's now depleted lands.

---

[7] *Annales de Vendôme*, 61, in *Recueil d'annales angevines et vendômoises*, ed. Louis Halphen, Paris 1906.

[8] *Historia sancti Florentii*, 280.

[9] *Gesta ambaziensium dominorum*, 81. Eudes had earlier granted Chaumont to Nivelon de Frétéval, see *Cartulaire blésois de Marmoutier*, ed. Charles Métais, Blois 1889–91, xxii.

[10] *Grande Chronique de Tours*, in *Recueil de Chroniques de Touraine*, ed. André Salmon, Tours 1854, 119; Bernard Bachrach, 'The Angevin strategy of castle-building in the reign of Fulk Nerra, 987–1040', *American Historical Review* 88, 1983, 547.

[11] Jean-François Lemarignier, *Le Gouvernement royal aux premiers temps capétiens (987–1108)*, Paris 1965, 95, note 106.

[12] *Recueil des Actes de Philippe 1er, roi de France (1059–1108)*, ed. Maurice Prou, Paris 1908, no. 75; *Archives de Loir-et-Cher. Clergé regulier*, ed. Guy Trouillard, Blois 1936, I, 227.

[13] *Gesta ambaziensium dominorum*, 81; *Gesta consulum andegavorum*, 51, in *Chroniques des comtes d'Anjou*.

Fulk Nerra's possession of Vendôme to the north, through his marriage with the heiress to that county, and his castles of Beaugency and Meung-sur-Loire which blocked the road to the royal demesne in the east, were formidable obstacles.[14] Only to the north-west in Maine was there potential for protected access to Chartres. But Angevin power was growing in Maine. Were either Fulk or his successor Geoffrey to control the whole county securely, then Tours must sooner or later fall to Angevin hands, and Amboise would become a serious menace to Blois and Chaumont. I shall argue that, from 1026 on to 1085, first Gelduin and then more importantly his son Geoffrey consistently attempted to impress on Eudes and his successors Thibaud III and Stephen-Henry the significance of Maine to the survival of their remaining Loire castles.

But the position there worsened dramatically for them in the 1040s. Thibaud III, who succeeded Eudes II in 1037 in Blois (his younger brother Stephen becoming count of Troyes and Meaux) derived no benefit from Fulk Nerra's death in 1040; indeed, Fulk's successor, the young Geoffrey Martel, proved an even tougher opponent than his father. In the summer of 1044 he laid siege to Tours, determined to annex it permanently. Thibaud III and his brother Stephen, with the now adult Geoffrey of Chaumont in attendance, marched up to attempt to raise the siege, and clashed with the Angevin army on 21 August 1044, on the field of Nouy. According to the Great Chronicle of Tours, Geoffrey Martel's stunning victory was to be explained by the banner of St Martin which he bore, and the consequent assistance of white-clad troops from heaven.[15] Thibaud was captured and faced with the prospect of a lifetime's incarceration if he refused to yield to the victor's demands. Within three days his resistance had crumbled. He surrendered Tours and the whole area around it, with the sole exception of his patronage of the monastery of Marmoutier, in return for Geoffrey's rather token recognition that he owed Thibaud homage for his new acquisitions.[16] It was hardly surprising that, after a disaster of this magnitude, Thibaud should increasingly regard Chartres rather than Blois as the kernel of his principality.

Thibaud's capitulation secured his own release quickly. It was not so for the large number of his soldiers – a figure of up to a thousand was given by Fulk le Réchin in his chronicle[17] – also taken on the field of Nouy. Among these was Geoffrey of Chaumont. His imprisonment at the fortress of Baugé lasted till around the end of 1044, during which time Chaumont was apparently in the charge of his enemy Lisois of Amboise.[18] Some light is shed on the conditions of his detention by a Marmoutier charter which describes how the abbot of that monastery was able to gain access to Geoffrey to obtain his confirmation of a gift made by one of his men of Maillé.[19] In exchange for his compliance in this matter,

[14] Bachrach 539, 547–8.

[15] *Recueil de Chroniques de Touraine*, 121.

[16] *Cartulaire de Marmoutier pour le Dunois*, no. 92 (a charter granted by Stephen-Henry in 1096): *Pater meus . . . in tantum caram habuit ut cum totam Turonicam cum civitate ipsa traderet Andegavorum comiti Gaufredo Martello, qui eum ceperat, in redemptionem sui, ipsam tamen id est abbatiam Majoris Monasterii, nominatim exceperet atque sibi in proprio dominio retineret. Gesta consulum andegavorum*, additions, 148, contains a version of the treaty between Thibaud and Geoffrey Martel.

[17] *Fragmentum Historiae andegavensis*, in *Chroniques des comtes d'Anjou*, 235.

[18] Olivier Guillot, *Le comte d'Anjou et son entourage au xie siècle*, Paris 1972, I, 331.

[19] This fortress in the immediate environs of Tours, which had remained in Gelduin's hands after

Geoffrey begged the abbot and his community to pray for his release, pressing into the abbot's hand a small piece of firewood to be placed on the altar of the monastery's church.[20] Despite the inadequacy of the token offered, the community's prayers were apparently successful. Geoffrey was released. As Thibaud's most important local henchman, he was included in the peace treaty with Geoffrey Martel, who undertook to restore to him (and to Gelduin who is here mentioned for the last time) his fiefs east of the river Vienne and St Cyr-en-Bourg, for both of which homage to the victor was required.[21] But the loss of Tours had tightened the Angevin noose around Blois and Chaumont. It was all the more essential to Geoffrey that Thibaud should try to prevent Maine from being swallowed up by his victorious enemy.

In this objective the house of Blois could find at least one group of allies whose interests coincided with their own, the Bellêmes. This notoriously aggressive and expansionist family controlled much of northern Maine through their fortresses at Alençon, Domfront and Bellême, two of which were captured by Geoffrey Martel in 1044, to their intense chagrin. Further south they exercised some authority through the bishopric of Le Mans which was in the hands of relatives from 971 to 1055.[22] Gervais, bishop from 1036 to 1055, seems initially to have had some success in limiting Angevin aggression in the area,[23] but it was short-lived. The events of 1044 were a serious blow. However, by 1047 at the latest he had enhanced his position with the acquisition of the lordship of Chateau-du-Loir;[24] though this was dangerously threatened by nearby Angevin fortresses, it commanded an important route to the north which could materially affect the survival of Blois lands on the Loire. Thibaud III was therefore eager to assist the bishop.

It was in Gervais's interests to reinforce the shaky position of Hugh, son of Herbert Wake-the-dog, as count of Maine, in order to frustrate Geoffrey Martel's ambitions in that quarter. Consequently Gervais probably had a hand in arranging the marriage between Thibaud III and Gersende, daughter of Herbert Wake-the-Dog, that took place between 1045 and 1047.[25] He was certainly responsible for the marriage of Berthe, Thibaud III's sister, to count Hugh in 1047. This union produced children, but so incensed Geoffrey Martel that he imprisoned the bishop for four years.[26] These two marriages set the seal on an alliance forged to protect eastern Maine from absorption into the Angevin orbit. Inevitably they precipitated a war between count Hugh and Geoffrey Martel.[27] If Gervais was the architect of

---

the loss of Saumur, was presumably lost by his son as a consequence of his peace treaty with Geoffrey Martel.

[20] Paul Marchegay, 'Chartes angevines des onzième et douzième siècles', *Bibliothèque de l'École des chartes* 36, 1875, 388.

[21] *Gesta consulum Andegavorum*, 58.

[22] *Actus Pontificum Cenomannis in urbe degentium*, ed. Gustave Busson and Ambroise Ledru, Le Mans 1901, 352.

[23] Guillot, i, 54–55 and note 251.

[24] Guillot, i, 333.

[25] *Actus pontificum*, 377; Michel Bur, *La formation du comté de Champagne v.950–v.1150*, Nancy 1977, 199 and note 22. Gervais's devotion to the hereditary claims of count Herbert's family was the principal reason for his conflict with Herbert Baco, regent for the young Hugh.

[26] *Actus pontificum*, 365, where the imprisonment in chains is said to have lasted for seven years, a timespan that does not fit with the rest of the events recorded.

[27] Fulk le Réchin, *Chroniques des comtes d'Anjou*, 236.

this risky policy, the lord of Chaumont will have favoured it, since his own and his lord's interests on the Loire were protected by it.

Yet the partnership did not last long. In 1049 Thibaud III repudiated his wife, thereby causing grave scandal in Christendom;[28] Gersende was sent off to northern Italy, where she married into the Este family.[29] In behaving so boorishly, Thibaud was not motivated by the usual medieval causes for divorce: Gersende had borne him a son, Stephen-Henry; nor does Thibaud's eye seem to have been caught by another woman, since he did not remarry for almost a decade. The beneficiary of his divorce was undoubtedly Geoffrey Martel, whose conquest of Maine (completed in 1052) was much aided by the disappearance from the scene of the more important of count Herbert Wake-the-Dog's two surviving daughters. If cause can be inferred from result, then Thibaud acted under duress in putting away Gersende.

The impression that the count of Blois yielded to *force majeure* is heightened by what happened afterwards. When his brother-in-law count Hugh died in 1051, Thibaud did nothing to protect the rights of his infant nephew Herbert, despite his obvious fondness for Berthe, now widowed for the second time. The field was left clear for Geoffrey Martel to march upon Le Mans.[30] And when, in 1052, bishop Gervais was finally let out of his Angevin prison, it was to the duke of Normandy, not to his old friend Thibaud, that he repaired.[31] It was as if a campaign, carefully planned between 1045 and 1047 to bring eastern Maine under Blois surveillance, had been abruptly and completely abandoned in 1049.

Coincidentally, Geoffrey of Chaumont's life took an unexpectedly sombre turn in the years after 1044. As far as can be seen, he was by now lord only of Chaumont and Pontelevoy.[32] According to the *Gesta*, at an unspecified date between 1044 and 1066, he made an arrangement for these that was apparently clean contrary to his own interests, and that facilitated the fortress of Chaumont's eventual subordination to Angevin rule. He undertook to hand over half of Chaumont and of all his other possessions to his niece Denise, whom he had brought up, on her marriage to Supplicius, son of Lisois of Amboise; on Geoffrey's death, Denise and Supplicius were to inherit the remainder of his lands.[33]

From the count of Anjou's point of view, this was an ideal arrangement. Chaumont would eventually come under the authority of Amboise, thus vastly strengthening the Angevin hold on this part of the Loire, and providing the opportunity for the conquest of Blois. Yet the marriage alliance and the fact that Geoffrey was not to be totally disappropriated would calm protest in the town. Furthermore Lisois of Amboise, who had held Chaumont in his grasp for a short time after the battle of Nouy, would feel satisfied that his son was to have permanently what he himself had enjoyed only for a few months. And on Geoffrey's death, the last remnants of Blois domination there would pass into

---

[28] John of Fécamp in *Patrologiae latinae cursus completus*, ed. J. Migne, t. 143, col. 799. The repudiation was discussed before pope Leo IX at the council of Rheims in October 1049; see Bur, 199 note 22.

[29] *Actus pontificum*, 376.

[30] *Actus pontificum*, 366.

[31] Guillot, i, 76 and note 336.

[32] Guillot, i, 332.

[33] *Gesta ambaziensium dominorum*, 87–88.

oblivion. Had the count of Anjou known that this event was to be postponed almost to the end of the century, he might have been less contented; but the immediate rewards were great enough to wipe out any anxiety about the future.

It is hard to conceive of circumstances in which Geoffrey of Chaumont would have made this arrangement entirely voluntarily. He was relatively young and strong;[34] there was no reason yet to abandon hope of producing an heir. It is odd that he had not married after his release from imprisonment. This may have been the result of temperament – he was known as Geoffrey the Maiden because he was prettier than most girls.[35] But marriage in the middle ages was rarely governed by personal preference. Perhaps he had been wounded in battle and became impotent. More plausibly political force was exercised on him, since his decision was unexpected. Even if he had decided to remain celibate, his sister Chana and her husband Frangelo of Fougères may have had a son whom he could have named his heir.[36] He had no ground for favouring Supplicius, whose father had long been his enemy. And to lose half his possessions was surely a harsh blow to one who had already been forced to surrender Saumur and much besides.

I suggest that the most plausible explanation for this act of self-sacrifice was that Geoffrey had committed some offence considered by the count of Anjou to be a breach of the terms of his release from prison, and that Geoffrey Martel was exacting his revenge. May the count have held the lord of Chaumont directly responsible for Thibaud's intervention into Maine, and may there therefore be a close connection between Geoffrey of Chaumont's loss of half his lands and count Thibaud's repudiation of his wife and abandonment of claims to Maine? Each certainly served Angevin interests remarkably well.[37]

But matrimonial alliances could not easily be controlled over long periods. If Geoffrey Martel was able to scotch one that seriously threatened his interests, he was apparently powerless to suppress a less important but still worrying one, that between Geoffrey of Chaumont's now widowed sister Chana and Raoul IV, viscount of Maine. This occurred after 12 September 1058 (the date of Raoul's first wife's disease) and 1060, when Chana is found signing a charter along with her new family.[38] It constituted a significant new link in the chain between the lords of Blois and Maine, and lasted at least until Raoul IV's death in 1067. It also provided Geoffrey of Chaumont with a further reason for concerning himself with the fate of Maine.

Between 1044 and the early 1060s Geoffrey seldom witnessed charters. Then, within a short space of time around 1064, he witnessed three gifts, all of them in the company of Thibaud III's son Stephen-Henry, who must by then have been in his middle to late teens. In all three cases, Stephen-Henry confirmed the gifts

---

[34] I have not taken seriously the *Gesta*'s, 109, claim that Geoffrey was a hundred years old when he died between 1098 and 1100 – though he was certainly a very old man.

[35] *Gesta ambaziensium dominorum*, 81.

[36] Eustace Avenel, 'The Bohuns of Hereford and Midhurst', *Herald and Genealogist* 6, 1871, 30 suggests, for reasons that he does not give, that there were two sons of this marriage. But he appears to have been wrong in ascribing Savary fitzCana to this marriage rather than to Chana's second marriage with Raoul IV, viscount of Maine; see below, note 89.

[37] For evidence of Geoffrey continuing to act as lord of at least half of Chaumont between 1050 and 1060, see *Cartulaire blésois*, no. 29.

[38] Robert Latouche, *Histoire du comté de Maine pendant le Xe et le XIe siècles*, Paris 1910, 130–31.

separately from his father.[39] The implication is that the young count had been established with a household of his own, and that Geoffrey of Chaumont was an important figure in that entourage. It was the start of a relationship between them which was to last to Geoffrey's death, and which imitated in warmth the friendship between Gelduin and Eudes II.

In the meantime, Thibaud III had not been inactive in looking for allies to halt the Angevin menace. Indeed, he found an important though temporary one in King Henry I who, between 1047 and 1050 was increasingly angered by Geoffrey Martel's friendship with the emperor Henry III.[40] The king's support for Thibaud took the form of a military campaign against the count of Anjou in late 1049, in which the young duke of Normandy also took part. William had already distinguished himself by reversing Geoffrey Martel's annexation of Alençon and Domfront, an act that earned for him the homage of the lord of Bellême and the goodwill of Thibaud.[41] Now, for the first time, we can see the rulers of Normandy and Blois cooperating against Anjou. The capture of Mouliherne, near Angers, was a firm response to Geoffrey Martel's aggression against Bellême lands.[42] Although King Henry was subsequently to perform a volte-face and by 1052 to ally with Geoffrey, the campaign of 1049 had demonstrated to Thibaud and William their common interest in ridding Maine of the Angevin menace.

I would suggest that by 1052 William and Thibaud had worked out an agreement whereby Thibaud surrendered any claim he and his son Stephen-Henry might have to Maine into William's hands. William, whose own rights in that county were negligible, was to build up his reputation as a good lord there by conspicuous generosity to Marmoutier, the monastery near Tours still under Thibaud III's patronage, which had solid landed interests in Maine.[43] More immediately, he was to shelter bishop Gervais of Le Mans, and to encourage the Bellême family in their opposition to Geoffrey Martel. Eventually, when circumstances favoured him, he was to attempt the full-scale conquest of Maine. The benefit to the Norman duchy in securing a safe southern frontier and in working with the Bellêmes was evident. The profit to Thibaud would lie in the safeguarding of his remaining Loire possessions at very little cost to himself. That such an agreement was in existence is implied when, some time after 1056 (perhaps as late as 1060), Thibaud's nephew Herbert, son of Berthe and count Hugh of Maine, arrived to take up residence at the court of William of Normandy.[44] By that time William had already led one successful campaign into Maine, in which he had obtained the homage of a leading lord, Geoffrey of Mayenne.[45]

Thibaud's anxiety after 1049 to find a third party to fight in Maine on his behalf

[39] *Cartulaire blésois*, nos. 32, 33, 40.

[40] Jan Dhondt, 'Henri Ier, l'Empire et l'Anjou', *Revue belge de philologie et d'histoire*, 25, 1946–47, 87–109.

[41] Jumièges, 126

[42] *Gesta Guillelmi*, 22. On Thibaud of Blois' participation in this campaign with 500 knights, see Bur, 200.

[43] For Thibaud's continued patronage of Marmoutier, see *Cartulaire pour le Dunois*, 37, no. 40, where, between 1073 and 1084, he was described as *loci istius Majoris scilicet Monasterii defensorem atque patronum*. For Marmoutier's lands in Maine, see *Cartulaire manceau de Marmoutier*, ed. Ernest Laurain, Paris 1945.

[44] Guillot, i, 87.

[45] *Gesta Guillelmi*, 78–80.

was inspired not only by his undistinguished showing thus far and any pressure that Geoffrey Martel might be applying, but also by his concern with the affairs of Champagne. The death of his brother Stephen, count of Troyes and Meaux, between 1045 and 1048, leaving one young son Eudes as his obvious successor, had given him new ambition. He took on the regency, temporarily reuniting the family lands as Eudes II had held them.[46] Immediately he involved his nephew in his own political network.[47] In 1048 Eudes, in the company of the duke of Normandy, was at the royal court at Senlis, where he was required by his uncle to sign away an important abbey on his lands to the benefit of King Henry, on whose support Thibaud was counting.[48] During the decade 1048–58 Thibaud concentrated almost exclusively on Champagne territory, especially on strengthening the frontier with Lotharingia.

Thibaud's attitude towards his young nephew is hard to gauge. On the one hand, he was restrained by family feeling. On the other, he no doubt felt some bitterness that he, the elder son of Eudes II who had clearly been intended by his father to inherit the more important part of the family domains, had after 1044 become the junior partner in terms of land-holding. Stephen's death offered him the opportunity at least to redress the balance at Eudes's expense. But any adjustment there might be in his favour at the end of Eudes's minority would need royal ratification. He could not afford to break with the king, even after 1052 when Henry launched his attack on William of Normandy. He therefore sent troops to the king's army attacking Normandy in 1054, and seems to have served personally in the 1057 campaign.[49] But Henry's failure in that quarter can have caused him no lack of sleep. Tergiversations on the king's part could not affect the real bond of interest between Thibaud and William.

Around 1058 Eudes III of Troyes and Meaux reached the age of majority, creating a dilemma for his uncle. At around the same time, Thibaud finally embarked on a second marriage; his bride was Adela of Bar-sur-Aube, a match which increased Thibaud's influence in Champagne and menaced his nephew's prospects, particularly since three sons were soon to be born to the couple.[50] It was inevitable that Eudes III should feel unhappy. In a charter conferring land on the bishop of Châlons, he spoke of obtaining his uncle's consent to the gift when good relations were restored between them.[51] But they never were. The death of King Henry in 1060 and the consequent minority of Philip I enhanced Thibaud's freedom of action. Whether Eudes actually revolted against him and was defeated or whether Thibaud simply manoeuvred the young heir out of his inheritance cannot be known. The much later story in the chronicle of Fountains abbey that accuses Eudes of having murdered a nobleman and being forced to flee from his home does not carry much conviction.[52] But in late 1063 or 1064, he left

[46] Bur, 199–200.
[47] Barbara English, *A study in Feudal Society. The Lords of Holderness 1086–1260*, Oxford 1979, 9–13.
[48] *Catalogue des actes de Henri Ier, roi de France (1031–1060)*, ed. Frédéric Soehnée, Paris 1907, no. 81.
[49] Bur, 201, 202.
[50] Bur, 230.
[51] Bur, 209.
[52] Oxford Bodleian MS B449, fol. 10: *Wilhelmus autem fuit filius Stephani filius Odonis qui fuit filius comitis Campaniae iunioris et propinquus Regis Francorum. Odo autem propter homicidium*

Champagne for good. He was welcomed in Normandy where, probably before 1067, he married the duke's sister Adelaide, and obtained through her control (for her lifetime only) of her dower lands in Aumale.[53]

The question of the Champagne inheritance thus feeds into the Normandy-Blois alliance in Maine. William's willingness to save Thibaud embarrassment and to distract Eudes III from his justified anger against his uncle can be interpreted as his *quid pro quo* for Thibaud's reinforcement of his position in Maine. David Bates has remarked that William's seizure of Maine looks like opportunism.[54] In so far as he had a claim to the county, the duke obtained it through protection of members of the houses of Blois and Bellême. William of Poitiers, in justifying his master's conquest in 1062, may well have fabricated the story of Herbert II's deathbed cession of the county to the duke of Normandy.[55] But Duke William could not have achieved his objective so cleanly or so easily if he had been facing opposition not only from Anjou (by now much weakened through the death of Geoffrey Martel in 1060) but also from Blois, the natural protector of Herbert II till his death in 1062, and of his mother Berthe after that date.

That active cooperation continued between the house of Blois and William of Normandy is demonstrated by a charter of 1062, in which William made concessions to a newly-established permanent ecclesiastical overseer for the monastery of Marmoutier's interests in Normandy.[56] The appointment of such an official was necessitated by the sheer scale of the duke's generosity to Marmoutier, especially in the years after 1052.[57] Since that monastery was still in the patronage of Thibaud III, it is not surprising that Geoffrey of Chaumont, Thibaud's most loyal henchman, was present at the ducal court at La Hougue to witness the charter. (He had family interests of his own there, for his uncle, once viscount of Blois, had become a monk at Marmoutier.[58]) Interestingly, also present was Roger of Montgomery who, since his marriage to Mabel of Bellême (c.1050–54), was fighting to secure the whole Bellême lordship[59] – an ambition favoured by duke William. It is unfortunate that no other evidence remains of what was discussed at

---

cuiusdam de magnatis terre fugit de terra sua et venit ad Wilhelmum Nothum qui fuit dux Normannorum et rex Anglorum, et petivit dari sibi sororem eiusdem Wilhelmi in uxore; quod et factum est, Archiepiscopo Rothomagensi adiuvante partes Odonis. Postquam autem nuptie celebrate sunt Odo rogavit eundem Archiepiscopum ut suggeret Regi dari sibi unde uxorem suam et regis sororem alere possit. Exposuit ei causam quare de terra sua fugisset. Dedit ergo Archiepiscopus Odoni civitatem Albermarliae ut in expeditionibus esset ipsius Archiepiscopi signifer, cum decem militibus. Suggessit ergo idem Archiepiscopus Regi ut aliquam possessionem daret eidem et exposuit ei causam ipsius. Qua audita dedit Rex Odoni Holdernesse. Chronica Monasterii de Melsa *auctore Thome de Burton*, ed. Edward Bond, London 1866, i, 89, contains much the same account, though expressed in more elegant Latin.
[53] Orderic, ii, 264; for the date, see English, 55 and note 10. Although the link between Odo and Archbishop Maurilius is attested only in the late Meaux chronicle, it is plausible, because Maurilius, who came from Rheims, will have been conversant with Champagne politics.
[54] *William the Conqueror*, London 1989, 39.
[55] *Gesta Guillelmi*, 88; Bates, 39–40. It is worth noting, however, that *Gesta consulum andegavorum*, 63 accepts the truth of Herbert's donation to William. Although this is far from contemporary evidence, it was not in Angevin interests to repeat the story if untrue.
[56] Fauroux, no. 150.
[57] For this, see Fauroux, nos. 137; 141; 150; 151; 157; 159; 161; 162; 163; 163 bis; 165; 228.
[58] *Cartulaire blésois*, no. 61; *Cartulaire de Marmoutier pour le Vendômois*, ed. Charles de Trémault, Vendôme-Paris 1893, Appendix, no. 17.
[59] Geoffrey White, 'The first house of Bellême', *TRHS*, 4th series, xxii, 1940, 86–8.

La Hougue. But given Geoffrey of Chaumont's concern for the future of Maine, and given his concern to safeguard the rights of Stephen-Henry, the security of whose surviving possessions on the Loire would be much enhanced by a Norman conquest of Maine, his presence is most unlikely to have been fortuitous. Indeed the timing of the charter suggests a link with the duke's successful invasion of the county in that year. Perhaps the gathering at La Hougue was a council of war?[60]

The next Norman assembly in which Geoffrey of Chaumont is known to have participated, that on 17 June, 1066 at La Trinité de Caen, was certainly a prelude to military action.[61] The dedication of La Trinité, in the presence of Duke William and his Flemish wife Matilda, has been interpreted as a vital part of the spiritual preparation for the invasion of England, which was imminent.[62] Those who witnessed William's gifts to the new abbey, among them Geoffrey of Chaumont, were the duke's closest allies in the forthcoming campaign. Geoffrey's position in the witness list to the charter, after the duke's relations and among the household officers, is a clear sign of his importance in Norman eyes, and corroborates the claim of the author of the *Gesta* that he was held in great respect by William.[63]

It must have been with the approbation of Thibaud III and Stephen-Henry that Geoffrey embarked on the English expedition. Their concern in the matter was twofold: while anxious to boost Norman prestige at the expense of the Angevins, they needed an emissary at the duke's court to ensure that Maine was not forgotten in the excitement of new conquests; and they may also have hoped that Eudes III of Troyes might acquire in England some more permanent base for his ambitions, far from Champagne. If the latter was their wish, it was indeed fulfilled; but not until 1087, when Eudes acquired the lordship of Holderness.[64] In the matter of Maine, they had rather more rapid success. Geoffrey of Chaumont may have been among the advisers who persuaded William to leave England in 1073 and reassert his authority in the county after the rebellion of 1069 had almost destroyed it.

The *Gesta*'s story that Geoffrey of Chaumont participated in the Norman conquest of England is therefore confirmed by the witness list of the charter of 17 June 1066. The *Gesta* also states that, prior to his departure, Geoffrey handed over to Supplicius of Amboise and his niece Denise the lordship of all his remaining possessions in Chaumont, Blois and the Touraine, which included the tithes of St Cyr-en-Bourg.[65] Later events suggest that he retained a part of these in fief. This gift was presumably intended to safeguard his properties in the event of his death in battle. In line with the spirit of his undertaking of about seventeen years before, it points to a certain cordiality having been achieved over time between himself and his appointed heir of the next generation. Indeed, Supplicius's subsequent wavering in his adherence to the count of Anjou, his father's traditional lord, is most easily explained in terms of the influence of Geoffrey upon him. Though the author of the *Gesta* does not mention it, in the year after Geoffrey of Chaumont's

---

[60] David Bates has pointed out that La Hougue, in the far north of the Cotentin, was not an obvious place for such a council.

[61] *Regesta*, i, no. 4. Davis mistakenly identified our Geoffrey as lord of Chaumont-en-Vexin. But there were no lords of Chaumont-en-Vexin called Geoffrey at this time; see *Dictionnaire de la Noblesse*, ed. François Aubert de la Chenaye des Bois and Badier, Paris 1864, v, 509–10.

[62] Bates, 65.

[63] *Gesta ambaziensium dominorum*, 89.

[64] English, 10.

[65] *Gesta ambaziensium dominorum*, 89.

departure with William the Conqueror Chaumont was besieged by an army led by the young king Philip of France, his tutor Baldwin of Flanders, and the two rival claimants to the county of Anjou, Geoffrey the Bearded and his brother Fulk le Réchin.[66] While the siege was soon raised, its purpose had surely been to reinforce Angevin lordship on Chaumont, an unnecessary step had Supplicius been regarded as dependably loyal. From now on the lords of Amboise were to face the opportunities and drawbacks of divided allegiance.[67]

Despite the absence of specific evidence that Geoffrey fought at Hastings, it seems quite likely that he did. If so, he may have been included by William of Poitiers, appropriately though inaccurately, among the men from Maine who broke through the English defensive shield wall.[68] The *Gesta ambaziensium dominorum* speaks of his service to William being rewarded with lands and huge amounts of moveable wealth, and of him being retained in William's immediate entourage.[69] But if he did indeed acquire lands in England – and that is a question to which we shall return – then like William himself he did not settle down on them. In 1069 he was back in France, witnessing a charter of Thibaud III to the abbey of St Père of Chartres;[70] perhaps his return to the court of Blois was made possible by William's own brief visit to Normandy in late 1068 and early 1069. It is, however, a clear indication that Geoffrey's links with Thibaud were still important. The coincidence of his arrival with the brewing of rebellion against William in Maine is also noteworthy.

Apart from a brief visit to Philip I's court in 1070,[71] I have discovered no trace of Geoffrey between 1069 and 1075. That he accompanied William on the great Maine expedition of 1073 seems probable, but cannot be proved. In 1075 he was back at the French royal court again. On this occasion, he had business of his own to transact there, obtaining from Philip confirmation of his father's original charter endowing Pontelevoy and of his own additions to the endowment.[72] What other missions he may have accomplished on that occasion, either for Thibaud or for William, we do not know. But between 1077 and 1079 he seems to have been a fairly regular attender at the king's court; he witnessed six royal charters in those two years (on three occasions in the company of Hugh of Le Puiset).[73]

The last of these charters, written in January 1079, may perhaps furnish a clue as to the motive for his frequent appearances there. The grant he witnessed on that occasion was made during the siege of Gerberoi, conducted by Philip and duke William.[74] This famous siege, one of William's few military failures, was the culmination of Robert Curthose's rebellion against his father. Philip's presence at the siege has always been hard to explain, since he had deliberately fanned the flames of discord between father and son by favouring Robert, to whom he had granted the castle of Gerberoi in the first place. Someone at the royal court will

---

66 *Cartulaire manceau*, ii, Sablé no. 2.
67 *Gesta ambaziensium dominorum*, 122.
68 *Gesta Guillelmi*, 192.
69 *Gesta ambaziensium dominorum*, 89.
70 *Cartulaire de l'abbaye de St-Père-de-Chartres*, ed. Benjamin Guérard, Paris 1840, i, 210. I have assumed that *Calido Monte* is an editorial error.
71 *Actes de Philippe I*, no. 52.
72 *Actes de Philippe I*, no. 75.
73 *Actes de Philippe I*, nos. 87, 89, 90, 91, 92, and 94.
74 *Actes de Philippe I*, no. 94; *Regesta*, i, no. 115a.

have persuaded him towards the end of 1078 to change his mind and support William. Given the real danger to Norman control over Maine posed by Robert's rebellion, Geoffrey of Chaumont springs to mind as the honey-tongued adviser.[75]

Before 1080 Geoffrey was back with Thibaud III and Stephen-Henry.[76] His presence there fits in with the narrative of the *Gesta*, which specifically attributes to his negotiation the marriage between Stephen-Henry and William's daughter Adela.[77] Though this was celebrated some time between 1081 and 1084,[78] it was probably arranged well before the event. Stephen-Henry will have been relieved to pull off this coup, since it revitalised an old alliance. Adela was to bear him at least four sons, and in other respects also the union seems to have been successful. The lady had not yet acquired the characteristics that were to make her formidable in her widowhood.

Geoffrey's long visit to the comital court on this occasion proved fortunate for the inhabitants of Chaumont. They were thrown into confusion at the end of 1081 or the beginning of 1082 when Supplicius died,[79] leaving his brother Lisois as regent for Hugh, his infant son, who was held hostage by count Fulk le Réchin of Anjou.[80] Lisois soon faced a rebellion, aimed at disinheriting Hugh, and perhaps connived at by Denise and her daughters. Gauzbert, the prévot of Chaumont and a considerable figure in ecclesiastical circles,[81] appealed to the town's one-time lord to come and sort out the problem. Geoffrey firmly reinforced the authority of Gauzbert and Lisois, thereby demonstrating his continued adherence to the settlement he had made more than thirty years before. The author of the *Gesta* comments that even his opponents recognised his authority in the matter, since they knew him to be a *familiaris* of count Stephen-Henry.[82]

Having established peace, Geoffrey of Chaumont then returned to England. Shortly afterwards, Lisois put diplomatic pressure on Fulk le Réchin to obtain the release of Hugh. When Geoffrey sailed to Normandy, in the company of William the Conqueror, for the wedding of Adela and Stephen-Henry, he was able to meet his young great-nephew again, and to take on the task of his education.[83]

I have argued that charter evidence corroborates the *Gesta*'s picture of Geoffrey of Chaumont as a man on close terms with both William the Conqueror and

---

[75] The closeness between Geoffrey of Chaumont and William the Conqueror, and his continuing concern in the affairs of Robert Curthose, is also suggested by his attestation, along with Robert, of William's subscription of the Préaux charter, either between 1077 and 1078, or after Robert's rebellion and between 1080 and 1081; *Regesta*, i, no. 288. On this, see Véronique Gazeau, 'Le domaine continental de l'abbaye de Notre-Dame et Saint-Léger de Préaux au XIe siècle', in Lucien Musset et al., *Aspects de la société et de l'économie dans la Normandie médiévale (x–xiie siècles)*, Caen 1988, 178 note 51. I am most grateful to Dr David Bates for this reference and for his comments on the dating of the charter.

[76] *Cartulaire de St-Père-de-Chartres*, i, 158. For my reading of the name, see note 70.

[77] *Gesta ambaziensium dominorum*, 97.

[78] Bates, 107 gives the date as c.1080; Bur, 231 says it occurred in 1084; Van Houts, 48 believes it was arranged between 1078 and 1082.

[79] *Cartulaire de Marmoutier pour le Dunois*, no. 142. No. 149 shows that Supplicius was still alive in 1080 when he contested a gift to Marmoutier.

[80] *Gesta ambaziensium dominorum*, 94.

[81] He witnessed the charter of dedication when Pope Urban II consecrated the church of Marmoutier; *Marmoutier. Cartulaire tourangeau et sceaux des abbés*, ed. Claude Chantelou, Tours 1879, 40.

[82] *Gesta ambaziensium dominorum*, 97.

[83] *Gesta ambaziensium dominorum*, 98.

Stephen-Henry of Blois. I have tried to give substance to this picture by suggesting that he acted as a go-between, above all in business relating to Maine. But there is one important element in the *Gesta*'s account that I have been unable to corroborate, the claim that William endowed Geoffrey with extensive lands in England.[84] Geoffrey of Chaumont does not feature in Domesday Book;[85] and none of the Geoffreys mentioned in it without identifying places of origin could be our Geoffrey unless the author of the *Gesta* was distinctly misleading about the size of his endowments. He might, of course, have been rewarded after 1086; but since it was clearly William the Conqueror who was his patron, not much after. And the narrative implies both that lands were bestowed on him shortly after his arrival in England, and that the story of his good fortune was soon well known in the Loire valley.

Geoffrey's appearance among some of William's tenants-in-chief as a witness to the foundation charter of Lewes priory gives at least some substance to the claim that he enjoyed status in England.[86] But the absence of evidence as to landownership is disconcerting, even if we accept a picture of great tenurial fluidity for the period 1066–1086.[87] If the *Gesta*'s credibility is to be sustained, one hypothetical explanation suggests itself: that Geoffrey followed his father Gelduin in deliberately preferring a frontier outpost as a basis for lordship. If so, he may have settled on the Welsh March, just beyond the frontier recorded in Domesday Book but in close contact with Roger of Montgomery and other members of the Bellême family, his former allies.[88] Alternatively, and perhaps more plausibly, he may have gone north to Durham, the bishopric of which was ruled from 1080 by William of St Calais, formerly abbot of St Vincent in Le Mans, and perhaps an old acquaintance. An attraction of this hypothesis is that it fits into the *Gesta*'s story that, shortly after the accession of William Rufus to the throne, Geoffrey obtained the king's permission to resign his English lands into the hands of his nephew Savary.[89] Had he been in any way connected with William of St Calais, such a step might have been a prudent reaction to that bishop's disgrace in 1088.[90]

[84] *Gesta ambaziensium dominorum*, 89.

[85] I am most grateful to Professor John Palmer for confirming this for me.

[86] *Chartes de l'abbaye de Cluny*, ed. Auguste Bernard and Alexandre Bruel, Paris 1888, iv, no. 3559. Charles Clay in *Early Yorkshire Charters. 8 The Honour of Warenne*, 1949, no. 2, argues that the charter probably dates from before December 1081. Geoffrey of Chaumont's fellow attestors were the Beaumont brothers, Robert Giffard, and Roger Mortemer. His presence on this occasion suggests a link with William de Warenne.

[87] See Robin Fleming, *Kings and Lords in Conquest England*, Cambridge 1993, 183–214.

[88] R.R. Davies, *The Age of Conquest. Wales 1063–1415*, Oxford 1991, 29 comments that Domesday Book may lead us to underestimate the scale of Norman penetration in the South-east of Wales.

[89] *Gesta ambaziensium dominorum*, 98. Despite Avenil's contention that Savary was the child of Chana's first marriage, see 'The Bohuns of Hereford' 430, he is specifically described as son of viscount Raoul when he witnessed a charter of donation some time between 1067 and 1080; see *Cartulaire de Saint-Vincent au Mans*, ed. R. Charles and Samuel Menjot d'Elbenne, Mamers 1886–1913 , no. 115. Although Savary fitzCana ultimately became lord of Midhurst (Avenil, 'The Bohuns of Hereford', 430; Orderic, vi, 32 and note 2), the gift was from Henry I, and therefore probably does not help in the detection of Geoffrey's lands. The prominence of the name Gelduin among Savary fitzCana's sons and descendants indicates that his Loire ancestry was not forgotten. I am most grateful to Dr Katherine Keats-Rohan for information on this.

[90] On this, see Margaret Gibson, *Lanfranc of Bec*, Oxford 1978, 160–1; 220–1.

Whatever his endowment, Geoffrey can never have spent much time in England. It may, however, be significant that he did not abandon a base there until after, but only shortly after, Eudes III of Champagne had been given the honour of Holderness.[91] When Thibaud and Stephen-Henry no longer had to fear the reappearance of their erstwhile rival, Geoffrey of Chaumont could re-establish himself in France. Some time between 1087 and 1091 he visited Normandy, accompanied by his nephew Savary.[92] There he went again to the abbey of La Trinité de Caen, this time witnessing duke Robert Curthose's gift to the nuns of that remarkable foundation. He also reappeared briefly at the court of King Philip.[93] But he spent most of the last decade of his life with count Stephen-Henry and countess Adela in places long familiar to him.[94] He must have been well into his eighties when, in 1097–8, he appeared before Adela to claim rights in three priories belonging to Marmoutier, rights which he voluntarily renounced when his old friend Gauzbert, prévot of Chaumont, testified against him.[95]

By this time, Lisois of Chaumont had recently died, and Geoffrey's great-nephew Hugh was lord of Chaumont and Amboise. Hugh, along with count Stephen-Henry (and possibly Geoffrey of Chaumont himself), was present at Marmoutier in 1096 on the occasion on which pope Urban II preached the crusade to the people. The *Gesta* tells that, when Stephen-Henry took the cross, Geoffrey provided his nephew with much gold and silver so that he might accompany his lord.[96] Thus the profits of the Norman conquest of England came to finance another great adventure in Western expansionism.

Hugh survived the crusade and acquired greater glory than count Stephen-Henry. But when he returned home after the battle of Ascalon, he found that his aged great-uncle had died and had been buried at Pontelevoy. The *Gesta* records that Geoffrey retained to the end all his faculties except his sight.[97] In his will, he had lavishly endowed the monastery of Marmoutier. So considerable was the legacy that the abbot thought it expedient to bribe Hugh into accepting its terms by the gift of an expensive palfrey.[98] Thus even after his death Geoffrey's English treasures had the power to stir emotions.

The Geoffrey of Chaumont revealed in the pages of the *Gesta* is a very perfect gentle knight. It is natural to suspect that he tells us more about mid twelfth-century ideals than mid eleventh-century facts. Yet surviving charter evidence bears out enough of the detail to still some scepticism. Indeed I have argued that the truth was perhaps more romantic even than the author of the *Gesta* knew: that Geoffrey's loyalty to the house of Blois and to the dukes of Normandy was a formative element in establishing a long-lasting political alliance which in the end

---

[91] English, 10.

[92] *Regesta*, i, no. 324.

[93] *Actes de Philippe I*, no. 121. Geoffrey's presence strengthens Prou's case that the charter dates from 1086–1090 or 1091.

[94] *Gesta ambaziensium dominorum*, 98.

[95] *Cartulaire blésois*, no. 74. The dating of the charter according to Pope Urban's visit, suggests a connection between Geoffrey's willingness to surrender his claim and the impression made by the pope's presence.

[96] *Gesta ambaziensium dominorum*, 101.

[97] *Gesta ambaziensium dominorum*, 109.

[98] *Cartulaire blésois*, no. 76.

made its mark both on French and on English history.[99] The friendships of princes can only be conducted through intermediaries; and Geoffrey always appeared at the time and place appropriate for the exercise of diplomatic gifts. He achieved the difficult feat of serving two lords faithfully. From what can be patched together of his life story, he deserved the *Gesta*'s epithet *vir mire strenuitatis et sapientissimus*.[100]

99   On this, see Michel Bur, 'Les comtes de Champagne et la "Normanitas": semiologie d'un tombeau', *ante*, iii, 1980, 22–32.
100 *Gesta ambaziensium dominorum*, 81.

PARIS, UN ROUEN CAPETIEN?
(DEVELOPPEMENTS COMPARES DE ROUEN ET PARIS SOUS LES REGNES DE HENRI II ET PHILIPPE-AUGUSTE)

Bernard Gauthiez

Cet article a pour origine une question que David Bates me posait il y a quelques années, à l'occasion du congrès de la British Archeological Association à Rouen en 1989. La teneur de sa question était celle-ci: 'Rouen n'a-t-il pas été, à la fin du XIIe siècle, une sorte de "Paris" angevin?'. Ma réponse fut alors que l'inverse paraissait plus probable, sur la base d'arguments urbanistiques que j'avais commencé à développer dans ma thèse sur Rouen.[1] C'est cette question qui va être ici traitée, principalement sous l'angle de la croissance comparée des deux villes à cette époque, en essayant de comprendre le lien entre leur développement et les circonstances politiques. Je n'aborderai ici qu'essentiellement les données d'ordre topographique. Sur la connaissance du rôle de Rouen à cette époque, et de la manière dont elle était perçue, je renverrai à l'article de David Bates, que je dois ici remercier pour me l'avoir communiqué avant sa parution dans *British Archeological Association Conference Transactions*, xii, 'Rouen from 900 to 1204: from Scandinavian settlement to Angevin "capital" '.

Les deux villes sont, peu avant 1150, des capitales de principautés au poids sensiblement égal. Elles présentent cependant à cette époque des visages très différents, témoins de deux histoires non parallèles et de sites aux contraintes propres (figure 1). Leur taille est assez comparable, et leur superficie urbanisée est du même ordre, un peu plus probablement pour Rouen avec environ cinquante hectares, un peu moins pour Paris, peut-être quarante hectares. Chacune est enclose par un mur construit depuis quelques décennies, malheureusement mal connu dans les deux cas. Les quartiers extra muros n'y sont pas de grande ampleur, toutefois les murs paraissent relativement pleins.[2] Cette situation semble représentative des principales villes des principautés de l'époque dans le bassin parisien, comme Chartres et Reims, de taille voisine à ce moment.[3]

Ces villes connaissent à partir du milieu du XIIe siècle, plus ou moins précocément, des développements considérables. Bien connus à Chartres et Reims, et plus

---

[1] Bernard Gauthiez, *La logique de l'espace urbain, formation et évolution; le cas de Rouen*, thèse de doctorat nouveau régime, Ecole des Hautes Etudes en Sciences Sociales, Paris 1991, i, 204–5.
[2] Sur Rouen, Gauthiez, 1991, 169; fig. 61, 180.
   Sur Paris, Anne Lombard-Jourdan, 'De la protohistoire à la mort de Philippe-Auguste', *Paris, genèse d'un paysage*, sous la direction de Louis Bergeron, Paris 1989, 3–52; Jacques Boussard, *Nouvelle histoire de Paris, de la fin du siège de 885–86 à la mort de Philippe-Auguste*, Paris 1976; Françoise Boudon, André Chastel, Hélène Couzy et Françoise Hamon, *Système de l'architecture urbaine, le quartier des Halles à Paris*, Paris 1977, 17 et 59.
[3] Ch. Billot, *Chartres à la fin du Moyen Age*, Paris 1987; P. Desportes, *Reims et les rémois aux XIIIe et XIVe siècles*, Paris 1979.

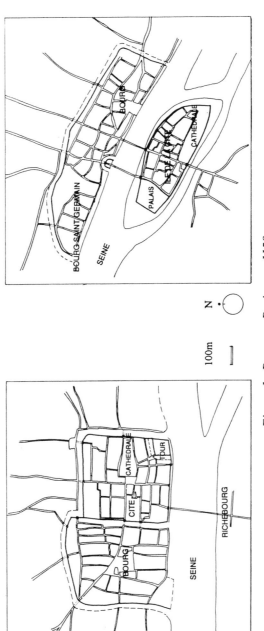

Figure 1. Rouen et Paris vers 1150
(dessin B. Gauthiez)

récemment à Rouen, ils résultent de politiques délibérées de la part des princes, ducs, roi ou archevêque dont elles sont les villes les plus importantes. Employer le mot capitale, au sens où nous l'entendons de nos jours, serait probablement abusif. Rouen et Paris seront cependant appelées à grandir plus que les autres d'une manière que nous allons maintenant étudier. Une question est aussi, bien sûr, de savoir comment Paris devint capitale, et, incidemment, si cela était aussi inéluctable qu'une tendance historiographique plus particulièrement parisienne tend à faire penser.

La première de ces villes à connaître une politique de développement fut Rouen.

Le développement de Rouen sous Henri II prit différentes formes. Certaines d'entre elles sont bien documentées, et surtout bien datées, ce sont le nouveau pont en pierre et la résidence royale de Quevilly. Le nouveau pont fut construit par Mathilde avant sa mort en 1167 en remplacement d'un pont localisé plus à l'est, renforcé par Geoffroi Plantagenêt. La chaussée qui le prolongeait en rive sud de la Seine fut probablement aussi réalisée à cette époque, modifiant l'ancien trajet d'approche de la ville de ce côté.[4] La nouvelle résidence royale de Quevilly, elle aussi sur la rive sud de la Seine, fit l'objet de travaux à la fin des années 1150. Elle fut affectée par Henri II à l'usage d'hôpital pour des lépreuses en 1185–88. Un certain nombre d'actes attestent de sa fréquentation par le roi.[5]

D'autres aspects de la croissance de la ville sont bien identifiés dans l'espace, leur datation est plus incertaine. Une nouvelle enceinte fut construite avant 1198, date à laquelle la porte Beauvoisine est citée.[6] Elle existait assûrément avant 1190, lorsque le mur de la cité est qualifié de 'vieux', à proximité du château de la Tour.[7] Vraisemblablement construite avant l'octroi de la charte communale, peut-être dans les années 1150–60, elle semble en place lors du siège de la ville par le roi de France Louis VI en 1174.[8] Nous pouvons donc avec une certaine confiance l'attribuer à Henri II. Un certain nombre de quartiers nouveaux, sous la forme de grands lotissements, apparaissent au tournant du XIIIe siècle à l'intérieur du secteur nouvellement enclos. Leur forme est conditionnée par la nouvelle enceinte, ils lui sont donc certainement postérieurs. Il s'agit tout d'abord de la paroisse St Patrice, attestée en 1189–94,[9] établie probablement sur le site de vignes ducales données en 1032 à l'abbaye de Cerisy.[10] La rue St Patrice adopte un tracé équidistant et régulier entre l'enceinte du XIe siècle et celle du XIIe. La paroisse St Godard est mentionnée pour la première fois en 1208.[11] La rue du Beffroi, à proximité de l'église est parallèle au nouveau mur, et fut donc vraisemblablement tracée le long de celui-ci.

Le quartier situé entre les actuelles rues de l'Hôpital, Beauvoisine, Thiers (maintenant rue Jean Lecauvet) et la place de l'Hôtel-de-Ville a pris la place de la

---

[4] Georges Dubosc, 'La maison des templiers de Rouen', *Bulletin des Amis des Monuments Rouennais*, 1911, 75; Gauthiez 1991, 133–35.

[5] Robert de Torigni, *Chronique*, éd. Léopold Delisle, Rouen 1872, ii, 331.

[6] Bibliothèque Municipale de Rouen (BMR), ms Y 44, no. 93.

[7] BMR, ms Y 44, nos. 228–229.

[8] Gauthiez, 1991, 183–89.

[9] Archives Départementales de la Seine-Maritime (ADSM), G 4369.

[10] ADSM, G 2, pouillé d'Eudes Rigaud; Fauroux, 192.

[11] ADSM, G 4296.

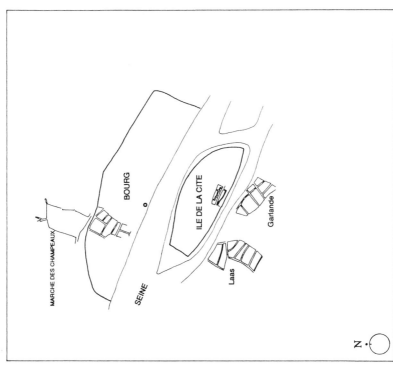

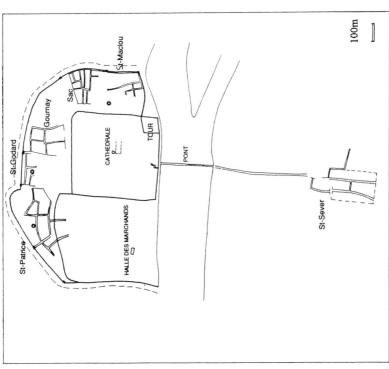

Figure 2. Principaux éléments de la croissance de Rouen et Paris entre 1150 et 1190 (dessin B. Gauthiez)

résidence d'un personnage du nom de Pierre de Gournay. Les rues du secteur reprennent toutes ce nom, et donnent ainsi son étendue. Elle était lotie déjà lorsqu'une rue 'Neuve devant St Ouen' est citée en 1195–1200.[12] Le réseau des rues du quartier s'organise au nord manifestement en fonction du tracé de la nouvelle enceinte. Le lotissement du quartier délimité au nord par la rue Eau-de-Robec et à l'ouest par la rue Damiette a une même logique, contrainte par la présence du mur à l'est. Les rues qui le parcourent portent dans les mentions anciennes le nom de 'rue du Sac'. Si la plus ancienne mention de ce nom n'est que de 1231, il est hors de doute que l'urbanisation est ici plus ancienne.[13] La paroisse St Maclou, citée en 1201–03, montre de même le développement de la ville vers l'est à cette époque.[14] Les rues Notre-Dame et des Crottes, qui forment un lotissement régulier, font partie de cette nouvelle paroisse. La rue des Crottes est mentionnée en 1206–17.[15]

La nouvelle enceinte, permettant de nouveaux lotissements dans les secteurs qu'elle protège, a donc eu pour conséquence d'induire un développement de la ville et de sa population. La paroisse St Vivien, attestée en 1208, s'est peut-être aussi formée à cette époque, mais à l'extérieur de la ville close.[16] Peut-être est-ce dans ce cadre qu'il faut insérer le Bourg Gilbert, cité en 1289 dans la paroisse St Martin sur Renelle, et le Bourg Tyart, évoqué en 1314 paroisse St Laurent.[17] Enfin, à cet ensemble il faut vraisemblablement ajouter le secteur au sud de l'église St Sever, en rive gauche, dont on sait qu'il est occupé au début du XIIIe siècle, et dont la forme suggère une urbanisation de la deuxième moitié du XIIe siècle.[18] La construction du nouveau pont fut certainement dans ce cas déterminante. Dans un autre registre d'opérations remodelant la ville et son aspect, le pavement du roi mentionné dans la paroisse St Vivien en 1218, en dehors de l'enceinte, indique que le pavage des principales rues de la ville fut probablement entrepris avant la fin du XIIe siècle.[19]

Du point de vue monumental, l'élément le plus remarquable est la construction de la tour St Romain, au nord de la façade principale de la cathédrale, vers 1160–65. Elle renouvelle le marquage de l'axe du castrum, face à la rue du Gros-Horloge, dans la continuité de l'urbanisme pratiqué au Xe siècle. Les travaux de reconstruction de la nef de la cathédrale vont bon train à la fin du siècle. En ce qui concerne la société rouennaise, il faut noter l'émergence d'une puissante bourgeoisie dès le milieu du XIIe siècle, ou avant, largement impliquée dans les affaires du duché et du royaume. Sa puissance transparaît dans les libertés réaffirmées vers 1150, puis dans la Commune, octroyée vers 1174.[20] De grandes

[12] ADSM, 14 H 18, no. 419.
[13] ADSM, 14 H 18, no. 199.
[14] ADSM, G 6872, fo 4.
[15] BMR, ms Y 44, no. 284.
[16] ADSM, 14 H 18, no. 125.
[17] ADSM, G 4329 et 6826.
[18] Gauthiez, 1991, 189–95 et 197–202.
[19] ADSM, 14 H 18, no. 185.
[20] Sur la cathédrale, Lindy Grant, 'Rouen Cathedral 1200–1237', *Medieval art, architecture and archaeology at Rouen*, BAA Conference Transactions, xii, 1993, 60–68. Après 1169: Arthur Giry, *Les établissements de Rouen*, Paris 1883, 11; avant 1176: L. Delisle, Elie Berger, *Recueil des actes de Henri II*, Paris 1916, 40, no. D, ii, 50.

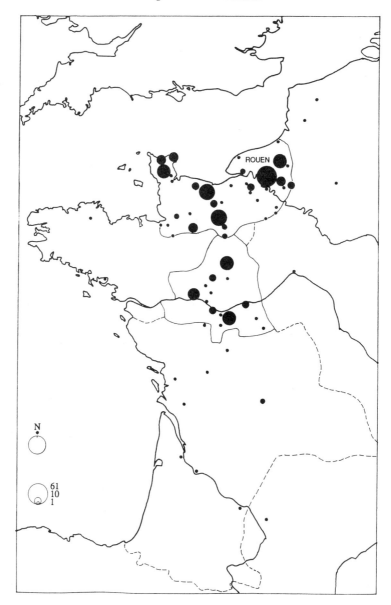

*Figure 3. Carte des lieux d'où les chartes de Henri II émanent
(d'après Berger, 1909, 61–62, dessin B. Gauthiez)*

Le gouvernement de Henri II s'exerce essentiellement à partir des prov-
inces à l'origine de son pouvoir continental, et surtout de la Normandie
(69% des actes, dont 15% pour Rouen), secondairement de l'Anjou (28%
du total). 3% seulement des actes proviennent d'autres territoires. Les
points soulignent remarquablement les routes suivies par le souverain, particulièrement entre Anjou et Normandie, de même que l'importance des
ports du Nord-Cotentin pour la traversée de la Manche, et les sites des
forteresses frontalières normandes.

résidences en pierre en montrent la réussite.[21] La Halle des Marchands, dans la paroisse St Eloi, est agrandie en 1192.[22]

Les sources concernant cette époque permettent de la sorte de dresser le portrait d'une ville que l'on qualifie souvent de Métropole (figure 2). David Bates a fait l'état des sources qui vont dans ce sens, jusqu'à la comparaison, sur un jeu de mots, entre Rouen et Rome. L'urbanisme pratiqué par Henri II à Rouen, à notre connaissance sans parallèle dans les grandes villes de l'ensemble Plantagenêt, lui donne ainsi des traits qui sont ceux d'une capitale. Rouen est la ville où le roi-duc a semble-t-il, sur le continent, le plus édicté d'actes, de sa résidence de Quevilly, et plus encore de la Tour. Cette supériorité n'est toutefois pas écrasante (figure 3).[23] La présence du gouvernement royal à Rouen se traduit par la résidence autour du château de personnages directement associés à la cour ou à l'exercice du pouvoir, par exemple Gocelin et Henri, cuisiniers;[24] Robert, cithariste;[25] Roger de Warwic, chapelain;[26] ou encore Baudri, sergent;[27] Hugues de Creiseio et Robert de Vieux-Pont, gardiens de la Tour.[28]

Plus significative encore est la présence d'un grand nombre de représentations ecclésiastiques extérieures, à la fois du royaume anglais et du duché normand, principalement dans la paroisse de la Tour, St Denis, avec par exemple Gautier de Coutances, avant qu'il devienne archevêque de Rouen en 1184;[29] Roger archevêque d'York;[30] Henri de Châtillon archidiacre de Canterbury;[31] Mauger évêque de Worcester;[32] l'abbaye St Etienne de Caen et les évêchés normands, Bayeux, Sées, Evreux, Lisieux, Avranches (figure 4).[33]

Par ailleurs, malgré l'absence de l'Echiquier de Normandie localisé à Caen, Rouen apparaît comme un centre financier majeur de l'ensemble anglo-normand. Les textes en font foi, et plus encore la localisation dans la ville des groupes sociaux les plus significatifs à cet égard. On constate ainsi, dans la paroisse Notre Dame de la Ronde et dans ses abords, une très forte concentration d'anglais, et particulièrement de grands du royaume, au nombre desquels Raoul Fils Etienne, Gautier de Coutances, Guillaume de Mandeville comte d'Essex, Bertrand le Chambellan, Robert comte de Leicester (figure 5 et 6).[34] On y trouve aussi de

[21] Bernard Gauthiez, 'Les maisons de Rouen XIIe–XVIIIe siècles', *Archéologie Médiévale*, xxiii, 1993, 132–141.
[22] Alfred Cerné, *Une ancienne Halle aux Marchands de Rouen*, Rouen 1933.
[23] Le nombre des chartes émanées par lieu est donné par Elie Berger, 1909, 61–62, note 3.
[24] Iocelinus Coquus, ADSM, G 2094 et G 4275. Henricus Cocus, BMR, ms Y 44, no. 258.
[25] Delisle/Berger, no. 472.
[26] ADSM, G 4278, 1171–90; BMR, ms Y 44, no. 228–229.
[27] Delisle/Berger, no. CCX.
[28] Hugues de Creseio, *Mémoires de la Société des Antiquaires de Normandie* (MSAN), xv, 1845, 22. Robert de Vieux-Pont, Maurice Veyrat, *Les baillis de Rouen*, Rouen 1953, 27.
[29] BMR, ms Y 44, nos. 85–86–87.
[30] BMR, ms Y 44, no. 228.
[31] ADSM, G 2094.
[32] ADSM, G 2094.
[33] Evêque de Bayeux, *MSAN*, viii, 1834, 427, début XIIe siècle; BMR, ms Y 44, no. 68, début XIIIe siècle. Evêque de Lisieux, ADSM, G 4275, 1189. Evêque d'Evreux, BMR, ms Y 44, no. 115, 1195–1200. Evêque de Sées, ADSM, G 2094, 1256. Evêque d'Avranches, ADSM, G 4223, 1322. Abbaye St Etienne de Caen, BMR, ms Y 44, no. 234, 1207, et no. 260.
[34] Raoul Fils Etienne, ADSM, 20 H 6 et G 4363. Gautier de Coutances, ADSM, G 4364. Guillaume de Mandeville, Léopold Delisle, 'Cartulaire Normand', Caen, 1882, no. 1095. Bertrand le Chambellan, ADSM, G 4279. Robert de Leicester, AN, S.5199, no. 56 et Delisle, no. 291.

Figure 4. Résidences des grands écclésias-tiques à Rouen, par paroisse (XIIe-début XIIIe siècle). A paroisse St Denis (dessin B. Gauthiez)

Cette figure, de même que les figures 5 à 8 et la figure 10, est tirée d'une base de donnée sur les noms de personnes résidant à Rouen, constituée d'après les sources suivantes:

ADSM, série G, 1098, 2094, 3529, 4262, 4264, 4263, 4265, 4266, 4272, 4273, 4275, 4276, 4278, 4279, 4280, 4281, 4282, 4287, 4289, 4290, 4295, 4296, 4297, 4298, 4299, 4301, 4302, 4303, 4304, 4305, 4306, 4307, 4309, 4311, 4312, 4313, 4320, 4321, 4322, 4324, 4325, 4327, 4331, 4332, 4333, 4336, 4339, 4341, 4343, 4345, 4346, 4347, 4351, 4352, 4353, 4354, 4356, 4358, 4359, 4361, 4363, 4364, 4365, 4366, 4368, 4369, 4370, 4371, 4372, 4408, 4616, 4617, 6872. ADSM, série H, 13 H 184, 14 H 18, 14 H 143, 14 H 350, 14 H 690, 20 H 1, 20 H 5, 20 H 6, 20 H 7. ADSM, Cordeliers. ADSM, Filles Dieu. BMR, ms Y 44. BMR, Tiroir 417. Archives Départementales de l'Eure, H 698. AN, S.5199. Bibliothèque Nationale, ms n.a. F.6190s, fo 135. Léopold Delisle, *Cartulaire Normand*, Caen 1882. Maurice Veyrat, *Les baillis de Rouen*, Rouen 1953. Robert de Torigni, *Chronique*, éditée par Léopold Delisle, Rouen 1872. *Regesta*. Fauroux. Berger, *Recueil des actes de Henri II*, Paris 1909–1916. 'Magnus Rotulus Scaccarii Normanniae', publiés par Léopold Delisle, *MSAN*, VIII. Thomas Duffus Hardy, *Rotuli Charta-rum in Turri Londinensi*, Londres 1837. J.J. Vernier, *Chartes de l'abbaye de Jumièges 825–1204*, Rouen 1916. 'Grands rôles de l'Echiquier de Normandie', publiés par Lechaudé d'Anisy, *MSAN*, XV, Paris 1846. *The register of Eudes of Rouen*, publié par Brown et O'Sullivan, New-York 1964. Joseph R. Strayer, *The royal domain in the bailliage of Rouen*, Londres 1976.

Il n'existe pas de liste de noms de personnes à Rouen pour les XIIe et XIIIe siècles. Ces données regroupent un peu plus de 1500 personnages. Elles ne représentent qu'une partie des sources disponibles (dont une bonne part reste à inventorier), mais permettent cependant, de par leur diversité, une exploitation de type statistique.

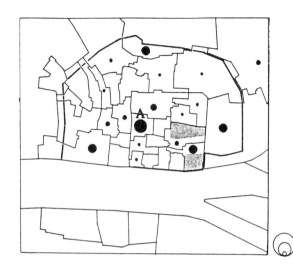

Figure 5. Résidences des anglais à Rouen, par paroisse (XIIe-début XIIIe siècle). A paroisse Notre-Dame-de-la-Ronde (dessin B. Gauthiez)

Figure 6. Résidences des grands du royaume à Rouen, par paroisse (XIIe-début XIIIe siècle). A paroisse Notre-Dame-de-la-Ronde (dessin B. Gauthiez)

Figure 7. Résidences des juifs à Rouen, par paroisse (XIIe-début XIIIe siècle).
A paroisse St Lô

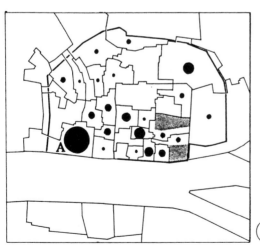

Figure 8. Résidences des grands bourgeois à Rouen, par paroisse (XIIe-début XIIIe siècle). (Familles de maires avant 1230 et Salehadin.)
A paroisse St Eloi

grands ecclésiastiques dont encore l'archidiacre de Canterbury et probablement Geoffroi évêque de Winchester.[35] Le quartier juif est localisé juste à côté de l'église Notre Dame de la Ronde, et l'on sait le rôle des juifs dans le financement des emprunts royaux et la protection dont ils ont pu jouir (figure 7).[36] De grands bourgeois y ont encore une résidence, comme Sylvestre d'Orgueil, certainement le Sylvestre le Changeur maire en 1209, dont la maison était située face à l'église Notre Dame De la Ronde, et même, au début du XIIIe siècle, un riche arabe converti lié aux Templiers, Laurent Salehadin (figure 8).[37] Certains de ces personnages possédaient deux résidences, l'une en ce point, l'autre dans le quartier le plus typique de leur groupe social, ainsi Henri de Châtillon archidiacre de Canterbury près de la Tour, Laurent Salehadin paroisse St Eloi, ou encore des familles de grands bourgeois comme les Le Gros, les Trentegerons ou les d'Orgueil, paroisse St Eloi aussi.[38]

Ainsi, autour de Notre Dame de la Ronde, collégiale et paroissiale de patronage royal, la seule dans ce cas à Rouen, et le long de la rue du Gros-Horloge à proximité de l'église, existait une espèce de coeur financier de la ville, concentrant dans un cosmopolitisme étonnant la richesse rouennaise. C'est là semble-t-il que pouvaient être mobilisés une large part des financements, d'origine juive ou bourgeoise, nécessaires aux souverains ou aux grands du royaume. On aimerait connaître les mécanismes de ce coeur financier, et particulièrement le rôle de la collégiale Notre Dame, dont les statuts seront réformés en 1251, peut-être parce qu'alors devenus inadaptés à une situation bien différente.[39] C'est que, bien sûr, le rattachement à la France fera disparaître l'essentiel de ces fonctionnements.

Ces éléments permettent de dresser une carte du 'système' des pouvoirs dans la ville: royal, ecclésiastique, économique et financier (figure 9). Sous ces aspects urbanistiques, gouvernemental et social, Rouen est bien à cette époque une capitale de fait, probablement jusqu'en 1204. Son rayonnement démographique, traduit par les lieux d'où proviennent une bonne partie de ses habitants, reste cependant assez largement limité à la Normandie orientale, avec toutefois un important contingent originaire d'Angleterre (figure 10). D'évidence, le rôle de capitale de Rouen s'étend, au moins en partie, à la rive nord de la Manche.

Le visage du développement de Paris est un peu différent. Il est plus tardif, puisqu'il ne démarre réellement que vers 1190, et semble moins systématique que celui de Rouen. Il faut tout d'abord mentionner quelques interventions antérieures,

---

[35] Henri de Chatillon, Delisle, no. 57 Geoffroi de Winchester, ADSM, G 2094.

[36] Sur les juifs de Rouen et leur rôle à cette époque, voir Norman Golb, *Les juifs de Rouen au Moyen Age*, Rouen 1985, 101–42.

[37] Sylvestre d'Orgueil, ADSM, 14 H 20, nos. 20, 103 et 110; ADSM, G 4359; BMR, ms Y 44, no. 247. Laurent Salehadin, AN, S. 5199, no. 57.

[38] Laurent Salehadin à St Eloi, AN, S. 5199, no. 65. Les Le Gros, AN, S.5199, nos. 65–67; ADSM, G 20 H 5; ADSM, G 4368 à St Martin sur Renelle. Les Trentegerons, AN, S.5199, nos. 59–65–67; ADSM, G 4289 et G 4356. Les D'Orgueil, AN, S.5199, no. 65; BMR, Tiroir 417.

Lucien Musset évoque la bourgeoisie citadine normande, ce qui concerne largement Rouen, '(très) liée à l'administration des Plantagenêt, aux finances royales et plus spécialement aux mouvements de fonds entre les trésors anglais et normands', 'Quelques problèmes posés par l'annexion de la normandie au domaine royal français', *La France de Philippe-Auguste, le temps des mutations*, colloque CNRS 29 sept.–4 oct. 1980, Paris 1982, 299.

[39] Delisle, no. 500.

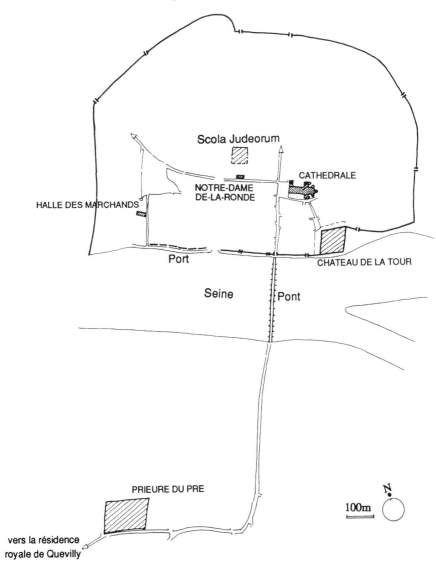

*Figure 9. Le 'système' des pouvoirs à Rouen à la fin du XIIe siècle
        (dessin B. Gauthiez)*

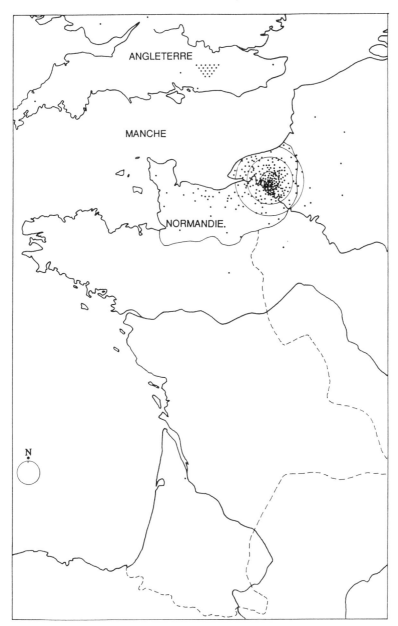

Figure 10. Origines géographiques des résidents à Rouen, d'après les noms de personnes des XIIe et XIIIe siècles (hormis les origines extérieures à la Normandie et à l'Angleterre après 1240) (dessin B. Gauthiez)

Cette carte montre le très fort rayonnement de Rouen sur la Normandie orientale, de même qu'une forte attirance sur la région correspondant à l'actuel département du Calvados et sur le sud de l'Angleterre. Les cercles autour de Rouen sont placés à 16, 40 et 60 km

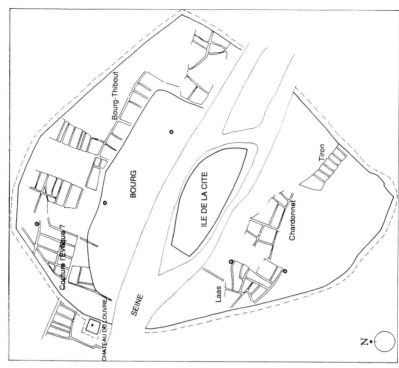

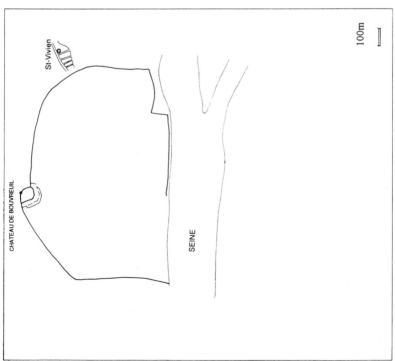

Figure 11. Principaux éléments de la croissance de Rouen et Paris entre 1190 et 1223 (dessin B. Gauthiez)

comme le percement de la rue Neuve devant la nouvelle cathédrale Notre Dame, vers 1163, et le lotissement du quartier adjacent.[40] En rive gauche, c'est le lotissement du clos de Garlande vers 1134, sur une vigne, dans le secteur de la rue d'Orléans et du début de la rue St Jacques.[41] Le nouveau marché est la première décision d'envergure qui puisse être rapportée au nouveau roi Philippe. A l'origine des halles de Paris, il est créé en 1181–83 hors les murs, aux Champeaux, par déplacement de la foire St Lazare, et entouré d'un fossé. Sa création entraine le lotissement du secteur au sud de la rue St Honoré (figure 2).[42]

Le second élément décisif est la construction d'un mur d'enceinte élargi pour protéger les abords de la ville et le nouveau marché. La décision est prise en 1190, à l'occasion du départ du roi pour la croisade. Le poids de la bourgeoisie parisienne apparaît alors pour la première fois.[43] Le nouveau mur, qui enclôt de vastes espaces libres, permet l'urbanisation de nouveaux secteurs, dont le quartier entre le marché des Champeaux et la rue St Denis sur des terres royales, et celui à l'ouest du marché, plus tardif, sur des terres épiscopales, peut-être la 'Couture l'Evêque' évoquée dans un texte de 1222. Plus à l'est apparaît le Bourg Thibout, probablement du nom d'un riche bourgeois.[44]

Une nouvelle enceinte est décidée, en rive gauche cette fois, en 1211.[45] Elle protège et induit de nouveaux lotissements, sur la volonté explicite du roi.[46] Petit à petit, surtout en fait à partir du milieu du siècle, leur succèderont de nombreux collèges, qui vont constituer une nouvelle partie de la ville, l''Université'.[47] Les nouveaux quartiers qui apparaissent dans ce secteur sont principalement le clos de Laas à partir de 1179, loti par l'abbaye de St Germain autour de la future paroisse St André des Arts;[48] le clos Bruneau en 1202 entre la clos de Laas, la Seine, le clos de Garlande et la place Maubert;[49] le clos de Tiron en 1214.[50] La croissance s'accélère au début du XIIIe siècle, et les nouveaux quartiers obligent à créer de nouvelles paroisses: St Leufroy vers 1205, St Eustache vers 1212, St Jean en Grève en 1213, St Jacques de l'Hôpital et St Sauveur en 1216, Ste Opportune en 1220, ceci pour la rive nord; St André des Arts et St Cosme en 1211, St Etienne du Mont en 1222 pour la rive gauche.[51] Le roi décide en 1186 de paver les rues principales de Paris.[52] Une nouvelle résidence royale, enfin, vient clore la liste des grandes réalisations urbanistiques attribuables au règne de Philippe-Auguste, c'est

---

[40] Jacques Boussard, *Nouvelle histoire de Paris, de la fin du siège de 885–86 à la mort de Philippe-Auguste*, Paris 1976, 186; Anne Lombard-Jourdan, 'De la protohistoire à la mort de Philippe-Auguste', *Paris, genèse d'un paysage*, sous la direction de Louis Bergeron, Paris 1989, 28.

[41] Boussard, 186; Lombard-Jourdan, 28.

[42] Boussard, 265.

[43] Boussard, 319–20; Halphen, *Paris sous les premiers capétiens (987–1223), étude de topographie historique*, Paris 1905, planches I et II.

[44] Lombard-Jourdan, 23; Boussard, 306.

[45] Boussard, 324 et 327.

[46] Rigord, 'Gesta Philippi Augusti', *Recueil des historiens des Gaules et de la France*, xvii, 1818.

[47] Raymond Cazelles, *Nouvelle histoire de Paris, de la fin du règne de Philippe-Auguste à la mort de Charles V, 1223–1380*, Paris 1972, 69s.

[48] Boussard, 183.

[49] Boussard, 186.

[50] Boussard, 321; Cazelles, 14.

[51] Lombard-Jourdan, 25–28.

[52] Boussard, 318.

le château du Louvre, construit vers 1200 du côté de la menace principale, vers la Normandie, pour d'évidentes raisons stratégiques (figure 11).[53]

La croissance de Paris s'accélère ainsi nettement au début du XIIIe siècle, à la faveur du rattachement de l'Artois, puis surtout avec l'annexion de la Normandie au domaine royal. La bourgeoisie parisienne, dont les statuts des environs de 1170 sont inspirés de ceux des marchands rouennais, pourra alors bénéficier d'une politique royale nettement défavorable à ces derniers, et l'administration du royaume pourra disposer de revenus considérablement accrus. Il peut paraître étonnant que cette nouvelle situation n'amène qu'assez tardivement le développement des représentations de grands ecclésiastiques et de grands féodaux du royaume. Les représentations en ville des grands du royaume apparaissent au milieu du XIIIe siècle avec celle d'Alphonse de Poitiers, frère du roi Louis IX. Elles se multiplient en fait surtout lors du règne de Philippe le Bel, à la fin du siècle.[54] Il en est de même semble-t-il pour celles des grands écclésiastiques. De ce point de vue, le retard par rapport à Rouen est en partie dû au fait que Paris n'est pas siège d'un archevêché. Il faut aussi se rappeler que Philippe-Auguste avait exclu les grands du royaume de son conseil.[55]

Le développement de l'Université, ou tout du moins du quartier qui l'abrite, est, on l'a vu, un fait tardif, puisqu'il n'est guère significatif avant le milieu du XIIIe siècle. Le premier collège à s'installer dans le futur 'Quartier latin' est en 1248 celui des Cisterciens, suivi en 1252 de celui des Prémontrés, et en 1254 de la Sorbonne. Ainsi, l'urbanisation ne remplira-t-elle la nouvelle enceinte de la rive gauche que dans le courant du XIVe siècle.

Les éléments topographiques à notre disposition montrent donc que Rouen est vers 1180 d'une taille nettement supérieure à Paris, et prend l'aspect d'une capitale sous l'égide de Henri II, bien avant que Paris ne fasse de même au tournant du XIIIe siècle à la suite d'une politique de développement délibérée menée par Philippe-Auguste. La croissance parisienne, largement plus tardive, ne sera suivie qu'avec retard de l'apparition des fonctions de représentation, liées en partie à la formation d'une cour.

Devant cette importance de fait prise par la métropole normande, la question doit être posée de savoir si Rouen aurait pu devenir capitale à proprement parler, donc royale. Il aurait fallu une fusion du royaume anglais et du duché normand, fusion difficile à imaginer, tant pour les anglais Winchester, et surtout maintenant Westminster et Londres, étaient attachées aux rites royaux;[56] on voit de plus mal les normands s'assujettir à un gouvernement basé Outre-Manche, pays à l'origine conquis. Et puis il y a une différence de statut. Eriger la Normandie en royaume, c'eût été braver une règle de légitimité alors bien établie, ou tout du moins en voie de renforcement, au mépris de l'inféodation reconnue au roi de France, même si Henri II ne rendit jamais hommage à son suzerain pour ses terres continentales.

---

[53] Boussard, 322–24.
[54] Cazelles, 19–21.
[55] John W. Baldwin, 'L'entourage de Philippe-Auguste et la famille royale', *La France de Philippe-Auguste, le temps des mutations*, colloque CNRS 29 sept.–4 oct. 1980, Paris 1982, 73.
[56] David Bates, *William the Conqueror*, Londres 1989, 71; Marjorie Chibnall, *Anglo-Norman England 1066–1166*, Oxford 1987, 21.

Enfin, pour reprendre les termes de Lucien Musset, 'l'aristocratie laïque . . . se sent de plus en plus anglaise', et l'on a vu combien cette évolution pouvait être sensible dans l'espace de la métropole normande.[57]

Rouen est ainsi une ville plus importante que Paris jusqu'à la fin du XIIe siècle, alors que les développements souhaités par Philippe-Auguste commencent à prendre leur effet, permis par l'accroissement des revenus royaux. La superficie enclose à Rouen atteint 85 hectares sous Henri II, celle de Paris fait plus que doubler en 1190, en passant à 114 hectares. En fait, à l'annexion de la Normandie par le roi de France en 1204, les deux villes paraissent s'équilibrer du point de vue de la superficie réellement occupée. Mais Rouen perd alors à la fois une bonne partie de son rôle politique, un immense territoire où exercer son commerce, de même que son rôle de plaque tournante commerciale et financière entre l'Angleterre et la Normandie. Paris connaît un sort inverse, accroît considérablement son aire d'influence géographique, et voit sa croissance stimulée par ce nouveau contexte et la stabilisation de la résidence royale dans ses murs. L'illustration monumentale en est la nouvelle enceinte de 1211 en rive gauche, qui porte l'ensemble protégé à 189 hectares, et les lotissements qui petit à petit emplissent l'espace enclos.[58]

C'est à ce moment que Paris, jusque-là capitale d'un petit royaume, devient réellement une métropole. La croissance de Paris, fortement encouragée par Philippe-Auguste, est parallèle à l'accroissement de son influence géographique. Elle amène par ailleurs la stagnation d'autres villes 'capitales' de principautés sur lesquelles s'étend la domination royale, comme Chartres, qui restera comme figée dans les limites de son enceinte de 1182, ou Reims, dont le développement s'arrête avec les lotissements des années 1180. Dans les deux cas, c'est à la suite de la mise sous tutèle royale de la famille comtale en 1201, avant la commise de la Normandie en 1202.[59]

Le droit fut ainsi pour Philippe-Auguste une arme décisive pour dominer ses vassaux et stopper la croissance des principales villes entourant Paris. A Rouen, il faudra attendre les décisions prises par son successeur, Louis VIII peu après son accession au pouvoir en 1224, pour relancer la croissance de la ville, d'ailleurs fort activement.[60] Philippe-Auguste aura maintenu Rouen immobile pendant vingt ans, à l'ombre d'un nouveau château, le château de Bouvreuil, mieux à même de la contrôler, tout en promouvant parallèlement le développement de sa capitale.[61] L'émergence de Paris au détriment des autres villes capitales de principautés à la fin du XIIe siècle fut donc largement due à la volonté et à la ténacité d'un roi.

Au vu des éléments que l'on peut connaître, une certaine similitude apparaît entre les politiques menées à Rouen par Henri II, puis par Philippe-Auguste à

---

[57] Musset, 1982, 293.
[58] 189 hectares, et non 272 comme cela a été souvent écrit, cf. Simone Roux, 'De Philippe-Auguste à François 1er', *Paris, genèse d'un paysage*, sous la direction de Louis Bergeron, Paris 1989, 58. Ces 272 hectares comprennent la superficie de la Seine, qui à notre sens doit être exclue.
[59] Billot, 89–94; Desportes, 60–72. Sur le rôle du droit et son utilisation par Philippe-Auguste, Georges Duby, *Le Moyen Age, 987–1460, de Hugues Capet à Jeanne d'Arc*, Paris 1987, 258–62.
[60] BMR; registre U 1, fo 16–18, janvier 1224, décision d'étendre aux quartiers protégés par l'enceinte de Henri II les privilèges de la ville. BMR, Tiroir 63, mai 1224, vidimus de 1279, mesures économiques favorisant le développement de la draperie et autorisations de lotir la berge de la Seine et les anciens fossés. Voir aussi à ce sujet Gauthiez, 1991, 241.
[61] Gauthiez, 1991, 206–8.

Paris, avec un décalage d'une génération. On peut ainsi se poser la question d'une possible influence de l'oeuvre de Henri II sur le souverain français.

La principale convergence concerne le rôle des enceintes nouvelles dans les deux villes. Celle que nous pouvons attribuer à Henri II à Rouen a été conçue, semble-t-il, pour favoriser le développement de nouveaux quartiers dans les secteurs protégés, jusque là largement libres de constructions. Ainsi, quatre nouvelles paroisses apparaissent à Rouen avant 1208. Il semble qu'il en ait été de même à Paris avec l'enceinte en rive droite de 1190, d'autant qu'avec celle de 1211 en rive gauche l'objectif royal est explicite, puisque le but est que la ville se remplisse: 'ut tota civitas usque ad muros plena domibus videretur'. Dans les deux villes, l'objectif fut atteint avec une totale réussite, de même que d'ailleurs à Chartres où un processus identique prit place après la construction d'une nouvelle enceinte en 1182.

On connait par certaines sources l'éducation de qualité que Henri II avait reçue de son père. L'Archevêque Rotrou la donne en exemple dans une lettre adressée au roi à propos de son fils Henri. On peut la citer dans une traduction de Charles de Beaurepaire au début de ce siècle: 'Nous savons, par expérience, tout le profit que votre royaume a tiré de l'éducation libérale que vous avez reçue dans les premières années de votre adolescence . . . S'il faut gouverner l'Etat, engager des batailles, tracer des camps, construire des machines de guerre, renouveler des retranchements, élever des citadelles; s'il faut enfin assurer le repos d'un peuple libre, le culte de la justice, le respect des lois, de bonnes relations avec les peuples voisins, les livres ne fournissent-ils pas . . . les leçons les plus parfaites? Un roi sans lettres, c'est un vaisseau sans rames, un oiseau sans ailes . . .'.[62]

Les préceptes de Rotrou trouvent un écho dans le *Liber de principis instructione*, de Giraldus Cambrensis: 'Pour vivre une époque sûre et heureuse . . ., il faut se prémunir (de la guerre et de ses calamités) . . . en enfermant les villes dans des murs, en les entourant de fossés, et en les munissant d'armes et de provisions en quantité suffisante, de même dans ce but (il faut) donner du coeur aux citoyens au moyen de libertés'.[63]

Chapelain déçu de Henri II, Giraldus Cambrensis s'adresse ainsi au futur Louis VIII en donnant précisément le gouvernement de Henri II lors de la première partie de son règne en exemple. Ce court passage est le parfait résumé de ce que l'on peut supposer de l'action du roi à Rouen. Du point de vue strictement militaire, au vu de l'humiliation de Philippe obligé en 1193 de lever le siège de la ville en brûlant ses machines de sièges, on sait qu'elle fut particulièrement efficace.

L'exemple cependant semble se limiter à l'utilisation de l'enceinte comme moyen de développement. Il n'y eut pas à Paris de politique de réorganisation de la ville telle qu'on la voit à Rouen autour du pont reliant les nouveaux aménagements de la rive gauche et la ville close dont la forme nouvelle, arrondie, a quelque chose d'idéal. Il n'y eut pas non plus d'encouragement comparable de la bourgeoisie, peut-être n'était-elle pas encore assez puissante. En résumé, l'urbanisme de Henri II fut celui d'une capitale, et de fait Rouen fut la seule ville

---

62 Charles Robillard de Beaurepaire, *MSAN*, xxv, 314–15.
63 Giraldus Cambrensis, *Liber de principis instructione*, *Opera*, viii, édité par G.F. Warner, Londres (RS) 1891, 44.

angevine à être ainsi traitée. L'urbanisme de Philippe Auguste à Paris consista, plus simplement, à faire grandir sa ville.

Cette étude sur l'évolution comparée de Rouen et Paris sur ces périodes permet d'avancer un certain nombre de conclusions. La première est que, longtemps avant Paris, Rouen prend de fait les aspects d'une capitale, que ce soit par sa taille ou par les activités liées au gouvernement qui y sont présentes. Le paradoxe est que la nation dont elle est alors la ville principale n'existe pas, ou plutôt est divisée en deux, sans qu'une union apparaisse possible dans la logique du XIIe siècle. Rouen est de plus située dans la partie au statut inférieur, le duché normand. L'élévation au statut de ville royale, seul à même de confirmer et peut-être de stabiliser cet état de fait, ne fut pas possible. La question du statut de la ville fut certainement posée, en effet, Richard et Jean réactivent à la fin du XIIe siècle la cérémonie d'investiture ducale dans la cathédrale Notre Dame. Lindy Grant a montré, dans son analyse de l'édifice, et en particulier du choeur construit vers 1220–30, qu'il était un 'uneasy compromise between Reims, the coronation church of the Capetian kings . . . and St Etienne at Caen, the house to which William the Conqueror bequeathed the ducal regalia'.[64] Jusqu'aux années 1230 certains rouennais, et non des moindres puisque le chapitre cathédral et l'archevêque sont concernés, ont donc pensé que Rouen pourrait retrouver son statut de métropole politique.

Notre Dame est aussi, en cette fin de XIIe siècle, et de manière réaffirmée, un mausolée dynastique, au travers de l'inhumation des restes de Henri le Jeune et de Richard Coeur de Lion.

En fait, les circonstances ont conduit à une évolution moins favorable, sous les coups de boutoir d'un Philippe Auguste tenace, inspiré – ironie de l'histoire – par la politique de Henri II, particulièrement à Rouen. L'influence fut technique, si l'on peut dire, mais aussi due à la puissance même de la métropole normande, longtemps dominante en taille et en richesse. On sait par ailleurs combien l'orgueil de Philippe Auguste avait pu être touché par la munificence de son vassal Plantagenêt, qu'il s'agisse de Henri II ou de son successeur Richard.

L'effacement de Rouen de la scène internationale laissa la place à des villes prêtes à prendre le relai. Paris bien sûr, qui bénéficia dans un premier temps surtout du champ économique libéré. Londres aussi qui, de première ville en Angleterre qu'elle était depuis déjà un certain temps, devint d'un coup la première ville du royaume. Les fonctions de capitale s'y affirmeront dans le courant du XIIIe siècle, avec par exemple la multiplication des résidences de grands du royaume à partir des années 1230.[65] Bordeaux fut la troisième ville à directement en profiter, en devenant la capitale des domaines anglais en France, reprenant une partie du commerce entre le Continent et la Grande-Bretagne, particulièrement celui des vins. Il peut paraître surprenant dans ce contexte que le développement de Rouen au XIIIe siècle, après 1224, ait été aussi vigoureux, et que la ville soit restée d'une taille proche de celle de Paris jusque vers 1250, et même jusqu'au XIVe siècle, puisqu'une évaluation quantitative récente lui donne une masse de

---

[64] Lindy Grant, cf. note 20.
[65] Jacques Heers, *La ville au Moyen Age*, Paris 1990, 460.

l'ordre de 70% de celle de la capitale française à cette époque.[66] L'explication est probablement à rechercher dans les fonctions respectives des deux villes. Rouen était vraisemblablement plus productive, plus tournée vers l'industrie et le commerce, en un mot avait une tradition plus entreprenante. Paris était plus dépendante du siège de l'administration du royaume. Les grands bourgeois rouennais, une fois l'orage passé, surent reconvertir leur activité, particulièrement vers la draperie. Il n'est pas indifférent, à cet égard, de constater qu'au début du XIVe siècle le patriciat rouennais prend une part déterminante au milieu royal à Paris et au financement des emprunts royaux.[67]

Une dernière conclusion se doit, à mon sens, d'insister sur l'importance prise par les décisions d'ordre urbanistique dans le développement de ces villes. Les politiques urbaines menées montrent la vision stratégique qu'avaient les souverains – du moins certains d'entre eux – de l'importance de leurs villes, notamment du point de vue démographique et économique. L'urbanisme fut bien souvent un outil déterminant dans l'affirmation et le développement de leur pouvoir. On voit combien il a pu jouer dans le jeu des puissances capétienne et angevine en cette fin de XIIe siècle.

---

[66] Bernard Gauthiez, 'La topographie de Paris, Florence et Rouen au XIVe siècle', séminaire à l'Institut de Recherche sur les Civilisations de l'Occident Moderne, Université de Paris-Sorbonne, 5 mars 1993, à paraître.
[67] Gauthiez, 1991, 268–69.

CHANGES IN ENGLISH CHANT REPERTORIES IN THE ELEVENTH CENTURY AS REFLECTED IN THE WINCHESTER SEQUENCES

David Hiley

Sequence Repertories

It was only to be expected that the changes at the top of the church hierarchy after the Conquest should have had consequences for the celebration of the liturgy, and, since chant is an essential component of the liturgy, caused changes in the repertories of chant to be sung. One of the categories of chant most affected was the sequence, the grand syllabic chant sung immediately after the alleluia of mass in the Middle Ages. Since the sequence was a relative newcomer in the Roman-Frankish liturgy established in Carolingian times, not hallowed by the authority of St Gregory, church musicians generally (not just in post-Conquest England) seem to have felt themselves relatively free to compose new sequences in response to local requirements. In doing so they often retained a traditional sequence melody while providing it with a new text. As is well known, something of this sort was already done by Notker of St Gall at the end of the ninth century. A large proportion of the sequences in pre-Conquest manuscripts from Winchester have texts unknown elsewhere, whereas nearly all the melodies used at Winchester can be found in other sources. The variability in choice of sequences between different churches can be seen, for example, in Table 1, which lists the sequences for Easter and Pentecost sung at Winchester before the Conquest, St Gall in the tenth century, St Martial at Limoges in the eleventh, and Saint-Évroul and Cambrai in the twelfth.

Sequence repertories are therefore a good starting point for investigations into the relationships between the liturgical uses of different churches or changes in liturgical practice.

It so happens that the only sizeable collections of sequences which survive from pre-Conquest England are those in the Winchester manuscripts Oxford, Bodleian Library, Bodley 775 and Cambridge, Corpus Christi College, 473, whereas practically all our post-Conquest collections are from different churches, and we have nothing directly comparable with them from Winchester itself, that is, no post-Conquest gradual, troper or missal from Winchester with the full cycle of sequences for the church year. Looking at the later sources from other churches, the indications are clear enough that rather little of the old Winchester repertory survived the Conquest. But it is more satisfactory to trace the changes within a single institution, and luckily this is possible, for the Winchester sources received numerous additions in the eleventh and twelfth centuries. Admittedly, they do not give us the full cycle of sequences which would have been required, but they

Table 1   Easter and Pentecost sequences in selected sources

WINCHESTER
Easter Sunday	*Fulgens preclara*
during the week	*Prome casta concio, Pange turma*
Pentecost Sunday	*Benedicta sit beata trinitas*
during the week	–

ST GALL
Easter Sunday	*Laudes salvatori*
during the week	*Is qui prius, Christe domine laetifica, Agni paschalis, Grates salvatori, Laudes deo concinat, Carmen suo*
Pentecost Sunday	*Sancti spiritus*
during the week	–

ST MARTIAL
Easter Sunday	*Fulgens preclara*
during the week	*Exultet nunc, Laetabunda, Stans a longe, Dic nobis, Candida concio, Prome casta concio*
Pentecost Sunday	*Benedicta sit beata trinitas, O alma trinitas deitas, O alma trinitas deus*

(no clear distinction is made between Sunday and weekday sequences, or between Pentecost and Trinity sequences)

SAINT-ÉVROUL
Easter Sunday	*Fulgens preclara*
during the week	*Prome casta concio, Concinat orbis, Laudes Christo redempti, Sempiterno devote*
Pentecost Sunday	*Sancti spiritus*
during the week	*Resonet sacrata, Eia musa, Alma chorus domini, Christe salvator*

CAMBRAI
Easter Sunday	*Fulgens preclara*
during the week	*(Eia) Dic nobis, Sancta cunctis letitia, Laudes salvatori*
Pentecost Sunday	*Fulgens preclara* (a different continuation)
during the week	*Sancti spiritus, Alma chorus domini, In omnem terram*

Sources:	WINCHESTER	Oxford, Bodleian Library, Bodley 775
	ST GALL	Sankt Gallen, Stiftsbibliothek 381, 376, etc.
	ST MARTIAL	Paris, Bibliothèque Nationale, lat. 1120
	SAINT-ÉVROUL	Paris, Bibliothèque Nationale, lat. 10508
	CAMBRAI	Cambrai, Bibliothèque municipale, 60

nevertheless tell us a good deal about the changes in practice consequent upon the Conquest.[1]

Both the Winchester manuscripts contain a collection of sequences as part of the main corpus of the manuscript. The date of the core collection in Corpus 473 may be placed in the last decade of the tenth century, that of Bodley 775 in the

1 The sequences were first listed by Walter Howard Frere, in *The Winchester Troper*, Henry Bradshaw Society 8, London 1894. There has been more than one edition of the texts local to Winchester. See, for example, E. Misset and W.H.J. Weale, *Analecta liturgica II: Thesaurus hymnologicus* 1–2, Lille and Bruges 1892, and *Analecta Hymnica* xl (1902). In preliminary studies for a critical edition with music I have investigated the sources of the original repertory and

middle of the eleventh century. These sequence collections are of great importance not only as witnesses to the Winchester sequence repertory but also because there is an almost total lack of contemporary collections from other centres in the whole English-North French area (nothing from Corbie, St Denis or Tours, for example). Both manuscripts remained in use for a considerable period of time. This is clear from, among other things, the revision of the musical notation in Bodley 775, very obvious evidence of a later effort to keep the manuscript in use. The notational signs for many sequences were erased and in some cases replaced by staff notation, which may be dated to the later twelfth century. Figure 1 shows, bottom right, the start of the sequence *Pange turma* with the original notation. For the sequence *Prome casta concio* (middle left) the notation has been erased and some stave lines entered, but no new notation. Top left is the end of *Fulgens preclara*, for which the new notation has been provided.

It is clear that the sequences with the later notation were still being sung at the later date. These are listed in Table 2. They are sequences for the highest feasts of the Temporale, excepting the sequence for Birinus.

Table 2 Sequences with revised notation

fol.	scribe	incipit	assignment
136r	E	Celica resonant	Christmas
137v	D	Laus armonie	John Evangelist
139v	E	Nato canunt	Circumcision
140r	E	Epiphaniam domino	Epiphany
142r	E	Fulgens preclara	Easter
145r	E	Rex omnipotens (notation incomplete)	Ascension
146r	E	Benedicta sit beata trinitas (notation inc.)	Trinity
159v	M	Caelum mare tellus	Birinus

Possibly it had been intended to renotate all the sequences whose notation was erased (Table 3).

Whole sides of some sequences were erased to create space for new pieces. It would seem that the sequences thus mutilated can hardly have been required any longer (Table 4).

Yet I do not understand why *Laude iocunda* should have been partly obliterated in this way, since after the Conquest it was easily the most popular sequence for St Peter. Nothing among the later additions would replace it, although it is true that two other sequences for St Peter were available, entered immediately before

compared both literary and musical variants in other sources. See 'The repertory of sequences at Winchester', *From Rome to the Passing of the Gothic: Western Chant Repertories and their Influence on Early Polyphony: A Conference in Honor of David G. Hughes*, Harvard University 1990 – publication in preparation; and 'Editing the Winchester sequence repertory of ca.1000', *Cantus Planus*, International Musicological Society Study Group Cantus Planus, papers read at the Third Meeting, Tihany, Hungary, 19–24 September 1988, ed. László Dobszay, Péter Halász, János Mezei and Gábor Prószéky, Budapest 1990, 99–113.

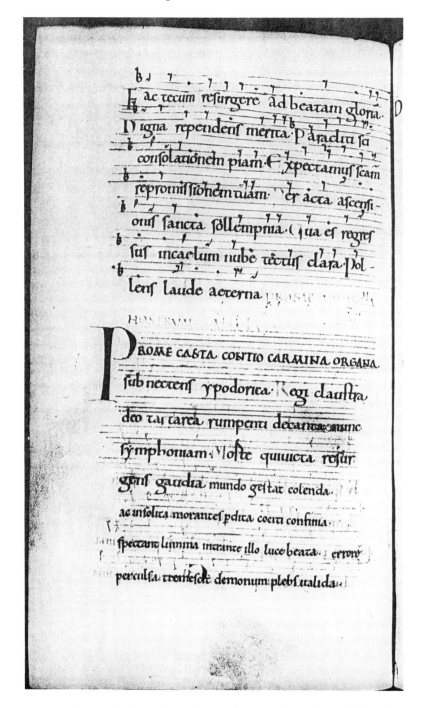

Figure 1. Oxford, Bodleian Library, MS Bodl. 775, fols 143v–144r
(reproduced by permission of the Bodleian Library, Oxford)

144

Dant suspiria fletuum alta repagula
quisic audax fregerit mirantur tunc
fortia. Sic ad supera redit cum turma
gloriosa & timida refouet discipulo
rum corda P recelsa huius trophea
admirantes flagitamus nunc uoce
dedliua. Virginum inter agmina more
amur pretiosa. colere ut pascha.
Galilea inquit sacrata presulgide con
tueri lucis exordia. PROSA EDUX
DNS ALLELVIA Pange turma corde
uultu xpo preconia. Concelebrans
ammiranda Pascbalia sacramenta.
O beneficia o quam mirifica. omni seclo
posita Alta polo micantia. Magna
solo fulgentia. Q uelic & ampla

:

Table 3 Other sequences whose notation was erased

fol.	*incipit*	*assignment*
143v	Prome casta concio	Easter week
147r	Alle caeleste	Annunciation BMV
148r	Exulta celum (i) (notation partly erased)	John Baptist

In the following case I am not sure if the notation for the first few verses, now missing, was ever entered:

| 157r | Alme caelorum (notation partly erased) | All Saints |

Table 4 Sequences partly erased to make way for new pieces

fol.	*incipit*	*assignment*
152r	Laude iocunda	Peter
178r	Salve mater Christi	BMV
178v?	(a sequence whose start is erased)	?
179v	Exulta celum (ii)	John Baptist
181r	Laudes . . . (notation partly erased)	All Saints?

Laude iocunda in the original collection. But on account of this erasure one is led to speculate that these two manuscripts, even with all their additions, cannot have been the only sources of sequences at Winchester in the later Middle Ages. I should suppose that there were at least a couple of other, newly compiled sequentiaries designed to replace the older manuscripts with their somewhat haphazard accumulation of alterations, replacements and additions to the Winchester sequence repertory. It looks rather as if Bodley 775 and Corpus 473 started life as formal reference books containing a complete record of the pieces required in various chant categories, and were then used more and more as informal notebooks in which recent arrivals and new creations could be jotted down. For during the same period in which the old sequences were altered, numerous new pieces were added to both manuscripts in a variety of hands. Figure 2 shows an opening where the text hand is the same throughout but two notators have been at work, one for *Magnus deus* (bottom left, top right), an earlier one for the *Alle cantabile* (ends top left) and *Fulget dies iocunda* (starts bottom right).

The added sequences in Bodley 775, which date roughly from the time of the Conquest onwards, and at any rate reflect the preferences of Norman musicians, are twenty-nine in number. Similar in nature are the eleven added sequences in Corpus 473. The order in which they were entered by various hands into the manuscripts can be ascertained roughly, but a demonstration of the paleographical layering of the additions would extend the length of this discussion to an undesirable extent, without being of paramount importance for what I wish to explain, namely, the Norman derivation of the additions. Rather brutally, in Table 5 I have arranged the sequences into liturgical order, which facilitates comparison with the old repertory.

If one were to combine the list of sequences with revised notation in Bodley 775 with those added to the two manuscripts, one would still not have a complete picture of the Winchester sequence repertory of the twelfth century. The number of sequences is undoubtedly too small, the feasts not represented are too important. It is inconceivable, for example, that Winchester alone should not have sung sequences on the Sundays of Advent, yet here the notation was not revised. There should be more sequences for the Blessed Virgin Mary and something for John the Baptist.

Table 5 also indicates concordances with sources from Normandy and elsewhere in North France. On the far right I have given in abbreviated form the probable area of origin of the sequence.[2]

When surveying the likely origins of the sequences added to the Winchester repertory, I shall not try to make a distinction between Bodley 775 and Corpus 473. My remarks are pitched at a more general level, where the fact that four of the eleven sequences in Corpus 473 are not in Bodley 775 is not of great significance.

For Christmas the original repertory had only *Celica resonant*, which was also known in Normandy and would have continued to be sung at Winchester after the Conquest. Now we have also *Sonent regi nato*, present in the repertory of Rouen cathedral, but not Norman monastic manuscripts, in the Norman-Sicilian books, and in Angers (96), Chartres and Paris. *Verbum legibus* (Corpus 473 only) is found elsewhere only in books of Cambrai (Cambrai, Bibl. mun. 60 and 78, neither with staff notation; I have not been able to find a transcribable version).

Gloriosa dies, the sequence previously sung at Winchester for Stephen, achieved no great distribution in North France, and was not used in Norman churches. *Magnus deus* was the widely-known replacement.

Pura deum, the old sequence for the Holy Innocents, was sung at Angers (97) and Cambrai, and also turns up in the ordinals of Mont-Saint-Michel, but was otherwise unknown in Normandy. *Celsa pueri* was the widely-known replacement.

We may assume that *Epiphaniam domino* continued as the main sequence at Epiphany. *Gaude virgo ecclesia Christi* is known outside Winchester only from the Barking ordinal and Hereford missals. It is therefore almost certainly a new English composition rather than a foreign import.

In the old corpus, *Fulgens preclara* was the original sequence for Easter Sunday and would have remained so. For Pentecost *Benedicta sit beata trinitas* was originally provided, but in the later Middle Ages this was regularly assigned to Trinity Sunday. Notker's *Sancti spiritus* was by then a standard choice for Pentecost.

The five Easter sequences added in Bodley 775 (none in Corpus 473) were all known in Norman uses and probably imported via Norman exemplars. But the distribution of the five in Normandy is not consistent. The four Pentecost sequences were likewise not sung everywhere in Normandy. There seems to be a particularly close relationship between the Winchester selection and that of Rouen cathedral manuscripts, also the manuscript London Royal 8.C.xiii, which, however, lacks the sequences for Pentecost. The case of the last sequence, *Gaude mater ecclesia*, is not uncharacteristic. Rouen books are the only continental

---

[2] My thesis *The Liturgical Music of Norman Sicily: A Study Centred on Mss 288, 289, 19421 and Vitrina 20–4 of the Biblioteca Nacional, Madrid*, University of London King's College 1981, compares sequence repertories in over sixty sources.

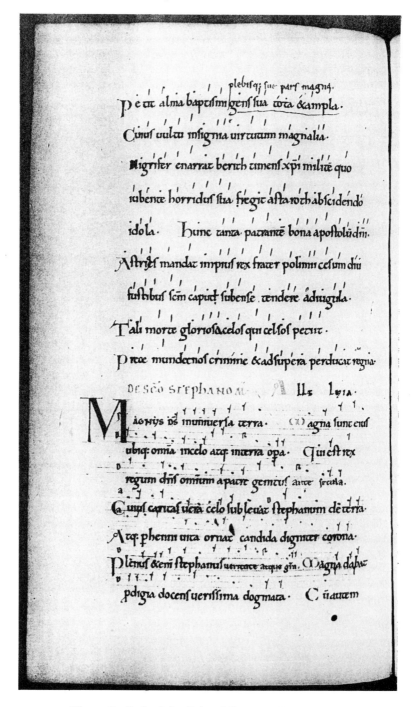

Figure 2. Oxford, Bodleian Library, MS Bodl. 775, fols 131v–132r
(reproduced by permission of the Bodleian Library, Oxford)

132

predicaret iam presencia. N re redempcionis nostra

gaudia. Intento insuperna celi patet ianua. O usq:

circū stanti plebi uoce publica. S acra plenis gracia.

Ecce deī uideo ā mirabilem g̃tam. C laritate fulgida.

tq: ihm stantem inuirtutis dei dextera. C ū hoc

audisse & mpia gens iudaica dans fremitū ēcrā quassat

lapidibus stephani membra. S ed stat fortiter

pariens martir & orat. N ec is xpe noxam statuas.

& iam accipe animā meam. E tcū hoc dixisset

indomino obdormiuit pace eterna. T u& nobis

martir ostephane sempiterna L impetra

gaudia amen. Alle luia

y laet dies iocunda inqua xpi gaudet aecclesia.

Promartiris eterna sci iusti palma & lucida.

tas tenera uirtus inquo sed ualida. M undi prospera

tempnit acuincit forcia. G racia quē deus

mira facit inipsa pollere infancia. P rophetie illi

Table 5 Concordances with the added sequences

Bodley 775	Corpus 473	AH vol.p/no.	incipit	assignment
x	x	50.282/212	Sonent regi nato	Christmas
	x	10.22/19	Verbum legibus	Christmas
x	x	53.353/220	Magnus deus	Stephen
x		53.264/162	Celsa pueri	Innocents
x	x	40.25/6	Gaude virgo ecclesia Christi	Epiphany
x		37.30/23	Iubilans concrepa	Easter
x		40.42/23	Psalle lirica carmina	Easter f2?
x		53.69/37	Dic nobis	Easter f3
x		40.39/21	Concinet orbis	Easter f4?
x		53.65/36	Laudes salvatori	Easter
x	x	53.322/200	Sancti spiritus	Pentecost
x		54.21/14	Laudes deo devotas	Pentecost
x		7.90/77	Eia musa	Pentecost f2
x	x	40.53/33	Gaude mater ecclesia filiorum	Pentecost f3
x	x	9.39/47	Gaude virgo mater ecclesia	Dedication
x		53.171/99	Concentu parili	Purification? (2/2)
x		53.186/106a	Aurea virga prime matris	Assumption? (15/8)
	x	53.359/223	Precelsa seclis colitur	Vincent (22/1)
x		54.52/35	Sancti merita Benedicti	Benedict (21/3, 11/7)
x		9.28/30	Laudamus te rex	Holy Cross (3/5, 14/9)
x		53.392/244a	Alma choors una laudum	Swithun (2/7)
x		40.288/337	Gaudens Christi presentia	Swithun (2/7)
x		37.265/306	Psallat ecclesia mater decora	Swithun (2/7)
x		40.269/314	Solennitate rutilans	Peter ad Vincula (1/8)
x	x	40.180/204	Dies sacra dies ista	Ethelwold (1/8, 10/9)
x		53.220/129	Alle cantabile	Bartholomew (24/8)
x		53.306/190	Ad celebres	Michael (29/9)
x		9.141/186	Supernam armonicam	Denis (9/10)
x		40.58/43	Alme deus cui serviunt	All Saints (1/11)
x		40.226/256	Fulget dies iocunda	Justus (10/11)
x		53.294/181	Sacerdotem Christi Martinum	Martin (11/11)
x		40.132/140	Clara cantemus	Andrew (30/11)
x		53.367/228	Clare sanctorum	Apostles

	Rou	Ou	Jum	Evr	Mi	Bec	Dij	Sic	Mag	Che	Par	Den	Cam	A96	A97	Fon	Cha	Fle	Origin
	Rou							Sic			Par			A96			Cha		late NFr
													Cam						late NFr
	Rou	Ou	Jum	Evr		Bec	Dij	Sic		Che	Par	Den	Cam	A96	A97	Fon	Cha	Fle	old Fr?[1]
	Rou	Ou	Jum			Bec		Sic		Che	Par	Den					Cha	Fle	late NFr
																			Winchester
y	Rou							Sic											Norman
y	Rou	Ou			Mi	Bec	Dij												Norman
y	Rou	Ou	Jum			Bec		Sic	Mag	Che	Par		Cam				Cha		old Fr?[2]
y	Rou	Ou	Jum	Evr		Bec		Sic		Che	Par								late NFr
y	Rou						Dij	Sic		Che			Cam						St Gall
	Rou	Ou	Jum	Evr	Mi	Bec	Dij	Sic		Che	Par	Den	Cam	A96	A97	Fon		Fle	St Gall
	Rou							Sic		Che	Par	Den							late NFr
	Rou	Ou	Jum	Evr	Mi	Bec	Dij	Sic	Mag										Norman
	Rou																		Norman
				Evr		Bec													Norman
	Rou																		St Gall
	Rou	Ou	Jum	Evr	Mi	Bec		Sic	Mag	Che	Par	Den	Cam		A97	Fon	Cha	Fle	late NFr
								Sic			Par							Fle	old Aquit.?
																		Fle	Fleury?
								Sic	Mag										Norman
	Rou	Ou		Evr	Mi			Sic							A97	Fon		Fle	late NFr
																			Winchester
																			Winchester
																			Winchester
																			Winchester
																Fon			Canterbury?
	Rou	Ou		Evr	Mi	Bec	Dij	Sic	Mag		Par	Den	Cam			Fon	Cha	Fle	old Aquit.
	Rou	Ou		Evr		Bec		Sic	Mag							Fon			late NFr
																			Winchester
																			Winchester
	Rou	Ou	Jum	Evr	Mi	Bec	Dij	Sic			Par		Cam			Fon			old German
																			Winchester
y	Rou	Ou	Jum	Evr	Mi	Bec	Dij	Sic	Mag	Che	Par	Den	Cam			Fon		Fle	St Gall

[1] North French?
[2] Aquitainian?

sources for it. In later English sources it turns up only in the Haughmond and Ronton graduals, which of all English uses have the most similarity to Rouen cathedral use. *Laudes deo devotas* is different, in that it was known in Paris, at St Denis, Chelles and Compiègne, and therefore may not have come to Winchester via Normandy.

No sequence in the old repertory can be unequivocally designated as a Dedication chant. The Dedication sequence *Gaude virgo mater ecclesia* is known on the continent only from the Saint-Évroul troper and the Bec missal. In such cases it is difficult to say whether the piece came to England from Normandy or travelled in the reverse direction.

Among the sequences that remain to be considered, that is those for the Proper of Saints and the Common of Saints, if for the moment we set on one side those for English saints, the highest number of concordances is once again to be found in the Rouen sequence repertory.

The Melodies

Among the sequences for the English saints *Alma choors* was a favourite Norman sequence from the Common of Saints, where it was possible to insert the required saint's name in certain verses to make it suitable for any local usage. The rest of the sequences for Swithun, Ethelwold und Justus were not sung abroad, but it is of interest to know what melodies were employed for them, and also for the other texts not known elsewhere. I could have excluded from this group *Alle cantabile* for Bartholomew, which may well have originated in Canterbury, although it is also in the Fontevrault gradual of the fourteenth century.[3] That is nine sequences in all, for which Table 6 gives the probable model melody.

In fact, most of the sequence melodies in this group were already known at Winchester before the Conquest, and indications of new Norman influence are rather sparse.

Gaude virgo ecclesia Christi for Epiphany uses the widely known melody 'Post partum virgo' or 'Greca', whose best-known text was *Hac clara die* for the Blessed Virgin Mary, already part of the original corpus at Winchester.

Both *Gaudens Christi presentia* and *Psallat ecclesia mater decora* for Swithun take up a widely-known melody, 'Quoniam deus [minor]', which at Winchester was already sung for *Caelum mare tellus* (Birinus; probably composed with *Magnus deus* in mind). The new sequence for Stephen, *Magnus deus*, also uses this melody.

Solennitate rutilans has the same melody as another sequence for Peter, *Nunc luce alma*, which is a relative newcomer to the international repertory. *Nunc luce alma* may well be a Norman composition. It is the almost universal choice in later English books for the feast of Peter's Chains, but is somewhat less common in North France (again almost always for Peter's Chains): Fontevrault, Chelles, two Sicilian books, in Normandy itself Rouen cathedral and St Ouen, Jumièges,

---

[3] Queen Emma had bought St Bartholomew's arm from the bishop of Benevento and given it to Canterbury. See R.W. Southern, *Saint Anselm and His Biographer: A Study of Monastic Life and Thought, 1059–c.1130*, Cambridge 1966, 23 n and 234–5.

Table 6   Model melodies used for texts known only, or first, at Winchester

Gaude virgo ecclesia Christi . . . spirituales – Epiphany
   melody 'Post partum virgo' or 'Greca', usual text *Hac clara die* (BVM), in old
   Winchester repertory

Gaudens Christi presentia – Swithun (2/7)
Psallat ecclesia mater decora . . . Swithunus – Swithun (2/7)
   melody 'Quoniam deus [minor]', usual text *Magnus deus* (Stephen), at Winchester
   Caelum mare tellus (Birinus; probably composed with *Magnus deus* in mind) in old
   repertory.

Solennitate rutilans – Peter ad Vincula (1/8)
   usual sequence *Nunc luce alma* (Peter), probably Norman.

Dies sacra dies ista – Ethelwold (1/8, 10/9)
   usual melody, 'Pretiosa', usual text *O alma trinitas*, at Winchester *Gaudet clemens*
   and *Alme caelorum* (both All Saints).

Alle cantabile – Bartholomew (24/8)
   melody 'Multifarie', usual text *Nato canunt omnia* (Christmas) already in old
   Winchester repertory.

Alme deus qui serviunt – All Saints (1/11)
   melody 'Quoniam deus [maior]', otherwise hardly known, but already in old
   Winchester layer for *Promere chorda* (Martin).

Fulget dies iocunda – Justus (10/11)
   melody 'Letabitur iustus', usual text *Concelebremus sacram* (Common of Saints),
   already used at Winchester for *Laurea clara* (Lawrence).

Clara cantemus – Andrew (30/11)
   melody 'In omnem terram', usual text *Laude iocunda* (Peter & Paul).

Mont-Saint-Michel and Bec. It is possible that the Winchester cantor was confronted with *Nunc luce alma* as a new piece for the feast of Peter's Chains, and
decided to write a fresh text for the new melody.

Dies sacra dies ista for Ethelwold puts to use an old melody, 'Pretiosa', which
was already known at Winchester, being used for *Gaudet clemens* and *Alme
caelorum*, both for All Saints.

Alle cantabile uses the melody 'Multifarie', associated chiefly with the
Christmas text *Nato canunt omnia*, already part of the old Winchester repertory.

Alme deus qui serviunt for All Saints was one of the first added sequences in
Corpus 473, and it is not surprising that its melody, 'Quoniam deus [maior]' is
already to be found in the old layer for the text *Promere chorda* for St Martin. It
was by no means a common melody, being found elsewhere only at Nevers, for
Deus quoniam magnus for the patron saint Cyricus.

Fulget dies iocunda for Justus also has an old melody, 'Letabitur iustus', used
at Winchester for *Laurea clara* (Lawrence) and abroad for texts of the Common of
Saints: *Concelebremus sacram* (Angers 97, Saint-Évroul, Aquitainian sources)
and *Convenite mellico* (only at Chartres).

Clara cantemus for Andrew has the melody 'In omnem terram'. The best-known text for this melody was *Laude iocunda* for Peter and Paul, but another text exists, *In omnem terram*, for the Common of Saints and other occasions:

Cambrai	Pentecost
Royal 8.C.xiii	Common of Saints
Rouen	Pentecost, Common of Saints
Fleury	Common of Saints
Chelles	Common of Saints

One would like to know whether the old *Laude iocunda* (Peter) or *In omnem terram* was the starting-point for *Clara cantemus*, the new Winchester piece. Except that the text for Andrew refers to the obvious fact that he was Peter's brother, I see nothing in the literary text to decide the matter, and there are no significant divergences in the music of the three pieces which could decide the matter one way or the other.

Thus far I have looked for concordances for the sequence texts added to the Winchester repertory, and, in the case of literary texts not known abroad I have looked to see if foreign (Norman) melodies were employed. The results of these searches indicate that, as one would expect, there is a fair degree of Norman influence upon Winchester practice, and some hints that Rouen cathedral usage played an important part in it. At this point one should acknowledge that the sources upon which one can draw for comparison are but patchily distributed in time and place, and it would be unwise to place too great weight on any one indicator. Our Rouen sequence sources are all of the thirteenth century and later, while from St Ouen we have but one late medieval missal with text incipits only for the sequences, and from Mont-Saint-Michel only ordinals with text incipits for the sequences. From Saint-Évroul we have the twelfth-century troper (one would dearly love to have at least one or two more of the twelve tropers mentioned in the twelfth-century library list of Saint-Évroul), from Jumièges a fourteenth-century gradual, from Bec a thirteenth-century notated missal. The only other source which may come from Normandy is the fragmentary troper London, BL, Royal 8.C.xiii, and in view of the concordances which have cropped up between this manuscript, Rouen and Winchester, it is particularly frustrating that its provenance cannot be more clearly determined.

It is somewhat disappointing that no new melodies appear to have been composed for the additions to the Winchester sequence repertory. The old repertory had only three, it is true. (Some possibly unique melodies in the original collection are only partially preserved, and there are organal voices for two sequences otherwise unknown.) But one might have hoped for at least one new creation. On this evidence, Winchester was less creative than Canterbury, where new melodies and texts for Alphege, Dunstan and Augustine appear to have been produced.[4]

---

[4] See my forthcoming article 'Chant composition at Canterbury after the Norman Conquest', *Festschrift Max Lütolf*.

The Literary Character of the Replacement Texts

The character of the literary texts of the sequences for St Peter is indicative of some of the various currents mingling in sequences of the 'first epoch'.

Laude iocunda, like many old West Frankish pieces (our sources are predominantly Aquitainian) makes play with musical imagery. 'Symphonia rythmica' (well-proportioned harmonious sounds) are to be joined with the words.[5] Two other texts were sung at Winchester before the Conquest, *Sanctus Petrus* and *Agmina leta*. *Sanctus Petrus* is another old West Frankish text, which treats the two saints Peter and Paul in absolutely even-handed parallelism, in that the first versicle of each pair is devoted to Peter, the second to Paul, with as much correspondence between matter and manner as the poet can manage. *Agmina leta* (known only from the Winchester books, the Crowland gradual, the Sherborne missal and the Book of Cerne) must be modelled upon *Sanctus Petrus*, for not only does it use the same melody, it adopts the same scheme of parallelism. There are one or two examples of the abstruse language which not infrequently turns up in Winchester texts, for example in verse 3. In 3a Peter vanquishes the sorcerer Simon (Acts 8), whereupon it is Paul's turn to perform a similar act (with reference to Acts 13): 3b. *Paulus herile sperma contorquens Elymae gemella obcaecavit lumina*.

Since both *Nunc luce alma* and *Solennitate rutilans* are ostensibly for the feast of Peter's Chains, Paul is not mentioned. In contrast to the above texts, *Nunc luce alma* strikes a rather conventional note, with a little musical imagery and a minimal reference to Peter's power to bind and to loose, to his possession of the key of heaven and his ability to loose our chains as his own were loosened. It is perhaps not surprising that a Winchester poet thought he might provide something more colourful. *Solennitate rutilans* mentions various events in Peter's life (which is a common way of compiling sequence texts): his calling, his abandoning of the fisherman's trade to be a fisher of men, and various miracles which he performed. There is nothing especially abstruse or elevated about it.

This rather homely narration of events from a saint's life is also a feature of some of the imported replacements for older sequences in the Winchester repertory. *Magnus deus*, for example, is of this type, whereas *Gloriosa dies* is not. *Celsa pueri* and *Pura deum* are both narrative. The older *Arce superna* for Benedict is long and laudatory in a general way (though clearly referring to a monastic saint); the effectiveness of the piece must have stemmed largely from the hypnotically repetitive melody. The new sequence for Benedict, *Sancti merita*, brings in as much as possible of Benedict's life and works.[6] For Michael, the old *Ecce pulchra* (if it was indeed intended for Michael) is really a sequence for All Saints or the Common of Saints, whereas *Ad celebres* is topical in the grand manner. For

---

[5] The significance of this vocabulary is discussed by Lars Elfving, *Étude lexicographique sur les séquences limousines*, Studia Latina Stockholmiensia 7, Uppsala 1962. On a passage in *Laude iocunda* (AH 7 no. 183) see Elfving p. 254.

[6] *Sancti merita Benedicti*, like most other Benedict sequences, draws upon the miracles recounted in the Second Dialogue of St Gregory (Migne *PL* 66, 125–204). The sequence is edited in *Eight Sequences for St. Benedict and St. Scholastica* by David Hiley with a translation of the text by Dom Augustine Morris OSB, Wimborne 1980.

Martin the old layer had *Promere chorda*, which is specific enough, and altogether less measured in tone than the popular *Sacerdotem Christi* (possibly German).[7]

It is not certain whether the new sequences for Swithun and Ethelwold replaced the old ones or supplemented them. In the case of Swithun, the tendency towards emphasis on the good deeds of the saint, as opposed to more neutral eulogia, is not discernible. In the old layer of Corpus 473 only, Swithun shared the sequence *Laude resonet* with Birinus: at least both are equally important, insofar as both are mentioned once and deeds of a generally saintly nature enumerated. Of the three new sequences for Swithun, *Alma choors* will do for any saint, as already mentioned, while *Gaudens Christi presentia* is in the old-fashioned enthusiastic Winchester style with learned-sounding expressions, and *Psallat ecclesia mater decora* takes up the musical terminology of the old West Frankish sequences. Only at one place is there a reference to the miracle-working relics of the saint. On the other hand, the old and new sequences for Ethelwold typify the older and newer style of text. *Laude celebret* (in Bodley 775 only) is a long, adulatory text which, as the melody requires, includes some acclamatory phrases (the first is 'Via lux veritas') found in all texts for this music. *Dies sacra dies ista* may be a humdrum effort, but it does refer quite specifically to notable events in Ethelwold's life, such as his nearly being poisoned, his driving of the clerics from the church of Winchester and installing monks, the effect of his curse upon the pilfering monk, and the prodigy of the flask of oil.[8] It is not possible to say whether there is any link between the sequence and the pre-Conquest lives of St Ethelwold by Wulfstan or Aelfric, wherein these events are naturally recounted.

In general the substitutions therefore favour topicality of content, directness and simplicity of expression.

Conclusions

It may be useful to summarise once again the direction from which the added sequences came to Winchester, that is, not their ultimate place of origin but the place from which Winchester probably received them, as indicated by the concordance patterns in Table 5. Judgement in such matters must often be rather subjective, dependent on the chance survival of sources, and based on such uncertain grounds as that a sequence is found in more Norman sources than any others. That our extant sources for many churches are of the thirteenth century and

---

[7] Two verses of *Promere chorda* are in direct speech, whereby they paraphrase passages likewise highlighted in direct speech from Sulpicius Severus' *Vita Sancti Martini*. Cf. Sulpice Sévère, *Vie de Saint Martin*, ed. Jacques Fontaine, I: *Introduction, Texte et Traduction*, Sources Chrétiennes 133, Paris 1967, p. 258 (Ep. 3, 3) and p. 338 (Ep. 3, 10).

In *Notker der Dichter und seine geistige Welt*, Berne 1948, Wolfram von den Steinen argued that *Sacerdotem Christi Martinum* itself replaced an older text, *Tuba nostrae vocis*, which already referred to Martin's most famous deed, his dividing his cloak with a beggar, and to his miracles. The more accomplished *Sacerdotem Christi* therefore avoided such allusions and focussed attention on Martin's universal veneration. See *Notker der Dichter*, ii, 125–7 (texts) and i, 435–8 (discussion). The usurpation of *Promere chorda* at Winchester may then have been due to a general sense that both text and melody were simply provincial.

[8] *Chronicon Monasterii de Abingdon*, ed. J. Stevenson, RS 2, 2 vols, 1858, ii.255–266, see §12, 15, 22, 21.

later demands an act of faith that they actually preserve more or less the same repertory as would have been known in Norman times.

Normandy (10):
> *Iubilans concrepa, Psalle lirica, Concinet orbis, Laudes salvatori, Sancti spiritus, Eia musa, Alma choors, Supernam armonicam, Sacerdotem Christi Martinum, Clare sanctorum*

Rouen? (2):
> *Gaude mater ecclesia filiorum, Concentu parili*

Normandy (Rouen?) or elsewhere in North France (2):
> *Sonent regi, Laudes deo devotas*

Normandy or elsewhere in North France (7):
> *Magnus deus, Celsa pueri, Dic nobis, Aurea virga, Precelsa seclis, Laudamus te rex, Ad celebres*

North France (1):
> *Sancti merita Benedicti*

North-East France (Cambrai?) (1):
> *Verbum legibus*

Normandy or England (1):
> *Gaude virgo mater ecclesia*

English (4):
> *Gaude virgo ecclesia Christi, Solennitate rutilans, Alle cantabile, Clara cantemus*

Winchester (5):
> *Gaudens Christi presentia, Psallat ecclesia mater decora, Dies sacra dies ista, Alme deus cui serviunt, Fulget dies iocunda*

The frequency of the concordances with Rouen and with the manuscript London, BL, Royal 8.C.xiii was noticed above. It would be easy to over-emphasise the significance of these connections. Royal 8.C.xiii contains a full collection of ordinary of mass melodies and tropes which does not in all respects coincide with the numerous pieces in this category added to Bodley 775. We have no comparable collection from Rouen. Although Royal 8.C.xiii is clearly affiliated to other Norman sources of ordinary of mass chants, including the Norman-Sicilian ones, it is not possible to determine its exact place of origin by repertorial comparisons.

The connection with Rouen may, however, be more than a freak indication from insufficient data, since, as is well known, the priest Walkelin of Rouen was installed as Bishop of Winchester after the Conquest. It is true that we have no information about liturgical initiatives on Walkelin's part. His brother Simeon had been a monk of Saint Ouen. When Simeon was elevated to the see of Ely, Godfrey of Cambrai became prior, and in the *Annales de Wintonia* there is at least a hint that Godfrey had some interest in liturgical matters.[9]

In summing up the results of this brief survey, it may be stated that Norman importations had a significant impact upon the Winchester repertory – that is, pieces composed in Normandy as well as sequences which came to England *via*

---

[9] David Knowles, *The monastic order in England: from the times of St Dunstan to the Fourth Lateran Council, 940–1216*, Cambridge 1963, 130, 178.

Normandy. A certain number of new sequence texts were composed in Winchester, but no new sequence melodies. Compared with the achievement of establishing the splendid repertories of the late tenth century – sequences, proper tropes, ordinary tropes, and polyphony – these may seem to be very modest efforts, and to reinforce the impression which David Knowles communicated many years ago: 'how small was the development that had taken place since the days of Dunstan'.[10] It is also a pity that whatever creative effort is discernible remains anonymous. But rarely do our relatively scarce sources allow us to pinpoint the place and date of composition with any accuracy. The attachment of a cantor's name to the composition usually remains no more than a hypothesis. Could one detect unmistakeable fingerprints of literary or musical style in these pieces, clues to the composer's identity, one would have come a good step further in removing the veil of anonymity, but at least in musical matters this is not possible.

Yet what we see at Winchester – the adoption of a large number of pieces known elsewhere, the addition of a few items in response to local needs – is the rule rather than the exception. Even in the largest collections, for example those in the Saint-Évroul troper or the Norman-Sicilian tropers, the proportion of new compositions is small. Thus in the Saint-Évroul troper there are 57 sequences, of which only one is unique: predictably, the one for Ebrulphus himself, with text *Solennis erit dies*, to one of the best-known of all sequence melodies, 'Mater' or 'Musa'. Furthermore, none of those for which the troper is the earliest source can be assigned to Saint-Évroul as place of origin. It is much easier to look at concordance patterns and establish a likely *area* of origin – Normandy, North East France, England, etc. – than to point to one institution. Cantors were on the whole unwilling to venture too far out on a limb, preferring to assemble pieces already sanctioned by use. That a very real change of use took place in England is abundantly clear. The sequences and ordinary of mass chants in sources of the twelfth century (the two St Albans sources, the later part of Caligula A.xiv) have almost nothing in common with the old Winchester repertory. The significance of the additions to Bodley 775 and Corpus 473 is that they show, uniquely, some of the steps taken at one particular institution to rejuvenate and refashion the repertories established in the age of Dunstan to reflect the needs and tastes of the age of Lanfranc and Anselm.

[10] Knowles, 557.

TOWARDS ADMISSION AND INSTITUTION: ENGLISH EPISCOPAL FORMULAE FOR THE APPOINTMENT OF PAROCHIAL INCUMBENTS IN THE TWELFTH CENTURY

B.R. Kemp

Some time before September 1142 Bishop Alexander of Lincoln supposedly notified the archdeacon of Buckingham that he had received and instituted Gloucester abbey's clerk, William son of Theodoric, as parson of the churches of Wraysbury and Langley Marish. The relevant part of his charter reads:

> Nos autem . . . predictum Willelmum suscepimus et eum in prenominatis ecclesiis personam instituimus . . .[1]

If this text could be relied upon, it would constitute a very early use in an English episcopal charter[2] of the later standard formula of 'institution' to represent the bishop's action in appointing to a parochial benefice. I hope to show in due course, however, that the charter's text, preserved only in a late thirteenth-century copy, is probably a forgery perpetrated some decades after its purported date. Indeed, one of the points I intend to make in the course of this paper is that, by careful analysis and dating of the various formulae found in this category of twelfth-century episcopal charters, possible or probable forgeries of this kind may be detected. Beyond that, however, the aim is to examine the process by which, after much diplomatic diversity, experimentation and development in the twelfth and early thirteenth centuries, the standard formulae of the later middle ages were arrived at.

The task is complicated by a number of factors. Firstly, it seems clear that English bishops did not begin to issue charters dealing specifically with the appointment of parochial incumbents until well into the twelfth century, in most dioceses not before about 1150, and that, when they did, the clerks and scribes who produced the charters, having few guides to help them, found it necessary to devise what they considered appropriate formulae by which to designate the relevant episcopal acts. This resulted in a considerable variety of diplomatic forms, often reflecting some common or basic attitudes, but, certainly for some decades, without any degree of standardisation. At first sight, this variety and apparent lack of precision in the use of terms can bewilder modern readers familiar with the fixed terminology of the later middle ages, and to some it may

---

[1] *Historia et Cartularium Monasterii Sancti Petri Gloucestriae*, ed. W.H. Hart, 3 vols, RS 1863–7, ii, no. 710. The charter is discussed in M. Brett, *The English Church under Henry I*, Oxford 1975, 145.

[2] The term 'charter', rather than 'actum', is used throughout this paper.

appear vague, unsophisticated or even at times verging on the careless. There has
been a consequent tendency to force twelfth-century formulae into a later mould
by translating them into what are considered to be their later equivalents. Although this practice may be justified to some extent, it can easily mislead and
should be avoided as far as possible, since it implies that the precise concepts of a
later age were of universal application in the twelfth century and, moreover, may
obscure one's view of how contemporaries understood the bishop's role in filling
parochial benefices.

Other problems arise in connection with formulae. Some terms commonly in
use were capable of bearing slightly different meanings, especially when also
employed by archdeacons, rural deans and others. Another potentially confusing
phenomenon is that bishops often used the same formulae for the appointment to
parochial benefices of either individual clerks or religious houses. The latter type
of appointment usually signified an early form of appropriation of a church to a
monastery, but, since English appropriations were rarely formalised in detail until
quite late in the century, and given the variety of formulae in use in this period, the
exact nature of some episcopal acts is not always clear. One must equally be alert
to the possibility that some episcopal charters in favour of religious houses,
though given in a bishop's name and authenticated by his seal, were composed
and written by the beneficiaries, a circumstance which might result in the inclu-
sion of idiosyncratic or archaic formulae quite different from those normally
employed by that bishop. Finally, since episcopal charters were rarely dated
before the last decade of the twelfth century,[3] it is frequently difficult to provide
accurate dates for the occurrence of particular formulae, especially when dealing
with charters from a long pontificate like Jocelin de Bohun's at Salisbury (1142–
84).

This paper makes no claims to completeness. It is offered as a provisional study
based mainly on printed collections of episcopal charters and on my own quite
extensive but far from exhaustive searches in manuscript sources. Since we have
no English episcopal registers before the thirteenth century (and very few before
its latter half),[4] bishops' charters of the twelfth century have first to be laboriously
gathered together from a great diversity of sources before any meaningful analyti-
cal work can begin. Happily, enough collections of such charters have already
been made and published to enable at least tentative conclusions to be reached. Of
great assistance have been the volumes already published in the British
Academy's *English Episcopal Acta* series, covering the dioceses of Lincoln,
Norwich and Hereford (for the whole of the twelfth century), and Canterbury and
York (for, respectively, the second and first halves of the century).[5] To these can

---

3   C.R. Cheney, *English Bishops' Chanceries 1100–1250*, Manchester 1950, 81–5. The exceptions
were mainly those which recorded judicial settlements.
4   See, in general, D.M. Smith, *Guide to Bishops' Registers of England and Wales*, Royal Historical Society, London 1981. The earliest surviving English registers (in roll form) are those of Hugh
of Wells, bishop of Lincoln 1209–35, and Walter de Gray, archbishop of York 1215–55.
5   *English Episcopal Acta*, British Academy 1980 – (continuing) [hereafter *EEA*]: I, *Lincoln
1067–1185*, ed. D.M. Smith, 1980; IV, *Lincoln 1186–1206*, ed. idem, 1986; VI, *Norwich 1070–
1214*, ed. C. Harper-Bill, 1990; VII, *Hereford 1079–1234*, ed. J. Barrow, 1993; II, *Canterbury
1162–1190*, eds C.R. Cheney, B.E.A. Jones, 1986; III, *Canterbury 1193–1205*, eds C.R. Cheney, E.
John, 1986; V, *York 1070–1154*, ed. J.E. Burton, 1988. I am grateful to Dr Julia Barrow for
permission to see her text of the Hereford volume before publication.

be added the volume on Chichester diocese published some decades ago by the Canterbury and York Society,[6] and a number of editions of individual bishops' charters from various dioceses, which have appeared since the 1930s.[7] In addition, many episcopal charters have been printed or calendared in editions of monastic and other cartularies or charter collections. Nevertheless, a large number remain in manuscript, and no comprehensive survey will be possible until the British Academy's project is complete.

One of the striking features of English episcopal charters as a whole in the twelfth century is their increasing concern with parish churches. This is hardly surprising, given the spread of the Gregorian reform programme and the consequent efforts of bishops to gain effective supervision over the churches in their dioceses. Where churches are mentioned in charters of the first half of the century, it is most often in the context of confirming lay or other gifts of churches to religious houses, reference being only rarely made to the clerks who will serve them. Confirmations of this kind continue to be granted throughout the century and beyond, but, mainly from about 1150, references to the service of churches and actual appointments of incumbents figure with growing frequency. By the early thirteenth century a significant proportion of surviving episcopal charters fall into this category. A number of reasons for this rise can be adduced: the increasing use of writing in general over the period; the growing need of bishops to forestall false claims to benefices by issuing charters to the rightful incumbents; and, especially after the English crown had asserted its right to deal with advowson disputes, the desire of patrons and incumbents to fortify themselves with documentary title against any challenge in the royal courts.[8] Even so, it is sobering to realise that, despite their increasing numbers, such charters as survive cover only a very small proportion of the appointments which took place. Thousands have gone unrecorded, or at least the records have not been preserved, and even where copious cartularies have survived from monasteries with several churches in their possession, they often contain few if any episcopal charters appointing incumbents to their churches. Any study of twelfth-century formulae needs to keep in mind the limited scope of the evidence.

By about the middle of the thirteenth century the procedures and formulae involved in the filling of parochial benefices had largely become standardised throughout the English church and, despite some continuing variation, remained

[6] *The Acta of the Bishops of Chichester 1075–1207*, ed. H. Mayr-Harting, Canterbury and York Society lvi, 1964.
[7] For example, A. Morey, *Bartholomew of Exeter, Bishop and Canonist*, Cambridge 1937, 135–59; A. Saltman, *Theobald, Archbishop of Canterbury*, London 1956, 233–534; *The Letters and Charters of Gilbert Foliot*, eds A. Morey, C.N.L. Brooke, Cambridge 1967; E.F. Kealey, *Roger of Salisbury*, Berkeley, Los Angeles and London 1972, 223–71; M.G. Cheney, *Roger, Bishop of Worcester 1164–1179*, Oxford 1980, 228–312.
[8] On these points, see M.T. Clanchy, *From Memory to Written Record: England 1066–1307*, 2nd edn, Oxford 1993, esp. chapter 2; Alexander III's decretal to William, bishop of Norwich (below, p. 165); J.W. Gray, 'The Ius Praesentandi in England from the Constitutions of Clarendon to Bracton' *EHR* lxvii, 1952, esp. 481–90. Several advowson cases recorded on the early Curia Regis Rolls turned on the production of episcopal charters of institution or the like, but the importance of having such a charter is revealed in a case as early as 1156 x 1161, in which the crown intervened and where the successful claimant produced a charter of Jocelin, bishop of Salisbury, *quae donationis titulum astruebat* (*The Letters of John of Salisbury*, eds W.J. Millor, H.E. Butler, C.N.L. Brooke, 2 vols, Oxford 1986 [rev. edn], 1979, i, no. 102).

essentially the same thereafter. In normal circumstances, after presentation of a suitable clerk by the true patron, the appointment comprised the acts of admission and canonical institution, performed by the bishop, followed by the clerk's induction into corporal possession of the benefice, carried out by the archdeacon. Admission signified that the bishop had accepted the clerk as a fit person to serve the church, and institution represented the commitment to him of the cure of souls. The ceremony of induction gave him formal and legal seisin of the benefice with all its rights and possessions.[9] (Basically the same procedures were followed when monasteries acquired benefices by episcopal acts of appropriation, but in these cases institution did not confer the cure of souls, which was committed instead to a separately appointed perpetual vicar.[10]) Both the bishop's and the archdeacon's acts could be performed by properly constituted deputies or commissaries, but this did not alter the succession of acts involved. It was thus a threefold process. Examples of it, using precisely these formulae, can in fact be found very early in the century. In 1204, for instance, Robert of Hardres, archdeacon of Huntingdon, announced that he had received a mandate from William, bishop of Lincoln, declaring that he had admitted and canonically instituted the abbot and monks of Colchester as parsons of Walkern church, and ordering the archdeacon to induct them into corporal possession of the church, which he had duly done.[11] Analogous cases, but with slightly different formulae, occur in the later twelfth century.[12] In that century in general, however, not only was parochial appointment not always seen or described as a threefold process, but, as has been mentioned, a variety of formulae were employed at different times to describe the stages that were involved. Moreover, diplomatic practice varied from one diocese to another and often from one bishop to another in the same diocese.

Nevertheless, as far as the acts performed by the bishop are concerned,[13] some basic trends can be detected. Firstly, the earliest episcopal charters dealing with parochial appointments were frequently couched in terms of gifts or grants. In this respect they resembled the charters issued by 'owners' or patrons when granting churches to clerks, for these, as Stenton long ago observed, were still in the mid-twelfth century commonly couched in 'the ordinary formulae of enfeoff-

[9] G.W.O. Addleshaw, *Rectors, Vicars and Patrons in Twelfth and early Thirteenth Century Canon Law*, St Anthony's Hall Publications 9, York 1956, 19–22; *Acta Stephani Langton Cantuariensis Archiepiscopi A.D. 1207–1228*, ed. K. Major, Canterbury and York Soc. 1, 1950, xxxv–xxxvi. Where the bishop himself was patron, admission and institution were replaced by collation (Addleshaw, 21), although occasionally thirteenth-century bishops speak of collation *and* institution.

[10] See, for example, the documents by which Eynsham abbey appropriated Histon church in 1268 (*The Cartulary of Eynsham Abbey*, ed. H.E. Salter, 2 vols, Oxford Hist. Soc. xlix, li, 1906–8, i, nos 19–22) and, for comment, B.R. Kemp, 'Monastic possession of parish churches in England in the twelfth century' *Journal of Ecclesiastical History* xxxi, 1980, 15–16.

[11] *Cartularium monasterii S. Johannis Baptiste de Colecestria*, ed. S.A. Moore, 2 vols, Roxburghe Club 1897, i, 126. The bishop's mandate does not survive, but his charter of admission and institution is *EEA* IV, no. 230.

[12] In 1191, for example, the archdeacon of Ely stated that the bishop of Ely had received (*suscepit*) and instituted the canons of Waltham in the *personatus* of Babraham church and had instructed the archdeacon to put them into corporal possession (*The Early Charters of . . . Waltham Abbey, 1062–1230*, ed. R. Ransford, Woodbridge 1989, no. 123).

[13] For the final act of induction or its equivalent, commonly performed by the archdeacon, see my paper 'Archdeacons and parish churches in England in the twelfth century', *Law and Government in Medieval England and Normandy*, ed. George Garnett and John Hudson, Cambridge 1994, 353–4.

ment', suggesting that 'no fundamental difference was recognised at this time between a church and the other profit-yielding appurtenances of an estate.'[14] Many charters of this kind are known, often from monastic patrons and usually without any indication that the diocesan had been involved, although, as Dr Brett has argued, lack of an episcopal charter or of reference to the bishop is certainly no proof that the latter had not acted.[15] What was being emphasised in these early patronal charters was that the recipient of a church was to hold it of the donor(s) as of his superior lord(s) in a quasi-feudal manner, though usually in free alms.[16] However, canon law asserted that churches were not to be given or conferred except by the bishop or on his authority.[17] It gradually became desirable, therefore, to have an episcopal charter recording the fact that the bishop, rather than the patron, had granted and confirmed the church to its new incumbent, even though such charters almost invariably stated that the bishop had acted in response to a presentation (sometimes a petition) from the patron. So, for example, some time in the early 1160s, Bishop Henry of Blois of Winchester conceded and confirmed Catherington church to Peter the clerk in free alms at the presentation of Nuneaton priory, to which he was to pay seven marks annually.[18] At first sight this does not look like the appointment of an incumbent, but the thirteenth-century endorsement on the surviving original charter, in calling it an institution, indicates that it was.[19]

Alternatively, many early episcopal charters focussed on the fact that, in response to the patron's presentation, the bishop had received a clerk into a church or benefice (using the verb *suscipere* or *recipere*). This marked a conceptual step forward from the language of grant and confirmation, since it carried with it the notion of positive approval of the presented clerk, which only the bishop or someone acting for him could give. It meant that, from the bishop's point of view, the clerk concerned was an acceptable person to serve the church. Quite often at this time no other episcopal act was mentioned, but in several examples reference was also made to the bishop's gift or grant of the church. The formula of 'reception', or its later form 'admission', continued to appear in most subsequent charters, but gradually, and at first occasionally, the bishop's act of 'institution' or the equivalent was recorded as well, and was sometimes mentioned on its own.[20] This

---

[14] *Documents Illustrative of the Social and Economic History of the Danelaw*, ed. F.M. Stenton, British Academy 1920, lxxiv.

[15] Brett, *English Church*, 144.

[16] An annual pension would normally be payable to religious patrons, but not to the laity.

[17] Brett, 141–3; Kemp, 'Archdeacons', 355–6.

[18] BL, Additional Charter 47855. The priory's charter to Peter the clerk, of possibly doubtful authenticity, makes no reference to the bishop, but clearly concedes the church to Peter as the new incumbent (BL, Add. Ch. 47854; see *The Heads of Religious Houses, England and Wales, 940–1216*, eds D. Knowles, C.N.L. Brooke, V.C.M. London, Cambridge 1972, 217 n. 2).

[19] A little earlier Archbishop Theobald of Canterbury conceded and confirmed to Edmund *presbiter* the church of Bekesbourne, which Robert of Hastings had conceded to him. That this was a parochial appointment is placed beyond doubt by Robert's charter notifying his men (of Bekesbourne) that, with Theobald's advice and concession, he has conceded the church to Edmund *sacerdos*, and requesting and requiring them *ut predictum Edmundum presbiterum vestrum diligatis, honoretis, serviatis, obediatis et illum ut decet per omnia intendatis* (Saltman, *Theobald*, 288–9; *Cartulary of the Priory of St Gregory, Canterbury*, ed. A.M. Woodcock, Camden 3rd ser. lxxxviii, 1956, no. 35).

[20] As Addleshaw pointed out (*Rectors*, 4), the use of *instituere* or *constituere* in the western Church from the early 12th century onwards represented the Gregorian Reform's revival of

development further enhanced the bishop's role in the sense that, having accepted the patron's candidate, he had now proceeded canonically to appoint him to the benefice on episcopal authority and to commit the cure of souls to him. That is not to say, however, that twelfth-century incumbents appointed without reference to institution or the like filled their benefices any less completely than those who were, or were to be, specifically instituted. The case was rather that the appropriate formulae changed as understanding of the bishop's role was refined, and particular forms which were perfectly adequate at one time were in due course either discarded or subjected to tighter canonical definition. It was, nevertheless, a gradual process, and older forms often overlapped for many years with those newly introduced. For example, long after 'institution' had made its first appearance, the verbs *suscipere* and *recipere* continued to be used alone and, as is clear from other evidence, were capable of subsuming the notion of institution. For instance, in c.1180 x 1181 Gilbert Foliot, bishop of London, announced that he had 'received' Walden priory into the *personatus* of Arkesden church (Essex), whereas both the archbishop of Canterbury, who after inspecting Foliot's charter confirmed the act, and the archdeacon of Colchester, who stated that he was present on the occasion, referred to the bishop's act in terms of 'institution'.[21] Clearly, to both of them, if Foliot had received, he had also instituted. Even some way into the thirteenth century, when the formula of reception had generally been replaced by that of admission, the latter could still quite often stand alone for the entire episcopal process.[22]

With this broad outline in mind, the next step is to focus our attention on a selected group of dioceses to see what formulae their episcopal charters employed in the twelfth century, what diplomatic changes took place, and the extent to which they individually approached the later medieval formulae of admission and institution. The dioceses to be considered are Salisbury and Chichester in the south, Lincoln and Norwich in the east, and Hereford in the west midlands.

In the diocese of Salisbury the first instances of appointment to parochial benefices occur among the charters of Jocelin de Bohun, whose pontificate extended over the exceptionally long period from 1142 to 1184, although none of the surviving cases is actually earlier than 1155. Not surprisingly, given that the bishop ruled at a time of considerable diplomatic development in this field, his charters employ a wide range of formulae in various combinations. What may well be the earliest example, dating from 1155 x 1165, contains unusually cumbersome phraseology, which seems to indicate a primitive stage in the emergence of appropriate formulae to describe the bishop's acts. The bishop declares that, at Robert son of Fulcred's presentation, he has conceded and given Padworth church and its dependencies to Robert de Port, clerk, and has canonically received (*recepisse*) him into the *personatus* and 'fulfilled in respect of Robert as much as belongs to our right' (*quantum ad ius nostrum pertinet in Rodbertum explevisse*).[23]

formulae for the appointment of incumbents which had been employed in Visigothic Spain in the 6th and 7th centuries, but whose use in this connection had since died out.
[21] *Foliot Letters and Charters*, no. 446; *EEA* II, no. 221; BL, Harley MS 3697, fol. 38v.
[22] *Acta Stephani Langton*, xxxvii and nos. 30, 74; below, n. 35.
[23] *Facsimiles of Early Charters in Oxford Muniment Rooms*, ed. H.E. Salter, Oxford 1929, no. 25. Robert son of Fulcred's letter (no. 26) simply informs the bishop of his gift and concession in (free) alms.

The final passage clearly refers to the clerk, but its meaning is somewhat obscure; it may have involved an order for induction or, conceivably, the equivalent of institution. At any rate, its lack of precision is notable. The formula of 'conceding and giving' the church was, as has been said, a common feature of early appointments, but it occurs again only rarely at Salisbury. Jocelin's twelve other surviving charters in this category employ much more concise formulae, but even so with little sign of an evolution of standard usage. Moreover, as in other dioceses, the same range of possibilities was apparently available irrespective of whether an individual or a religious house was being appointed to a benefice.

Certain general observations may, however, be made. Firstly, in contrast with the complicated terminology of the example discussed above, the dispositive clauses of Jocelin's other charters commonly refer to one episcopal act only. Thus, in 1166 x 1177 he merely received (*suscepisse*) a clerk as parson of the churches of Shinfield and Swallowfield; between 1158 and 1182 he 'constituted' a clerk as parson of Powerstock church; in 1177 x 1184 he instituted Gloucester abbey in the *personatus* of Boyton church; and in c.1180 x 1184 he received (*recepisse*) a clerk as perpetual vicar of Englefield church.[24] In one such case, however, a supplementary term was introduced into the confirmatory and sealing clause: in 1165 x 1178 the bishop stated that he had received (*recepimus*) an individual as parson of Upavon, but in the final clause referred to this act as *hanc nostram concessionem et institutionem*.[25] This is a further illustration of the fact that reception could imply institution. Most of Jocelin's remaining charters speak of two episcopal acts in the dispositive clauses, using various combinations of formulae. In c.1170 x 1182, for instance, Jocelin received (*suscepimus*) and canonically constituted the canons of Southwick priory as parsons of Swindon church; in c.1170 x 1184 he received (*suscepisse*) and canonically invested a chaplain as perpetual vicar of Tockenham church; and in c.1173 x 1178 he received (*suscepisse*) and canonically instituted an individual as parson of Winterbourne Bassett church.[26] The latest surviving charter of Jocelin's pontificate refers to three acts involved in the appropriation of two Windsor churches to Waltham abbey: it declares that he has instituted and 'inparsonated' the canons in these churches, and has caused them to be inducted into corporal possession by his officials.[27]

Secondly, despite the variety of formulae employed in Jocelin's charters, the two verbs, *suscipere* and *recipere*, were those most frequently used to designate the act of receiving a clerk to a benefice (the equivalent of the later admission), with no real sign that either was preferred at any particular time. The verb *admittere* occurs only once, in a charter of c.1170 x 1184 recording the admission

---

[24] *The Cartulary of Carisbrooke Priory*, ed. S.F. Hockey, Isle of Wight Records Series 2, 1981, no. 25; *Charters and Documents illustrating the History of the Cathedral, City and Diocese of Salisbury*, eds W.(H.) R. Jones, W.D. Macray, RS 1891, no. 37; *Hist. et Cart. Glouc.*, i, no. 112; *Reading Abbey Cartularies*, ed. B.R. Kemp, 2 vols, Camden 4th ser. xxxi, xxxiii, 1986–7, ii, no. 796.

[25] PRO Transcripts, PRO 31/8/140A, no. 343; calendared, *Cal. Docs France*, no. 175.

[26] Winchester, Hampshire Record Office, Southwick Priory Register I, fol. 3v – calendared (incompletely), *The Cartularies of Southwick Priory*, ed. K.A. Hanna, 2 parts, Hampshire Record Series ix–x, 1988–9, i, no. I 22; PRO, C115/K2/6683, fol. 275r; BL, Cotton MS Vespasian F.xv, fol. 170v – translated, *The Lewes Chartulary: the Wiltshire . . . portion of the Lewes Chartulary . . .*, eds W. Budgen, L.F. Salzman, Sussex Record Society, additional volume, 1943, no. 47.

[27] *Early Charters of Waltham*, no. 111.

of a priory to a church at a layman's presentation, in effect a preliminary stage in an appropriation process.[28] Similarly, the two verbs used to describe the act of institution, *constituere* and *instituere*, occur in roughly equal numbers, although no instance of either can be certainly dated earlier than the 1170s. As we have seen, however, in one case, which may be as early as the later 1160s, the term 'institution' was introduced into the sealing clause. Finally, we should note Jocelin's employment in 1184 of the verb *inpersonare* in tandem with *instituere* to represent the appropriation of the Windsor churches to Waltham abbey. Though not found again at Salisbury, *inpersonare* occurs in the episcopal charters of other dioceses, and we shall need to return to it later.[29]

A survey of Jocelin's charters thus reveals that, while the terms 'admission' and 'institution' certainly occur, they never appear together and, even towards the end of the pontificate, there was no general trend in favour of their combination. The nearest approach is the linking of *suscipere* and *instituere* in the charter of c.1173 x 1178, where also, for the first time at Salisbury, *instituere* is qualified by the adverb *canonice*.[30] In the course of the two succeeding pontificates, however, admission and institution gradually gained ground. Bishop Hubert Walter (1189–93) has left few charters of any kind, largely because he was abroad for most of his pontificate,[31] but they include one relevant case, dating from 1193 and involving the appointment of an abbey as parson, in which the formula of 'canonical institution' appears with that of 'gift and concession',[32] and, most significantly, during his absence his officials (un-named) made two parochial appointments by means of admission and institution, these being the earliest known instances of the joint formula in Salisbury diocesan charters.[33] Furthermore, admission and institution occur together in four charters of the next bishop, Herbert Poore (1194–1217), at dates ranging between 1196 and 1215, most of the others having one or other of these terms alone.[34] In the charters of his successor, Richard Poore (1217–28), institution is the term most frequently employed, but there is no preference for the joint formula of admission and institution, which occurs only once.[35]

At Salisbury, then, after considerable diplomatic variation under Bishop

[28] Southwick Priory Register I, fol. 3r–v; calendared, *Southwick Cartularies*, i, no. I 21.

[29] See below, pp. 171–2.

[30] See note 26, last reference. *Canonice* occurs in 3 other charters of Jocelin, qualifying the verbs *admittere*, *constituere* and *investire* (see note 26, first two references, and note 28).

[31] He was overseas from early 1190 to the spring of 1193 (C.R. Cheney, *Hubert Walter*, London 1967, 32).

[32] Oxford, Christ Church, Archives, Notley charter roll, mem. 10.

[33] *Reading Cartularies*, ii, no. 696; Taunton, Somerset Record Office, DD.WO. 37/20/1.

[34] For Herbert Poore's charters mentioning both admission and institution, see BL, Cotton MS Tiberius D.vi, fol. 145r; PRO, C115/K2/6683, fol. 151r; Hertford, County Record Office, D/E AS 2; *Calendar of the manuscripts of the Dean and Chapter of Wells*, 2 vols, Royal Commission on Historical Manuscripts 1907–14, i, 526.

[35] Only 6 relevant charters of Richard Poore have come to light so far. The single case of admission and institution (with induction) is PRO, E315/61, fol. 113v, but collation and institution are combined in 3 charters, 2 relating to churches in the bishop's patronage, the third not (*Salisbury Charters*, nos. 136, 165, 173). Admission occurs alone in *Carisbrooke Cartulary*, no. 36, and institution alone in Oxford, Bodleian Library, MS Ch. Berkshire 1211. It is notable that neither *instituere* nor any other verb is ever qualified as *canonice*, although 2 institutions are said to have been made *auctoritate pontificali*. For the use of collation where the bishop was not the patron (not exceptional at this time or earlier), cf. *Acta Stephani Langton*, xxxvi and nos. 53, 68.

Jocelin, a certain trend towards the later standard formulae had set in by the early thirteenth century, but it was by no means fully established as late as the 1220s.

Turning to the diocese of Chichester, we find that, although its episcopal charters contain one early reference to a patron presenting prospective incumbents to the bishop, archdeacon or (rural) dean,[36] no examples of parochial appointments as such have survived from before the rule of Bishop Seffrid II (1180–1204). His charters show that, by his time at least, the joint formula of admission and institution was that most commonly employed, appearing in seven out of ten cases, the earliest dating probably from 1187 x 1189,[37] with the variant form of reception (*recepisse*) and institution in an eighth.[38] In the remaining two cases, both from quite early in his pontificate and both concerning the appointment of individuals, institution appears either alone or with the formula of 'concession, gift and confirmation'.[39] Moreover, in almost every case the institution is said to have been made *canonice*. The short pontificate of the succeeding bishop, Simon of Wells (1204–07), has left two charters in this category, one of which refers to the admission and canonical institution of an individual parson, the other to the concession of a church to a monastery and the canonical institution of its abbot as parson.[40] This evidence suggests that the standard joint formula was in more regular use at Chichester slightly earlier than at Salisbury.

In the diocese of Lincoln, apart from Bishop Alexander's charter with which this paper began, the earliest instances of parochial appointments occur in the pontificate of Robert Chesney (1148–66), and even then they form a minute proportion of his surviving charters. Their formulae, however, are instructive, and one of the first examples displays a similar sort of involved terminology to that found in Jocelin of Salisbury's early charter. In 1152 x 1164 Bishop Chesney declared that, at the request and presentation of Walden priory, he had assigned Kirkham church to Ralph de Diceto, canonically received him (*suscepimus*) into its *personatus* and confirmed the church to him in perpetual alms.[41] The concept here of assigning the church to the recipient is clearly akin to that of a gift or grant, but is interestingly not expressed in the normal language of enfeoffment. The same verb (*assignare*) occurs in another of the bishop's charters, of 1153 x 1166, in which he also states that, at the presentation of three lay patrons, he has received (*suscepimus*) a clerk into the *personatus* of a church and 'introduced', or inducted, him.[42] The reference to induction is notable, since this part of the process was later on normally allocated to the archdeacon or rural dean, but here it may be the equivalent of investiture, a symbolic act carried out by the bishop on the occasion of a clerk's appointment, usually by the handing to him of a ring or,

---

[36] *Acta of Chichester*, no. 5 (cf. *Foliot Letters and Charters*, no. 399). Omitted from *Acta of Chichester* is a charter of Bishop Hilary, dating from the 1160s, by which he conceded a church to Haughmond abbey and 'invested' the abbot, but this was probably not an appointment to the benefice (*The Cartulary of Haughmond Abbey*, ed. U. Rees, Cardiff 1985, Appendix C, no. ii, and cf. nos. iii–iv).

[37] *Acta of Chichester*, nos. 75, 93, 99, 100, 123–5; the earliest is probably no. 93.

[38] *Acta of Chichester*, no. 92.

[39] *Acta of Chichester*, nos. 120, 117.

[40] *Acta of Chichester*, nos. 152, 143.

[41] *EEA* I, no. 277.

[42] *EEA* I, no. 278.

less commonly, a book.[43] The situation is far from clear, however, for the same two verbs used here by Bishop Robert, *suscipere* and *introducere*, occur together in a charter of Geoffrey Plantagenet, bishop-elect of Lincoln 1173–82, appointing a religious house to the *personatus* of a church, but in this case the rural dean is further instructed to 'invest' the monks with the church, while another of Geoffrey's charters states that he has received (*suscepimus*) and canonically instituted the same religious house into the *personatus* of another church, and orders the rural deal to 'introduce' and put the monks into corporal possession of the church.[44] Whatever the precise meaning of *introducere* in these charters may have been, it is clear that, apart from the verb *suscipere*, no other formula was regularly employed. It is notable, however, that in the second of Geoffrey's charters the term 'institution' makes its first certain appearance in Lincoln episcopal charters. The four known parochial appointments among the charters of the next bishop, Walter of Coutances (1183–85), show a preference for *recipere* as a slightly later alternative to *suscipere*, but otherwise maintain the emphasis on the act of reception into a benefice. Two speak of the diocesan receiving into a *personatus*, another of his receiving into a perpetual vicarage, and the fourth (known only from a reference to its having been produced in the king's court in 1206) of his receiving and instituting to a vicarage.[45] If the 1206 record can be trusted, this is only the second authentic mention of institution in the appointing clauses of a Lincoln episcopal charter. The pontificate of Bishop Hugh of Avalon (1186–1200) produced a great increase in the number of charters concerned with parochial appointments. A variety of terms continued to be employed, but the most frequent formula was a combination of *recipere* and the fairly recently introduced *instituere*.[46] This represented a definite move towards the later *admittere* and *instituere* together, of which there is indeed one example among the charters of this bishop.[47] It is clear from the charters of his successor, William of Blois (1203–06), that by then admission and institution had become the normal joint formula for parochial appointments in this diocese; of the bishop's eight surviving charters of appointment no fewer than seven employ the combination,[48] and there is no occurrence at all of *recipere*. Moreover, *instituere* was by now regularly qualified by the adverb *canonice*. At Lincoln, then, the standard later medieval formulae had been arrived at by very early in the thirteenth century.

In the diocese of Norwich a somewhat different series of developments can be seen. Although the bishops concentrated from the start on the language of gift and concession, from a comparatively early date they combined it with that of

---

[43] See below, p. 170.

[44] *EEA* I, nos. 293, 292.

[45] Respectively, *The Boarstall Cartulary*, ed. H.E. Salter, Oxford Hist. Soc. lxxxviii, 1930, no. 2; *EEA* I, nos 321, 317; *CRR* iv, 260. The Boarstall cartularly text, in favour of Coventry priory, states further that, at the latter's presentation, the bishop has 'given and conceded' the church to Master Roger of Rolleston and, with his and the priory's consent, has 'conceded' to Master William de Pentir the perpetual vicarage of the church.

[46] For example, *EEA* IV, nos. 6, 10, 54–5, 77–8, 81, 85, 89, 136, 140. Occasionally, one or other of these terms was used alone (e.g., nos. 13–15, 76, 188A). *Suscepisse* occurs in no. 88A, and the exceptional combination of *recepisse* and *contulisse* (where the bishop was not patron) is found in two charters (*Cartulary of Oseney Abbey*, ed. H.E. Salter, 6 vols, Oxford Hist. Soc. 1929–36, iv, no. 343; vi, no. 964).

[47] *EEA* IV, no. 180.

[48] *EEA* IV, nos. 230, 234–5, 268, 272, 287, 290.

institution. The earliest charter of parochial appointment survives from the time of Bishop Everard (1121–45). Unfortunately, its date cannot be defined within narrower limits, but its very simple phraseology suggests that it might be quite remarkably early: the bishop merely says that he has given (*dedisse*) St Andrew's church, Tattersett, to Roger the priest, to hold for life, at the presentation of Castle Acre priory and of the parishioners.[49] Everard's successor, William Turbe (1146/7–1174), has left an unusally large number of charters in this category, comprising at least nineteen for individual clerks and at least four appointing monasteries to benefices, making a total greater than I have found for any other English diocese before 1175. This may in part reflect the fact that the bishop received from Pope Alexander III a decretal advising him, in order to frustrate fraudulent claims, to issue letters to parsons of churches in his diocese (presumably on their appointment).[50] Be that as it may, apart from two charters containing only the formula of reception (*suscipere*) and a third mentioning only institution,[51] the rest employ the terminology of a grant in one form or another. The commonest version is 'concession and gift' (*concedere et dare*), replaced occasionally by 'gift and concession' or by one of these terms in isolation. Moreover, in most cases the 'concession and gift', etc., are specifically said to have been made *canonice*, and there is usually no reference to free alms.[52] These were therefore canonical acts by the bishop, quite different from any lay grant of a church. Four of William's charters go further, however, for they state that, as well as canonically conceding and giving a church to an individual presentee, he has also canonically instituted him as parson.[53] To take one example, in c.1154 x 1168 the bishop announced that, at the presentation of Holme St Benet's abbey, he had canonically conceded and given the church of Potter Heigham to Thomas of Ludham, clerk, and canonically instituted him as parson in the same.[54] The other three, none of which is later than 1171, employ identical formulae. Moreover, on two further occasions, one as early as 1146/7 x c.1153, the bishop canonically instituted monasteries in parochial benefices.[55] The formula of canonical institution was thus well established in Norwich diocese at a relatively early date, perhaps some twenty or more years before the regular mention of institution in the charters of Salisbury, Chichester and Lincoln. Furthermore, Bishop Turbe's fully developed formulae were generally maintained in the charters of his successor, John of Oxford (1175–1200), showing that this was the preferred style of the Norwich episcopal writing office,

---

[49] *EEA* VI, no. 27.

[50] 'Decretales', in *Corpus Iuris Canonici*, ed. E. Friedberg, 2 vols, Leipzig 1879–81, ii, 2.28.4. The full text is given in *Patrologia Latina*, ed. J.P. Migne, 221 vols, Paris 1844–64, cc, cols 928–30. See also *EEA* VI, lvi.

[51] *EEA*, VI, nos. 66, 88, 81.

[52] For example, *EEA* VI, nos. 61, 70, 106, 131. Perpetual alms is occasionally mentioned, as in no. 157.

[53] *EEA* VI, nos. 58, 74, 87; *St Benet of Holme 1020–1200*, ed. J.R. West, 2 vols, Norfolk Rec. Soc. ii–iii, 1932, i, no. 95.

[54] *St Benet Holme*, i. no. 95.

[55] *EEA* VI, no. 81; *Newington Longeville Charters*, ed. H.E. Salter, Oxfordshire Rec. Soc. iii, 1921, no. 122. In addition, a charter of Walchelin, archdeacon of Suffolk, states that he was present when William *recepit et instituit* Blythburgh priory in Blyford church, but the bishop's charter refers only to his having conceded and given the church to the priory (*Blythburgh Priory Cartulary*, ed. C. Harper-Bill, 2 vols, Suffolk Records Soc., Suffolk Charters II–III, 1980–1, i, nos. 124–5).

not simply that of one bishop's clerks. As in the roughly contemporary pontificate of Hugh of Avalon at Lincoln, John of Oxford's charters exhibit a further increase in the number dealing with parochial appointments. Some variation in formulae is evident, much of it resulting perhaps from composition by monastic beneficiaries, but the great majority of the charters are couched in the preferred Norwich formulae of *concedere et dare* and *instituere*, only the latter being now usually qualified by *canonice*.[56] The charters of the next bishop, John de Gray (1200–1214), exhibit the same preference, but with the addition of 'confirmation' immediately after 'concession and gift'.[57] The term 'admission' does occur in the charters of both John of Oxford and John de Gray, but so rarely, and never in the dispositive clauses of appointments, that it must normally have been assumed in the verbs *concedere et dare*.[58] Thus, while the later standard formula of institution appeared in regular use relatively early at Norwich, the later equally standard use of admission had not been adopted there by the early thirteenth century.

The episcopal charters of Hereford diocese present yet another pattern of development. From the earliest examples onwards, with very few exceptions, they avoided the quasi-feudal language of gift and concession, opting instead for the formula of reception or its equivalent. The evidence begins with the pontificate of Robert de Bethune (1131–48), whose charters include the appointment of an incumbent at the exceptionally early date of 1131 x 1137 (possibly 1134). The phraseology here is notable in that, despite the date, there is no reference to a grant of the church, but rather the bishop declares that he has received (*suscepi*) Stephen the priest into the vicarage of Holme Lacy and 'committed the cure of souls to him'.[59] The latter formula does not recur in Hereford episcopal charters, and I have not so far found it elsewhere,[60] but, in emphasising the spiritual aspect of the appointment, it clearly amounts to institution. The charters of the next bishop, Gilbert Foliot (1148–63), similarly include only one example concerned with the appointment of individual clerks. It involved the settlement in c.1155 x c.1158 of a dispute between one clerk and his uncle, both of whom claimed rights in the same church. By mutual agreement the bishop 'constituted' the nephew as parson and, on his presentation, received (*suscepimus*) the uncle into the vicarage of the church.[61] The use of different formulae for the two appointments is interesting, but its significance should probably not be exaggerated. What is more important is the fact that, in the form of 'constitution' (which Foliot was later to use quite frequently as bishop of London), the formula of institution had appeared at Hereford in the 1150s and, either as 'constitution' or as 'institution', was to appear in almost all later charters of parochial appointment in the diocese. On two occasions,

---

[56] For example, *EEA* VI, nos. 164–5, 170, 175, 183, 188, 190, 195.

[57] For example, *EEA* VI, nos. 334, 341–2; *St Benet Holme*, i. no. 100. 'Confirmation' occurs in most of the relevant charters of William Turbe and John of Oxford, but not in the primary clauses of appointment.

[58] For 'admission', see *EEA* VI, nos. 191–2, 412A.

[59] *EEA* VII, no. 15. In another charter (no. 16) the bishop 'conceded' the *plenus personatus* of a church to Gloucester abbey, but the exact force of the grant is uncertain.

[60] This statement applies only to clauses of appointment, since cure of souls is sometimes mentioned in other clauses.

[61] *Foliot Letters and Charters*, no. 326. In c.1155 Foliot 'constituted' a monk of Gloucester as parson and prior of Bromfield in the process of converting that ancient collegiate church into a dependent priory of Gloucester abbey (ibid. no. 303).

however, each involving the appropriation of a church to Gloucester abbey, Foliot employed the formula, not of 'constitution', but of 'inparsonation', as he was to do once again in his early years at London.[62] It was not repeated at Hereford. On the other hand, though mostly avoided by Foliot, the formula of reception or the like was regularly included by later bishops, generally in combination with that of institution. For example, Bishop Robert Foliot (1174–86) on two occasions received clerks to churches and canonically instituted them as parsons.[63] His successor, William de Vere (1186–98), also used the verb *recipere* (with *instituere*) twice in this context, but on three other occasions he chose what in some dioceses seems to have been the earlier preferred verb, *suscipere*.[64] The details of de Vere's appointments suggest no reason why *recipere* or *suscipere* should have been selected in any particular case, implying that the two were regarded as simply interchangeable. In one instance, however, in c.1190 x 1198, both were discarded in favour of *admittere*. In this first appearance of 'admission' in Hereford episcopal charters, de Vere announces that, at the presentation of Shrewsbury abbey, he has admitted Peter of Hopton to the chapel of Aston Eyre and canonically instituted him as perpetual vicar in the same.[65] The standard joint formula of later times had arrived. It was not, however, to become fixed at Hereford for several decades. Bishop Giles de Braose (1200–1215) adopted it twice, but on a third occasion reverted to *suscipere* alone,[66] and as late as the pontificate of Hugh Foliot (1219–34) we find three appointments made with the verbs *recipere* and *instituere*, and only a fourth, probably dating from 1233 very near the end of his rule, with *admittere* and *instituere*.[67] Clearly, standardisation was not to be achieved at Hereford until well into the thirteenth century. Nevertheless, though often not expressed in the specific terms of admission and institution, these two acts were in effect regularly mentioned together in Hereford appointments from the last quarter of the twelfth century.

The general picture emerging from these surveys is one of considerable variation. It is confirmed by the evidence from collections of individual bishops' charters in other dioceses. One particularly interesting group comprises those of Roger, bishop of Worcester (1164–79), one of the English bishops most versed in canon law and frequently appointed as a papal judge-delegate, whose charters throw light on the formulae which a prelate of his standing, or his clerks, considered appropriate in the making of parochial appointments. Five cases involving individual incumbents are known. The earliest, dating from 1164 x 1176, speaks of the bishop's having received (*suscepisse*) a clerk as perpetual vicar,[68] while the others, all later, refer either to admission or to institution (in one case 'constitution'),

---

[62] *Foliot Letters and Charters*, nos. 304–5, 384. For 'inparsonation', see below, pp. 171–2.
[63] *EEA* VII, nos. 135, 152. The syntactical awkwardness in no. 152 should be noted.
[64] *EEA* VII, no. 182; *Hist. et Cart. Glouc.*, ii, no. 590 (*recipere*); *EEA* VII, nos 203, 221; *The Shrewsbury Cartularly*, ed. U. Rees, 2 vols, Aberystwyth 1975, ii, no. 35lb (*suscipere*).
[65] *EEA* VII, no. 235.
[66] *EEA* VII, nos. 256, 284, 279. In a fourth case (no. 245), where the patron had not presented within the canonically prescribed period, the bishop collated (*contulimus*) and instituted to a perpetual vicarage.
[67] Respectively, *EEA* VII, nos. 317–8; *Haughmond Cartulary*, no. 271; *EEA* VII, no. 333.
[68] *The Cartulary of Cirencester Abbey*, eds C.D. Ross, M. Devine, 3 vols, Oxford 1964–77, ii, no. 375.

but never to the two in combination.[69] It is instructive to note that the two examples of admission are dated 1178, the year when another charter used institution, revealing that alternative formulae could be employed in the same year. In addition, two charters of Roger as a papal judge-delegate make provision for the future institution of parsons.[70] Notably absent is any reference to the bishop giving or granting a church to a new incumbent.

The charters of Gilbert Foliot as bishop of Hereford have already been noticed. As bishop of London (1163–87) he made a much larger number of parochial appointments, employing a wide range of formulae with, on the whole, only limited progress towards standardisation. By the time of his death the preferred formulae seem to have been a combination of *concedere* and *personam* (or *vicarium*) *instituere*,[71] but even in the 1180s this might be varied by the substitution of *conferre* for *concedere*, and of *constituere* for *instituere*.[72] Most of his institutions (or constitutions) are said to have been made *solempniter* or *cum solempnitate* rather than *canonice*, which he never uses. Moreover, his charters mostly omit the notion of reception or the like, although the verb *suscipere* occurs in the dispositive clauses of four charters, and there are single instances of *recipere* and *admittere*.[73] In general, despite their more variable formulae and the total absence of *canonice*, Foliot's London charters approach closer to those of Norwich diocese than any others I have examined.

The charters of twelfth-century archbishops of Canterbury have been printed for all pontificates from Theobald's (1139–61) to Hubert Walter's (1193–1205).[74] In addition to confirmations of parochial appointments made by bishops in other dioceses, a few charters are concerned with the archbishops' appointments in Canterbury diocese itself. Theobald has left four examples (all relating to individuals), three of which employ various formulae of gift and concession, the fourth, dating from 1154 x 1161, that of 'constitution'.[75] None survive from Thomas Becket's rule, but Richard of Dover (1174–84) and Baldwin (1184–90) have each left four, and Hubert Walter eleven, those appointed comprising religious houses as well as individual clerks.[76] There is precious little sign of the systematic evolution of standard formulae over these three pontificates. For instance, although 'institution' is mentioned in most of Richard's and Hubert's charters, it occurs only once under the intervening archbishop, Baldwin. Similarly, 'admission' is found in half the charters of Richard and Hubert, but not at all in Baldwin's. On the other hand, however, whereas the terminology of a grant is

---

[69] M.G. Cheney, *Roger, Bishop of Worcester*, Appendix I, nos 32, 34 (admission); no. 20; *The Cartulary of Worcester Cathedral Priory*, ed. R.R. Darlington, PRS lxxvi, 1968 for 1962–3, no. 169 (institution).

[70] Cheney, *Roger of Worcester*, Appendix I, no. 69; *The Cartulary of Newnham Priory*, ed. J. Godber, 2 parts, Bedfordshire Hist. Rec. Soc. xliii, 1963–4, i, no. 94.

[71] For example, *Foliot Letters and Charters*, nos. 376, 387, 404, 467–8.

[72] *Foliot Letters and Charters*, nos. 403, 433 (*conferre*; in the latter case the bishop was certainly not the patron); 434, 457 (*constituere*).

[73] *Foliot Letters and Charters*, nos. 367, 370, 393, 398 (*suscipere*); 446 (*recipere*); 395 (*admittere*).

[74] See above, notes 5 and 7. The charters of Stephen Langton, archbishop 1207–28, have also been printed (see above, note 9).

[75] Saltman, *Theobald*, Charters, nos. 63, 97, 146, 226 (the last refers to 'constitution').

[76] *EEA* II, nos 114, 144–6 (Richard); 248–9, 268, 289 (Baldwin); *EEA* III, nos. 351, 373, 384, 392–3, 402, 449–50, 518, 589, 600 (Hubert).

mostly eschewed in Richard's charters, it appears in all of Baldwin's and in half of Hubert's. To what extent this puzzling picture is due to changes of personnel in their respective writing offices is unclear, but it stands in striking contrast with the sort of continuity evident, for example, at Norwich. Nevertheless, it is notable that at Canterbury both 'admission' and 'institution' (regularly described as canonical) appear already in fairly regular use under Archbishop Richard. Furthermore, in one case, dating from 1182 x 1184 and involving the institution of a monastery, the two terms occur together.[77] Precisely the same combination was employed in two of Hubert Walter's charters, in one case for the appointment of an abbot as parson on behalf of his monastery, in the other for that of (remarkably) the bishop, prior and convent of Rochester as parson.[78] No example survives, however, of the use of the joint formula in the appointment of individuals before the death of Hubert Walter.[79]

It would be tedious to carry our investigation of English episcopal charters further. My impression is that, although new peculiarities may well come to light in other bishops' charters, the general picture I have drawn – of variety in the early stages and of halting and uneven progress towards the later standard formulae – is not likely to need major modification. It is, however, worth comparing the formulae we have encountered with the canons of ecclesiastical councils and synods held in England between the late eleventh and early thirteenth centuries. Although the earliest canon concerned with the transfer of churches pre-dates by more than half a century the first surviving episcopal charters of appointment to benefices, it and later canons probably helped to establish the diplomatic framework in which such charters were couched. In Lanfranc's Winchester council of 1072 it was decreed that 'no one shall put a priest in a church without the authority of the bishop, who shall entrust (*commendet*) the cure of souls to him'.[80] The legatine council of John of Crema at Westminster in 1125 prohibited the unlawful ejection of anyone who had been ordained (*ordinatus*) in a church by the bishop, and forbade anyone to claim a church by hereditary right or to 'constitute' a successor to himself in any ecclesiastical benefice.[81] The latter was repeated in Alberic of Ostia's legatine council of 1138, also at Westminster, where it was further enacted that, 'when anyone has received investiture (*investitura*) of a church from the bishop', he shall swear not to give or promise it to another.[82] In Archbishop Richard of Canterbury's Westminster council of 1175 a proposition was discussed (but not implemented as a canon) to the effect that 'no one shall presume to enter upon a church *absque . . . impersonatione diocesiani episcopi*', while the canons actually promulgated by the council included the provision that 'henceforth no

---

[77] *EEA* II, no. 114.

[78] *EEA* III, nos. 450, 589.

[79] Moreover, only one such example, dated 1224, is known from his successor's pontificate (*Acta Stephani Langton*, no. 65), although Langton used *recipere* and *instituere* in 1213 x 1215, and *conferre* and *canonice instituere* in 1222 (nos. 31, 53).

[80] *Councils and Synods, with other Documents relating to the English Church, I, Part II, 1066–1204*, eds D. Whitelock, M. Brett, C.N.L. Brooke, Oxford 1981, 606, canon 5.

[81] *Councils and Synods . . . 1066–1204*, 739–40, canons 9, 5. The form *ordinare* is in my experience very rare in English episcopal charters, but it was used by Bishop Chesney of Lincoln in c.1164 x 1166: *ordinavimus per manum Nicholai archidiaconi Hunted' Adam de Stivecle personam ecclesie de Walden'* (*EEA* I, no. 169).

[82] *Councils and Synods . . . 1066–1204*, 775, canons 5–6.

sons of priests shall be instituted (*instituantur*) as parsons in their fathers' churches'.[83] The use of the verb *instituere* here is the earliest appearance of the formula in English ecclesiastical legislation, but thereafter it established itself in this context as the standard form. Thus, in Hubert Walter's provincial council at Westminster in 1200 two canons employed it in reference to parochial appointments.[84] Moreover, by 1215, though not apparently in the twelfth century, the other term that was later to be standard, *admittere*, had made its first appearance in English diocesan statutes. Admission to a cure of souls without presentation to the bishop was forbidden in the statutes of an unknown diocesan of before 1215, and in 1219 the statutes of William of Blois, bishop of Worcester, enacted that no one other than a priest was to be admitted to a church whose estimated value did not exceed five marks.[85] It is notable, however, that no twelfth-century English canons contained the formula of reception, which, as we have seen, was in common use in many dioceses. Equally, the language of gift and concession was eschewed, but otherwise ecclesiastical legislation in England exhibited broadly the same sort of range and use of formulae as episcopal charters, although the latter were certainly more variable.[86]

Two of the formulae found in these conciliar texts, 'investiture' and 'inparsonation', need further discussion, since, although the former eventually passed out of regular use and the latter died out altogether, they each occur in a number of twelfth-century episcopal charters. Investiture (*investitura*) is the more difficult to deal with because its precise meaning in any given context is not always clear. In episcopal charters it normally stood for the act of institution or its equivalent. This is clearly the sense in which the term was used in the canons of the Westminster Council of 1138 as well as in certain papal decretals directed to English prelates, including that of Alexander III to Archbishop Richard of Canterbury in 1180.[87] As far as the central middle ages were concerned, investiture was an older term for ecclesiastical appointment than 'institution', by which it was in due course replaced. The usage arose from the fact that, when appointing to a benefice, bishops customarily handed to the new incumbent a symbolic object, usually a ring, thereby investing him with the spiritual care of the benefice.[88] The ceremony asserted ecclesiastical as against lay investiture, the attack upon which was central to the Gregorian Reform programme. In a few English episcopal charters of the twelfth century it was this aspect of the process that was mentioned rather than

[83] *Councils and Synods . . . 1066–1204*, 978, item i; 984, canon 1.
[84] *Councils and Synods . . . 1066–1204*, 1067–9, canons 10, 14.
[85] *Councils and Synods . . . 1066–1204*, 1073–4, statute 7; *Councils and Synods . . . II, Part I, 1205–1265*, eds F.M. Powicke, C.R. Cheney, Oxford 1964, 56, statute 11.
[86] How far the diplomatic of episcopal charters was directly influenced by the terminology of English canons and statutes is difficult to say, but it is likely that, in some cases at least, English bishops and their clerks took their cue in part from the canons of Lateran and other papal councils (which themselves found echoes in English canons), or, perhaps more importantly in the second half of the 12th century, from papal decretals addressed to English prelates. A full study of this last aspect has not been feasible, but a cursory examination of the relevant decretals of Alexander III (1159–81) included in Gregory IX's 'Decretales' (see above, note 50) and of some others has revealed that a variety of terms occur (*admittere, recipere, curam animarum committere, instituere, investire, introducere*, etc.), but that *instituere* is the most frequent.
[87] *Decretales ineditae saeculi xii*, eds S. Chodorow, C. Duggan, Vatican City 1982, no. 38.
[88] P. Thomas, *Le Droit de Propriété des Laïques sur les Églises et le Patronage Laïque au Moyen Age*, Paris 1906, 144–5; Addleshaw, *Rectors*, 21.

any act of institution or the like. So, as we have seen, Bishop Jocelin of Salisbury in c.1170 x 1184 received and invested a chaplain as vicar of a church; and in 1161 x 1182 Bishop Richard Peche of Coventry, at the presentation of Burton abbey, invested the archdeacon of Coventry with the church of Ilam.[89] Rather earlier, in 1138 x 1143, Bishop Robert Warelwast of Exeter requested Bishop Simon of Worcester and the archdeacon of Gloucester to invest one of his clerks as parson of St Mary's church, Gloucester, which he had 'given' him.[90] The investiture of religious houses also seems usually to have signified institution. In 1165 x 1179, for example, Bishop Nicholas of Llandaff, at Margaret de Bohun's presentation, gave Caldicot church to the canons of Lanthony and canonically invested them, an act which his successor, Bishop William, confirmed in 1186 x 1191 as an institution.[91] On occasions, however, the act appears to have symbolised little more than the bishop's confirmation of a layman's gift of a church to a monastery without specifically appointing that monastery to the benefice.[92] As a further complication, investiture carried out by archdeacons or rural deans normally denoted, not institution, but the equivalent of induction of an incumbent (individual or corporate) into a benefice.[93]

The term 'inparsonation', which was discussed at the Westminster Council of 1175 and which, as we have seen, occurs in some English episcopal charters, was clearly used normally as a synonym for institution, in the particular sense of making someone a parson in a church, or of putting someone into the *personatus* of a church.[94] In some dioceses it appears, like investiture, to have been a forerunner of the formula of institution. It seems to have been used chiefly in dioceses on the western side of England and in parts of Wales, and mainly in the second and third quarters of the twelfth century. Its omission from the final canons of the 1175 council may indicate that it was not generally acceptable or that it was by then passing out of fashion, even though it continued occasionally to be employed, especially by archdeacons and others, into the early thirteenth century.[95] In the areas where it was in most frequent use it served for the appointment of

---

[89] Above, p. 161; 'The Burton Chartulary', ed. G. Wrottesley, in *Collections for a History of Staffordshire* V, part i, William Salt Arch. Soc. 1884, 54.

[90] PRO, C115/K2/6683, fol. 34v.

[91] *Llandaff Episcopal Acta 1140–1287*, ed. David Crouch, South Wales Rec. Soc., Cardiff 1988, nos. 21, 36.

[92] See, e.g., Bishop William of Norwich's confirmation (in effect) to Nuneaton priory of Earl William of Gloucester's gift of a church, probably c.1159 (*EEA* VI, no. 136), and Bishop Hilary of Chichester's charter to Haughmond abbey (above, note 36).

[93] Thomas, *Droit de Propriété*, 145–8. See, e.g., Ralph archdeacon of Stafford's investiture of Osney abbey in Shenston church on an order from papal judges-delegate to 'introduce' the abbey 'into corporal possession', c.1170 (*Oseney Cartulary*, v, no. 578E), and a rural dean's 'induction' of Newnham priory 'into corporal investiture and possession' of Hatley church on instructions from the archdeacon of Bedford's official to put the priory into the same, c.1170 x 80 (*Newnham Cartulary*, ii, no. 923); and cf. *EEA* I, no. 293.

[94] On *inparsonare*, and particularly on related formulae, see W. Petke, 'Von der klösterlichen Eigenkirche zur Inkorporation in Lothringen und Nordfrankreich im 11. und 12. Jahrhundert', in two parts, *Revue d'Histoire Ecclésiastique* lxxxvii, 1992, esp. 48–51, 387, 390, 398 n. 190.

[95] In c.1180 x c.1183 Robert archdeacon of Buckingham 'inparsonated' Dunstable priory in a church (*A digest of the Charters . . . in the Cartulary . . . of Dunstable*, ed. G.H. Fowler, Bedfordshire Hist. Rec. Soc. x, 1926, no. 150). In the king's court in 1217 a plaintiff challenged the admission and inparsonation of a clerk in a church by Herbert, late bishop of Salisbury (1194–1217) (*Bracton's Note Book*, ed. F.W. Maitland, 3 vols, London 1887, iii, no. 1354).

individual or corporate incumbents. As early as c.1139, for example, Bishop Roger of Chester 'inparsonated' a clerk in Trentham church at the presentation of Matilda (the Empress).[96] In 1138 x 1150 Bishop Simon of Worcester received and 'inparsonated' a clerk in the church of Oldberrow[97], and in 1151 x 1153 Archbishop Henry of York 'inparsonated' a canon of York in Bubwith church,[98] while, between 1148 and 1166, Bishop Nicholas of Llandaff 'inparsonated' clerks in two churches and, on another occasion, referred to a similar act by his predecessor, Bishop Uthred (1140–48).[99] On the other hand, some bishops seem to have regarded the formula as particularly appropriate (though not exclusively so) for the appointment of a monastery to a parochial *personatus*, clearly in an early form of appropriation. Thus, in c.1158 Gilbert Foliot of Hereford, responding to a request from Matilda de Wattevile that he 'appropriate' Taynton church to Gloucester abbey, 'inparsonated' the abbey's sacrist in the church; at the same time he 'inparsonated' the Gloucester monks in another church and conceded to them the *plenus personatus*.[100] As bishop of London, Foliot in 1163 x 1172 'invested' and 'inparsonated' the Hospitallers in Harefield church,[101] although he did not employ the formula for other appropriations, nor did he ever use it for the appointment of individual clerks. Similar examples in other dioceses include the 'inparsonation' of Kenilworth priory in Charlton Horethorne church by Bishop Robert of Bath in c.1159 x 1166 and, as late as 1184, Bishop Jocelin of Salisbury's 'institution' and 'inparsonation' of Waltham abbey in the Windsor churches, mentioned earlier.[102] In the last case the combination of two terms which to all intents and purposes meant the same thing seems extraordinary, particulary since 'inparsonation' had not been employed earlier at Salisbury. Occasionally, however, 'inparsonation' carried out by archdeacons and the like equated to induction.[103] Finally, it is worth noting that, although the term was clearly derived from the words *persona* and *personatus*, once coined it would be extended to vicars and vicarages, though not to my knowledge in episcopal charters. For example, a document of 1148 x 1158 referred to Nicholas archdeacon of Bedford, who was to hold a church of St Neots priory for life, as *quasi vicarius inpersonatus*.[104]

The terms 'investiture' and 'inparsonation' are thus of considerable interest in the history of episcopal diplomatic, but it is clear nevertheless that neither was very widely favoured as a formula for parochial appointment in England. Apart from them, the evidence we have considered reveals that, for much of the second half of the twelfth century and a little earlier, bishops' charters concentrated mainly on the acts of granting churches to their new incumbents (whether individual or corporate) and/or of receiving them into the benefices concerned. The

---

[96] BL, Harley MS 3868, fol. 35r–v.
[97] Evreux, Archives départementales de l'Eure, II F.2463 (Wootton Wawen cartulary), fol. 26v.
[98] *York Minster Fasti*, ed. C.T. Clay, 2 vols, Yorkshire Arch. Soc., Record Series cxxiii–cxxiv, 1958–9, i, 53–4; for the date, see *EEA* V, no. 133.
[99] *Llandaff Episcopal Acta*, nos. 7–8, 28.
[100] *Foliot Letters and Charters*, nos. 304–5.
[101] *Foliot Letters and Charters*, no. 384.
[102] BL, Harley MS 3650, fol. 51r; *Early Charters of Waltham*, no. 111.
[103] E.g., in the 1190s Bernard prior of Newburgh, official of the archbishop of York, 'inparsonated and inducted into corporal possession' a clerk whom the archbishop had already 'received and instituted' (BL, Cotton MS Vespasian E.xix, fol. 73v).
[104] BL, Cotton MS Faustina A.iv, fol. 39v.

regular use of the formula of 'admission', in place of 'reception', appeared only in the last two decades of the century (and then not everywhere), although it is occasionally found earlier. Likewise, the canonical act of 'institution' was, save at Norwich, relatively rarely mentioned before the last quarter of the century, even though, as we have seen, it could be represented by 'investiture' or 'inparsonation', or alternatively was often implied in the formula of 'receiving' to a benefice.

With these findings in mind, we may now return to the alleged charter of institution by Bishop Alexander of Lincoln with which this paper began. If genuine the charter would date to before September 1142, since it is addressed to R. archdeacon of Buckingham (probably Richard de Urville), who by then had been succeeded by archdeacon David.[105] To recapitulate, the charter declares that the bishop has received (*suscepimus*) and instituted Gloucester abbey's clerk, William son of Theodoric, as parson of the churches of Wraysbury and Langley Marish. It contains more than this, however, for it begins with a reference to the abbey's letters presenting the clerk to the bishop and requesting that he 'institute' him, and continues after the clause of institution with an instruction to the archdeacon to announce in his chapter that the clerk has been 'instituted'.[106] The act of institution is thus referred to three times in a text of modest length. This degree of repetition, which is rare in such charters, gives the impression that the writer was anxious to establish beyond any doubt that a clerk presented by Gloucester abbey had actually been instituted by the diocesan. That would not be enough to invalidate the charter, since, if the formula of institution was only now being introduced into charters of parochial appointment, it might well have been thought necessary to repeat it more frequently than was later to be the case. Additional doubts are cast on the charter's credibility, however, by the facts that (a) no other charters of parochial appointment by Alexander survive (let alone any employing the formula of institution),[107] and that (b), as we have seen, reference to institution does not occur in later Lincoln charters before the time of Bishop-elect Geoffrey (1173–82) and only becomes common under Hugh of Avalon (1186–1200).[108] Alexander's use of the verb *suscipere* would be far less problematical, but, even so, it is found at Lincoln mainly between the later 1150s and early 1180s, in the charters of Robert Chesney and Geoffrey. In short, my belief is that Alexander's supposed

[105] John Le Neve, *Fasti Ecclesiae Anglicanae 1066–1300, III, Lincoln*, compiled by D.E. Greenway, London 1977, 39–40.

[106] See above, note 1.

[107] In 1186 x 1192 the archdeacon of Buckingham stated that Alexander had 'admitted' and 'instituted' the abbot of Osney in Stone church (*Oseney Cartulary*, v, no. 624), but no episcopal charter survives and, of course, use of these formulae in the 1180s does not establish their currency in Alexander's time.

[108] See above, p. 164. Moreover, I have not found *instituere* used in the appointing clauses of episcopal charters in other dioceses dating certainly as early as before 1142, although provision for future 'institution' is made in a charter for Pontefract priory by Archbishop William FitzHerbert of York, 1143 x 47 *or* 1153 x 54 (*EYC* iii, no. 1476). On the other hand, institutions by archdeacons in Lincoln diocese are known from the 1160s onwards, and one isolated case, in which Henry archdeacon of Huntingdon apparently received (*recepimus*) and instituted (*instituimus*) St Neots priory in a Huntingdon church, dates from Bishop Alexander's time (BL, Cotton MS Faustina A.iv, fol. 42r). This charter's text may later have been interpolated, however, since, apart from the problem of an archidiaconal institution *sede plena* (unless the act was effectively an induction), the bishop's confirmation refers only to the donor resigning the church to the priory by the archdeacon's hands (*EEA* I, no. 54).

charter of institution is a forgery which, by comparison with the other Lincoln evidence, should be dated to somewhere in the period c.1160–c.1185. If it is a forgery, the intention was clearly to prove that, certainly in Bishop Alexander's time, Gloucester abbey had exercised the right of presentation to the two churches concerned. In that case, was there an occasion, within the period suggested, when Gloucester needed to furnish such proof? To answer this question a brief history of Gloucester's troubled possession of the churches in the twelfth century is required.[109] The churches were given to the abbey by Robert Gernun in 1112 x 1113, the gift being confirmed at that time by Henry I and Bishop Robert Bloet of Lincoln (and subsequently by Henry II and Bishops Alexander and Robert Chesney).[110] However, when Robert Gernun died without heirs, Henry I granted his estates to William de Montfichet; when the latter died, his son and heir Gilbert de Montfichet was a minor, and wardship was granted to Earl Gilbert (of Pembroke).[111] In the 1140s, despite the fact that William de Montfichet had recognised Gloucester's rights, the earl sought to overturn them by intruding a clerk Payn into the two churches, whereupon Abbot Gilbert Foliot complained to Bishop Alexander, who delegated the case to David, archdeacon of Buckingham, before whom in his synod the matter was settled in favour of the abbey.[112] This was clearly a dispute over patronage, but, in view of the suggested period of the forgery, it is unlikely to have occasioned the latter's perpetration. Gloucester's problems were not yet at an end, however, for, apart from a conflict with one of Bishop Chesney's clerks in 1148 x 1163,[113] a more serious dispute occurred in the early 1170s when Gilbert de Montfichet, who had come of age by 1156,[114] challenged the abbey's right of patronage in the two churches, reviving in effect the claim made by his guardian in the 1140s. This was regarded by the monks as so serious a matter that they obtained from Gilbert Foliot, now bishop of London, a testificatory letter detailing the history of the two churches, with particular attention to the conflict in the 1140s,[115] as well as letters addressed to the pope from Bishop Nicholas of Llandaff, who had been a monk at Gloucester at (or soon after) the time of Robert Gernun's original gift, and from Bishop Roger of Worcester, Gloucester's diocesan, both of whose letters date from 1173 x 1174.[116] This is most likely to have been the dispute which led to the production of the forgery, since some such document was needed to clear the matter up by showing that the abbey had successfully exercised the patronage of the two churches before the first challenge mounted by Earl Gilbert in the 1140s. Moreover, its formulae of reception and institution accord well with a date in the 1170s.

---

[109] Since Langley was also known as Laverstoke in the 12th century (see *Hist. et Cart. Glouc.*, ii, no. 711), documents concerning the church employ either name.
[110] *Hist. et Cart. Glouc.*, ii, nos. 698–9, 703, 700, 711. For the date of the original gift, see ibid., i, 118.
[111] See Nicholas bishop of Llandaff's testimony in 1173 x 74 (*Hist. et Cart. Clouc.*, ii, no. 714; *Landaff Episcopal Acta*, no. 15), and I.J. Sanders, *English Baronies*, Oxford 1960, 83.
[112] See the testimonies of Nicholas bishop of Llandaff (previous note) and of Gilbert Foliot as bishop of London (*Hist. et Cart. Glouc.*, ii, no. 708; *Foliot Letters and Charters*, no. 371), and David archdeacon of Buckingham's charter (*Hist. et Cart. Glouc.*, ii, no. 706).
[113] *Hist. et Cart. Glouc.*, ii, no. 711; *Foliot Letters and Charters*, no. 115).
[114] Sanders, *Baronies*, 83 n. 1.
[115] See note 112.
[116] See note 111 and *Hist. et Cart. Glouc.*, ii, no. 715; Cheney, *Roger of Worcester*, Appendix I, no. 24.

More momentously, the results of our survey also undermine the credibility of a well-known charter of Henry of Blois, bishop of Winchester, to which great importance has been attached by historians of vicarages in the twelfth century. Apparently dating from the 1150s, it concerns the appointment of a perpetual vicar at Christchurch, Twinham (Hampshire), and the assignment to him of specified items of income, as his predecessor had had them.[117] This has been seen as an early prototype of the perpetual vicarage with assigned revenues, which was to become increasingly common in England from the later twelfth century. Christopher Cheney hailed it as revealing 'the complete arrangement . . . in being at Winchester' in the 1150s, adding that 'nothing quite like this can be found elsewhere at so early a date', and Dr Peter Hase has remarked upon 'the revolutionary nature of Henry's actions'.[118] Both accepted the charter as genuine, but, while the details of the vicar's endowment may not in themselves be suspicious, apart from their supposed early date, the clause of appointment raises serious doubts. It reads:

> Noverit universitas vestra nos, ad preces et ad presentationem Reginaldi prioris et regularium canonicorum Christi ecclesie de Twynham, admisisse Robertum capellanum ad perpetuam vicariam eiusdem Christi ecclesie et ipsum inde canonice instituisse . . .

The reader is thus asked to believe that, as early as the 1150s, an English bishop 'admitted' and 'canonically instituted' a vicar, using the standard later medieval formulae which we have not found elsewhere at this time and which, moreover, Henry of Blois himself did not employ again, save in a related charter for Christchurch priory. This second charter, which has been dated 1161 x 1170, reiterates the 'admission' and 'canonical institution' of Robert in the Christchurch vicarage and provides for similar vicarages in the priory's other churches in the diocese, to which the bishop will 'admit' and 'canonically institute' suitable vicars presented by the priory.[119] The rather later date of this charter perhaps makes it marginally more credible, but, even so, its consistent use of the later joint formula is, to say the least, remarkable. The joint formula is not found at all in the surviving charters of Henry's successor, Richard of Ilchester (1174–88), and only begins to appear at Winchester in those of Godfrey de Lucy (1189–1204).[120] It seems most likely, therefore, that both of Henry's texts are forgeries dating at the earliest from the later twelfth century. A forged text does not, of course, necessarily mean that the act it purports to record never took place, but nevertheless, if these charters are indeed later forgeries, they raise at least the possibility that Henry of Blois did not play the significant role in the development of English vicarages which is usually credited to him. Such a conclusion would conveniently remove the difficulty faced by historians in explaining why, if perpetual vicarages of the kind described

---

[117] L. Voss, *Heinrich von Blois, Bischof von Winchester, 1129–71*, Berlin 1932, 159–60, Anhang IV a.

[118] Cheney, *From Becket to Langton*, 134; P.H. Hase, 'The Mother Churches of Hampshire', in *Minsters and Parish churches: the local church in transition 950–1200*, ed. J. Blair, Oxford 1988, 58.

[119] Voss, *Heinrich von Blois*, 161–2, Anhang IV c.

[120] I am indebted for information on the Winchester charters to Dr Michael Franklin, whose edition was published after this volume went to press.

(i.e. with specifically assigned revenues) had been established by Henry as early as the 1150s, no other bishop appears to have followed his example for the best part of a generation, and most not until much later in the century.[121]

These cases illustrate the way in which close analysis of the diplomatic of episcopal charters, and of diplomatic development over the century, can enable probable forgeries to be detected. The application of these techniques is only possible, however, because the twelfth century saw so much diversity and change in the formulae of episcopal appointments to benefices. Only very gradually and unevenly did the trend in favour of admission and canonical institution set in towards the end of the century. It heralded the eventual triumph of that neat joint formula over the fascinating range of alternative forms which had proliferated in earlier decades, some of which were still to have plenty of life left in them well into the thirteenth century.

---

[121] The next case after the 1150s known to me is the ordination of the vicarage at Gazeley by Bishop William Turbe of Norwich in (probably) c.1161 x 1174 (*Stoke by Clare Cartulary*, eds C. Harper-Bill, R. Mortimer, 3 vols, Suffolk Records Soc., Suffolk Charters iv–vi, 1982–4, i, no. 87; *EEA* VI, no. 152), but here the bishop's title, unique among his surviving charters, may cast doubt on the act's authenticity. In northern France, however, what amounted to a vicarage of this kind was ordained at Tours-sur-Marne as early as 1099 (Petke, 'Von der klösterlichen Eigenkirche . . .', 382–6). It is true also that in England by the 1150s, and in one case not later than 1140, bishops were occasionally requiring the establishment of vicarages when appropriating churches to monasteries, but without detailing the endowment of these vicarages (Cheney, *From Becket to Langton*, 133–5; Kemp, 'Monastic possession of parish churches', 22–3; cf. a charter of Alexander of Lincoln, ? c.1133 x 1148, *EEA* I, no. 21).

BURHGEAT AND GONFANON:
TWO SIDELIGHTS FROM THE BAYEUX TAPESTRY

Derek Renn

A scene embroidered two-thirds of the way along the Bayeux Tapestry brings together my two otherwise diverse subjects.[1] A figure wearing a conical helmet, coat of mail and sword holds a lance which bears a flag with streaming tails; he is about to take the reins of a ready-saddled horse from a groom. The armed figure is usually identified as William, duke of Normandy. Just to his left is a building of at least two and probably three storeys beside a turret with a large wide-open door, drawn as if William had just emerged from it.[2] I believe that the artist intended to represent something other than a church and prayer before battle and so I propose to look at all the representations of towers in the Tapestry (except those on mottes) and to compare them with those contemporary buildings with large upper openings which have survived in England.[3]

My second theme is the flags of the Tapestry. An analysis suggests that most of them were drawn to indicate movement; and that three of the four war banners mentioned by the chroniclers can be identified at two different stages of the battle.

I am grateful to Matthew Bennett, Claud Blair, John Blair, Marjorie Chibnall, Dione Clementi, John Cowdrey, Brian Durham, Sandy Heslop, Christopher Lewis, David Parsons, Ian Peirce, John Weaver and Ann Williams for advice and argument, even if not always followed.

[1] Citations of the Bayeux Tapestry throughout will be BT followed by three numbers giving respectively (a) the scene number written on the backing linen and used on the *dépliant* sold at Bayeux, (b) the plate number in *The Bayeux Tapestry*, a comprehensive survey, ed. Sir F.M. Stenton et al., revised and enlarged edition, London 1965, and (c) the plate number in *The Bayeux Tapestry; The Complete Tapestry in Colour*, ed. Sir D.M. Wilson, London 1985. Roman numerals on pages 187 to 192 refer to the gonfanons listed in Appendix 2 (page 198).

[2] BT 48, 53, 51. The Tapestry shows William frequently (but not exclusively) on a large black horse in Brittany, in Normandy and at Hastings (sic). The dramatic crash of an enormous black stallion during the subsequent battle may be coupled with the preceding picture of such a horse being axed and the following picture of the unhorsing of a rider by a soldier on foot grabbing the girthband, as the incidents described in the *Gesta Guillelmi*, 196–8 and the *Carmen*, xxv, xxvii, 32–4, 93, 96, 97.

[3] *Med. Arch.* xiv, 1970, 224–5, reviewing *Chateau Gaillard III: European Castle Studies: Conference at Battle, Sussex, 19–24 September 1966*, ed. A.J. Taylor, Chichester 1969, with reference to A.J. Taylor, 'Evidence for a pre-Conquest Origin for the Chapels in Hastings and Pevensey Castles', 144–51. For towers on mottes in the Bayeux Tapestry, see Arnold Taylor, 'Belrem', *ante* xiv , 1992, 1–23.

The burhgeat

In the scene representing Harold's return from Normandy, his landfall is watched by a group of men in and on a very curious building.[4] The main structure is four storeys high: the topmost has been missed by most commentators on the Tapestry because its three round-topped openings (the central one slightly larger than the others) do not stand out from the chequer-work on black-and-white photographs. Below this storey is another from which a face looks out through a tall round-headed frame. More faces peer out through three shorter round-topped openings in the storey below and finally at the bottom is the largest round-headed opening of all, reached up three steps. Level with the second storey of the tower is a platform on which stands a figure looking (like all the others) at the approaching ship. One hand shields his eyes either from the sun or from bad news. The platform is supported at one end by the tower and by a central column with moulded base and capital. At the other end is another pillar, with three small steps (or another moulded base?) at its foot and a dragon-head finial at the top. The wavy lines under the ship run on in front of the platform but slope away from the right-hand part of the tower and may indicate a pier or jetty standing at the seaside. The curving lines might indicate a wooden tower and platform, although the diagonal chequer-work of the top and ground storeys is used to denote masonry elsewhere in the Tapestry.

At the very beginning of the Tapestry is a comparable structure attached to a hall.[5] This also has a ground-floor round-headed doorway up three steps and a top floor with three windows, the central one higher than the others, both groups surrounded by chequerwork. But this tower has flanking turrets, the gateway is ornamented with capitals and bases to the jambs and there is only one intermediate storey, with a three-cusped ceiling, and the Tapestry indicates that it is some distance from the coast: Harold rides some distance both before embarking and after disembarking.

After that return, attached turrets can be seen in the succeeding 'debriefing', 'deathbed' and 'Halley's Comet' scenes.[6] Freestanding turrets flank the 'Harold/William conversation + Aelfgiva' scene and also follow the building of Hastings castle.[7] The 'open and shut' pair may signify gatetowers, and the other be the turret at Hastings represented again in the next scene.

One other three-storey tower with an attached turret is shown here, namely that from which Duke William emerges to mount his horse before riding to battle.[8] To Arnold Taylor's identification of this structure with the central elements of the church now within Hastings Castle,[9] I then added the idea that the embroidery might be meant to indicate a lord's seat in an upper room (rather than an apse), with an upper doorway opening into space. Perhaps this links with the previous scene in which William sits high alongside Hastings castle and a turret.[10] The

---

[4] BT 24, 30, 27.
[5] BT 1, 1, 1.
[6] BT 25, 31/2, 28/9; BT 27, 33, 30; BT 32, 35, 32.
[7] BT 14/5, 18/9, 16/17; BT 45/6, 51 and detail, 50. E.F. Freeman, 'The identity of Aelfgyva', *Annales de Normandie* xli, 1991, 117–34.
[8] BT 48, 53, 51.
[9] Note 3.
[10] BT 46, 51, 50.

castle was erected within an Early Iron Age hillfort which had probably become the site of the tenth-century *burh*; therefore the pre-Conquest tower might have had a secular origin.[11] Three steps from ground level into both sides of the tower as well as into both turrets are shown, just like those into the buildings previously described, and the large central opening of the top floor may be a doorway opening into space, Finally, attention may be drawn to the curious building whose oddly-tiled roof is being set on fire just before William sets out from Hastings.[12] Its upper storey has a large central doorway opening into space.

Where was the four-storey tower? Harold's landfall is unknown. Bosham, from whence he set out, is a possibility and the church tower there has a monumental east arch and three upper storeys with small windows. But the drawing is very different from that of the Bosham church shown earlier in the Tapestry.[13] This tower is not topped off with a cross, as other buildings are in the embroidery, to indicate a religious use; indeed it has a very lived-in look with large openings at three levels.

Just across the harbour from Bosham at Warblington church is the upper part of a small tower with round-topped openings above roof level to north, south and west which are big enough to stand up in (Figure 1).[14] The foundations of two secular stone towers of eleventh-century date have been excavated overlooking harbours near Bosham. Building S18 at Portchester Castle was originally associated with a large timber hall before being rebuilt as a tower 6m. each way with two rows of posts inside.[15] Itself associated with late Saxon burials, it was demolished about 1100. At Church Norton (Selsey), there were tower foundations about 9m. each way, with a smaller and slighter stone-based building alongside. Pottery evidence indicated a Saxo-Norman date.[16] Neither of these latter towers was clearly ecclesiastical in purpose; the building of churches nearby (but not on the same site) after the towers had been demolished suggests a change of use. A stone secular building 6m. square in Tanner Street, Winchester, was incorporated later into the nave of St Mary's church.[17] At Chilham and Eynsford castles in Kent, multi-storey buildings (10m. or so each way) have been found below Norman work.[18]

Oxford has two four-storey towers connected only later with a church. St George's Tower (in the castle) is wrongly oriented and the plans made before the rebuilding of the early Norman crypt shew no congruence with the tower. Apart

[11] P.A. Barker and K.J. Barton, 'Excavations at Hastings Castle 1968', *Arch. Journ.* cxxxiv, 1977, 80–100 especially 83.
[12] BT 47, 52. 50.
[13] BT 3, 3, 3.
[14] E.A. Fisher, *The Greater Anglo-Saxon churches: an Architectural-Historical Study*, London 1962, Plates 277 and 278. Figures 1 to 15 are diagrammatic and only intended to shew the size and positions of large upper openings, overlaid on to one elevation for economy.
[15] B.W. Cunliffe, *Excavations at Portchester Castle Vol. II: Saxon*, Report xxxii of the Research Committee of the Society of Antiquaries of London, London 1976, 49–52, 60.
[16] F.G. Aldsworth and E.D. Garnett, 'Excavations on "The Mound", Church Norton, Selsey in 1911 and 1965', *Sussex Archaeological Collections* 119, 1981, 217–220.
[17] M. Biddle, 'Excavations at Winchester 1971: Tenth and Final Interim Report, Part II', *Antiqs. Journ.* lv, 1975, 295–337 especially 308–13.
[18] A.W. Clapham, 'An Early Hall at Chilham Castle', *Antiqs. Journ.* viii, 1928, 350–3; V. Horsman, 'Eynsford castle – a reinterpretation of its early History in the light of recent Excavations', *Archaeologia Cantiana* cv, 1988, 39–58.

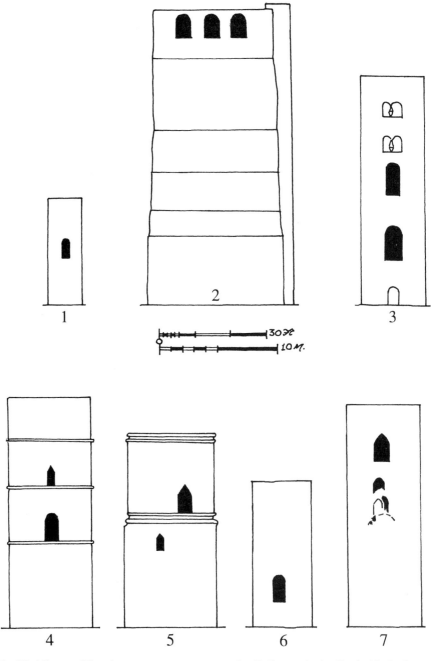

1   Warblington (Hants)
2   St George in the Castle (Oxford)
3   St Michael at the Northgate (Oxford)
4   Earl's Barton (Northants)
5   Barnack (Northants)
6   Wickham (Berks)
7   Guildford (Surrey)

Figures 1–7

from a restored east arch and narrow west window the only openings are four round-headed doorways in the parapet (Figure 2). Standing on the bank of the Thames beside the Saxon east-west street, St George's Tower might be associated with the first west gate of the town. The motte (which presumably dates from the foundation of the castle in 1071 and carried a tower at least from the thirteenth century) effectively neutralized St George's Tower by blocking its view over Oxford.[19]

David Parsons has suggested that the church tower of St Michael at the Northgate was originally a pedestrian gate-tower into the city, a *burhgeat* or secular tower. A large tall blocked doorway exists at first floor level in the south wall; the west window here has been altered at least twice, and there is another large doorway higher up in the north wall, all below two tiers of belfry openings with central balusters (Figure 3).[20]

In his magisterial survey of Anglo-Saxon buildings, Harold Taylor has referred to the use of church towers for the storage of valuables, the display of relics from galleries and also for private use by the founder and his family.[21] As well as St Michael, Oxford, four or five other Anglo-Saxon church towers appear both in Taylor's table of towers with upper doorways opening into space and also in a list of turriform naves compiled by David Parsons, which may have been of secular origin.[22]

Brian Davison has drawn attention to the defensive earthworks around Earl's Barton church.[23] There are no less than six – possibly seven – upper doorways opening into space from this tower, with its all-over decoration of narrow pilaster strips (Figure 4). Another such decorated Saxon tower is at Barnack with not only a similar upper doorway into space but also internal masonry which Baldwin Brown interpreted as a 'seat of judgment' on the west side, which was formerly accompanied by ranges of oak benches round three sides of the tower (Figure 5).[24] A third church tower with elaborate decoration is St Peter's, Barton-on-Humber, but there the upper doorways were intended from the first to open into the east and west annexes, and the evidence for a previous tower there is slender.[25] But the

[19] E. King, *Vestiges of Oxford Castle*, London 1796; Royal Commission on Historic Monuments, England, *Inventory of . . . City of Oxford*, London 1939, 156–8; T.G. Hassall, 'Excavations at Oxford castle, 1965–73', *Oxoniensia* xli, 1976, 232–308 especially Fig. 2, 252–4 and J. Cooper, 'The Church of St George in the Castle', 306–8.

[20] B. Durham et al., 'Oxford's Northern Defences: Archaeological Studies 1971–1982', *Oxoniensia* xlviii, 1983, 13–40 especially 14–18, 33–5; Council for British Archaeology Churches Committee *Newsletter*, 22, 1985; T.G. Hassall, *Oxford, the Buried City*, Oxford 1987, 22–3. I am grateful to Brian Durham for showing me the draft of his forthcoming monograph, and to David Parsons for providing Appendix I in elaboration of his side of the argument.

[21] H.M. Taylor, *Anglo-Saxon Architecture* iii, Cambridge 1978, 826–7, 887–94.

[22] M. Audouy et al., 'The tower of All Saints' Church, Earl's Barton, Northamptonshire: its construction and context', *Arch. Journ.*, forthcoming.

[23] B.K. Davison, 'The Origins of the Castle in England', *Arch. Journ.* cxxiv, 1967, 202–11 especially 208–10.

[24] H.S. Syers, 'The building of Barnack Church', *Reports and Papers of the Associated Architectural Societies* xxiii, 1895–6, 143–51 extended as 'Barnack Church', *Journ. BAA* second series 5, 1899, 13–28.

[25] W. and K. Rodwell, 'St Peter's Church, Barton-on-Humber: Excavations and Structural study 1978–81', *Antiqs. Journ.* lxii, 1982, 283–315 but cf. H.M. Taylor, 'Old St Peter's Church, Barton-on-Humber', *Arch. Journ.* cxxxi, 1974, 369–73. Sir David Wilson, 'Defence in the Viking Age; private defence', in *Problems in Social and Economic Archaeology*, ed. G. de G. Sieveking et al.,

church stands immediately outside a Middle Saxon enclosure which was levelled in the Late Saxon period when a large square mortared foundation was built on the line of the bank just east of the church, together with an oven and three wells. It might be the base of a secular tower, connected with the adjoining manorial site. A formerly freestanding Saxon tower at Wickham (Berks) has two blocked doorways about 3m. up, with no lower openings (Figure 6).[26] At St Mary's church, Guildford the central tower has four narrow flint pilasters on each face, cut into by early Norman and later arches.[27] There are traces of external arcading and the size of the upper openings to east and west (each at two levels) are commensurate with doorways opening into space (Figure 7).

Elaborate ornament and large upper doorways are unusual in pre-Conquest towers. Such towers draw the eye, particularly to their upper openings, and may be called 'towers of display'. An abbey like Jumièges had an obvious need for display but (apart from Deerhurst) the other churches with upper openings into space seem to have been manorial in origin, and the towers may involve the secular arm and its needs as well as the Church's. A church must have a ground-floor entrance somewhere, but this could be blocked in an emergency, and a stone tower might not be a death-trap, since stout timber takes a long time to burn through.

The definition and function of the *burhgeat* mentioned in Wulfstan's 'Of People's Ranks and Laws' has provoked much debate, but a consensus view would be 'entrance to a protected enclosure'.[28] The accompanying *bellhus/an* may

London 1976, 443–4 suggested the stone church towers of Barton-on-Humber, Earl's Barton and Barnack as integral fortifications. See also G. Baldwin Brown, *The Arts in Early England II: Anglo-Saxon Architecture* second edition, London 1925, especially 273–294, 330–2 and J.T. Micklethwaite, 'Something about Saxon church building', *Arch. Journ.* liii, 1896, 293–351 especially 335 and *Arch. Journ.* lv, 1898, 340–9.

[26] Fisher (note 14 above), 386; H.M. and J. Taylor, *Anglo-Saxon Architecture* II, Cambridge 1965, 660–2.

[27] J.H. Parker, 'The church of St. Mary Guildford', *Arch. Journ.* xxix, 1872, 170–80; F.W. Holling, 'Early foundations of St Mary's church, Guildford', *Surrey Archaeological Collections* lxiv, 1967, 165–8.

[28] F.W. Maitland, *Township and Borough*, Cambridge 1898, 489–92; *Domesday Book and Beyond*, Cambridge 1987 reprint, 184, 190 (as a seat of justice); F.M. Stenton, 'The Thriving of the Anglo-Saxon Ceorl', expanded version of a 1958 lecture printed in *Preparatory to Anglo-Saxon England: Being the collected papers of Frank Merry Stenton*, ed. D.M. Stenton, Oxford 1970 (as a fortified dwelling); Davison, 'Origins' (note 23 above) especially 204; B.K. Davison, 'Sulgrave', *Current Archaeology* 2, 1969, 19–22 (but the thinwalled building turned out not to be turriform, see B.K. Davison, 'Excavations at Sulgrave Northamptonshire, 1960–76', *Arch. Journ.* cxxxiv, 1977, 105–14). R. Allen Brown, 'An Historian's approach to the origins of the Castle in England', *Arch. Journ.* cxxvi, 1969, 131–46 (with Davison's reply 146–8), reiterated in *Origins of English Feudalism* (Historical Problems: Studies and Documents 19), London and New York 1973, 80–2, 145 and *English Castles*, third edition, London 1976, 46–9 (town or manor gate); H.R. Loyn, 'Towns in Anglo-Saxon England: the evidence and some possible lines of enquiry', in *England before the Conquest: studies in primary sources presented to Dorothy Whitelock*, ed. P. Clemoes, Cambridge 1971, 115–28 especially 119–20 (fortified centre); Ann Williams, 'A Bell-house and a Burh-geat: Lordly Residences in England before the Norman Conquest', in *The Ideals and Practice of Medieval Knighthood*, ed. C. Harper-Bill and R. Harvey, iv, 1992, 221–40, especially the reference to Adam of Cockfield's manorhouse in Bury St Edmunds with its 140 foot high timber belfry. The whole catalogue of requirements (. . . *burgrete*) is later used in the pretended original Berkeley charter from duke Henry to Robert fitzHarding of early 1153 (*Regesta* iii, no. 309). The Irish round towers (from 950 A.D. onward) were usually called *cloicthech* (bellhouse): M. Hare

derive from the Germanic words for peace and protection and not necessarily require a bell.[29] David Parsons has suggested to me that some early towers fulfilled several of the requirements for a ceorl's promotion: the gate, the chapel and the belfry, might be all in one building. So I have appropriated the term '*burhgeat*' in this paper to mean a free-standing building of at least two storeys, the upper with large openings, whose architectural detail suggests a date no later than the twelfth century. Its purpose might be either secular or religious, or a joint corporate venture with compatible objectives. An open gallery or a large upper doorway can only have been for display (of people or of relics) and not for defence, particularly if the openings go down to the floor level. Shooting slits need breast-high defence and only a small opening for missiles; the cross-shaped openings in the embrasures at Earl's Barton would be impossible to shoot through. Even if the Tapestry designer was not showing actual buildings but using conventional symbols, the symbols should have been recognisable by those who saw the Tapestry when new.

St Leonard's Tower at West Malling (Kent), can perhaps therefore be seen as an early Norman essay at a *burhgeat*, its two surviving upper floors having large openings into space on all four sides, external arcading and no groundfloor entrance (Figure 8).[30] The nearby early Norman church tower originally had an east annexe of similar width and length, giving a unitary plan.[31] A clear example of this plan in use can be seen in the upper floor of the church tower of Brook (Kent) where the altar recess is flanked by large openings (which seem to have originally gone down to floor level) clearly visible from the nave and lit by the tower windows, an 'ecclesiastical theatre', probably due to prior Ernulf of Christ Church, Canterbury (1093–1107).[32] Richard Gem has drawn attention to the military and domestic architectural features of another unitary church at Shipley (Sussex), Templar work of c.1140. The openings in each face of the top storey of the tower are very large – 3m. high and 1m. wide.[33]

Several eleventh-century castle gatehouses carry on this *burhgeat* idea. Probably the first in England is that at Exeter, 7m. square with three floors over the

and A. Hamlin, 'The Study of early church architecture in Ireland; an Anglo-Saxon viewpoint', in *The Anglo-Saxon Church . . . in honour of H.M. Taylor*, ed. L.A.S. Butler and R.K. Morris, CBA Research Report 60, London 1986, 131–45.

[29] R. Morris, *Churches in the Landscape*, London 1988, 255.

[30] Unpublished notes by H. Sands in the library of the Society of Antiquaries of London correcting inter alia G.T. Clark, 'St Leonard's Tower, West Malling', *The Builder* xxxix, 1880, 640–2. U.T. Holmes, 'The Houses of the Bayeux Tapestry', *Speculum* iii, 1959, 179–83, plate V reproduces a carving from Moissac of a tall building with a large arch to the ground floor, two major round-topped openings above and two oculi to the second floor below a ridged roof.

[31] J. Newman, *West Kent and the Weald*, Buildings of England 29, ed. N. Pevsner, Harmondsworth 1969, 375; G.M. Livett in A.W. Lawson and G.W. Stockley, *A History of the parish church of St Mary the Virgin, West Malling, Kent*, West Malling 1904.

[32] S.E. Rigold, 'The demesne of Christ Church at Brook', *Arch. Journ.* cxxvi, 1969, 270–2.

[33] R.D.H. .Gem, 'An Early church of the Knights Templars at Shipley, Sussex', *ante* vi, 1983, 238–46. Gem has separately argued that the original west front of Lincoln Minster had a fortified aspect and intent: R.D.H. Gem, 'Lincoln cathedral: Ecclesia Pulchra, Ecclesia Fortis', in *Medieval Art and Architecture at Lincoln Cathedral*, BAA Conference Transactions 1982, 9–28. The only apparent defensive feature – the skied machicolations over the side recesses – could have been simply for liturgical use.

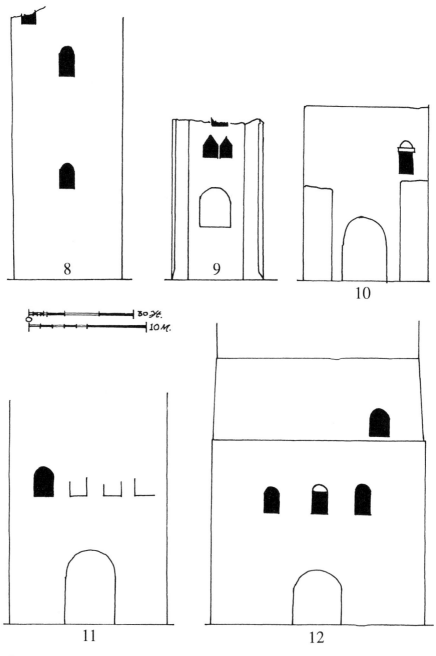

8   St Leonard, West Malling (Kent)   9   Exeter Castle (Devon)
10 West gate Lincoln Castle   11 Inner gate, Ludlow Castle (Salop)
12 Richmond Castle (North Yorks)

Figures 8–12

gatepassage.[34] The first floor is blind, but those above have triangular-headed openings – doors and windows – leading to platforms both inside and outside over the forearch (Figure 9). The West Gate at Lincoln castle as rebuilt seems to have been openbacked above the gatepassage with a doorway to the platform in front (Figure 10).[35] The inner gatehouse at Ludlow (Salop) originally had four large openings at first-floor level and two loops to the next higher floor (Figure 11). The masonry suggests that originally only the facade was built, with flanking vaulted chambers.[36] At Richmond castle, the simple doorway was converted into a square gatehouse and by the early twelfth century the upper floor had been added, with three tall openings (the central one with a plain tympanum) on the outside looking over the town, cut straight through the wall (Figure 12).[37] Over 1m. wide and 2m. high, they cannot have been meant for defence. On the staircase leading up from this floor is another opening which gave access to a wooden gallery on the inside of the castle. The second phase of the tower of Bramber Castle formerly had at least two openings one metre wide and two to three metres high above the wide arch of the gatepassage (Figure 13).[38] Another opening survives leading to a dogleg passage in a side wall; fallen masonry fragments suggest that part of the front wall had a gallery as well.

The main gatehouses to the episcopal castles of Newark and Sherborne probably date from the 1130s. At Newark, three former windows can be traced over the gatepassage, with two more one storey higher and positioned between them (Figure 14).[39] The north-west gate to Sherborne castle has an opening 2m. each way in each of the four walls at first floor level, three of them being outside the curtain wall (Figure 15).[40]

The gatehouses of the castles of the Angevin kings after 1154 lack large upper 'display' openings as do the surviving ones of Henry de Blois which all seem to date from after his return from exile in 1159.[41]

A late medieval carved oriel bracket at New Buckenham (Norfolk) represents a timber castle, with a large stone gateway having two-storey turrets and rooms

---

[34] S.R. Blaylock, 'Exeter Castle Gatehouse; architectural survey', *Exeter Archaeology 1984–5*, 18–24.

[35] E. King, 'Observations on antient castles', *Archaeologia* vi, 1782, 261–6.

[36] D.F. Renn, ' "Chastel de Dynan": the first phases of Ludlow', in *Castles in Wales and the Marches: Essays in honour of D.J.C. King*, ed. J.R. Kenyon and R. Avent, Cardiff 1987, 55–73. The decorated gatehouse at Tickhill (Yorks) appears to have traces of gallery windows over the entrance arch, and may date from Roger de Busli's time: M. Chibnall, 'Robert of Bellême and the castle of Tickhill', *Droit Privé et Institutions Régionales: Études offertes à Jean Yver*, Paris 1976, 151–6.

[37] G.T. Clark, 'Richmond Castle', *Yorkshire Archaeological Journal* ix, 1886, 33–54. I cannot find any evidence for the earlier tower shown on the folding plan in Sir Charles Peers, *Richmond Castle, Yorkshire*, London 1953.

[38] K.J. Barton and E.W. Holden, 'Excavations at Bramber Castle, Sussex, 1966–67', *Arch. Journ.* cxxxiv, 1977, 11–79 especially 15, 16, 30, 37.

[39] H.S. Braun, 'Newark Castle', *Transactions of the Thoroton Society* xxxix, 1935, 53–91.

[40] Royal Commission on Historic Monuments, England, *Inventory . . . Dorset I: West*, London 1952, 64–6, folding plan and plate 90.

[41] M. Biddle, *Wolvesey: the old bishops' palace, Winchester*, London 1986; M.W. Thompson, 'Recent excavations in the keep of Farnham castle, Surrey', *Med. Arch.* iv, 1960, 81–94 and *Farnham Castle, Surrey*, London 1961; J.N. Hare, 'Bishops Waltham Palace, Hampshire . . .', *Arch. Journ.* cxlv, 1988, 222–54 especially 225–6.

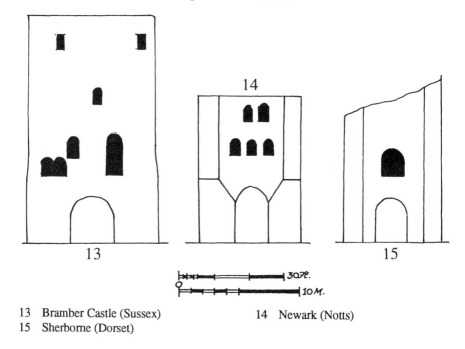

13   Bramber Castle (Sussex)   14   Newark (Notts)
15   Sherborne (Dorset)

Figures 13–15

flanking the main arch, with another row of three doorways one above, all twelve openings having round heads.[42]

Such galleries weakened the passive defensive capability of a gatehouse, and must have been designed for display, analogous to today's box at the theatre, the balcony of Buckingham Palace or the declaration of an election result. Although features designed to give the occupier a dramatic context can be found in later castle architecture (for example the approach to the audience chamber and its setting at the Wakefield Tower, London, Knaresborough and Warkworth, or the heraldic panels over the entrance at Bodiam, Herstmonceux, Hylton, Kirby Muxloe or Warkworth), this concept of public exhibition does not seem to have outlasted the middle of the twelfth century in England.[43] Whether motivated by considerations of comfort or safety, later medieval magnates preferred not to demonstrate their *dominatio* by displaying themselves from a staged setting over the castle gate.

[42] P.A. Barker and R.A. Higham, *Timber Castles*, London 1992, 161–4.
[43] P.E. Curnow, 'The Wakefield Tower, Tower of London', in *Ancient Monuments and their Interpretation: essays presented to A.J. Taylor*, ed. M.R. Apted et al., Chichester 1977, 155–89 especially 163–71 and pl. XID; P. Dixon, 'The donjon of Knaresborough: the castle as theatre', *Chateau Gaillard* xiv, 1988, 12–39; B.K. Davison on Warkworth, Oxford symposium on recent work on medieval castles, 9 October 1982. Heraldic panels are usually only treated in the guide-book on sale at the castle, but special mention should be made of B.M. Morley, 'Hylton Castle', *Arch. Journ.* cxxxiii, 1976, 118–34.

The gonfanon

Thirty-seven flags are embroidered on the Tapestry, including the two 'plastic' (cut-out) wyverns which Brooks and Walker identified as one and the same Saxon standard which, with its white-bearded bearer, his sword still sheathed, is shown falling before a horse which treads on the wyvern.[44] The standing figure carries a conical shield and holds the wyvern on a stout spike-topped pole (XXXI), whereas the unprotected toppling figure has dropped a thin 45 staff carrying the wyvern (XXXII).[45]

Although the figures are technically wyverns (with two feet) they presumably represent the dragon of Wessex. Is it simply coincidence that St Vigor of Bayeux was a dragon-slayer?[46] Nearly two hundred years later, King Henry III ordered a dragon standard with jewelled eyes and a simulated flickering tongue.[47] Such flags were valuable trophies: King Henry I paid 20 silver marks for the standard of King Louis after the battle of Brémule.[48]

Brooks' and Walker's identification of the same standard being shewn twice (albeit with slight differences) led me to look at the rest of the flags to see if others were duplicated to identify an individual (or a group) as they moved through the narrative. The flags (like any of the details of the text and drawings) may have been altered from those of the original Tapestry story, but there does seem to be an underlying unity.

The remaining thirty-five flags have the fly (that is, the side of the flag furthest from the support or hoist) in the form of three or more narrow strips usually tapering to points (tails). Five of them are masthead pennants, three-tailed without a field between hoist and fly. Four occur on the ships of the invasion fleet, and one on the English ship carrying the news of Harold's coronation to Normandy.[49] I can see no special significance in these pennants, English and Norman alike, and therefore exclude them from further study here. We are now down to thirty flags (plus the two 'plastic' wyverns mentioned above) which are all carried just below the head (either a blade or a barbed point) of either a thin staff (embroidered as a single row of stitches)or a stout pole (two parallel rows of stitches with contrasting colour between). Only a minority of the lances shewn carry flags, and consequently I see them (as Allen Brown did) as marking out the leader of an army or at least of a fighting unit (*conroi*). A long flag with a split fly is usually called a

---

[44] N.P. Brooks and H.E. Walker, 'The Authority and interpretation of the Bayeux Tapestry', *ante* i, 1978, 1–34. H.E.J. Cowdrey suggested that it was dropped by one man and picked up by another: 'Towards an interpretation of the Bayeux Tapestry', *ante* x, 1987, 59–60.

[45] The Roman figures in brackets refer to the numbering of Appendix 2, page 198.

[46] D. Bernstein, *The Mystery of the Bayeux Tapestry*, London 1986, 31.

[47] *Calendar of Close Rolls, 1242–47*, London 1916 , 201.

[48] Orderic vi, 240/1; see 242/3 for the cognizances thrown away and changed in 1119.

[49] Appendix 2, M. Repair work may conceal another on the English ship earlier under way carrying Harold to Ponthieu (BT 5, 5, 6), but it is more likely that this was intended to be a masthead cap (truck) like that embroidered on the ship (probably the same one) about to anchor. The largest ship of the invasion fleet (BT 38, 43 and detail, 42) has a large square object at the masthead, quartered and topped by a cross. Usually this is identified with Poitiers' signal lantern, but it might be William's symbol: C. Erdmann, *Die Entstehung des Kreuzzugsgedankens*, Stuttgart 1935, trans. by M.W. Baldwin and W. Goffart as *The Origin of the Idea of Crusade*, Princeton 1977, 198; T.A. Heslop, *'Image and Authority': English seals of the 11th and 12th centuries*, chapter 2 (forthcoming). But to be a flag it should have either been offset from the mast or given tails/pennants like the others.

gonfanon (meaning a war flag) more properly hung from a cross staff.[50] Here I shall use the term 'gonfanon' to mean not only a flag with split tails but also the lance to which it is attached.[51] Many such flags are held upright, gripped at shoulder height. Riders usually hold the gonfanon in their right hand, butting it into their stirrup, managing the reins and their shield in the left hand. Those on foot hold the gonfanon in their left hand whilst gesturing with the right. There are exceptions: where Harold is given arms by William (VIII) and in the heat of battle, where 'Eustace' transfers the gonfanon (XXX) to his left hand and stirrup to point out William, and also where the dragon standardbearer (XXXII) uses his left hand to hold his shield. Sometimes a rider holds his gonfanon in front of him, either at an angle or almost horizontal (e.g. II, V).[52] Usually the lance is held at the point of balance, but there are instances (e.g. IX) where it appears to be held near the butt.

At the beginning of the Tapestry, none of the figures is in full military array: Guy of Ponthieu and his men have shields and weapons, but it is not until William's expeditionary force reaches Mont St Michel that the first two figures in chain mail and helmets appear in the throng, the first man bearing a lance with a flag (I). After the crossing of the Couesnon and the attack on Dol, everyone is in armour. The Norman *Consuetudines* required war to be announced by the wearing of the hauberk (*lorica*), the carrying of the flag (*vexillum*) and the sounding of the horn (*cornu*).[53] Here we have the first two elements; the latter two will be seen later during the seaborne invasion.

Is the standardbearer William himself? The infulae at the nape of the neck are shown elsewhere on representations of the duke in the Tapestry, where he gives

[50] Erdmann, 42 distinguishes the war banner, with a flag attached to a staff, from the holy banner, with its flag hung from a transverse bar. Dione Clementi suggested to me that the flag was first attached to a lance as an improvised signal. The earliest gonfanon carried by a tenant-in chief comes in the Otto-Evangeliar (983–1002): H. Schnitzler, *Rheinische Schatzkammer* i, 1957, Koln 1957, tafel 102, p. 30. If the free end was split in two, this could indicate the tenant-in-chief of an imperial tenant-in-chief. For the Lombard and Norman gonfanons in southern Italy, J. Deer, *Papsstum und Normannen*, Koln 1972, 23 and D. Clementi, 'Stepping-stones in the making of the Regno', *Bullettino dell' Istituto Storico per il Medievo* 90, Roma 1982/3, cap. II. Wace (*Roman* iii.6, 405/6 cited by M. Bennett, 'Wace and Warfare', *ante* xi, 1988, 46) distinguished between the gonfanons of the barons and the pennants of the knights.
[51] J.F. Verbruggen, 'La tactique militaire des armées des chevaliers', *Revue du Nord* xxix, 1947. A. Ailes, 'The Knight, Heraldry and Armour: The Role of Recognition and the Origins of Heraldry', in *The Ideals and Practice of Medieval Knighthood*, ed. C. Harper-Bill and R. Harvey, iv, 14, notes 56, 57. For the significance of the left hand, see Cowdrey, 'Interpretation' (note 44 above), 57–9.
[52] The lances are not technically couched. Using the arm as well as the hand to support the lance's weight is only commonsense, and the blow might be delivered using the momentum imparted by the forward movement of the horse. Couching was designed to weld man, horse and lance together to unhorse a mounted opponent, and the Normans had no such opposition here. They were moving uphill, and consequently the lanceheads were held higher than was usual to attack men on foot. Once the target has been struck, if the lance remains unbroken, the holder risks a broken arm or a fall unless he lets go or pulls it out instantly. If William was armed with the stump of a lance at the end of the day (*Gesta Guillelmi* 202), this does not prove he had been using a couched lance. For the literature on couching see in particular, F. Buttin, 'La lance et l'arrêt de cuirasse', *Archaeologia* xcix , 1965, 77–178 especially 80–2, D. Nicolle, 'The impact of the European couched lance on Muslim military tactics', *Journal of the Arms and Armour Society* x, 1980, 6–40 and J. Flori, 'Encore l'usage de la lance . . .', *Cahiers de civilisation médiévale* xxxi, 1988, 213–40.
[53] C.H. Haskins, '*Consuetudines et Justicie* of William the Conqueror', *EHR* xxiii, 1908, 502–8, expanded in *Norman Institutions*, New York and London 1918, reprinted 1960, Appendix D section 4.

arms to Harold (VIII) and also when he sets out from Hastings (XVII).[54] This first flag is sewn very delicately. The hoist has three spaced bands wrapped round the staff, the field (between hoist and fly) carries a thin upright (red) cross between vertical bands and the fly has three long pointed tails. The cross on the field of the gonfanon does not reappear in the Tapestry until the army reaches Hastings (XIV), when it appears in a very different form (p. 191). Although this cross appears in Montfaucon's engraving (but with expanding equal arms), it might be an eleventh-century change to link the two events, the beginning of hostile action after the invasion of Brittany and of England.[55]

The red cross makes an Englishman think of St George, who had appeared to support Roger de Hauteville at the battle of Cerami in 1063 with 'a white banner bearing a wondrous cross'.[56] Almost certainly this appearance is commemorated by the remarkable tympanum over the south door of St George's church at Fordington (Dorset) where the saint carries a large gonfanon on a launcegay, with a lengthwise plain cross and three tapering tails.[57] He is triumphing over three tumbled figures with conical shields to the obvious relief of two praying mailed figures with kite-shaped shields. The style is very close indeed to that of the Tapestry. This St George's church was in existence by 1091, and so this tympanum may have predated the appearance of the saint (together with Demetrius and Mercurius) leading a heavenly host with white banners (no mention of crosses) in support of the crusaders at Antioch in 1098.[58]

Can this gonfanon be the papal banner given to the duke of Normandy?[59] Here, at the start of the Breton campaign of 1064 it would be an anachronism, since Harold was then supporting William and Edward the Confessor was still alive.

After trying several classifications, I found two groups of approximately equal size and have attempted to distiguish individual flags within each group. Some inconsistencies remain, as so often with an attempt to explain the details of the Bayeux Tapestry.

The thirty gonfanons may be divided between the seventeen which have a border round all four sides of the field, and the thirteen which are simply striped, or rolled up so that it is uncertain whether they have a border or not. I will call the latter 'simple' and the former 'bordered' gonfanons. In the Tapestry there are several cases where a gonfanon of one type held erect is followed by another

---

[54] C. Stothard, 'Some observations on the Bayeux Tapestry', *Archaeologia* xix, 1820, 184–91; I. Peirce, 'Arms, Armour and Warfare in the Eleventh Century', *ante* x, 1987, 241 note 22; Cowdrey, 'Interpretation' (note 44 above), 60.

[55] Dom B. de Montfaucon, *Les Monuments de la Monarchie Francaise I*, Paris 1729, plates XXXV–XLIX; *II*, Paris 1730, Plates I–IX.

[56] Erdmann (note 49 above), 135 citing Geoffrey Malaterra, *RIC 2*, II, 33, 141.

[57] S. Alford, 'Romanesque Architectural Sculpture in Dorset: a Select Catalogue and Commentary', *Proceedings of the Dorset Natural History and Archaeological Society* 106, 1984, 1–22 especially 1–5. The dragon does not appear until the twelfth century: Erdmann (note 49 above), 278.

[58] Orderic v, 112/5.

[59] The gift of a papal banner is mentioned by William of Poitiers (*Gesta Guillelmi* 153, 184), and Orderic ii, 142/3 but C. Morton argues that it did not arrive before 1070 at the earliest: 'Pope Alexander II and the Norman Conquest', *Latomus* xxiv, 1965, 362–82. Several papal banners were awarded in 1063/4: Erdmann (note 49 above) 154, 185–9 explains the distinction between a feudal investiture and a holy war symbol.

sloped forward and finally one held horizontally. I suggest that this indicates the same group (*conroi*) moving through the scenes of action.

If we first consider the Breton campaign, then a 'simple' gonfanon is held upright at Mont St Michel (I), sloped forward as Rennes is passed (II) and finally held horizontally to receive the keys of Dinan (VI). This last scene also has four 'bordered' gonfanons. Two (III, IV) stand upright, with very long staves embroidered right across the lower border of the Tapestry. They have shields leaning against them, perhaps belonging to the mailclad pair of attackers with a flaming torch in each hand who seem to be getting in each other's way. The other two 'bordered' gonfanons are held horizontally, one (V) by Conan in both hands and carrying the keys on its point, the other (VII) by one of the recipient's riding companions. If the 'bordered' gonfanon bearers were meant to be distinguished from the 'simple' ones, this runs counter to the explanation of them being William's men besieging Dinan. Other explanations are

a separate *conroi* (with a 'bordered' gonfanon) threatens to fire Dinan and takes the keys to hand over to the superior leader who has a 'simple' gonfanon or

Conan is the holder of the 'bordered' gonfanon; he takes Dinan by threats, surrenders and finally makes off or

a muddle by the artist or embroiderer, which could be resolved by reversing the gonfanons offering and receiving the keys. Montfaucon shows the recipient's gonfanon (VI) differenced with a central disk, which might support this explanation.

The next scene shows Harold receiving a gonfanon (VIII) from William which has two disks inside the border and four tails, just possibly captured (Breton) arms made to look more important. We do not see this gonfanon again for certain, which is only to be expected: Harold would be unlikely to flaunt signs of his new vassalage on his return to England.

We now move on to the embarkation of the invasion fleet. The leading figure wears a mantle and carries a partly-furled gonfanon (IX), perhaps indicating that the war would begin at the English shore and not in Normandy. Something of the same idea can be seen today in the casing of military colours. The sloping staff is being held at its lower end, probably so that it can be seen by the whole army.

On the great ship of the fleet, the hornblowing figure on the sternpost slopes his small 'simple' gonfanon (X) towards England. On landing, two figures with rolled-up gonfanons (XI, XII) on poles across their horses'necks gallop up to a more leisurely rider who holds his 'simple' gonfanon (XIII) erect. Next a mounted scout has planted his 'simple' gonfanon (XIV) on the hill but points (double-jointedly) to it from the saddle.

Staying with the 'simple' gonfanons, three are successively held erect (XXI), then forward (XXII) and then horizontal (XXIII) as William orders the advance. This action is then repeated with 'simple' gonfanons (XXIV, XXV, XXVI) differenced with three disks on the field, ending just as the Norman horses reach the massed English foot. Finally a 'simple' upright gonfanon (XXVII) can be seen between the first two Englishmen, and crossed by a broad-bladed axe. Since none of the English can spare a hand from spear and shield for either axe or gonfanon (it is remarkable that the first Englishman here is also a greybeard, indicating a veteran) the latter gonfanon must be Norman insignia.

My interpretation is that the first *conroi* to disembark goes scouting, rallying on the hill. When battle begins, their gonfanon is lowered for action and then after engagement, raised to rally. Another *conroi* then follows them into action.

We now turn to the 'bordered' gonfanons. Two figures oversee two stages of the building of Hastings castle: first, the collection of the labourers (XIV) and then the halfbuilt structure (XV). The cross (p. 189) now reappears; a fat one on the first upright gonfanon may be then shown 'reversed' as the four disks embroidered on the second. Both figures are wearing mantles like William as he gets news of Harold, seated and holding a stout pole displaying a gonfanon (XVI) with a fat cross and four tails. He then stands outside the Hastings *burhgeat* grasping an erect gonfanon (XVII) charged with a single disk.

As the advance quickens to a gallop, there are two 'bordered' gonfanons on poles borne like the rolled-up pair carried by the first men galloping off the boat earlier: the first (XVIII) has five tails and a quatrefoil charge, the other (XIX) is semi-elliptical, with a charge which has been described as a bird or a chalice and nine short flamelike tails.

At the far right of the massed English infantry stands yet another bearded man, with both hands grasping a gonfanon (XXVIII) charged with a central disk and five tails. On his left he is protected by an axeman, to his right are four spearmen with shields, the furthest away providing breast-high protection by poking his spear between the second and third shields.

A fallen triangular gonfanon (XXIX), with four tasselled indented streamers, appears before the deaths of Harold's brothers. Worsaae identified this 150 years ago as the *danbrog*, the Viking warflag to be seen associated with the raven on the coins of Anlaf Cuaran, ruler of Northumbria 941–44. The bird on the nine-fringed flag shewn earlier (XIX) could be a raven and so might be intended to represent the same flag.[60]

'Eustace' holds an elaborate gonfanon (XXX), charged with a cross with four small disks in the quarters and another four in a strip before the fly and points to William who pushes back his helmet. This flag is another candidate for the vexillum given by pope Alexander II to William. *'[E]. . .cius'* is suspect, not least because the standardbearer is elsewhere named as Thurstan fitz Rou.[61] If Eustace's name was interposed in the Tapestry for political reasons, the damage to the border may have been later censorship.

This gonfanon is the one clear case in the Tapestry of a cross formy with expanded ends which we find in later pictures, e.g. on crusaders' helmets and on their gonfanons at the battles of the First Crusade at Ascalon, Dorylaeum, Nicaea and Antioch on the glass formerly in a window at St Denis.[62] There Robert of Flanders' banner also had four disks between the limbs of the cross formy. This

[60] G.J. French, 'On the banners of the Bayeux Tapestry and the earliest heraldic charges', *Journ. BAA* 13. 1857, 113–30 especially 129; *Encomium Emmae Reginae*, ed. A. Campbell, Royal Historical Society Camden third series lxxii, 1949, 96–7; Ailes (note 51 above), 8 note 34; *Coinage in Tenth-century England from Edward the Elder to Edgar's reform*, ed. C.E. Blunt et al., Oxford for the British Academy 1989, chapter 14 , especially 221–2.
[61] M. Bennett, 'Poetry as History? The Roman de Rou of Wace as a source for the Norman Conquest', *ante* v, 1982, 33 n. 68; Freeman, 'Identity' (note 7 above), 134; Erdmann (note 49 above), 197–9.
[62] BN Ms Fr15634 (i) engraved in Montfaucon (note 55 above), i, Paris 1729, plates l–liv and reproduced in R. Allen Brown, *The Normans*, Woodbridge 1984, 118–19, 126–8.

glass must have dated from the middle of the twelfth century at earliest, and so cannot be used as contemporary evidence for the gonfanons of the First Crusade. But the cross formy with disks design appears on the reverse die of William's coinage, both as duke of Normandy before 1066 and also on his English coins after 1080. It does not appear on the lance flags carried on the royal counterseals before 1100, however, which are simple separate streamers, without a field.[63] Neither William I nor Rufus wished to acknowledge papal authority after 1066. The cross was simply Christian (and used as a *signa* for attestations); the flag, if originally papal, acquired a wider use in and after the First Crusade. We might expect a more explicit emblem of St Peter, but the earliest image of a papal banner – the mosaic in the Lateran Tribune of the banner given by Leo III to Charlemagne – is of a three-tailed gonfanon sprinkled with tiny stars and six disks coloured like archery targets.[64]

The gonfanon with a plain cross occurs several times in the Scylitzes manuscript (1057 x 1081) borne by the Byzantine forces (as supporters of Christ) against the Muslims.[65] The similar standard here may be a Christian banner, appearing first (I, perhaps as an anachronistic 'papal amendment') at the start of the Breton campaign, three times at Hastings *ceastra* (XIV, XV and XVI with four 'tails'), once (XVIII with 5 'tails') during the advance and finally in elaborate detail (XXX) at the crucial point of the battle. This may be pushing symbolism too far, and the cross emblem may simply identify William at various points of the narrative where he is not otherwise obvious.

This leaves two 'bordered' flags to be accounted for; one (XVII) with three tails and a central disk held by William before setting off from Hastings and another (XXIX) with five tails and a central disk held by the unarmed (but mail-clad and protected) man on the right of the English line, Both flags appear to be heavily oversewn, and the disks may be the result of bad repairs. The first might have been intended as a cross but crowded out by the expanded border. A similar explanation for the other flag is that this was the 'Fighting Man' personal standard of Harold.[66] Or is this the gonfanon given to Harold by William two years before at Bonneville-sur-Touques, which has lost a disk and gained a tail?

Five tails may denote kingship, potential in William and factual in Harold.

[63] A.B. and A. Wyon, *The Great Seals of England*, London 1887 especially plate 2. Dr Heslop tells me that the swallowtailed second seal of William II is a forgery. Ailes, 15 n. 58.

[64] D.L. Galbreath, *A Treatise on Ecclesiastical Heraldry, part 1: Papal Heraldry*, Cambridge 1930, 1; Erdmann (note 49 above), 185.

[65] A.B. Hoffmeyer, 'Military Equipment in the Byzantine Manuscript of Scylitzes in the Biblioteca Nacional in Madrid', *Gladius* v, Granada 1966, especially figures 19, 28, 34.

[66] *Gesta Guillelmi* 224 and *Carmen* 24/5, possibly derived from the Cerne Giant hillfigure as suggested by E.M.C. Barraclough, 'The Flags of the Bayeux Tapestry', *Armi Antichi* i, 1969, 117–24 especially 120.

APPENDIX I

The West Tower of St Michael at the Northgate, Oxford

David Parsons

The text on which this appendix is based was originally drafted in the mid 1970s in response to the archaeological discoveries made around the church in 1972–73.[67] The investigations made it clear that the nave of the church, which is a later medieval addition to the Anglo-Saxon tower, stands directly on the line of the pre-Conquest rampart, so that it was not possible to imagine a conventional church in this position until the town wall was moved to the north at a date which is uncertain, but may be c.1100.[68] The tower was therefore interpreted by me as a free-standing structure associated with the defences and forming part of a gate-house arrangement. Ecclesiastical use of an upper floor as a gate chapel was not excluded, but the tower was regarded as an essentially secular structure and the existence of a church in the Anglo-Saxon period discounted.

This position must be modified, however, in view of the clear evidence of Domesday Book that the priests of St Michael's owned property in the city. This implies a collegiate foundation by 1086, which must have been provided with a church at a date when the original line of the Anglo-Saxon rampart was still functioning as the town defence at this point. Various suggestions have been put forward as to where this church might have been located. The upper part of the reconstruction diagram in the excavation report suggests a position on Ship Street with the church built into the tail of the rampart and entirely separate from the tower.[69] A more recent interpretation by the Oxford Archaeological Unit shows the church taking the place of the rampart behind a postulated section of masonry wall adjacent to the gateway, with the tower added only after the deflection of the wall to the north.[70] Given that a blocked opening was discovered in the south wall of the tower at first-floor level, it is not unreasonable to suggest a building, possibly the church, to the south of the tower, with a connexion between the two at gallery level or leading from the tower into the roofspace of the adjoining building. There are various objections to this particular interpretation, one of which is that as drawn it takes no account of the eccentrically-placed blocked door in the west wall of the tower, a point of some significance in the understanding of the uses that may be suggested for the tower. There is also an assumption, which I do not share, that openings in the north wall of the tower make it unsuitable for a defensive role and require it to be protected on that flank by the re-aligned city north wall.

A further possibility is suggested by this last interpretation, namely that the church itself formed part of the Anglo-Saxon defences at this point, with the tower already in existence and doubling as the west tower of the church and the gate tower of the town. This suggestion receives some support from the results of

[67] Durham et al. (note 20 above), 14–18, 33–35.
[68] Durham et al., 33.
[69] Durham et al., 33, Fig. 6A.
[70] Hassall, 'Buried City' (note 20 above), 22 fig. C.

archaeological work carried out at Repton (Derbyshire) in recent years. The line of the Viking defences has been established, and the termination of the ditch to the east of the chancel shows that the church building was incorporated as part of the defensive system.[71]

There are thus several different interpretations which can be put forward for the sequence of events at the north gate of Oxford and for the status of the buildings, actual or postulated:

(i) the tower was part of the north defences of the town in the Anglo-Saxon period and not attached to the church of St Michael; the deflection of the wall line, perhaps after the Norman Conquest, enabled a new church to be built to the east of the tower;

(ii) The Anglo-Saxon church was towerless and stood inside the north gate; in the late eleventh century the line of the wall was moved to the north, and it incorporated a gate tower attached to the north side of the church; the church was subsequently replaced by a building attached to the east side of the tower;

(iii) an Anglo-Saxon church with west tower formed the town defences at this point, taking the place of the rampart attested further to the east; the tower simultaneously acted as part of the gateway structure.

All these propositions merit discussion, but in the context of the present paper it seems appropriate to follow the argument of the original draft of this Appendix, which examined in more detail the first of the three possibilities. This was by no means the first attempt to interpret the tower of St Michael's as a gate-tower: in discussions and at conferences archaeologists and historians have been wont to speculate about a possible function for the tower in connexion with the Anglo-Saxon gateway. If the tower is regarded as flanking the actual entrance, with the gates hung on the line of the north wall of the tower, there are no problems of interpretation. However, attempts to see the tower as part of the entrance itself have foundered on the lack of a doorway at ground level which could have given access to the interior of the town. The rubble fabric of the lower part of the south wall of the tower has been rebuilt at some stage, and there is no apparent evidence for a former door. There are however some slight hints that a door once existed in the appropriate position. A plinth-like course of squared stones at the base of the tower fabric begins on the north side close to the north-west quoin, returns along the west face and continues along the south face for a short distance, after which it is hidden by modern paving surrounding the church porch. By inspection from above, however, it is possible to identify the continuation of this feature into the angle between the tower and the south-west buttress of the nave. On the west and north the stones project only about 2.5 cm from the face of the tower. They hardly constitute a plinth in the true sense of the term, and seem mostly not to be original. Fisher dismisses the feature as modern, drawing attention to the fact that it crosses the blocking of the west doorway, which he rightly says 'a plinth would not do'.[72] Figure 16 shows diagrammatically the arrangement of the stones, and it is clear that the two stones covering the blocking of the west door respect the jambs of the

[71] M. Biddle and B. Kjølbye-Biddle, 'Repton and the Vikings', *Antiquity*, lxvi (1992) 36–51, esp. fig. 2.
[72] Fisher (note 14 above), 233.

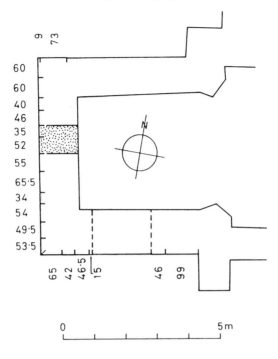

*Figure 16. Measured diagram of plinth at
St Michael by the Northgate Oxford*

opening; it is therefore possible that the 'plinth' predates the blocking of the doorway, which appears to have been carried out in the eighteenth century. The two stones concerned could have been inserted with the blocking marterial as a cosmetic effect. Be that as it may, there appears to be a gap in the line of 'plinth' stones on the south elevation measuring 1.86 metres, which would be consistent with a doorway in this position still in use at the time that the 'plinth' was inserted. The stone immediately to the west of this gap is also anomalous, measuring only about 15 cm, whereas most of the stones are between 34 and 73 cm in length. This may indicate that a small space between the stone on its immediate left and feature to its right had to be filled. If there had been no doorway here, one would have expected a much longer stone in this position.

The suggestion of a doorway in this position has a further attraction. Excavation evidence has shown that the eastern frontage of Cornmarket Street in the Anglo-Saxon period was more that seven metres behind the present line. A pedestrian walking up this side of the street would have been heading directly towards the postulated entrance to the tower. It is wise, however, to have some reservations about this evidence. Not only is the face of the plinth not visible on the south side, but is also unclear how much original walling existed here when it was fitted. Canon Martin has recorded a substantial rebuilding of the south-west quoin earlier this century, but the extent of this reconstruction is not clear from the recent stone-by-stone survey of the interior walls.[73] It appears from Martin's account that the plinth may not have been added to the tower until the demolition of the adjoining shop on the north side about the beginning of this century. A plan of the church in the parish records shows the parish bakehouse in this position apparently in the early eighteenth century, and its west wall aligned with the west front of the tower.[74] The 'plinth' could not have been constructed with this building in situ. If not twentieth-century in date, it must be pre-eighteenth.

Accepting provisionally, then, that there may have been an Anglo-Saxon south door, the ground-floor arrangements of the tower seem ideal for part of a gateway structure. There was presumably a large gate across Cornmarket Street abutting the west wall of the tower and giving access to vehicles and animals. When the gate was closed, the tower would afford pedestrian access by means of the original west door and the postulated south door. The dog-leg route through the tower could be seen as a version of the traditional defensive device attested for many periods and types of structure. The nature of the west door itself enhances such a suggestion. Its two most obvious characteristics are its very small size and displacement north of the axial line of the tower. These characteristics argue equally against the door's having originally been the entrance to a church and for its suitability as part of a defensive structure. In particular, its position north of the centre line of the tower leaves a good stretch of tower wall available on the town side of the opening (just over 3 m) for the abutment of the presumably wooden gate structure.

The interpretation of the tower as an essentially secular structure does not preclude the use of part of it for religious purposes. The association of churches and chapels with town gateways is well established, at least from the time of Gregory of Tours. In Oxford itself there were further examples at the Southgate (another St Michael's), the Eastgate (Trinity chapel), at Smithgate (Lady chapel) and if the eastern defences of the Anglo-Saxon town followed the line currently proposed, the church of St Mary the Virgin may be the successor of a pre-Conquest church associated with the original Eastgate. Elsewhere there are examples of churches, some of them Anglo-Saxon in origin, on or close to town gateways: St Mary at Cricklade, St Martin at Wareham, several St Botolphs at gates to the City of London, and in the later medieval period at Canterbury and at Winchester, where the chapel still exists over Kingsgate. The phenomenon of gate chapels is an under-researched topic, but it is clear at a superficial level that an ecclesiastical role for part of St Michael's tower would not be out of the ordinary. The dedication, if original, may have applied to the tower itself: St Michael, the protector of souls, was often associated with physical or symbolic defence.[75]

Note. The original draft went on to consider St Michael's tower in the context of Anglo-Saxon turriform churches, a discussion which will appear in M. Audouy et al., 'The tower of All Saints' Church, Earl's Barton, Northamptonshire: its construction and context', *Archaeological Journal*, forthcoming.

---

[73] R.R. Martin, *The church and parish of St Michael at the Northgate, Oxford: a history*, Oxford 1967.
[74] T.G. Hassall, personal communication 21 December 1976.
[75] Morris (note 29 above), 56.

APPENDIX II

The Gonfanons of the Bayeux Tapestry

Column 1 of the table below, p. 198 is the serial number used elsewhere in the text for identification. The masthead 'tails' (M) are not numbered.

Column 2 gives the nearest word of the inscription, with a slash (/) as near as possible to where the gonfanon occurs. Where there are long breaks in the inscription (during the battle for example) the last preceding word is given.

Column 3 gives the scene number as written on the backing linen and reproduced on the *dépliant* sold at Bayeux.

Column 4 gives the plate number in Stenton's edition and

Column 5 gives the plate number in Wilson's edition (note 1 above, p. 177)

The usual style of gonfanon is a rectangular flag (divided vertically) with three tapering 'tails' at the fly flown just below the lancehead on a slender lance held by a rider at the point of balance, or by a pedestrian at shoulder level.

Column 6 shows whether the lance is held

vertical (V), horizontal (H) or sloped forward (A), with the butt in the stirrup (S) or on the ground (G)

in the left (L) or right (R) hand, near the butt (U) or lies on the ground (F) and whether the flag's field has a border (B) or is a wyvern (W) and gives the number of crosses (C) and disks (D). The number of 'tails' (T) is specified, unless it is the usual three, and a final P means that the flag is supported on a stout pole, not a thin javelin.

Brackets surround doubtful items dealt with in the text.

Column 7 consists of notes. Although some of the colours of Stothard's engraving are wayward, the only significant differences noted are between Montfaucon's engraver and subsequent photographers.

Table of gonfanons in the Bayeux Tapestry

Column 1	2	3	4	5	6	7
I	EXERCIT/VS	16	21	18	VSRC	
II	VER/TIT	18	24	21	AR	
III	CONTRA/	19	26	23	VGB	
IV	DI/NANTES	19	26	23	VGB	
V	/ET	19	26	23	HLRB	Montfaucon D
VI	CV/NAN	20	26	23	HR	
VII	CLA/VES	20	26	24	ARB	
VIII	HAROL/DO	21	27	24	VGLBD2T4	Also Wilson page (22)
M	ANGLI/CA	34	36	33		
IX	MAGN/O	37	42	39	AR(U)	
M	NAVIGIO;/	38	42	40		
M	MARE/	38	42	40		
X	VENIT/	38	43	42	A(G)L	Sternpost dwarf
M	PEVENSAE;/	38	44	42		
M		38	44	42		Also Stenton VIII
XI	VERV/NT	40	46	44	AR(U)P	
XII	H/ESTINGA	40	46	44	AR(U)P	
XIII	/VT	40	46	45	VSR	
XIV	IV/SSIT	45	50	49	VGLBC	
XV	H/ESTENGA	45	51	49	VGLBD4	D4 as negative C?
XVI	WILLELMO/	46	51	50	VGLBCT4P	
XVII	MILITE/S	47	53	51	VGLBD	
XVIII	C/ONTRA	48	55	53	ARBCT5P	
XIX	HAROL/DVM	48	55	53	ARBT9(U)P	Oval, short fringes
XX	DISSET/	49	57	55	V(G)R	Rider pointing?
XXI	DVX/	50	59	57	V(S)R	Montfaucon D
XXII	SV/IS	50	59	57	AR	
XXIII	VI/RILITER	51	60	58	HR	
XXIV	SAPIENTER:/	51	61	59	VSRD3	
XXV	PRELIVM:/	51	61	60	ARD3	
XXVI	EXERCITV/	51	62	61	HRD3(U)	
XXVII		51	63	61	VG	
XXVIII		51	63	62	VGLRBDT5P	
XXIX	/REGIS	52	65	65	FBT4	Triangle, tasselled square lower fringe Also Stenton XI
XXX	CI/VS	55	69	68	V(S)LBCD4+4	Montfaucon no shaft, no E
XXXI	HIC/	57	71	71	FW	
XXXII	/HARO	57	71	71	VGRWP	

ARCHBISHOP STIGAND AND THE EYE OF THE NEEDLE

Mary Frances Smith

Stigand, the last English bishop of Winchester and archbishop of Canterbury, was one of the most influential and wealthy figures of the late Anglo-Saxon period.* Yet he remains one of the most enigmatic, owing primarily to his unsavory reputation cultivated by post-Conquest Norman propagandists. While no words remain from those who overtly supported him, there must have been many who either helped him or clung to his coat tails through fifty of the most turbulent years in all of English history. Indeed, during his long career this one churchman flourished in the reigns of five English kings and survived four years into the Conquest as the kingdom's most important prelate. At the same time, Stigand amassed a fortune in land equal to or greater than those of the kingdom's earls, and, in some areas, even Edward the Confessor. His personal territorial interests were widespread, spanning ten counties and comprising some of the most valuable estates found in Domesday Book. Yet land was only one component of Stigand's power. He maintained an immense lordship in East Anglia and other counties, indicating that many lay people as well as ecclesiastics sought the benefit of his protection and influence. Beyond his already immense personal wealth, Stigand controlled the lordships of Canterbury and Winchester, the kingdom's wealthiest sees, a combination that made his power truly unrivaled among ecclesiastics. This evidence suggests, therefore, that characterizations left to posterity by post-Conquest sources, ranging from greedy pilferer to simoniacal usurper and even murderer, are woefully inadequate. It is the purpose of this paper to provide a clearer picture of this most important figure by reconstructing the events of Stigand's life where possible, analyzing the nature and composition of his private and ecclesiastical lordships, fitting him into a more realistic picture of the church in which he served, and suggesting practical reasons why he acquired such a negative reputation in the decades that followed his death.

It is perhaps ironic that Stigand's career as a member of the Anglo-Saxon episcopacy began as a result of another conquest of England, that of Cnut the Dane. The *Anglo-Saxon Chronicle* records that Stigand was appointed as a royal priest to *Assandun* in 1020.[1] That his first appointment should be to Cnut's

---

* I would like to thank the members of the Battle Conference for their warm welcome and helpful suggestions, especially Drs Marjorie Chibnall, Simon Keynes and David Bates. Above all, I am grateful to Professor Robin Fleming and Dr Christopher Lewis, whose constant help and encouragement made this paper possible.

[1] *ASC*, s.a. 1020 (F): 'And in this year the king went to Ashingdon, and had a minster built there of stone and mortar, for the souls of the men who had been slain there, and gave it to a priest of his who was called Stigand.' Dorothy Whitelock notes that the word 'priest' was commonly used to mean royal chaplain in the later part of the *Anglo-Saxon Chronicle*. Stigand is also styled 'the

symbolic victory church, at a time when the new king was purging England of all potential political enemies, is evidence of Stigand's royal favor.[2] The favor that Stigand found at Cnut's court was perhaps due in part to his Anglo-Norse background. He was apparently from a prosperous Anglo-Scandinavian family centered in East Anglia, a family that represented the kind of conciliation that Cnut would have found desirable as a conqueror who intended to stay.[3] Hindsight suggests, however, that Stigand's favor at this time was due primarily to Ælfgifu Emma, Cnut's new wife and the widow of Æthelred 'the Unready'. In one version of the *Anglo-Saxon Chronicle* he is called her 'advisor', suggesting the possibility that his association was with her rather than Cnut.[4] In either case, Stigand was clearly acceptable to Cnut as a representative of the king's church. What role he played at Cnut's court over the next twenty years is difficult to determine. The sources are silent, with the exception of a few charters. They make it clear that Stigand was active in Cnut's court in the 1030s, witnessing a handful of Cnut's extant charters in this decade.[5]

The connection to Emma is generally considered the reason behind Stigand's next appointment as bishop of Elmham in 1043, so soon after the exiled King Edward's ascension to the throne.[6] Although Elmham was one of the poorest bishoprics in the kingdom, it was not a bad career move for a Norfolk man, providing Stigand with the opportunity to consolidate his personal holdings while serving in Edward's episcopate. It does not look as though Stigand was at court much while he held this bishopric: he does not attest any of Edward's extant charters as bishop of Elmham before 1046, and only two after. One of the reasons for this may have been the minor setback that Stigand experienced in the first year of his episcopacy, when he was implicated in a plot with Emma and was briefly removed from office. While the exact nature and extent of Emma's disgrace is unknown, it is clear that she was, at the very least, withholding from her son Edward access to her fortune stored at Winchester, which she had done to Harold Harefoot, as well, in 1035.[7] If one suspect account is to be believed, Emma hoarded this money in the hopes of backing Magnus of Norway in an invasion and

---

king's chaplain' in a Bury document published in *Monasticon*, iii, 154, no. 21; *The Works of Gervase of Canterbury*, ed. W. Stubbs, RS 1879, ii, 363; *ASC*, s.a. 1051 (F) [1052]; and Worcester, i, 193.

[2] See K. Mack, 'Changing thegns: Cnut's conquest and the English aristocracy', *Albion* xvi, 1984, 375–87.

[3] Stigand's name is Old Norse while his brother Æthelmær's is Old English (Olof von Feilitzen, *The Pre-Conquest Personal Names of Domesday Book*, Uppsala 1937, 184, 374). They have a sister who is a substantial Domesday landholder in Norfolk but she is simply called *mulier soror Stigandi* (*Domesday Book*, ii, 116a–b).

[4] *ASC*, s.a. 1043 (C); '. . . forðam he wæs nehst his modor ræde, and heo for swa swa he hire rædde' (*Two of the Saxon Chronicles Parallel*, ed. vol. 1, C. Plummer, Oxford 1892–99, s.a. 1043). But this statement may be unreliable since it appears only in this version, which is generally hostile to both Stigand and Earl Godwine, and the context is incriminatory.

[5] P.H. Sawyer, *Anglo-Saxon Charters: An Annotated List and Bibliography. Royal Historical Society Guides and Handbooks*, London 1968 (hereafter cited as S), nos. 967, 969 (1033); 975 (1035); 979 (1027x32). These charters are most likely all from the 1030s. Other royal priests attest on three and Stigand appears once by himself. Another charter, although dubious, contains an authentic confirmation by Harthacnut of one of Cnut's charters, on which Stigand attests as *capellanus*. The charter on which this is based is dated 1028x1035 (S 982).

[6] *ASC*, s.a. 1043 (C), 1042 (E) [1043].

[7] *ASC*, s.a. 1035 (C,D), 1043 (C,D), 1042 (E) [1043].

takeover of England.[8] Whatever the case, as her advisor, Stigand was implicated and suffered both removal from office and confiscation of lands in late 1043.[9] But his restoration in early 1044 indicates that his involvement in whatever it was that Emma did to annoy her son did not hold up under close scrutiny.[10] Rather, Stigand may be seen to be firmly back in Edward's favor by 1046, when he first appears as an episcopal witness to two royal charters and was therefore attending court.[11]

Emma, too, was exonerated, but was perhaps forced to lead a more retiring life afterwards at Winchester, where she had a commanding presence. Besides holding extensive property there, Emma was a kinswoman of the current bishop, Ælfwine, and a patron of both Old Minster and New Minster.[12] Thus it is not surprising that when the see of Winchester became vacant in late August of 1047, Stigand was translated to the bishopric.[13] Here, close to his patron and back in the favor of the king, Stigand was active at court, attesting all of Edward's extant charters from the years 1047 to 1052.[14] But he was clearly far more involved in the politics of the realm than the charter evidence shows. Having learned the importance of appearing neutral, Stigand played mediator between King Edward and the rebellious Earl Godwine, just four years after his appointment to the bishopric.[15] The reasons for Godwine's rebellion are complicated: he seems to have been goaded into action as a result of Edward's foreign and domestic policies, which encouraged the influence of his continental friends, especially that of his newly appointed archbishop of Canterbury, Robert of Jumièges. Ordered to appear at a trial for crimes of a now unclear nature, Godwine refused without the surety of safe conduct and hostages. It was Stigand who delivered the unhappy news to Godwine for a final time that Edward had denied the earl's request, news which precipitated the family's flight from England. And, according to Edward's anonymous encomiast, the failure to mediate this dispute successfully left Stigand weeping abundantly.[16] Doubtless his disappointment was very real. As a member of the Anglo-Saxon church on the episcopal fast-track, Stigand cannot have been any happier than Earl Godwine

---

[8] This account is based on a St Augustine tradition, which Frank Barlow has shown to be the likely product of a hagiographer's imagination. Although there may have been rumors to this effect, Emma's subsequent exoneration makes such a treasonous act doubtful (F. Barlow, 'Two Notes: Cnut's Second Pilgrimage and Queen Emma's Disgrace in 1043', *EHR* lxxiii, 1958, 649–56).

[9] *ASC*, s.a. 1043 (C). The Abingdon version of the *Anglo-Saxon Chronicle* is the only one to mention Stigand's involvement (see above, note 4).

[10] *ASC*, s.a. 1043 (E) [1044]. Barlow suggests the possibility that Emma's 'disgrace' was precipitated by her over-involvement in the king's business and that it was she who appointed Stigand and not Edward. This would more plausibly account for Stigand's removal from office; it is unlikely that, as the chronicler suggests, he advised Emma to go against the king, her son (F. Barlow, *Edward the Confessor*, Berkeley 1970, 76).

[11] S 1014, 1015 (1046). From the period 1044 to 1047, there are fourteen extant, authentic charters that Stigand could have attested. That he only appears on two is probably insignificant given that bishops of Elmham both before and after Stigand rarely attest charters.

[12] According to one Winchester tradition, Emma gave generously to the foundations, including ornaments of gold, silver and precious jewels, clothing and lands given to her by King Æthelred as dower lands, all for the good of her soul (*Annales de Wintonia* in *Annales Monastici*, ed. H.R. Luard, RS 1865, ii, 18, 24–5).

[13] *ASC*, s.a. 1047 (C), 1048 (D) [1047], 1045 (E) [1047].

[14] S 1017–1023.

[15] *Vita Eadwardi*, 34.

[16] *Vita Eadwardi*, 36.

with the forced introduction of the Norman, Robert, into Canterbury. Even if he held no hope of higher office, which is unlikely, Stigand would not have welcomed the threat to his favored position at court.[17] Moreover, it seems that the Canterbury community, according to canonical law, had already elected one of its own, who was, coincidentally, a kinsman of Earl Godwine.[18] The appointment of an obscure and malleable monk would have suited Stigand's purpose, if he himself were not elected. Moreover, that this monk was a kinsmen of Godwine suggests that Stigand would have supported his appointment, although it is difficult to know how close the bishop was with the kingdom's most powerful family at this time. Certainly, as a political realist, he would have desired the quick diffusion of a situation which gave unbridled authority to foreign favorites. But it is also likely that Stigand had a personal relationship with the family, inescapable due to his own position as bishop of Winchester in Godwine's earldom of Wessex. Whatever the connection, in 1052 Stigand once again intervened between the two parties after Godwine's threat of military action forced Edward to come to terms.[19] The result was the restoration of Godwine and his family to their previous position and the flight of a number of the Normans to the Continent. Among this group were Archbishop Robert, who died shortly after complaining of his expulsion to the pope, Ulf bishop of Dorchester, and William bishop of London, who was soon recalled.[20]

The unexpected flight of Robert of Jumièges left the see of Canterbury vacant, although in name only, considering it could not canonically be filled while Robert was still living. Why Edward decided to fill the position immediately and not wait until Robert's death is unknown. The king may have been able to propose Ælfric, the monk who had reportedly been canonically elected by the community, but he chose not to and instead appointed Stigand. He was, indeed, a logical if uncanonical choice, given his close association with both Edward and Godwine, and the likelihood that a candidate would have to be palatable to both. After all, Stigand had not taken sides during Godwine's rebellion, but had represented the best interests of the kingdom. Hence, he was elevated to the see of Canterbury in 1052.[21] Regardless of Edward's motives, Stigand was obviously aware of his

---

[17] It was thought that Robert, besides being a foreigner, had completely replaced the king's Anglo-Saxon councilors, Godwine and Stigand included, and '. . . with the authority derived from this promotion intruded himself more than was necessary in directing the course of the royal councils and acts; so much so, indeed, that according to the saying, "Evil communications corrupt good manners", through his assiduous communication with him the king began to neglect more useful advice' (*Vita Eadwardi*, 28). The encomiast's pro-Godwine stance is corroborated by two versions of the *Anglo-Saxon Chronicle* which record that subsequently the English '. . . outlawed all the Frenchmen who had . . . given bad counsel in this country' (*ASC*, s.a. 1052 (C,D)).

[18] In reference to Robert's appointment, '. . . all the clergy protested with all their might against the wrong' (*Vita Eadwardi*, 19). Although the account of the election only appears in the *Vita Eadwardi*, it is probably true; the Peterborough chronicler relates that Robert got what he deserved because '. . . he had obtained the dignity when it was not God's will' (*ASC*, s.a. 1052 (E)).

[19] *ASC*, s.a. 1052 (E). None of the accounts describing his role in this affair suggest that Stigand supported Earl Godwine against the king. Reconciliation was clearly in his best interest, and Stigand remained Edward's 'advisor and chaplain' throughout (*ASC*, s.a. 1051 (F) [1052]).

[20] *ASC*, s.a. 1052 (C,D,E). 'Florence' of Worcester notes that William was recalled because he was a 'good-natured man' (Worcester, i, 210). Ulf's appointment in 1049 seems to have caused bad feelings from the beginning. See F. Barlow, *The English Church 1000–1066*, London 1979, 215–6.

[21] *ASC*, s.a. 1053 (C) [1052], 1052 (E), 1051 (F) [1052].

uncanonical position, performing only administrative functions at this time, such as attendance at the king's court.[22] Indeed, Stigand appears to have been watching the situation in Rome very closely. Knowing that he could not hope to obtain a pallium from any pope of the reformed party, he was poised in 1058 to take advantage of the intrusion into the papacy of Benedict X, who sent him a pallium almost immediately.[23] It was only after he received his pallium that Stigand consecrated Æthelric to the bishopric of Selsey and Siward to Rochester.[24] Unfortunately, however, Benedict was expelled from the papacy in the following year, and the pontiff's untimely expulsion meant that Stigand had gambled and lost. Where before he possessed no pallium of his own, he was now in possession of a tainted pallium, granted by a man excommunicated for simoniacally obtaining the apostolic see.[25] Thus English episcopal appointees thereafter sought consecration elsewhere.[26] But Stigand did manage to bless several abbots, and ironically, consecrated William the Conqueror's nominee, Remigius, to the see of Dorchester in 1067.[27] And, while much is made after the Conquest of Stigand's uncanonical position, we know that he maintained at least cordial relations with the reformed papacy, with whose legates he sat in the council that elected Wulfstan to Worcester in 1062.[28] As Barlow notes, 'nothing at all can be put against the case that Stigand always acted as a bishop and was regarded as one'.[29] But it was to Ealdred that William the Conqueror turned for consecration in 1066, although under any other circumstances his first choice would have been the archbishop of Canterbury.[30] Nevertheless, Stigand survived four years into the Conquest as archbishop, accompanying William to Normandy in 1066 and attesting several of the Conqueror's charters.[31] Perhaps it took William those four years to feel secure enough to depose the wealthy and influential archbishop, whose favor he seems to have curried in these years. Or, more likely, William waited until after the death of Ealdred in 1069, a prelate whose deposition would have been both difficult and

---

[22] S 1024–6 (1052–5). Charter witness lists for the early years of Stigand's archiepiscopate have serious chronological problems, but they do indicate that he was in constant attendance at court. He was also performing some pastoral duties according to 'Florence' of Worcester, who records that he wore Robert's pallium during Mass (Worcester, ii, 5).

[23] *ASC*, s.a. 1058 (D,E,F).

[24] *ASC*, s.a. 1058 (E,F).

[25] That the tainted pallium was a problem is evident from 'Florence' of Worcester's account of Stigand's deposition (Worcester, ii, 5).

[26] Wulfstan of Worcester went to Ealdred for consecration in 1062 and Walter of Hereford and Giso of Wells to Pope Nicholas in 1061 (Worcester, i, 218, 221; *Historiola de primordiis episcopatus Somersetensis* in *Ecclesiastical Documents*, ed. J. Hunter, London 1840, 16).

[27] For the abbots, see *ASC*, s.a. 1061 (E) and *Liber Eliensis*, ed. E.O. Blake, Camden, 3rd series, xcii, 1962, 168, 201. For Remigius's consecration, see his profession in *Councils and Synods with other documents relating to the English Church, vol. i, part II: 1066–1204*, ed. D. Whitelock, M. Brett and C.N.L. Brooke, Oxford 1981, 573–4. In a recent pamphlet, David Bates considers William's motives in sending his first appointee to Stigand for consecration when the Conqueror had secured a papal banner to remove the archbishop eventually. Bates suggests that Remigius's touchiness concerning the archbishop of York's claims on his diocese in the 1070s indicates that his profession to the archbishop of Canterbury was designed to avoid setting any precedent for York's jurisdiction over Lincoln (D. Bates, *Bishop Remigius of Lincoln, 1067–1092*, Lincoln 1992, 7, 19–21).

[28] William of Malmesbury, *Vita Wulfstani*, ed. R.R. Darlington, Camden, 3rd series, xl, 1928, 18.

[29] Barlow, *English Church*, 305.

[30] *ASC*, s.a. 1066 (D,E).

[31] *ASC*, s.a. 1066 (D). *Regesta*, i, nos 5, 22–3, 26, 28.

embarrassing. Although extremely worldly, Ealdred had no current problems with the papacy and was responsible for the legitimate consecration of the Conqueror. Whatever his reasons, by 1070 William felt ready and doubtless obliged to carry out the reform of the English church authorized by the papal banner he had received before the Conquest.[32] Stigand, his brother Æthelmær, and a few abbots were deposed at the Easter council at Winchester in 1070, Stigand for having assumed the pallium of the still-living Robert, and his brother, ostensibly, for being married.[33] Stigand spent the remaining two years of his life imprisoned at Winchester, a visibly shaken and defeated man.[34]

These are the events which frame the fifty-year career of an important royal priest. But apart from scant mentions in contemporary chronicles related to these events, very little is known either about Stigand's personal life or the spiritual nature of his pontificate. We are fortunate, however, to possess a significant amount of information from Domesday Book regarding his personal landhold-ings and lordship, as well as the great episcopal endowments he controlled. An analysis of landholdings attributed to Stigand, Canterbury, and Winchester, and the lordship associated with these holdings, indicates that the later chroniclers, who focused on his immense wealth and power, were not far off the mark. Indeed, Stigand's political influence, especially in the courts of Cnut, Edward, and Harold Godwineson, and the huge fortune he amassed, combined to make him a lord among the kingdom's greatest.

In terms of the value and composition of his *personal* holdings, Stigand was by far unrivaled among ecclesiastics. For a royal priest he was immensely wealthy. Simon Keynes places Regenbald the Chancellor, one of Edward's wealthiest royal priests, in a class of his own with holdings valued at £40 per annum.[35] But Stigand's personal interests alone were worth more than £750 overall and were spread over ten counties (see Appendix). Even his fellow archbishop, Ealdred, controlled only some £300, which included the income of the lands of the arch-bishopric of York. Among laymen, the value of his personal holdings was worth almost double that of both Siward earl of Northumbria,[36] and the kingdom's richest thegnly families.[37] In fact, in some shires he was absolutely the richest pre-Conquest landholder. Comparatively, Stigand held more land in Norfolk than King Edward, and about the same in Suffolk and Dorset. There were no royal estates in Hertfordshire, where Stigand held more than £80.[38] Similarly, he had not quite double the family of Earl Godwine's holding in Suffolk and about the same in Gloucestershire.[39] In terms of post-Conquest comparison, Stigand would have ranked among the richest according to Corbett's Class 'A' list of greater

---

[32] *Monumenta Gregoriana*, ed. P. Jaffé, Berlin 1865, 414–16.

[33] 'Florence' of Worcester gives the fullest account of the depositions, citing three reasons in Stigand's case: holding Winchester in plurality, assuming the previous archbishop's pallium, and receiving his own pallium from the excommunicated Pope Benedict (Worcester, ii, 5).

[34] *De gestis pontificum*, 37.

[35] S. Keynes, 'Regenbald the Chancellor (*sic*)', *ante* x, 1987, 196–7.

[36] R. Fleming, *Kings and Lords in Conquest England*, Cambridge 1991, Table 3.1.

[37] Ansgar the Staller is believed to have been worth £485, Wulfweard White and Eadgifu the Fair £300 each (K. Mack, 'Kings and thegns: aristocratic participation in the governance of Anglo-Saxon England', unpublished research paper, Santa Barbara 1982, Appendix I).

[38] Fleming, *Kings and Lords*, Table 3.3.

[39] Fleming, *Kings and Lords*, Table 3.1.

Domesday tenants-in-chief, whose demesne lands ranged in value from approximately £100 to £1,000.[40] Based on these brief comparisons of the value of his own estates, Stigand was clearly among the wealthiest landholders in the kingdom, both before and after the Conquest.

In addition, just a glance through Little Domesday provides a sense of the magnitude of Stigand's personal and tenurial lordship. In East Anglia alone, where the bonds of soke and commendation are most comprehensively reported, more than one thousand thegns and freemen called Stigand their lord in one way or another.[41] Among these were at least five important thegns, Hagni, Osmund, Ketel, Offa, and Algar.[42] Generally, though, Stigand courted middling thegns, and built a network of freemen who are, by and large, unnamed in Domesday Book. His interests were intensely local, unlike those of Earl Harold, for example, whose men were from far wealthier and influential thegnly families.[43] Outside of Little Domesday, soke and commendation are unfortunately either sporadically reported or suppressed. In spite of this, in at least six other counties, Stigand had another hundred men, again all modest landholders. Included in these six counties are two, Middlesex and Buckinghamshire, where he held no land personally but where either Canterbury or Winchester had considerable holdings.[44] If the original returns were available, we might also expect to find more of Stigand's men, at the very least, in the counties of Gloucestershire, Dorset, Hampshire and Kent, where he did hold land. From a financial standpoint, then, Stigand benefited directly from the leases, rights of personal soke and commendation, and the soke that he held over whole hundreds in Norfolk and fifty burgesses in Norwich.[45] Moreover, as a lord, Stigand was bequeathed heriot in several extant thegnly wills.[46] He clearly benefited, too, from lordship in terms of rights that are less easily defined, and the prestige associated with such a great following. Although it is impossible to assess the value of the various components of Stigand's lordship, it was clearly enormous.

The analysis of Stigand's wealth has thus far concentrated on overall and comparative value, and breadth of distribution. However interesting, it provides only a one-dimensional picture; more questions are suggested by these results than are answered. For example, how did Stigand acquire such a huge fortune in land? Was he predatory like so many of his peers or simply savvy? Did he exploit the sees he occupied or benefit primarily from his favored position at court? While

---

[40] W.J. Corbett, 'The Development of the Duchy of Normandy and the Norman Conquest of England', *Cambridge Medieval History* v, 1926 (reprinted 1968), 505–13. See also C.W. Hollister, 'The greater Domesday tenants-in-chief' in *Domesday Studies*, ed. J.C. Holt, Woodbridge, Suffolk 1987, 219–48.

[41] Despite that unnamed men could, at times, be one and the same, these figures indicate instances of lordship. They are also significantly underestimated due to inconsistent reporting.

[42] *Domesday Book*, ii, 130b, 153a, 254a, 186a, 152b.

[43] Fleming, *Kings and Lords*, 73–4.

[44] In Middlesex, where one man was commended to Stigand, Canterbury held the large manor of Hayes (*Domesday Book*, i, 127r). In Buckinghamshire, where he had ten free men and one sokeman, Winchester possessed Wycombe, to which two of these men appertained (*Domesday Book*, i, 143v), and Canterbury leased three large manors (*Domesday Book*, i, 143v).

[45] *Domesday Book*, ii, 116a, 139b.

[46] *Anglo-Saxon Wills*, ed. and trans. D. Whitelock, Cambridge 1930, no. 34: 'And I grant to Archbishop Stigand, my lord, the estate at Harling ... and ... I grant to him as my heriot a helmet and a coat of mail and a horse with harness and a sword and a spear'. See also nos. 29 and 31.

these questions cannot be answered in every instance, there is enough information to suggest that Stigand acquired land through a variety of methods, and although the real Stigand was by no means pristine, his reputation as a merciless predator is not wholly deserved. The following analysis demonstrates the complexity of Stigand's dealings by investigating, where possible, the circumstances under which he acquired land. Because the nature of his tenurial relationships with religious houses was largely responsible for his posthumous reputation, it will be considered first, followed by a similar analysis of his lands with episcopal, royal, and patrimonial connections.

Of the approximately £750 worth of land that Stigand held personally, at least a third was held either by lease or outright encroachment of ecclesiastical houses other than his own. In East Anglia alone, where he held £325, at least £125 is attributable to his relationships with the three abbeys of Bury St Edmund's, Ely, and Peterborough, and the church of St Michael, Norwich. Further afield, Stigand benefited from connections not just to Ely but to the abbeys of St Albans, Bath, and Abingdon, and the churches of St Oswald's and St Martin's, Dover. Stigand's relationships with these institutions account for another £125 of land outside East Anglia, including his entire holding in Gloucestershire. Overall, then, Stigand obviously exploited his positions in Edward's episcopacy toward the accumulation of at least a third of his landed interests from ecclesiastical houses.

The nature of this exploitation, of course, varied from place to place and from house to house. In East Anglia, Stigand maintained complex relationships with Bury St Edmund's and Ely. A clear picture of his connection to the former, however, is stymied by the long and complicated relationship of Bury to the bishopric of Elmham, doubtless exploited to the hilt by Stigand. It is, indeed, difficult to disentangle Stigand's holdings from the bishopric's, and both of these from Bury's. The evidence is clear in some cases, however. In Norfolk, Stigand held Grimstone and Hunstanton, valued at £5 and £4 respectively, which had been bequeathed to the abbey circa 1038 by Ælfric, bishop of Elmham. Hunstanton was bequeathed to the abbey itself and Grimstone to Leofstan 'the dean' of Bury.[47] In a similar transaction, Stigand's successor and brother, Æthelmær, bequeathed four estates to Bury, two of which he apparently received from the abbey before he was made bishop.[48] These two transactions establish a firm connection not just between Elmham and Bury, but between Stigand's family and the abbey. Whether this relationship was cordial is another matter. Several extant writs emphasize Bury's independence from the bishopric during the 1040s,[49] and later Abbot Baldwin fought off further encroachment when Bishop Arfast attempted to move the post-Conquest bishopric to Bury.[50] These documents suggest a very uneasy relationship of long duration between the abbey and the diocesan bishopric, a situation apparently exacerbated by Stigand and his family.

In Suffolk, however, according to Bury tradition, Stigand's approach was less ambiguous. One of his most valuable manors, Mildenhall, assessed at £40, had

---

[47] *Domesday Book*, ii, 142a, 135b–136a; *Anglo-Saxon Wills*, no. 88.
[48] *Anglo-Saxon Writs*, ed. and trans. F. E. Harmer, Manchester 1952 (reprinted 1989), no. 35. These two holdings were meant to revert to Bury on Æthelmær's death, but were retained by his successor (*Anglo-Saxon Writs*, 204–5).
[49] *Anglo-Saxon Writs*, nos. 8–13.
[50] *Anglo-Saxon Writs*, 141–3.

been given to Bury by King Edward upon the dispossession of his mother, and an authentic writ declared that the land and the soke of Mildenhall belonged to St Edmund's.[51] The connection between Emma, Bury, and Stigand, is suggestive. That Stigand acquired this property against the wishes of the monks is evident in a passage contained in a Bury history, which states that he begged the lease of Mildenhall from them, a request they dared not refuse.[52] It further notes that he kept the property when he was translated to Canterbury. Despite the Confessor's writ, it took the community at Bury more than a hundred years to recover Mildenhall, which King William annexed with Stigand's other East Anglian property upon his deposition. In fact, the abbey had to repurchase it from Richard I in 1189.[53] Stigand further deprived the abbey of the Suffolk manor of Hintlesham, worth £10, which Leofgifu bequeathed, no later than 1044, to the abbey where she would rest for all eternity,[54] and he possessed Moulton, which had been bequeathed to one Sibriht in Ælfric's will.[55] The bequests and the transactions surrounding Mildenhall show that Stigand and his family were intimately associated with both the East Anglian lay landholders and the monks of Bury St Edmund's, who were themselves connected. This is not surprising, given that both Stigand and his brother were successive bishops of Elmham and given Stigand's immense personal lordship in the area. Obviously the relationship between Stigand and Bury could be hostile at times, although it is impossible to know how things were between them on a day-to-day basis. In any event, it was profitable for Stigand to have a neighbor like Bury, although the same cannot always be said in the reverse.

Ely Abbey maintained a similar, though more cordial, relationship with Stigand. In Norfolk, he held a life-lease for Methwold at £20, and Croxton at £10, by a grant of the abbot.[56] Stigand also held Thorpe St Andrew and its berewicks, valued at £12, to which Ely made a claim.[57] Outside of East Anglia, Stigand had leased the manor of Snailwell (£15) in Cambridgeshire from Abbot Leofsige,[58] but held Wood Ditton (£15), in the same county, by questionable means. According to Domesday Book, 'this manor lay [in the lands of] the Church of St Etheldreda of Ely TRE, but Archbishop Stigand took it away; the men of the hundred do not

---

[51] *Domesday Book*, ii, 288b–289a; *Anglo-Saxon Writs*, no. 9. This is property that Emma forfeited during her 'disgrace' which Stigand managed to get by lease when he was reinstated.
[52] *Monasticon*, iii, 154, no. 21: '. . . qui frequenter ad nos divertens, et graviter expensis et aliis exactionibus onerans, petiit a nobis ut villam de Mildenhall ei ad tempus accommodaremus: cui propter potentiam quam tunc habuit in tota Anglia, et maxime in nobis nondum per curiam Romanam plene exemptis, contradicere non audebamus.'
[53] *Anglo-Saxon Writs*, 436; *Monasticon*, iii, 154, no. 21.
[54] *Domesday Book*, ii, 289a–b; *Anglo-Saxon Wills*, no. 29. This is a very interesting will containing a bequest to Stigand, not of either of the two properties he holds, but of an estate at Willesham. According to Domesday, however, 'Aelfled, a free woman under the patronage of Harold, held Willisham TRE' (*Domesday Book*, ii, 351a–b). Either Stigand never received it (which is unlikely given his acumen), or perhaps he sold it or traded it for Bramford or another property.
[55] *Domesday Book*, ii, 372b.
[56] *Domesday Book*, ii, 136a, 136b. See also *Liber Eliensis*, Appendix D. Domesday Book records that these estates were supposed to be for the victualing of the monks.
[57] *Domesday Book*, ii, 137b–138b, 140b. There is a suspicious charter, not authentic in its present form, in which Thorpe is one of many properties confirmed to Ely (S 1051).
[58] *Domesday Book*, i, 199r.

know how'.[59] Thus the transactions with Ely and Bury illustrate the variety of Stigand's tactics, from leases to outright encroachment. It must be said, however, that the distinction may have been purely semantic. One other East Anglian holding, Well (£9), may have belonged originally to Peterborough Abbey.[60]

The value of Stigand's estates acquired from ecclesiastical houses in Gloucestershire was quite high, at more than £75. Moreover, these estates accounted for his entire holding in this county so distant from his dioceses, and must have had something to do with the king, since it was here that he held his Christmas court. Stigand probably acquired the manor of Tidenham for his use during this yearly excursion.[61] Assessed at £25, he held it by a lease from Bath Abbey, granted by Abbot Ælfwig and the community in the early 1060s. Preserved in Bath's twelfth-century cartulary, this lease provides a great sense of the type of terms that Stigand negotiated. It records that 'Abbot Ælfwig and all the community at Bath have let 30 hides of land at Tidenham to Archbishop Stigand for his lifetime in return for 10 marks of gold and 20 pounds of silver, and after his death it shall revert to the holy monastery with its produce and its men, entirely and completely as it is then, and in addition one mark of gold and six porpoises and 30,000 herrings [shall be given] annually'.[62] Not all of Stigand's dealings in Gloucestershire were so clear-cut, however. One of the most derogatory statements about him appears in the chronicle of the monastery of Abingdon, principally in reference to the Gloucestershire manor of Cerney, valued at £16. Here it is said that Stigand extorted (*extorsit*) the manor when he was bishop of Winchester in return for his support of the appointment of its abbot, Spearhavoc, to the bishopric of London.[63] Doubtless the chronicler, who had nothing good to say about either man, exaggerated his claim in anger over the loss of the manor. No formal charges of simony were ever made against Stigand, and the transaction was apparently concluded with King Edward's approval. This last piece of information suggests that Stigand's acquisition of Cerney, which the post-Conquest chronicler attributed to extortion, may actually have been the result of a bona fide lease, but because such leases were both embarrassing and problematic after the Conquest, the history of the estate was rewritten.[64] The remainder of Stigand's Gloucestershire holdings – Churchdown, Hucclecote, Norton, Swindon, and Compton Abdale – most likely once belonged to St Oswald's Priory.[65] Assessed together at more than £30, they are perhaps evidence that Stigand took advantage of the minster's decline, as did the

---

[59] *Domesday Book*, i, 189v. S 958 records Cnut's grant of Wood Ditton to Ely. See also *Liber Eliensis*, 168.

[60] *Domesday Book*, ii, 221b. S 1448, an authentic charter of Bishop Æthelwold records the gift of land at *Well* in Norfolk to Peterborough (c.963). This is a common place-name, so it is difficult to know if the charter definitely refers to this holding. The TRW landholder was the Benedictine monastery of St Stephen's of Caen, founded by William the Conqueror.

[61] *Domesday Book*, i, 164r. Presumably the lease encompassed two other smaller properties worth £1 each bearing the title Tidenham (*Domesday Book*, i, 166v, 167v).

[62] *Anglo-Saxon Charters*, ed. and trans. A.J. Robertson, Cambridge 1939, no. 117.

[63] *Domesday Book*, i, 169r; *Chronicon monasterii de Abingdon*, ed. J. Stevenson, RS 1858, i, 462–3.

[64] Domesday records, with ambivalence, that 'this manor is claimed for St Mary's Church at Abingdon, but all the county testified that Archbishop Stigand had held it for ten years during King Edward's lifetime' (*Domesday Book*, i, 169r).

[65] *Domesday Book*, i, 164v.

post-Conquest archbishops of York, who would absorb all but two of its extensive holdings.[66]

Three estates held by lease round out Stigand's holdings with ecclesiastical connections – Redbourn in Hertfordshire (£16), Deal in Kent (£7) and Taverham in Norfolk (£1). He held them, respectively, of St Albans, the Canons of St Martin's, Dover, and the church of St Michael, Norwich.[67] These estates eventually reverted back to their lessors, but not without difficulty in the case of Redbourn. As of 1086, Archbishop Lanfranc held the manor, but it was returned to St Albans during the abbacy of Paul, a kinsman of Lanfranc's, sometime between 1086 and 1093.[68]

Stigand's remaining twenty-four properties included two with episcopal connections, five resulting from royal patronage, and seventeen acquired through some unknown means. In the first case, Stigand does not seem to have encroached significantly on the lands of the sees he occupied, although Domesday Book is not altogether clear on this matter. Only for the enormous manor of East Meon in Hampshire, assessed at seventy-two hides and valued at £60, is the evidence straightforward. Domesday Book records that Stigand held East Meon 'for the use of the monks', but that 'later he had it for his lifetime'.[69] It is quite possible that he held other manors of Canterbury and Winchester in such a way, but the evidence is not forthcoming.[70] In Norfolk, another large manor probably came to Stigand when he was bishop of Elmham. Mileham and three of its six berewicks, assessed at £30, were located in the hundred of Launditch, very near North Elmham.[71] Because of its size and proximity to the episcopal see, Stigand could have acquired this manor in connection with his first episcopacy, but since Elmham's cartulary does not survive, this remains an open question.[72]

Royal favor accounts for the acquisition of five of Stigand's estates, although

---

[66] Founded by Æthelflæd of Mercia, St Oswald's enjoyed royal patronage throughout the tenth century, but steadily declined as the locus of power shifted to Wessex. The erosion of its extensive holdings by the late Anglo-Saxon period precipitated its absorption into the jurisdiction of the archbishop of York by the end of the eleventh century (Carolyn Heighway et al, 'Excavations at Gloucester, 4th interim report: St Oswald's Priory, Gloucester, 1975–1976', *Antiqs Journ.* lviii, 1978, 118–123).

[67] *Domesday Book*, i, 135v, 1v; ii, 201b. See also S 1228 which records St Albans' acquisition of Redbourn between 1042 and 1049. As for the Taverham lease, it should be noted that Stigand also held the lessor, the church of St Michael (*Domesday Book*, ii, 116a–b).

[68] Thomas Walsingham, *Gesta Abbatum Monasterii S. Albani a Thoma Walsingham*, ed. H.T. Riley, RS 1867, i, 54. This was not the only time Lanfranc, in seizing Stigand's lands, failed to honor the reversion of leases. In Hertfordshire, he appropriated two holdings of Ælfric Black, a man of Stigand's, which were leased from Westminster Abbey, and one that the same man held from St Albans. Only the St Albans property was eventually returned, under the same conditions as Redbourn (R.P. Abels, 'An Introduction to the Hertfordshire Domesday' in *The Hertfordshire Domesday*, ed. R. Erskine and A. Williams, London 1989, 22–4).

[69] *Domesday Book*, i, 38r.

[70] It is not always clear from Domesday Book if Stigand was holding manors of Canterbury and Winchester for personal use. Where the property had been part of the endowment of the see both before and after Stigand's tenure, its value was not included in the computation of his personal holdings. It should be noted, however, that this possibility does exist and that the ambiguity itself is perhaps meaningful.

[71] *Domesday Book*, ii, 136b–137a, 140a–b.

[72] There is, however, a spurious charter in connection with Belaugh, a berewick of Mileham, which King Edward purportedly confirmed with many other Norfolk properties to the church of St Benedict of Holme (S 1055).

many of the undocumented estates may also have been royal gifts. In four cases the connection is clear: Barham and Bishopsbourne in Kent, Sturminster Marshall in Dorset and Duxford in Cambridgeshire. Barham, assessed at £40, had been an early acquisition of Christ Church, Canterbury's. By 1066, however, 'Archbishop Stigand held this manor, but it was not the archbishopric's, but was of King Edward's demesne farm'.[73] Doubtless Stigand held Bishopsbourne (£20), also once a Canterbury property, because of its association with Barham.[74] In nearby Dorset, Stigand held Sturminster Marshall, which, valued at £66, was the most valuable of all his holdings.[75] Bequeathed in the will of Alfred the Great to his youngest son, this manor had an impressive provenance.[76] It may have come to Stigand as a grant when he was a royal priest of Cnut, since it was during the 1020s and 1030s that Cnut established a number of Scandinavian thegns in Dorset.[77] Duxford in Cambridgeshire, assessed at £5, was also a royal gift that Stigand shared with the thegn Horwulf from King Edward's farm.[78] And finally, the manor of Wymondham in Norfolk, valued with its berewick at approximately £70 and assessed at only four carucates, looks like a royal gift, although there is no direct evidence. Stigand seems to have received a huge tax break on it, which certainly implies royal favor.[79] Although the manors acquired through royal gift were small in number, they represented some of the most valuable in all of Domesday Book. Stigand therefore must be seen as a valued and influential primate and royal advisor.

Little can be said of his remaining seventeen properties, except that they were acquired by one or a combination of the means described above, or were part of Stigand's patrimony. The latter is likely true for his nine remaining estates in East Anglia, valued at over £100.[80] Certainly lands at Hellesdon, Wroxham, and Taverham in Taverham hundred are suggestively close to the borough of Norwich, and were probably part of Stigand's inheritance.[81] The final eight holdings under

---

[73] *Domesday Book*, i, 9v. Barham is not included in S 1047, a post-Conquest list of Canterbury's property supposedly confirmed by King Edward sometime during his reign. Its exclusion indicates that it had been alienated for some time, or Lanfranc surely would have tried to recover it. For the early history of this land, see N.P. Brooks, *The Early History of the Church of Canterbury*, Leicester 1984, 131.

[74] *Domesday Book*, i, 3v; S 1259.

[75] *Domesday Book*, i, 80r.

[76] *Alfred the Great: Asser's Life of King Alfred and other contemporary sources*, ed. and trans. S. Keynes and M. Lapidge, London 1983, 175.

[77] S. Keynes, 'The lost cartulary of Abbotsbury', *Anglo-Saxon England* xviii, 1989, 230.

[78] *Domesday Book*, i, 196r.

[79] *Domesday Book*, ii, 137b, 141a. Wymondham was an enormous manor, with sixty villeins, fifty bordars and eight slaves. Another eighty-seven freemen appertained to it. There is no TRE value recorded in Domesday Book, only that the jurisdiction alone was worth £20. Although the value of Stigand's lands tended to increase TRW, the value of the soke alone indicates that it must have been nearly as valuable TRE.

[80] Toft Monks (£12), Earsham (£11), Snettisham (£52), Hellesdon (£5), Wroxham (£3), Denham (£2), Burgh Castle (£5), Bramford (£10) and Bungay (£5). *Domesday Book*, ii, 141a, 138a, 142a–b, 271a–b, 228b–229a, 331a, 445a, 289a–b, 288a. Bramford had been bequeathed to an unnamed kinsman of Leofgifu, but somehow ended up in Stigand's hands (*Anglo-Saxon Wills*, no. 29).

[81] *Domesday Book*, ii, 271a,b, 228b–229a, 201b, 116a–117b. Stigand's family ties to Norwich are well-documented. He himself held sake, soke and commendation over 50 of the 1,238 burgesses, while his sister had 32 acres of the 80 acres available to all of them. Stigand also held the church of St Martin and 12 acres, and the church of St Michael's and 112 acres, not of his bishopric. His brother, Æthelmær, bishop of Elmham, held the church of Sts Simon and Jude of his patrimony.

discussion were spread over three counties – Pyrton at £16 (Oxfordshire), Standon, Pirton and Broxbourne at £65 (Hertfordshire), and Biggleswade, Dunton, Stratton and Holme at £25 (Bedfordshire).[82]

By all accounts, Stigand was enormously wealthy, and the preceding analysis reveals that his fortune was the result of inheritance, royal favor, and shrewd if occasionally unscrupulous dealings with English churches. In general, however, it does not look as though Stigand expropriated the holdings of his own bishoprics. Neither Winchester nor Canterbury suffered major depredations at the hands of Stigand, with the exception of the Winchester manor of East Meon, discussed above. Enough ambiguity exists in Domesday Book, however, to obscure the exact nature of Stigand's control of the episcopal endowments of Winchester and Canterbury, but control them he did. Together, the value of these two endowments exceeded £2,000, and an analysis of their composition rounds out the discussion of Stigand's landed interests.

By the time of Stigand's appointment in 1047, Winchester had long been a wealthy and distinguished see, with a history of close ties to the West Saxon court and a reputation as a center of monastic reform. Charter evidence indicates that the bulk of its endowment was granted during the tenth century, and that neither Stigand nor any of his eleventh-century predecessors did much to augment it.[83] Despite the slowdown of largess, by contemporary standards the see was immensely wealthy. Within the city itself, the ecclesiastical presence was impressive. The three minsters and the bishop's residence occupied more than one quarter of the area enclosed by the city's walls,[84] and the bishop collected in the vicinity of £70 per year in rents from approximately a third of the total tenements.[85] By far, however, the bulk of Winchester's wealth came from its rural estates. Composed of more than sixty holdings in Hampshire and eight nearby counties, the pre-Conquest value of Winchester's demesne lands was just over £1,000. Forty Hampshire estates, accounting for some £600, surrounded the city of Winchester within a twenty-mile radius. More than twenty of these were for the supplies of the monks. Two large and valuable estates, Chilcomb and Easton, bordered the city on virtually every side.[86] The remainder of Winchester's holdings were fairly diverse and included nearly thirty estates, valued at more than £400, in the counties of Surrey, Berkshire, Wiltshire, Buckinghamshire, Cambridgeshire, Hertfordshire, Oxfordshire, and Somerset. Of these, the ancient hundredal manor of Taunton in Somerset, Farnham in Surrey, and Downton in Wiltshire, were valued at more than £50 each, and were jewels in Winchester's crown.[87] Indeed, Winchester's endowment

---

[82] *Domesday Book*, i, 157r, 142v, 138r, 217r, 216r.

[83] Of the approximately eighty-five extant Old Minster charters, only fifteen or so were composed after the year 1000.

[84] *Winchester in the Early Middle Ages: An Edition and Discussion of the Winton Domesday*, ed. F. Barlow, M. Biddle, O. von Feilitzen and D.J. Keene, *Winchester Studies*, Oxford 1976, i, 464. Although the figures concerning the bishop's wealth in the city are based on data from the 1148 survey, Biddle states that they are reliable as TRE figures as well. This is based on the observation that the great fiefs were established by 1057, and that the composition of the king's fief was basically static between 1057 and 1148 (*Winchester Studies*, 456).

[85] *Winchester Studies*, 369.

[86] *Domesday Book*, i, 41r, 40r.

[87] *Domesday Book*, i, 87v, 31r, 65v. Taunton was assessed at £154 TRW.

was characterized by large and valuable manors, granted overwhelmingly from the early royal fisc.

That Stigand controlled this vast holding cannot be doubted, but his overall effect on it is difficult to determine. No evidence for obvious losses exists, with the exception of a handful of leases granted before or during Stigand's pontificate. Yet the loss to the monks was minimal, as the leases were overwhelmingly granted from the bishop's separate lands.[88] Domesday Book implies, however, that Stigand held several manors personally, but its compilers stopped short of indictment with the exception of East Meon.[89] Unfortunately, the community is silent on the matter of Stigand's pontificate, so we can only assume that there were few, if any, complaints while he was there.

In terms of wealth and prestige, it was the archbishopric of Canterbury that represented the pinnacle of Stigand's career. Besides being the primatial see, Christ Church could trace its history of royal and secular endowment back to the early seventh century.[90] And, by 1052, when Stigand took the helm, its holdings were immense, although confined to the south-east. Like Winchester, Canterbury had interests in the city itself, but its fortune lay in the nearly eighty properties it held directly in seven counties, at a total value of about £1,150. In Kent alone, the archbishop held nearly thirty estates in demesne worth about £575, while the monks had another twenty estates valued at more than £250. Like that of Winchester, Canterbury's endowment consisted of some very large and very valuable manors, such as the Kentish manors of Otford, Aldington, and Wingham, assessed at more than £60 each.[91] Property in Kent accounted for three-quarters of Canterbury's holdings, while the remainder comprised some twenty-five estates in the counties of Sussex, Surrey, Essex, Middlesex, Suffolk, and Oxfordshire. These estates added another £300 to the value of the already considerable endowment in Kent.

Stigand himself does not appear to have significantly altered the composition of Canterbury's landed endowment, but he does seem to have confirmed leases on at least eleven valuable properties to the family of Earl Godwine. Valued at nearly £300, these leases were a tremendous loss to the community.[92] Other laymen were holding at least ten additional leases, valued at more than £100. Stigand's successor, Archbishop Lanfranc, went to considerable trouble to recover these lands, which were most likely leased by Eadsige, Stigand's predecessor, but subsequently confirmed by Stigand himself. Only partially successful at the trial of Penenden Heath in 1075, Lanfranc doggedly pursued the matter. An extant memorandum of an inquest held three or four years later, a twelfth-century obituary notice of William the Conqueror, and Domesday Book itself attest to Lanfranc's eventual success in recovering these estates which had been carried off well

---

[88] Seven holdings were leased out in Hampshire for £47 (*Domesday Book*, i, 40r–40v,41v) and three in Wiltshire for £43 (*Domesday Book*, i, 65v). Only one, valued at £5, was leased from the monks' Hampshire holdings.

[89] See, for example, the entry for Yavington: 'The bishop himself holds Yavington. Archbishop Stigand held it' (*Domesday Book*, i, 40v).

[90] See Brooks, *Early History*, 100–7.

[91] *Domesday Book*, i, 3r, 4r, 3v.

[92] For a discussion of these leases, see Fleming, *Kings and Lords*, 81–2, especially note 111.

before the Conquest.[93] Only Folkestone remained permanently alienated, and, valued at £110, it was a considerable loss. While Stigand himself was not responsible for the substantial erosion of Canterbury's endowment, his maintenance of the status quo cannot have endeared him to the community.

Altogether, between the value of his own holdings and those of Canterbury and Winchester, Stigand was worth nearly £3,000, a truly staggering figure. Only the king and his earls controlled anywhere near this kind of wealth. The results of this analysis make it easier to understand, on several counts, why Stigand acquired the reputation of a worldly prelate, far more concerned with amassing his own personal fortune than looking out for the spiritual well-being of his flock. These calculations represent a conservative estimate of his wealth, but nonetheless Stigand was clearly one of the richest men in pre-Conquest England. He was undoubtedly one of the most well-connected, with ties to five kings, not to mention Ælgifu Emma, who was a pivotal figure throughout this period. At the very least, Stigand sought and received the cooperation of Earl Godwine and his son Earl Harold, cooperation necessitated by the occupation of overlapping geographical spheres of influence.[94] The importance of Stigand's relationship with this powerful family should not be overemphasized, however, because in no way can Stigand be seen merely as a Godwine man: he did not share the earl's exile and he owed his continuous prosperity far more to his favor at court than to the West Saxon earl, whose interests generally coincided with his own.

If Stigand's reputation with kings and secular lords was favorable because of his great wealth, the same cannot always be said for the many religious houses who, sometimes against their will, contributed to it. Even so, Stigand's contemporary reputation with English religious houses was quite mixed, and seems to have suffered its real decline only after his death. Indeed, there is evidence that he had a good reputation with several houses, including Old Minster Winchester, St Augustine's and Ely, where his name and the day of his death were inscribed in their necrologies.[95] Moreover, he was honorably buried at Winchester, where his body lies to this day.[96] Several houses, Winchester and Ely included, recorded also that Stigand gave them expensive crosses and other liturgical items.[97] One late Bury chronicle mentions nothing of the abbey's problems with Stigand, only that he gave them a great cross.[98] The attitude of the houses with which Stigand had a relationship was doubtless ambivalent, and is perhaps best expressed by the Ely chronicler, who declared that he maintained the abbey's interests in exchange for land.[99] Moreover, Domesday Book records that several religious houses held

---

[93] F.R.H. Du Boulay, *The Lordship of Canterbury: An Essay on Medieval Society*, London 1966, 39–42. See also D. Bates, 'The Character and Career of Odo, Bishop of Bayeux', *Speculum* 1, 1975, 3,9.

[94] Compare Stigand's holdings with those of the Godwinesons in Fleming, *Kings and Lords*, Figure 3.2.

[95] B.L. Cotton Vitellis E. xviii, ff. 2r–7v; Brit. Mus. Vitell. Cxii, fo. 120; Cambridge, Trinity College 0.2.1, fos k1–13, fo. k2v.

[96] '. . . honorifice sepultus est' (*Annales de Wintonia*, 29).

[97] *Annales de Wintonia*, 25; *Liber Eliensis*, 168. The gift of a great, ornamented cross is also recorded in Ely's necrology (see note 95).

[98] *The Chronicle of Jocelin of Brakelond concerning the acts of Samson Abbot of the Monastery of St Edmund*, ed. H.E. Butler, London 1949, 5.

[99] *Liber Eliensis*, 168.

leases of Winchester and Canterbury during Stigand's tenancy of these sees.[100] Accordingly, the relationship could also be beneficial, in ways that are unfortunately not nearly as well documented. Evidently Stigand provided protection and patronage, and in return benefited from life-leases, the subjects of which were meant to revert to the lessors upon his death.

Yet because Stigand's pontificate was interrupted by the Norman Conquest, the terms he negotiated were not fulfilled according to contemporary practice. As a result of his deposition, Stigand's lands were seized by the crown and the religious houses with which he had made arrangements almost without exception lost their land because of their former association with him. Thus it is not surprising that his reputation declined. By the twelfth century, for example, Winchester asked Savigny for reciprocal prayers only for Ælfwine and Walkelin, Stigand's predecessor and successor, but not for Stigand himself.[101] His name, moreover, has apparently been expunged from all surviving Christ Church obituary lists.[102] A tradition, espoused by the Ely chronicler and co-opted by later writers, holds that Stigand also assumed vacant abbacies in order to profit from them. But despite allegations that at various times he held Winchester, Glastonbury, St Albans, St Augustine's and Ely *in manu sua*, large gaps in abbatial appointments, which would suggest Stigand was involved in this kind of exploitation, do not occur with any certainty. Rather, this tradition is undoubtedly the result of bad feelings over the permanent loss of property, and grew as a consequence of festering ill-will.[103] Indeed, in the aftermath of the Conquest, it is understandable that English religious houses would find it necessary to distance themselves from Stigand, if not altogether alter for posterity the nature of their relationship with him. After all, the players and the rules had changed at all levels: royal, ecclesiastical, and secular. The ensuing scramble to recover lands and the need to re-establish title to them through royal confirmation is sufficient acknowledgment of the intense upheaval in landholding practices that took place after the Conquest. Association with Stigand generally meant loss of land, not for any personal reasons, but because he was on the losing side of a very thorough war of conquest. Thus English bishops and abbots, who may once have profited greatly from Stigand's attention, largely abandoned their benefactor's memory in favor of protecting their abbey's or bishopric's financial interests.

What we have, then, in terms of evidence concerning Stigand's life and career is unfortunately very slim or very suspect. Charter attestations provide glimpses of his regular participation in court activities, and a handful of writs directed to Stigand demonstrate the exercise of diocesan administrative functions. Occasional mentions of the archbishop in the *Anglo-Saxon Chronicle* are, for the most part, perfunctory; when they do give details other than chronological facts, entries

---

[100] Winchester leased *Chingescamp* in Hampshire to the Abbot of Ely (*Domesday Book*, i, 40v) and Canterbury leased Brasted, Kent to one Abbot Alnoth (*Domesday Book*, i, 4r), although Christ Church's own survey records that Brasted was leased to 'young Wulfnoth' and that it was in a different hundred (*The Domesday Monachorum of Christ Church Canterbury*, ed. D.C. Douglas, London 1944, 86).

[101] Barlow, *English Church*, 225n.

[102] See R. Fleming, 'Christchurch's Sisters and Brothers: An Edition and Discussion of Canterbury Obituary Lists', *The Culture of Christendom: Essays in Medieval History in Memory of Denis L.T. Bethel*, London 1993, 115–53.

[103] *Liber Eliensis*, 168.

focus on the problems associated with his uncanonical position and not on any-thing remotely personal. Only the portrait of Stigand as the weeping bishop in the *Vita Eadwardi Regis* is at all intimate. Yet even this sounds more like a literary *topos* than an act necessarily characteristic of Stigand. No letters survive, nor any *vitae*, which given the speed and thoroughness of the Conquest, were never produced if they had ever been intended. Moreover, both the Winchester and Canterbury communities are remarkably silent regarding Stigand's tenure; the bulk of contemporary evidence comes from houses that were not his own. Domesday Book, although impersonal, is the only truly comprehensive evidence of Stigand's achievements. But as we have seen, it records not the measure of the man, but the measure of his accomplishments – the accumulation of staggering wealth, a lordship rivaled only by earls, and widespread financial interests.

Why, then, despite his achievements, has Stigand remained a kind of stock background figure? Practical reasons account for many post-Conquest mis-representations of actual events in Stigand's career, where ecclesiastical houses had a financial interest in dissociating themselves from him. But the interests that shaped the history of the late Anglo-Saxon church were not primarily, or even secondarily, financial. By the twelfth century, when so many of our sources were compiled or composed, there was a different conception of the pre-Conquest church – English and Norman – and new principles for the writing of its history. This new conception, and the reasons for its emergence, are the final consider-ations of this paper.

It is not surprising that over time the events of the Conquest underwent consid-erable revision, both factual and thematic. Anglo-Norman writers did not simply re-record the history of the late Anglo-Saxon church, inaccurate as it often was, but in addition they refashioned it. After all, historians were no longer Norman monks who considered the English church innately decadent, but rather products of a mixed heritage. They needed a paradigm, as Antonia Gransden has convinc-ingly shown, that would accommodate both their English heritage and the rhetoric of the Conquest. They found it in the conception of an English ecclesiastical history characterized by peak periods of reform and low periods of decadence.[104] Hence they could celebrate the success of their Norman predecessors in reforming the late Anglo-Saxon church, without sacrificing the rich heritage of the Northumbrian Renaissance and tenth-century monastic reform. By the twelfth century, the Con-quest had become an inevitable stage in England's ongoing ecclesiastical history.

Just as the paradigm itself was a literary construct, so was the accompanying notion that the late Anglo-Saxon and Norman churches were fundamentally dif-ferent institutions. The similarities in and interconnections between the two are almost never mentioned in contemporary chronicles and have, by and large, also failed to attract the interest of modern historians. In fact, King Edward was half-Norman by birth and brought up in exile in the ducal court. Moreover, he was related to at least one important member of the Norman episcopacy, his maternal uncle Archbishop Robert of Rouen. In the time of Duke William's minority, and in the last years of his own exile, Edward witnessed first-hand Archbishop Robert's administration of the Norman church and his crucial role in stabilizing the

---

[104] A. Gransden, 'Traditionalism and Continuity during the Last Century of Anglo-Saxon Monas-ticism', *Journal of Ecclesiastical History* xl, 1989, 202–7.

duchy.[105] According to Norman practice, the duchy's leading prelate was also a powerful secular lord, in this case the count of Évreux.[106] He had been appointed by his brother, Duke Richard II, in keeping with the Norman custom of reserving the most powerful offices, both secular and ecclesiastical, for loyal kinsmen. Nepotism and the blending of offices gave Norman bishops unprecedented power and wealth and dramatically increased their importance as political instruments. Edward had to be impressed with the use the Norman dukes made of such an episcopacy against a predatory aristocracy, and it doubtless helped shape his future ecclesiastical policy. He learned, too, that political considerations were more important than canonical precepts. Indeed, despite Duke William's elaborate show of regard for ecclesiastical sensitivity, in matters of political exigency even he unhesitatingly violated canon law – in the appointment of his half-brother, Odo, to the bishopric of Bayeux, and his second cousin Hugh to the bishopric of Lisieux, when they were both under the required canonical age. Edward's ecclesiastical policy included many of the same practices as his Norman counterpart: the fostering of a wealthy and powerful episcopacy, at least at the highest levels; the appointment of loyal favorites; and, when necessary, the blatant disregard of canon law. So it seems clear, ironically, that Norman political and religious institutions had a far greater effect on King Edward and his church than the practices of the indigenous church, despite the contrary view of Norman monk-historians.

Although they fail to acknowledge the important similarities in England's and Normandy's pre-Conquest churches, Anglo-Norman writers were not blind to the faults of Normans and Anglo-Normans. Indeed, a comparison of their treatment of various bishops from different periods shows that by the twelfth century, historians were openly critical of worldly bishops and obvious breaches of canon law. In a study of the life and career of Odo, bishop of Bayeux, David Bates has convincingly shown that modern scholars have, by and large, accepted Orderic Vitalis's characterization of Odo, when it is clear that the monk was 'none too sympathetic towards the churchman who meddled in politics'.[107] Indeed, Orderic has trouble throughout his work reconciling what he considers the baser characteristics of Odo's nature (tyranny and oppression) with his obvious enrichment of the church. Also critical of episcopal worldliness, William of Malmesbury seems completely astounded by the enormity of Odo's wealth.[108] Roger of Salisbury, another rich and powerful bishop, is at once admired and disdained for his position and wealth; William, whom he knew quite well, says rather sarcastically that '. . . Roger was a man who knew well how to adapt himself to any situation according as the wheel of fortune changed'.[109] William wrote this after Roger's disgrace and death, but as Edward Kealey notes, his treatment of the bishop became increasingly critical over the years, and he seems to have agreed, in the end, with William of Newburgh, who saw Roger as an ambitious and greedy man given more to castle-building than spirituality.[110] These portraits are not unlike those of Stigand himself. William of Malmesbury, astounded as he was by Odo's

105 For a discussion of Edward's participation in Norman court activities, see S. Keynes, 'The Æthelings in Normandy', *ante* xiii, 1990, 187–94.

106 D. Douglas, 'The Earliest Norman Counts', *EHR* lxi, 1946, 129–56.

107 Bates, 'Character and Career', 2.

108 Bates, 'Character and Career', 3.

109 E. Kealey, *Roger of Salisbury, Viceroy of England*, Berkeley 1972, 9.

110 Kealey, *Roger of Salisbury*, 8.

wealth, thought that a key was found in Stigand's possession after his death that unlocked an immense treasure he had hidden on his estates.[111] Even though twelfth-century historians maintain a distinction between the Anglo-Saxon and Norman episcopacies on a thematic level, their portraits of worldly bishops, whether English, Norman or Anglo-Norman, subvert this distinction in their considerable uniformity.

One final observation should be made about the material with which these writers worked. In our age of print and electronics, historians are faced with so much material to sift through that it can be overwhelming. More often than not, twelfth-century historians had little more than a name, a date of death, and a few unrelated pieces of information from which to construct an interesting narrative. Chroniclers of secular matters solved the problem like hagiographers, constructing a plausible version of the way they believed things should have happened or how someone would have acted in a given situation. When Orderic Vitalis accuses Stigand of perjury and homicide, for example, he is no doubt simply projecting his belief that Stigand was capable of these crimes.[112] We are not obliged to believe that Stigand actually committed them, since Orderic never substantiates these accusations nor are they corroborated anywhere else. Eadmer similarly writes of *mala et horrenda crimina praedicabantur de Stigando*, none of which he describes, but he clearly believed Stigand capable of the worst, even if he did not know exactly what that was.[113] Even when information was available, it was easy to perpetuate mistakes, like that of confusing Stigand with the post-Conquest bishop of Selsey of the same name, which seems to have begun with 'Florence' of Worcester and was incorporated into later chronicles.[114] And, occasionally, wishful thinking on the part of the writer was responsible for a version of history that was plainly false. In his desire to promote the see of Lincoln, Gerald of Wales fabricated for Remigius, the see's first bishop, a canonical election and a consecration at the hands of Lanfranc, when the bishop's own profession admits he was consecrated by Stigand.[115] It is possible that Lincoln's official history had already been rewritten by the time Gerald attempted to canonize Remigius, but this is doubtful since the bishop was such an unlikely candidate for other reasons.[116]

Monks were clearly not the most reliable informants of episcopal and secular life, but they controlled the ecclesiastical press, and it is through their eyes that we see the rest of the world. Their judgment of the late Anglo-Saxon church was often too harsh. A rich, powerful and worldly episcopacy was neither an exclusively eleventh-century phenomenon nor particularly English. Since the great campaign for lay endowment in the tenth century, Anglo-Saxon bishops like St Æthelwold and St Dunstan were involved in worldly affairs to an unprecedented degree, and Norman bishops from the beginning were unabashedly ducal and often family appointments. Political considerations remained the motivation behind episcopal appointments throughout the Anglo-Norman world far beyond the Conquest, and

---

[111] *De gestis pontificum*, 37.
[112] Orderic, ii, 236.
[113] Eadmer, *Eadmeri Historia Novorum in Anglia*, ed. M. Rule, RS 1884, 9.
[114] Worcester, i, 193; Gervase, ii, 363.
[115] Giraldi Cambrensis, *Vita S. Remigii*, ed. J.F. Dimock, RS 1877, vii, 14; *Canterbury Professions*, ed. M. Richter, Canterbury and York Society, 1973, no. 32.
[116] For a discussion of Gerald's motives, see *Vita S. Remigii*, xvi–xxiii.

really only culminated, as a *modus operandi*, with the appointment of Anselm to Canterbury. By William of Malmesbury's time, though, increased sensitivity to the spiritual requirements of the office spelled the waning, but not the end, of the courtier bishop.

Stigand's rise from obscurity to the heights of wealth and power, if not always smooth, was nothing short of phenomenal. His survival and prosperity throughout this period of constant upheaval can only be a credit to his personality, something we know almost nothing about. That he was immensely wealthy is certainly now obvious. That he used his ecclesiastical positions as a point of departure in the acquisition of this wealth, sometimes at the expense of religious houses, is also unmistakable. But that he had ecclesiastical friends who found his patronage beneficial is also apparent. To accomplish so much must have taken a man of considerable tenacity, unreserved ambition and great charisma. But in practical terms, he was not so unique; what was true of Stigand had generally been true of bishops, both Norman and Anglo-Saxon, up to the twelfth century. St Oswald and Archbishop Ealdred were noted pluralists, St Æthelwold was clearly obsessed with property, and even St Dunstan had uncanonically assumed the position of archbishop under circumstances not so very different from Stigand's.[117] In Normandy, the prevalence of wealthy and sometimes married bishops with secular titles speaks for itself. Stigand's greatest weakness at the time of his downfall was neither simony nor his tainted pallium, but his close ties to the Anglo-Saxon nobility and throne that he supported until the last possible moment. Based on this analysis of his holdings and the extent of his lordship, it appears that Stigand's real sin after the Conquest was that he was too rich, too powerful, and too well-connected to the surviving Anglo-Saxon aristocracy for William's comfort and was deposed along with them for reasons as much political as spiritual.

[117] *Memorials of St Dunstan, Archbishop of Canterbury*, ed. W. Stubbs, RS 1874, 38.

APPENDIX

TRE Values by County
(Rounded to the nearest £5)

County	Stigand	Canterbury	Winchester
Bedfordshire	25	—	—
Berkshire	—	—	50
Buckinghamshire	—	—	30
Cambridgeshire	35	—	30
Dorset	65	—	—
Essex	—	65	—
Gloucestershire	75	—	—
Hampshire	60	—	600
Hertfordshire	80	—	5
Kent	70	830	—
Middlesex	—	40	—
Norfolk	240	—	—
Oxfordshire	15	10	35
Somerset	—	—	85
Suffolk	90	30	—
Surrey	—	65	55
Sussex	—	105	—
Wiltshire	—	—	150
TOTAL	£ 755	£ 1,145	£1,040

FREE ALMS TENURE IN THE TWELFTH CENTURY *

Benjamin Thompson

In 1257 the English clergy at a council in London complained:[1]

> Although kings and princes and others grant possessions and liberties to churches in free, pure and perpetual alms, without retaining any service or imposing any burden; nevertheless when disputes arise about these between ecclesiastics or between laymen and clerics, their holders are compelled to litigate in the secular court.

Underlying the clergy's protest was the demand that the 'liberty of the church' be preserved inviolate. The medieval church defined itself by its separation from the secular order: the papacy in the eleventh century wanted the clergy and their institutions to be marked out from the 'world', and their separation from the secular order and its evils to be enforced through the unifying and exclusive control of the pope.[2]

One consequence of this was the need to separate clerical property from lay jurisdiction, and subject it only to the courts of the church. Ecclesiastical tenure is therefore one area in which to test the nature and extent of the clerical separation in the world in practice. It posed a peculiar problem for the reformers, because (as the complaint shows) much church land had been given by laymen; indeed the very reform of the church was backed by princes. Land focuses the tension between on the one hand lay patronage and support for church reform, and the ideals of that reform which rejected lay involvement on the other, because, as the basis of most medieval wealth, power, and status, it was the meeting-point between clergy and laity where the stakes were highest. How well, then, were the papal ideals reflected in the tenure of land by churches? There is little need to address the demesne or dower land (glebe) of churches, which were recognized to belong to ecclesiastical control, although this is not the whole story. Nor is it necessary to worry much about lands which were acknowledged to be 'lay fee', which were subject to lay jurisdiction and often owed secular services: it is enough to record that churches did in fact accept these and hold them. Our

* I am most grateful to Dr David Dumville and Dr Christine Carpenter for their valuable comments on an earlier draft of this piece, as well as to the participants at Battle for the stimulating suggestions which many put forward in discussion. Needless to say the many remaining imperfections are my own.

1 *Councils and Synods with Other Documents relating to the English Church, II, 1205–1313*, ed. F.M. Powicke and C.R. Cheney, Oxford 1964, 545 [34].
2 E.g. B.J. Thompson, '*Habendum et tenendum*: lay and ecclesiastical attitudes to the property of the church', in *Religious Belief and Ecclesiastical Careers in Late Medieval England*, ed. C. Harper-Bill, Woodbridge 1991, 199–203.

concern here is with the lands held by monasteries and other collegiate churches between these two categories, which came to be identified as lands held 'in free alms' (frankalmoin). This tenure has confused historians for a century as to whether it lay in the secular or ecclesiastical spheres, as regards both contemporary perception and actual control. A primary task here, therefore, is to assess how far frankalmoin embodied the reformers' ideals of separation from the world.

Frankalmoin also offers a perspective from which to view law and jurisdiction in the twelfth century, especially in the light of current debate, in part focused on the views of Professor Milsom.[3] On the one hand post-Conquest historians are tending to diminish the significance of the Angevin reforms by arguing for Henry I's anticipation of many of its features and questioning the existence of the 'truly feudal world' Milsom posited.[4] But on the other, common lawyers want to re-emphasize the deliberate and far-reaching nature of the changes, against Milsom's picture of small changes within a framework of contemporary ideas which had unintended and revolutionary consequences.[5] It is not clear that he can be wholly wrong in both directions. Frankalmoin ought to be a medium through which to approach both the nature of early-twelfth-century landholding society, and the impact of Henry II's reforms on English law and custom – the before and after of the legal transformation. Moreover, ecclesiastical tenure adds the dimension of ecclesiastical jurisdiction, and thereby complicates it, which may enhance our understanding of the legal reforms themselves. (The more technical legal aspects of the tenure after c.1164, including the history of the assize *Utrum*, will have to be addressed in a second paper, but outline suggestions will be offered here.) Ecclesiastical tenure must therefore be set in the context of post-Conquest society, and its development alongside the changes of the century after 1066, particularly in the light of current understanding of such background.[6]

The third aim of this contribution is to investigate free alms tenure for its own sake, since debate about its nature goes back to Maitland (albeit sporadically), and has been recently revived. Whereas lawyers from the fourteenth century to the nineteenth assumed that the essence of free alms tenure was freedom from secular service, Maitland, finding that lands held in free alms owed all sorts of secular services, preferred to see the essence of the tenure in the immunity of such land from secular jurisdiction.[7] Audrey Douglas, in her turn, has taken apart Maitland's conclusion, finding that only a more restricted category of property was immune from lay jurisdiction. Instead, she, like Elisabeth Kimball before her, resorts to the assertion that the fundamental characteristic of free alms tenure was the spiritual

---

[3] S.F.C. Milsom, *The Legal Framework of English Feudalism*, Cambridge 1976; *Historical Foundations of the Common Law*, 2nd edn, London 1981.

[4] E.g. Stephanie L. Mooers, 'A re-evaluation of royal justice under Henry I of England', *American Historical Review* xciii, 1988, 340–58; John Hudson, 'Life-grants of land and the development of inheritance in Anglo-Norman England', *ante*, xiv, 1992, 67–80.

[5] Paul Brand, 'The origins of English land law: Milsom and after', *The Making of the Common Law*, 1993, 203–25.

[6] Some of the discussion after the paper was given took the story behind 1066; but I have steadfastly maintained my politically incorrect stance (through ignorance) and have not investigated Anglo-Saxon 'alms'.

[7] F. Pollock & F.W. Maitland, *The History of English Law before the time of Edward I*, 2nd edn, Cambridge 1898, reprinted 1968, ii, 240–51.

quality of its service.[8] But, because this service was 'indefinite' in later common law, these two – in common with all other writers – did little more than simply acknowledge the primary importance of the spiritual function, and focused their attention instead on the issues of services and jurisdiction.

This priority needs to be reversed: we should first assess the function of frank-almoin tenure, the fundamental aim which lay behind gifts in free alms. Only then shall we be on firmer ground in trying to understand those secondary features of services and jurisdiction which have proved so baffling. In suggesting answers to these three layers of questions, therefore, I shall proceed by analysing first the function of grants to the church, and then the tenurial consequences of those aims between the conquest and 1150. Changes within that period, will, for this paper, have to be skated over. I will then look quite briefly at free alms in the era of Henry II and the common law to assess the effect which the Angevin reforms had upon ecclesiastical tenure.[9]

As far as the evidence is concerned, we are naturally heavily reliant on charters, particularly before Henry II.[10] I want to treat the documents which we rather loosely assemble under that name precisely as evidence – as more important for the evidence they offer of events, of which we rarely have other glimpses, than as instruments significant in themselves. In particular, it is important to regard them as the products of negotiation. A charter attested and marked the end of a process of dealings (or even, in early cases, of many transactions) which stretched over many years, and in which the parties to the charter as well as others participated.[11] Even if they were drafted by beneficiaries, and so must be assumed to record the ecclesiastical point of view, it was precisely that view in which the donor was concurring – indeed which he was buying – when he granted land to an ecclesiastical institution.[12] If donors did not have the means to articulate their side of the story, it may be that they had no story to articulate. Nevertheless, if we suspect that lay donors had a greater sense of *de facto* control over their religious, which did not get reflected in the charters, that too may be significant. Variants and changes in terminology obviously need to be taken account of, particularly in the time before form settled down and drafters felt free to express what they meant

[8] Elisabeth G. Kimball, 'The judicial aspects of frank almoign tenure', *EHR* xlvii, 1932, 1–11; 'Tenure in frank almoign and secular services', *EHR* xliii, 1928, 341–53; Audrey W. Douglas, 'Frankalmoin and jurisdictional immunity: Maitland revisited', *Speculum* liii, 1978, 26–48; 'Tenure in *elemosina*: origins and establishment in twelfth-century England', *American Journal of Legal History* xxiv, 1980, 95–132. Two contributions by David Postles, for which I am grateful to the author for advance copies, are important: 'Gifts in frankalmoin, warranty of land, and feudal society', *Cambridge Law Journal* l, 1991, 330–46; 'Tenure in frankalmoin and knight service in twelfth-century England: interpretation of the charters', *Journal of the Society of Archivists* xiii, 1992, 18–28.

[9] There is no space here to be diverted by engaging with previous views as I go along, nor would it help the clarity of my exposition to do so. Some comments may be found in my 'From "alms" to "spiritual services": the function and status of monastic property in medieval England', *Monastic Studies* ii, 1991, 227–61.

[10] I cannot claim to have looked at a systematic selection for this paper: but I trust I have cast the net widely enough not to have been too drastically misled as to my analysis.

[11] See Paul R. Hyams, 'The charter as a source for the early common law', *Journal of Legal History* xii, 1991, 173–89, at p. 174; V.H. Galbraith, 'Monastic foundation charters of the eleventh and twelfth centuries', *Cambridge Historical Journal* iv, 1934, 205–22.

[12] On beneficiary drafting, see e.g. R.B. Patterson (ed.), *The Charters and Scribes of the Earls and Countesses of Gloucester to A.D. 1217*, Oxford 1973.

rather than to transcribe formulae; yet just as the fact of variation may be more important than its details, so that settling down is itself an important part of the story.[13]

The function of many grants to the church before the middle of the twelfth century was stated unambiguously in the charters. Some opened with some general motive such as 'pro Dei dilectione', 'pro Dei amore', 'ad honorem sancte ecclesie' or 'intuitu pietatis et amore religionis'.[14] To this were added the crucial phrases which became standard, 'pro redemptione anime mee', 'pro salute animarum nostrarum', or simply 'pro animabus', to which shorter or longer lists of relatives, lords and others were attached.[15] The grammatical conjunction of these phrases with the executive verbs of the charter – later 'do, concedo, et confirmo' – was universal in deeds recording donations. The specific linking of the act and the aim was sometimes emphasized when separate phrases such as 'hoc autem facio' or 'hanc donationem feci pro anima . . .' were included.[16] The terminology states simply but clearly the primary object of gifts: the intended beneficiaries were the souls of those already dead and of those yet to die.

How were the souls to benefit? How did these grants secure or help towards the salvation of individuals? Early preambles offer plenty of guidance on this score, and episcopal charters and statements are particularly revealing. They often dwelt on the relationship between temporal goods and spiritual benefits. This purports to be Henry I addressing the monks of Norwich: 'Kings and dignitaries of the whole world rejoice in these obsequies, and earthly kings purchase by a happy commerce eternal things with temporal, abundant heavenly goods with earthly ones, and endow the holy church with temporal goods'.[17] These 'eternal goods' were to avoid hell and to secure remission of sins and eternal bliss, which objects were encapsulated in phrases such as 'I have done this so that I might acquit and liberate from danger of hell the souls of . . .', and 'so that God Almighty will repay you with absolution and remission of all your sins in this world and concede perpetual life in the next', no less than the more common 'pro remissione peccatorum'.[18]

Elsewhere, Archbishop Theobald was more succinct: 'res ecclesie sunt redemptio peccatorum, oblationes fidelium'.[19] Similarly, Herbert Losinga, bishop of

---

[13] Hyams, 'The charter as a source'.
[14] Examples in these notes are intended to be minimal; perusal of the collections cited will provide more instances of the same or similar phrases. *Charters of the Honour of Mowbray, 1107–1191*, ed. D.E. Greenway (British Academy, Records of Social and Economic History, new series, i), 1972, nos. 5, 7, 10, 15; *Feudal Documents from the Abbey of Bury St Edmunds*, ed. D.C. Douglas (British Academy, Records of Social and Economic History, viii), 1932, nos. 185, 191; 'Charters of the earldom of Hereford, 1095–1201', ed. David Walker, *Camden Miscellany XXII*, Camden Society, 4th ser., i, 1964, 1–77, nos. 17, 104.
[15] Examples do not need to be given; *Bury*, no. 190, has the first phrase.
[16] 'Hereford', no. 3; *Blythburgh Priory Cartulary*, ed. C. Harper-Bill (Suffolk Records Society: Suffolk Charters, ii–iii), 1980–1, i, no. 42.
[17] 'Exultant in eis obsequiis reges et dignitates totius orbis et felici commercio de temporalibus eterna, de terrenis mercantur celestia bona abundanter, terreni reges sancte ecclesie largiuntur temporalia bona . . .'. *Charters of Norwich Cathedral Priory*, i, ed. Barbara Dodwell (Pipe Roll Society, lxxviii, new ser. xl, for 1965–6), 1974, no. 3.
[18] 'Hereford', nos. 94–5, 105; *Bury*, no. 185. *Norwich*, no. 112: 'pro redemptione vite mee meorumque omnium peccatorum absolutione'.
[19] *Liber Eliensis*, ed. E.O. Blake (Camden Society, 3rd ser. xcii), 1962, no. 126.

Norwich, urged his monks: 'Vacate elemosinis. quia sicut aqua extinguit ignem, ita elemosina extinguit peccatum.'[20] If Herbert, quoting Ecclesiasticus, was making a general statement about alms extinguishing sin, his successor Everard put the same idea in a charter: 'Great is the mercy of our redeemer, who gives a remedy for our sins in the distribution of alms.'[21] Everard thought that gifts of land were distributions of alms, and alms in some way cancelled out sin. (Of course, formally it did not: it remitted punishment or penance, as early indulgences had it, 'whoever makes alms shall have pardon of forty days of his penance'.)[22] This was the common assumption: gifts to the church were 'alms' because they helped in the remission of sins and therefore the attainment of eternal life. There is nothing at all mysterious in the use of the word to describe grants of land, particularly in a world where laymen had as yet an unsophisticated grasp of the precise mechanism of salvation. Even bishops encouraged the perception of a direct trade-off between alms and sins, a profit and loss account in the 'happy commerce' of temporal for eternal things. The lands of the church were 'alms' because they had been given for spiritual objects. The development of the formula '*in* alms', '*in elemosinam*', which (although much older in other parts of France) had just begun in Normandy by 1066, was a direct consequence of this perception.[23] Moreover, ecclesiastical property could continue to be described simply as 'alms' or 'the alms of churches' long after free alms formulae had become settled.[24]

If a grant to a church constituted an act of almsgiving, it was in itself a good work. The gain to be had, especially in founding a monastery, arose from and was embedded in the act itself. Charters relate not only the donation of land but also the foundation of the new church (monastery) to the 'soul-saving' clauses. So Herbert of Norwich: 'for the redemption of my life and the absolution of all my sins I have built at Norwich in honour of the Holy Trinity a church, which I have constituted and consecrated the mother-church of Norfolk and Suffolk'.[25] Equally a layman, Roger Bigod: 'for the common safety and remedy of our souls I give to God and the Virgin and the blessed apostles Peter and Paul and the church of Cluny, the church which I have begun to establish and build at Thetford'.[26] It was the work of a moment (although in the case of a foundation a long one) which brought spiritual benefit, because it was in itself an act of almsgiving, a good work. Another East Anglian example is even more explicit: 'Since faithful men who are devoted to God perform many good works for their souls, and in particular it is thought that salvation is to be found in the construction and endowment of holy mother church, . . . I, Robert Malet, hoping by a similar work to invoke the

---

20 *The Life, Letters, and Sermons of Bishop Herbert de Losinga*, ed. E.M. Goulbourn & Henry Symonds, 2 vols, Oxford and London 1878, ii, 26.
21 'Magna est misericordia redemptoris nostri, qui et in elemosinarum largitione nostrorum posuit remedia peccatorum, et pro temporalibus eterna comutat.' *Norwich*, no. 116.
22 *Norwich*, no. 108.
23 Emily Zack Tabuteau, *Transfers of Property in Eleventh-Century Norman Law*, Chapel Hill, 1988, 36–41; Jean Yver, 'Une boutade de Guillaume le Conquérant: note sur la genèse de la tenure en aumône', *Etudes d'Histoire du Droit Canonique*, Paris 1965, i, 783–96.
24 *Bury*, no. 206; R.C. Van Caenegem, *Royal Writs in England from the Conquest to Glanvill* (Selden Society, lxxvii), 1972, 279, n. 1; see below, note 46.
25 *Norwich*, no. 112.
26 *Monasticon*, v, 148.

mercy of God, for the souls of . . . construct a church to the use of the monks at Eye, and I place in it a convent of monks.'[27]

Establishing a monastery also brought further benefits to the founder, as is clear from the omitted phrases in the same preamble: 'for in churches the sins of those who build them are washed away by the prayers of religious men and the mercy of God, the poor are sustained by alms and other benefits, and other offices of charity are administered.' Founding convents established monks and good works which were to last for ever – 'monachos qui ibi Deo serviant usque ad finem' in the case of Norwich.[28] These good works could equally be termed 'alms': the penance imposed on those who fought and killed at Hastings could be performed by founding a church or endowing one and so procuring perpetual alms ('vel ecclesiam faciendo vel ecclesiam largiendo perpetua elemosina redimat').[29] At Battle Abbey, these were specifically termed 'bona opera'.[30]

The donor shared in these good works by confraternity, by his or her association with the prayers and alms and other activities of the monks. Confraternity was not only a general assumption, but also a specific institution, which was common amongst the religious themselves: as such it appears in early charters, such as those of Nigel d'Aubigny, by which laymen were explicitly granted the same obsequies and other intercessory arrangements as a monk or an abbot of the house.[31] Confraternity in this form was one step away from actually becoming a monk, either in retirement or right at the end, *ad succurrendum*, for adopting the habit itself was still seen as the surest way to heaven.[32] This was particularly true before lay religious practice was significantly affected by the development of purgatory and the acknowledgement that works performed long after death could help the soul.[33] In its developed form in the later twelfth century confraternity therefore offered 'a share in all benefits and prayers which are and shall be performed in this house for ever'.[34] It was commonly assumed that founders of religious houses were within the confraternity, sharing in the spiritual benefits, as were many other donors.

Alms terminology therefore accurately described the nature of grants of land to

[27] *Eye Priory Cartulary and Charters*, ed. V. Brown (Suffolk Records Society: Suffolk Charters, xii), i, no. 1.

[28] *Norwich*, no. 1.

[29] *Councils and Synods with Other Documents relating to the English Church, I (871–1204)*, ed. D. Whitelock, M. Brett and C.N.L. Brooke, 2 vols, Oxford, 1981, i, 583.

[30] *Battle Chronicle*, 66–7.

[31] *Mowbray*, nos. 1, 13; *Bury*, no .175 ('recepti me . . . in fraternitatem et in participationem omnium beneficiorum suorum'); *Charters of the Anglo-Norman Earls of Chester, c.1071–1237*, ed. Geoffrey Barraclough (Record Society of Lancashire and Cheshire, cxxvi), 1988, no. 2. See in general, H.E.J. Cowdrey, 'Unions and confraternity with Cluny', *Journal of Ecclesiastical History* xvi, 1965, 152–62; Rev. Preb. Clark-Maxwell, 'Some letters of confraternity', 'Some further letters of confraternity', *Archaeologia* lxxv, 1926, 19–60; lxxix, 1929, 179–216.

[32] *Norwich*, no. 106; C. Harper-Bill, 'The piety of the Anglo-Norman knightly class', *ante*, ii, 66, 69–76.

[33] Clive Burgess, ' "A fond thing vainly invented": an essay on purgatory and pious motive in later medieval England', in *Parish, Church, and People: local studies in lay religion, 1350–1750*, ed. S.J. Wright, 1988, 59–62; R.W. Southern, 'Between Heaven and Hell', *Times Literary Supplement*, 18 June 1982, 651–2 (review of J. Le Goff, *La Naissance du Purgatoire*).

[34] *Stoke by Clare Cartulary, BL Cotton Appx. xxi*, ed. Christopher Harper-Bill and Richard Mortimer, 3 vols (Suffolk Records Society: Suffolk Charters, iv–vi), Woodbridge 1982–4, nos. 11, 14, 15 (i, 9, 11).

the church. The two subtly overlapping meanings of 'alms', both describing good works, point towards the two ways in which benefactors were to benefit from their gifts. Their sins would be washed away and salvation procured both by the act of foundation itself, and by the works to be done perpetually by the religious, supported by the land.

In assessing how these intentions affected the nature of ecclesiastical tenure, it is important to be clear how far it was equated with secular modes of tenure, and therefore whether the monks' works were thought of as services, in the sense of rents or military service. In the period between the Conquest and the end of the twelfth century, it was rare for donors to require the religious to perform particular works for them in return for their grants. Where they did so it usually involved a work which required specific material provision, such as a light, a pittance for an anniversary, or food for a pauper.[35] Moreover, it was often couched in the form of a grant by the monks to the donor, rather than a condition of the grant.[36] Nevertheless, there are odd indications of an assumption that the monks' works were services owed to the donor. Charters reserved 'no secular service' (implying that there was spiritual service to be done), or no services 'preter orationes', or even 'sine omni retentione temporalis servitii preter elemosinam puram' and 'so that they be bound to do service from this land to no-one except God'.[37] The orthodoxy in the later common law was that spiritual services could not be enforced because they were indefinite and unspecified.[38] What we do not know, and can hardly hope to, is what actually happened within the relationship between donors and their churches. The patronage and protection exercised by the founding family, and in particular its heavy involvement in the early years, may have allowed its members some role in the arrangement and performance of the monks' works and hence the patrons' benefits.[39]

It is more likely, however, that lay donors, unlike prelates, did not interfere in this way, because most of them were as yet ignorant of clerical functions (as indeed were many churchmen) and of precisely how they were to be saved. The whole point of monastic foundation was to get the monks to secure salvation for you, to have your sins remitted vicariously. First the founder made a spectacular gift, in itself a great act of almsgiving, which the family made sure both God and the world saw. Then he left it to the professionals, the religious who were called in from whatever monastery or order, to save his soul and their own in the best way

[35] *Mowbray*, nos. 1, 7 (paupers); *Norwich*, no. 111 (anniversary); 'Hereford', nos. 96, 119; *Mowbray*, no. 9 (lights); 'Hereford', no. 108 (chantry). See Thompson, ' "Alms" to "spiritual services" ', n. 52.
[36] See n. 31 (Mowbray); *The Monastic Constitutions of Lanfranc*, ed. M.D. Knowles, London and Edinburgh 1951, 114–15; Cowdrey, 'Unions and confraternity with Cluny', pp. 157–8; *Stoke by Clare Cartulary*, nos. 11, 14, 15, 289, 302, 321, 513, 540, 560. As late as 1276 the nuns of Marham addressed a benefactor thus: 'nos temporalia bona sua predicta nobis in hac parte collata spirituali remuneracione quantum in nobis est sibi recompensare volentes', Norfolk Record Office, Hare MS 1, fo. 68v.
[37] *Blythburgh*, nos. 31, 35; *Monasticon*, v, 69; 'Hereford', no. 68; *Mowbray*, no. 17. Douglas, 'Tenure *in elemosina*', n. 55; *The Cartulary of Shrewsbury Abbey*, ed. Una Rees, 2 vols, Aberystwyth 1975, no. 288; Postles, 'Tenure in frankalmoign', n. 7.
[38] *Littleton's Tenures*, ed. Eugene Wambaugh, Washington, DC 1903, II, vi, §136 (p. 67); Kimball, 'Tenure in frank almoign', 341–4.
[39] See the precise works at note 35.

they knew how, according to their particular way of life. Spiritual activities were fundamentally under ecclesiastical control because that was what the clergy were there to do, so that it is no surprise to find the emerging ecclesiastical jurisdiction having cognizance of and control over them.[40] The monastic custumals laid down how the monastic day was to be lived, what liturgy was to be sung and said, and what obsequies were to be performed for dead brethren as well as confratres.[41] Indeed, twelfth-century donors had an increasing amount of choice of different approaches to the religious life, from old Benedictine and particularly Cluniac liturgy, to the different paths of Cistercian isolation and asceticism, and the pastoral emphasis of the canons. But donors chose a package, usually controlled centrally by a religious order, rather than a DIY kit to put together themselves: this was not their sphere of activity. We cannot, therefore, think of spiritual services as part of tenure between monasteries and donors, nor of a strict commerce of material for spiritual benefits. Rather we need to think of exchange between them, indeed of a gift-exchange whose character was the continual – but not precisely or quantifiably reciprocal – exchange of benefits through time: each act of donation or protection (spiritual or material) elicited a response from the other party which in turn created an obligation to further exchange.[42]

If there was no precise commercial exchange between the parties, however, there was some sort of tenure between them approximating to the tenure between lords and secular tenants, which provided the context within which the relationship operated. Walter of Gloucester confirmed in perpetual alms land granted by his ancestors 'which they and their predecessors held ('tenuerunt') of me and my ancestors'; and Hubert de Munchensy equally wished that the monks of Colne 'teneant de me et heredibus meis'.[43] Glanvill formalized this in the writ of right for free alms, where the tenant 'clamat tenere de te in liberam elemosinam'.[44] Indeed, there may have been a closer link between lords and churches than was the case with secular tenants precisely because clergy and monks did not do homage for their possessions.[45] Alms were occasionally seen as parts of the demesne, as Henry II said when taking Cirencester under his protection, 'de mea dominica elemosina' and ' sicut meas proprias . . . de propria elemosina mea'.[46] We do not need to go as far as Milsom's concept of a 'charitable subscription' charged on the demesne to suggest that this loose tenure on the one hand defined the closeness of the patronal family and its monastery, but on the other provided the context for the relationship between them to be conducted flexibly through time.[47]

Nevertheless, donors did have two particular expectations of tenure by religious

---

[40] Littleton thought that this was still the case for frankalmoin, *Littleton's Tenures*, §135; see *Councils & Synods II*, ii, 964 [5].

[41] E.g. *Udalrici Cluniacensis Monachi Consuetudines Cluniacenses*, in *Patrologia Latina* cxlix, cols 651–2, 767–78 (esp. 777–8); *Constitutions of Lanfranc*, 120–32.

[42] Dr Chibnall pointed out in discussion that confraternity had to renewed for each new patron, mirroring the secular process of renewal of seisin: both provided occasions for contact in the generations which succeeded the original parties.

[43] 'Hereford', no. 60; *Cartularium Prioratus de Colne*, ed. J. L. Fisher, Colchester 1946, no. 65.

[44] *Tractatus de legibus et consuetudinibus regni Anglie qui Glanvilla vocatur*, ed. G.D.G. Hall, London and Edinburgh 1965, xii, 3 (p. 137); *Early Registers of Writs*, ed. E. de Haas and G.D.G. Hall (Selden Society, lxxxvii), 1970, 18, 33, 34 (but see 110).

[45] *Glanvill*, ix, 2 (106).

[46] *Cartulary of Cirencester Abbey*, ed. C. Ross, 3 vols, 1964–77, i, nos. 63, 71, 74.

[47] Milsom, *Legal Framework*, 91.

houses, which flowed from their spiritual aims in granting these alms. In the first place, perpetuity was constantly emphasized in phrases such as 'in perpetuum possidendum' 'jure perpetuo', 'perpetualiter', 'perhenniter', and also 'in perpetuam elemosinam'.[48] Secure tenure was essential to both the modes by which souls benefited. The gift itself attracted the mercy of God, but not if it was reversed: Warin fitzGerold implored Henry II to maintain and confirm his gifts to Bury so that no wrongdoing would be able to violate them or bear away ('auferre') his soul.[49] Equally, the perpetual benefits of confraternity depended on perpetual tenure of the means of their support.[50] Grants of lands and churches were grants of capital, and would only realize the income to support perpetual good works through secure tenure in time. Furthermore, the secular benefits which flowed from monastic foundation reinforced an expectation of perpetuity on the part of families which were establishing visible symbols of lordship already achieved, and prestige to be acquired in the future. The special closeness in the relationship between founder and monastery depended upon its maintenance through time: the monks remained the focus for the family's spiritual provision down the generations, taking responsibility for the salvation of ancestors and heirs, and offering a demonstration of the family's antiquity and local lordship to the world. In the early fourteenth century the last earl Warenne self-consciously confirmed the grants of his six predecessors (since the conquest) to Castleacre priory, the centre of the family's lordship in East Anglia.[51]

Two subsidiary points arise here. In early grants, perhaps for fifty years after the conquest, perpetual tenure – although almost universally intended – receives less emphasis than the fact of the grant.[52] This balance derives from a number of interconnected factors. At the level of spiritual intention, it is probably a symptom of the undeveloped perception of purgatory: the more pressing need was to balance the spiritual books at the time of death, than to make provision for the future. But it equally corresponds to the uncertainty of securing perpetual tenure, and therefore to the delayed development of hereditary language until land had in fact been inherited: indeed, Professor Holt found that such language developed in part through expectations of perpetuity in grants to the church.[53] The conquest made a difference not because there was no expectation of inheritance and perpetual tenure, but because these could only arise from experience and therefore custom. Connected in turn to this is the possibility that 'perpetual' did not mean the same

---

[48] Examples are hardly necessary: early charters in any collection show a rich variety of phraseology. One confirmation translates the 'in perpetuam elemosinam' of the grant it is confirming as 'tenendam in perpetuum', *Bury*, nos. 177–8. See Holt in note 53.

[49] *Bury*, no. 189.

[50] Such perpetuity was guaranteed, for example, in the foundation deeds of Norwich (*Norwich*, nos. 1, 260). The addition to later common form for recipients, 'Deo et ecclesie sancte . . . et monachis ibidem servientibus', of 'et servituris' embodies the same implication, e.g. *Blythburgh*, no. 35.

[51] BL Harley MS 2110, fo. 13v. For some more continuing relationships, see e.g. Thompson, '*Habendum et tenendum*', 226, 229–31; this is a central theme of my Ph.D. thesis and the book which will emerge from it.

[52] Postles, 'Gifts in frankalmoin', 333–4. Early charters from some collections illustrate the point, especially Nigel d'Aubigny's restorations, which inform the argument which follows; *Mowbray*, nos. 1–15.

[53] J.C. Holt, 'Feudal society and the family in early medieval England: II. Notions of patrimony', *TRHS*, 5th ser. xxxiii, 1983, 193–220, esp. pp. 199–204.

as 'in sempiternam': a grant of a benefice could be made to a clerk who was clearly only to hold it for life, yet it was to have 'perpetual validity'.[54] 'Perpetual' seems to have meant something like 'as long as it matters', 'as far as I am concerned', or perhaps 'as far as we can reasonably bind the future from here'. Those who used it had a healthy sense of what was practicable, and were not expressing unwonted confidence in the stability of the world in the future.

Donors secondly emphasised freedom from secular service in the early charters, usually in some variant of 'liberam et quietam et absolutam de omni servicio et exactione seculari'. The language of these phrases leaves no room for doubt that freedom is to do with immunity from secular exaction. Lords often intended to take no secular services from the property which they granted to churches; and the king could exempt his ecclesiastical tenants-in-chief from burdens such as geld and other royal exactions.[55]

Such insistence on immunity from secular burdens may have flowed from the developing ecclesiastical ideology of the late-eleventh century. Some new orders in particular were keen to avoid paying any dues from their land, as part of their rejection of the world itself.[56] But a general immunity of free alms land is not even supported by Gratian: he exempted only the lands annexed to churches (what we would think of as glebe), and allowed royal and other burdens on lands given by donors or purchased.[57] Moreover, in England it was far too late to start imposing an ideology of the freedom of church land when the greatest ecclesiastical landowners owed military services, as well as homage, for their baronies.[58] I suggest that the insistence on freedom by donors and churches was essentially a practical matter: the land was to provide material support for spiritual activities, by supporting monks, rather than being diverted into secular services. (Some charters, indeed, mentioned not only the construction of monasteries, but also the feeding and clothing of the monks as resulting from the grant.)[59] The last thing donors wanted was the money being spent on secular exactions. Here is Roger earl of Hereford in the mid-twelfth century: 'I quitclaim all rents and customs on this land which they hold in alms so that they may without vexation or disturbance serve God according to their order, and the more freely and devotedly pray for me and my friends living and dead'.[60] Lands were to be quit of services the better to support the salvation of the donors.

This suggestion has the virtue of explaining why the freedom of land given in

---

[54] *Norwich*, no. 135; the common later form which emerged in a most interesting discussion on this point was the 'perpetual vicar'.

[55] Examples are again unnecessary; see note 37, and kings quit-claiming royal exactions at Norwich and Worcester: *Norwich*, nos. 2, 15; *The Cartulary of Worcester Cathedral Priory*, ed. R.R. Darlington (Pipe Roll Society, lxxvi, new ser. xxxviii, for 1962–3), 1968, nos. 6, 9, 30.

[56] 'Hereford', no. 73: 'libere et quiete, sicut decet ecclesiam Dei oblationes fidelium pacifice et tranquille possidere'; also no. 37. Postles, 'Tenure in frankalmoin and knight service', 21; Douglas, 'Tenure *in elemosina*', 118–19.

[57] *Corpus Iuris Canonici*, C XXIII, Q viii, cc. 24–5 (ed. E. Friedberg, Leipzig 1879–81, i, col. 962).

[58] H.M. Chew, *The English Ecclesiastical Tenants-in-Chief and Knight Service*, Oxford 1932.

[59] Above, notes 25–7; *Norwich*, no. 112, divided up properties for different purposes ('De hiis rebus divido et ad opera et ad alia ecclesie necessaria, videlicet ad victum et ad vestimenta monachorum, tribuo ea . . .'); *Shrewsbury*, no. 2; *Worcester*, nos. 3–4 ('ad victum'); 'Hereford', no. 18 ('ad vineam faciendam ad missas celebrandas'); *Mowbray*, no. 10 ('ad coquinam monachorum').

[60] 'Hereford', no. 17.

alms was never absolute: it was quite thinkable to grant land 'free of all service whatsoever, for a rent of . . .' or 'for the service of a knight's fee', or even Danegeld.[61] In the light of this, we may have to modify our conception of what 'free' meant, to denote something like 'free except what is specified'. Like 'perpetuity', 'freedom' was not absolute, but depended on context. The essence of a free tenure was not that it was quit of service: in fact the whole point of it was to procure some form of service. But it was to be immune from burdens beyond what was specified (or what custom laid down certainly, such as the terms of military service). The freedom of 'free alms' did not therefore derive, as has been suggested, from owing a 'free service', but from immunity from burdens which were not specified or unavoidable.[62] The donor's object was to grant land as freely as possible so as to produce the maximum substance for the church's support.

Freedom and perpetuity were therefore integral to frankalmoin, as the phraseology which was more commonly used from the mid-twelfth century testified, 'in liberam et perpetuam elemosinam'. Yet these two characteristics were important only because of the fundamental spiritual object of such grants: they were secondary qualities arising from the primary role of endowments in procuring salvation for their donors.

How were donors and their churches to protect the grants against diminution and interference, and thereby secure their spiritual purposes? (For these purposes the possibility of donors changing their minds barely affects the argument, although to believe that it did not happen is, as Paul Hyams put it in the parallel secular context, 'to believe in a world without sin'.)[63] To do so, they had to take into account the two different axes of lordship and of time. They needed to square their lords, whose interest lay in the services owed from the fee now being diminished by the grant. And they had to persuade the future to respect the grant being made now, particularly once they themselves were dead.

The more difficult of the two problems involved the future, because of the inability of donors to dictate to it and the lack of mechanisms to enforce their desires. The problem of time, to put it crudely, is that you lose personal control when you die. In part donors needed to prevent future seignorial exactions on the land granted,[64] but more importantly they focused their uncertainty on their heirs.[65] They wanted to prevent changes of mind by heirs which, the evidence of the writs of the two Henrys shows, did indeed happen.[66] Perhaps bishops felt even more vulnerable, since their successors had no blood interest in their grants: Herbert of Norwich firmly forbade his successors to change the arrangements he

---

[61] *The Cartulary of Missenden Abbey*, ed. J.G. Jenkins (Buckinghamshire Archaeological Society), 1938, no. 71; *Mowbray*, no. 22. Kimball, 'Tenure in frank almoign', esp. 347, n. 2; Postles, 'Tenure in frankalmoign', 22.

[62] Cf. the argument at Douglas, 'Tenure *in elemosina*', 105–7: this is a tendentious reading of Glanvill, for 'in liberam elemosinam' follows only 'clamat tenere de te . . '; the phrase does not include 'in liberum servicium', which only applies to the earlier tenures mentioned.

[63] Paul R. Hyams, 'Warranty and good lordship in twelfth-century England', *Law and History Review* v, 1987, 437–503, at p. 465.

[64] Some phrases focused future security on the freedom from exaction; *Bury*, no. 190.

[65] *Bury*, no. 178 is a sale, but makes the point: 'ne venditionem aliquatenus defraudare presumant . . . sicut volunt succedere in meam hereditatem'.

[66] Van Caenegem, *Royal Writs*, nos. 42, 47, 80, 127, 176.

had made in founding the cathedral priory.[67] These and many other statements show that this was a real issue, because it could not be completely squared at the time of donation. Donors revealed their sense of insecurity in various clauses expressing the intention that heirs should respect their grants for ever: one of the most insecure was Nigel d'Aubigny, who ordered his brother and heir not to violate his grants – in which he gave back everything he himself had taken from churches and laymen![68] These clauses evolved into the common form 'quare volo et firmiter precipio ut monachi firme et libere et quiete et honorifice in perpetuum teneant et habeant'.[69] Grants were made in solemn ceremonies involving oaths and other rituals; and clauses of warranty began to appear in Stephen's reign by which donors bound their heirs to maintain gifts and warrant tenants.[70]

The trouble was that without a mechanism which gave some grounds for believing that terms laid down at a particular moment would be enforced there-after, these aspirations expressed little more than pious hope addressed to an uncertain future. The most obvious procedure was to associate heirs in one's grants and to secure their confirmations, an institution known as the *laudatio parentum*; the heirs were, of course, spiritual beneficiaries since grants were made almost universally 'for the souls of me and my heirs and successors'. This got one a little way into the future, but more importantly it was positive as well as negative: heirs would inherit the power by which the lord had made his grant, and they would therefore have power (in the worst case) to reverse it and resume the land, or, what the donor hoped would be the norm, to protect the church's tenure.[71]

For this was a seignorial world, a world structured largely around the power of lords, the extent and distribution of whose lands determined the political make-up of any particular locality. Each lord was largely autonomous in his own fee, with the crucial exception of the interest which the lord's lord retained, all the way up to the king. Some donors laid down that the monks were to answer to no-one except the lord (i.e. the donor) alone, a feature mirrored in or mirroring royal grants under Henry I as well as Henry II, and often linked to the concept of 'elemosina propria' or demesne alms.[72] It was therefore not so much necessary for donors to square their lords in order to make secure grants to monasteries; it was unthinkable not to. Lords were concerned at least with the services from the land, which a religious house might not be able or willing to fulfil so readily as the lay donor. Lords were therefore associated in grants to the church: their consent was secured and they issued charters which in all essentials resemble those of their granting tenants except that they omitted the crucial word 'do', leaving the confir-matory 'concedo' and 'confirmo'.[73] Warin fitzGerold made a grant to Bury already

---

[67] *Norwich*, nos. 112, 260: the latter is Anselm, equally conscious that a successor might infringe or change the foundation.

[68] *Mowbray*, nos. 3, 5.

[69] Postles, 'Gifts in frankalmoign', 335–8.

[70] Ibid., 338–46.

[71] *Bury*, no. 179: 'quamdiu vixero manutenebo id quod constans sit et post me volo quod heredes mei hoc similiter faciant.' *Missenden*, no. 70 (1150), associates a whole host of sons in the gift. Postles, 'Securing the gift in Oxfordshire charters in the twelfth and early thirteenth centuries', *Archives* xix, 1990, 183–91; 'Gifts in frankalmoign', 341–2.

[72] 'Hereford', no. 37; *Cirencester*, no. 71; *Norwich*, nos. 26, 30. S.E. Thorne, 'The assize *Utrum* and canon law in England', *Columbia Law Review* xxxiii, 1933, 428–36, at n. 24.

[73] *Missenden*, no. 70, is a confirmation of a grant 'de feodo nostro', made by the tenants 'coram

noticed, which not only had a first witness 'Gaufridus dominus meus', but was followed by a confirmation of the same Geoffrey de Mandeville in the same terms, 'cum *predicta* libertate et immunitate et quiete ab omni servicio', as well as 'intuitu Dei et sue fidelitatis'.[74] Since in a seignorial world these confirmations were genuine concessions, they brought the lords who granted them within the circle of spiritual beneficiaries, and therefore might include the magic words 'pro anima mea':[75] indeed, many tenants, particularly in early grants by tenants-in-chief, had already included their lords among the beneficiaries, such as Peter Valoines, in founding Binham 'for the soul of my lord king William, who conquered England, gave me this manor, and by whose assent and licence I initiate this work'.[76]

This worked both ways, for lords consulted with their barons before making grants: 'locutus sum cum meis baronibus'.[77] Moreover they encouraged those tenants to make grants of their own to their houses, which were honorial monasteries, reflecting the glory both of the family and of its dependants; the cartulary of Stoke-by-Clare is full of grants from Clare tenants.[78] Confirmations were therefore naturally addressed to tenants, 'fidelibus et baronibus et hominibus suis francis et anglis', just like royal grants.[79] They had to be addressed to those who needed to know about them, sometimes those in a specific place, for the lord's tenants and ministers in the locality were those he relied on to protect grants. The strong seignorial context of all this is obvious: this was a world dominated by lords, in which the honour formed a central, if not exclusive, focus of political and social organization. Lords and their courts were important because it was lords and tenants who had the local power to defend and maintain a religious house and its tenure of lands.

Lords were therefore not so much a problem for donors in securing their grants; they were part of the answer. Indeed until 1135 they were the main part of the answer, because they, under the aegis of the ultimate overlord, the king, were in control of their world. The lord was indeed sometimes the king, but in any case a royal confirmation was worth having, so that donors such as Peter Valoines, Warin fitzGerold and many others secured royal confirmations, even imagining that this would (in a case of 1135) give the grant 'perpetua stabilitate'.[80] Perhaps Henry I's record shows that he did indeed intend to enforce perpetuity in grants, particularly where he wanted to show favour in cases brought to his attention.[81] The logic of the tenurial structure already seems to have been pointing upwards, towards the development of a common law.

nobis', i.e. in the lord's court; *Norwich*, no. 134 is another example at lower levels in the tenurial hierarchy, but the royal charters confirming episcopal grants were also seignorial confirmations, e.g. *Norwich*, nos. 1 ff. passim.

[74] *Bury*, nos. 190–1.

[75] *Bury*, no. 188.

[76] *Monasticon*, iii, 345; Galbraith, 'Monastic foundation charters', 220.

[77] *Chester*, no. 2; *Bury*, no. 170, 'sunt testes mei homines'.

[78] *Stoke-by-Clare Cartulary*, passim.

[79] *Gloucester Charters*, nos. 5, 11 ff. 'Volo ut omnes barones mei sciant', *Bury*, no. 176.

[80] *Bury*, no. 173. At *Norwich*, nos. 8–9, Henry I implies that this will indeed be the effect of his confirmation. Interesting examples of donors who urgently requested royal-seignorial confirmation of their restorations are *Mowbray*, no. 2; *Bury*, no. 189.

[81] See above, note 66.

Nevertheless 1135 was the end of such security for the moment, so that it is not surprising to find another jurisdiction, quite outside the landholding structure, emerging to guarantee grants: that of the church itself. Indeed, Archbishop Theobald confirmed a grant of King Stephen, which seems an extraordinary reversal of roles.[82] Perhaps this development might have taken place even without the interruption in royal authority: some of the guarantees involving heirs, such as oaths and anathema, were spiritual sanctions and so were implicitly subject to ecclesiastical jurisdiction. More important, the church, if its sanctions were respected, offered a mechanism to guarantee title in a more distant future than could be achieved by associating living lords and heirs in grants, because it was itself a perpetual institution; there would always be bishops and popes to fulminate against invaders of ecclesiastical property. Moreover the church was developing a network of courts backed by these authorities, as well as systematized law (especially after 1140) and sophisticated procedures for hearing cases. It also had a natural predilection for an ecclesiastical tenant against a lay opponent, and an inherent self-interest in perpetual tenure. Monasteries therefore got their property, lands as well as churches, confirmed and taken into special protection by bishops, archbishops and popes, which presupposed that these authorities would hear disputes and enforce solutions.[83]

The flaw in this development lies in the sad fact that spiritual sanctions were not always automatically respected; indeed they tended to have to be enforced by secular power. The church under Theobald only appears relatively strong because secular authority was weak and divided, and was failing to provide the protection and stability essential to monastic possession. Donors had to turn to the church because of this failure; but it seems that spiritual protection could not guarantee very much in practice, and monasteries in some areas suffered depredations.[84] Ecclesiastical jurisdiction was actually at its strongest when co-operating with the lay power: as even Anselm put it in one confirmation, 'et regia et nostra auctoritate'.[85]

Donors and churches, therefore, tried to secure their grants by all means available to them, by words and oaths and by confirmations, associations and commitments from various different authorities, including king and church. On the one hand this is symptomatic of a society in which power was quite widely distributed, and was certainly not centralized in one authority (although neither was it devolved to 'sovereign' lordships). But on the other, it encapsulates the dilemma of those seeking to bind the future: in the end there was in principle no single authority which could offer much guarantee of security to any particular arrangement made beyond around a generation in the future. It seems hard to doubt that this was exacerbated by the intervention of the Anarchy, which diffused power and forced landholders to look for a variety of different guarantees in various different jurisdictions. This might not have been necessary had, say, Henry II

---

[82] *Bury*, no. 183.

[83] For a particular notification see *Missenden*, no. 76. The sections containing episcopal and papal charters in cartularies show these authorities at work, as well as collections of episcopal and papal *acta*. For more detail, see Thompson, ' "Alms" to "spiritual services" ', 244–6; especially the charters in A. Saltman, *Theobald Archbishop of Canterbury*, 1956.

[84] Ibid.; most obviously in East Anglia, C. Harper-Bill, 'Bishop William Turbe and the Diocese of Norwich', *ante*, vii, 1984, 142–60, at p. 150; R.H.C. Davis, *King Stephen*, 3rd edn, London and New York 1990, 77–81.

[85] *Norwich*, no. 260.

succeeded Henry I and come to the common law by the straighter route of continuing his grandfather's lordly kingship.

Freedom from secular services and perpetual tenure were therefore ideal features of grants to the church, to judge from charters before 1150. They derived from the spiritual intentions which lay at the heart of grants, since grants were conceived both as gifts to poor religious (which were meritorious in themselves), and increasingly as support for perpetual good works (which would bring cumulative spiritual benefits). By this time, freedom and perpetuity had probably become intimately associated with the notion of alms, which above all encapsulated the spiritual intention: certainly the phrase 'in perpetual alms' was already common. Frankalmoin was beginning to represent a shorthand for the convergence of all these ideas.[86]

Nevertheless, although the use of 'alms' terminology was almost universal in gifts to the church by 1150, still in most such grants and many thereafter the intended perpetual nature and immunity from exaction continued to be expressed in clauses separate from the 'alms' formulae.[87] There was as yet no automatic understanding that 'in perpetuum' and 'libera' were synonymous with 'elemosina'. The 'pro anima' element too, despite its closeness to the alms idea, was expressed independently of 'alms' formulae. Even if, therefore, 'alms' was increasingly understood to include all three ideas, it did not yet include them so automatically that they did not have to be stated.

Indeed, it is still the great variety of phraseology which is striking in charters of c.1150, and certainly of the eighty years before. There was even great variety in the nature and form of documents, ranging from odd notes containing pieces of information addressed to specific individuals who needed to know, to general announcements approximating to later standard forms, whose object was to gain maximum publicity. We must remember that charters record occasions, which were the culminations of negotiations at which individual deals were finalized and brought to fruition. They were drafted, albeit under the general guidance of custom, to make specific bargains between specific parties at particular times in particular places. Certainly some charters of the time of Henry I look 'settled' in terminology by later standards; but equally others of the 1170s were still very unsettled and idiosyncratic in their phraseology. Scriptoria and scribes who were not under central supervision naturally varied greatly in their practices, and so reflected not only many different sorts of bargains, but also different perceptions

---

[86] The fact that 'alms' formulae could even be used of grants not made primarily for spiritual intent, such as sales, shows that the terminology could provide a shorthand for those features when they were applied in other contexts. *Bury*, no. 177, looks like a gift of c.1150 made for souls, in perpetual alms, but the confirmation which follows says that the donor 'vendidit' the land. On the other hand, that the lord here avoids both alms terminology and spiritual intent, and accepts cash, and other examples, show deliberate attempts to avoid such usages when the thrust of the concession was not a gift, e.g. *Missenden*, nos. 70–1 (where 'alms' is only used of the rent which is remitted), 160.

[87] Collections which are easy to follow chronologically, such as the *Bury* and, especially, 'Hereford', charters, show donors spelling everything out well into the second half of the twelfth century. Sophisticated early 'free alms' formulae at *Mowbray*, nos. 9, 17, nevertheless include additional 'freedom' clauses. *Chester*, no. 63 (1146–7) is a confirmation, free and quit and 'pro anima' with no 'alms' formula at all, which I think quite rare by 1150.

of what was important about a grant to the church, what had to be written down, and what it was important to communicate to the world and to the future. Charters testify to an exchange which was not centrally regulated, a massive free market. They witness first and foremost a relationship between donor and recipient which was more important than any of the panoply of powers and jurisdictions around it, based as it was on a strong spiritual bond. Even if central regulation was occasionally called upon in particular circumstances, especially under Henry I, this was to enforce arrangements made locally and particularly.

That said, these transactions were made under the guidance of custom – quite strong custom – which was both common, and perhaps increasingly standardized. It is conceivable that settled terminology in free alms grants was a result of ecclesiastical sophistication at this point, which guided custom into particular forms in a fairly centralized way: for the church was an institution with an increasingly strong central orientation and with its own systematic law, and had no doubt done at least as much as the laity to increase expectations of freedom and perpetuity. But this is not to say that we can yet speak of a free alms 'tenure'. Criteria will vary, but for me the absence of a central jurisdiction with the will and the power to enforce a standardized custom, or law, is crucial: no consistency, no tenure.

What made 'free alms' into a tenure were Henry II's innovations in government for which he has earned the accolade 'the founder of the common law'. Frankalmoin acquired definite characteristics which donors, churches and other parties could be confident would be enforced in a consistent manner. Glanvill seems to have assumed that the characteristics of frankalmoin were well known.[88] In charters, 'In liberam et perpetuam elemosinam' increasingly became standard form; the decreasing use of subsidiary phrases such as 'ab omni exactione seculari' and 'perpetualiter' suggests that they were no longer necessary, because freedom and perpetuity were now inextricably located in the notion of 'alms'.

What allowed this to happen was the imposition by and in the royal court of uniform standards and categories, particularly with respect to land. The creation of the common law amounted to the consistent enforcement throughout the realm of a common set of customs. Henry signalled his willingness to intervene between lords and tenants so as to enforce the customary terms of tenure between them. Up to then tenure had been a flexible matter, decided in the lord's court by the interaction between the lord and his tenants, the lord's will being guided by the customs of the fee. The relationship was fundamentally flexible and political, because external authority rarely dictated decisions about grants, inheritance, or the performance of services. Henry now offered his court to all free men as a forum for the systematic consideration of such issues, through writs and procedures which were predictable (and fixed in price). He offered the writ of right to those who claimed to hold a tenancy of a lord by hereditary right; and he offered speedy remedies to heirs refused succession and tenants unjustly deprived by their lords. Henry was not attempting to destroy the power of the lords, around whom the political world was structured: no king could conceive of doing so for at least

---

[88] *Glanvill*, ix, 2, xii, 3, 25, xiii, 24 (pp. 106, 137, 148, 163): in the last case he has the advantage of us, for we have not yet worked out what was meant; see Douglas at note 8.

another two centuries. But he proposed to regulate feudal relationships, in part as a consequence of the Anarchy. The effect of his offer (whether intended or not) was to transform arrangements which had been customary and flexible and subject to local political interaction, into fixed terms which in principle would be enforced by a jurisdiction external to the relationship. The result was to make the crown a fount of justice for all free men, giving them recourse to the royal court, even – perhaps particularly – against their lords.[89]

The effect on frankalmoin is evident in the records. On a political level, the revival of royal authority provided the stability which enabled ecclesiastical jurisdiction to function more effectively, and so to enable Theobald to reverse the depredations.[90] In legal terms, Henry provided the church with the best mechanism yet available for securing perpetual tenure. At last a jurisdiction which was in itself perpetual offered to provide systematic enforcement of the customs of tenure. Hence Glanvill offered a variant of the writ of right for tenants who claimed to hold of their lords in free alms – ecclesiastical institutions.[91] In providing extra protection, the new actions catered for precisely the situation the original donors had been impotent to control, the failure of their heirs to respect their grants or to protect them against other wrongdoers. Moreover, since the offer of royal jurisdiction itself gradually destroyed the power of the lords to protect their tenants and churches, ecclesiastical institutions increasingly took to the royal courts to defend their lands instead.[92] The systematic and consistent enforcement of declared custom by a single authority meant that law had arrived: and churches were not slow to appreciate the benefits and use the royal remedies and the mechanisms for enforcement which backed up the decisions. Equally, in charters the formula 'In perpetuam elemosinam' now became almost standard: it could be used with confidence.

Services were also affected by Henry's regulation of tenurial relationships. Henry himself seems to have supposed that the essence of alms was the absence of service.[93] On the early plea rolls, we see the justices enforcing freedom from service where it was specified, and preferring to exempt land from service in cases where 'free alms' or some variant was in the charters.[94] From then on, discussions of frankalmoin all started from a presumption of freedom from secular services.[95] Such freedom, however, was only an ideal, a starting-point. We have already seen that grants could be made in alms – and even 'quit of all service' – which nevertheless imposed service. The 'libera' appears to mean 'no service except what is specified.' To that one might add 'and unavoidable': for this is just the

---

[89] I follow Milsom in general; see notes 3, 5. R.C. Palmer, 'The origins of property in England', *Law and History Review* iii, 1985, 1–50, 375–96, has tried to work out the chronology.

[90] See above, note 84.

[91] *Glanvill*, xii, 3 (p. 137).

[92] Douglas, 'Tenure *in elemosina*', 120–3. The early plea rolls show churches involved, e.g. *Curia Regis Rolls*, 1922–; *Pleas before the King or his Justices, 1198–1212*, ed. D.M. Stenton, 4 vols (Selden Society lxvii–viii, lxxxiii–iv), 1948–9, 1966–7. Since I shall attempt a detailed analysis of churches using the royal actions elsewhere, I shall not give detail here.

[93] Warren, *Henry II*, 538, where he seems to define lay fee as one for which a secular service was owed.

[94] Douglas, 'Tenure *in elemosina*', 116–20.

[95] Kimball, 'Tenure in frank almoign', 341–4.

moment when it was becoming harder to grant or acquire land completely quit of secular burdens, because of the nature of the tenurial structure.

Services had originally been due from tenants rather than their lands, within the personal relationship with their lords (most obviously exemplified by the Conqueror and his companions, who became his tenants-in-chief).[96] Early donors were substantial enough to have the flexibility to exempt particular parcels of land from services, and to support them elsewhere if necessary. If they were kings, they could always grant alms completely freely (not that they always did). Tenants-in-chief held much in demesne, so that they could grant land on which no specific services had ever been imposed: it would be quit 'as freely as ever I or my ancestors held it', which suggests that frankalmoin did not itself offer any particular immunity from service.[97] Even if they were granting land which had rendered scutage and had now escheated from a tenant, they could absorb the service on the demesne or elsewhere:[98] after all, many were found in 1166 to have too many knights' fees.[99] Where their tenants were granting land once burdened with service, they could afford to be flexible for the same reasons, especially when grants were being made to their own houses: David Postles has now shown us some of these negotiations.[100] What is significant about his evidence is that all the examples date from the 1150s onwards. As more lesser donors proposed to make grants to religion, more parcels of land were being offered whose specific service-burdens the donors themselves could not absorb, and might not be able to get their lords to remit. One solution was for the religious to buy the lord out. Another was for them to accept the service due to the overlord, which came to be called 'forinsec' service, outside the direct tenurial bargain between lord and church. From Richard Mortimer's evidence of the early distribution of scutage within the honour of Clare, we might expect to find these problems arising earlier: it does prompt one to wonder how important a role the 1166 *Carte* played in finally cementing the relationship between land and fiscalized military service burdens.[101]

The result was that much more land came to the church unavoidably burdened with services which the royal court would enforce since, in the case of services if not that of title, it had a natural bias towards those higher up the scale since the king himself was affected. As the church acquired and was given more property, it was increasingly unable to avoid the consequences of the tenurial structure within which land was held. In the light, therefore, of the circumstances of this world, the ideal of freedom of alms failed in practice: 'free alms' came to mean 'as freely as is possible in the circumstances'.[102] This may explain the increasing addition to frankalmoin formulae of 'pure alms' to re-emphasize freedom: certainly Bracton

---

[96] J.C. Holt, 'The introduction of knight service in England', *ante*, vi, 1983, 89–106.
[97] 'Hereford', nos. 94–5, 105–7 ('sicut umquam illam melius tenuerunt antecessores mei'); also no. 91, 'de meo dominio'; *Mowbray*, no. 11 ('totum dominium . . . sicut unquam melius et quietius habui'); *Bury*, no. 173.
[98] *Bury*, no. 175 ('et servicium quod de predicta terra antiquitus fiebat de residuo feodi mei perficiam').
[99] *The Red Book of the Exchequer*, ed. Hubert Hall, 3 vols, RS, 1896, i, 186–445; *EHD*, ii, 968–81.
[100] Postles, 'Tenure in frankalmoign'. The lord in *Missenden*, nos. 70–1 released some service, at least in one case as a spiritual gift. The lord in *Bury*, no. 178, was bought out.
[101] Richard Mortimer, 'Land and service: the tenants of the honour of Clare', *ante*, viii, 1985, 177–97; Holt, 'Introduction of knight service', esp. 105–6.
[102] Tabuteau sketched a similar view for Norman frankalmoin, *Transfers of Property*, 36–41.

thought that pure alms were even more immune.[103] But even this word could not avoid forinsec services demanded by overlords higher up the chain. On the other hand, the practical significance of this failure ultimately diminished as services became eroded, particularly by inflation (although John's scutages must have been burdensome).

The royal court took cognizance of the free tenurial structure and the service burdens within it, imposing consistency on and ultimately replacing the customary procedures and negotiations which had been used both to secure perpetual tenure and to establish the distribution of service-burdens. In doing so it found that, whereas it could enforce donors' aspirations to secure tenure, it could not honour their hopes for the immunity of their alms from burdens demanded higher up the scale. Under royal control, frankalmoin gained its perpetuity, but lost flexibility and therefore freedom.

The fact that consistency in frankalmoin was a result of royal control tells its own story as far as the jurisdictional question is concerned. Nevertheless, jurisdiction did not become unified overnight in the crown: it remained multiple and mixed for some time to come, in the case of the church courts up to the Reformation and beyond. The clergy did not abandon ecclesiastical jurisdiction, because it was still useful to have as much protection as possible. Pleas about land appear before bishops and pope in the first half of the thirteenth century, and in some cases churches pursued their objects in both jurisdictions.[104] Nor did they abandon the protection of their lords, which, since that power was firmly based in the locality, was probably their first line of defence against other demands and usurpations. Indeed the legal records themselves illustrate the norm of patronal families maintaining the properties which were the foundation of their spiritual security, in that lords often acted for their monasteries in the royal court, as the earl Warenne did for Castleacre in 1200.[105] It may be that religious houses often relied on their warrantors, their lords and patrons, for some time into the thirteenth century; and this may explain why they appear on the rolls rather less than one might think.[106]

The main problem with this picture of donors and churches seeking protection wherever they could get it, and increasingly resorting to the consistency and security which royal jurisdiction offered, is presented by the assize 'Utrum' and the puzzle which it still presents. In clause nine of the Constitutions of Clarendon of 1164, Henry II appeared to allow cases over 'elemosina' to go to the church courts, subject to a preliminary hearing before the royal court to determine whether the land in question was lay fee or alms.[107] This is not the place to untie this Gordian knot (which I propose to try elsewhere); so I shall simply cut it with a few observations.[108] The Constitutions were never 'enacted', and were produced

---

[103] Pollock & Maitland, i, 245–6; *Bracton on the Laws and Customs of England*, ed. G.E. Woodbine, trans. S.E. Thorne, 4 vols, Camb., Mass., & Selden Society, 1968–77, ii, 93–4.

[104] Douglas, 'Tenure *in elemosina*', 123–6; e.g. *English Episcopal Acta, IV: Lincoln 1185–1206*, ed. D.M. Smith, 1986, nos. 232, Appx. II (31); Jane Sayers, *Papal Judges Delegate in the Province of Canterbury, 1198–1254*, Oxford 1971, 179–83, 332–3, 351–3.

[105] *Curia Regis Rolls*, i, 161; Milsom, *Legal Framework*, 51.

[106] The lack of religious houses is my impression from initial work on the plea rolls.

[107] *Councils & Synods, I*, ii. 880–1.

[108] Douglas, 'Frankalmoin and jurisdictional immunity', is illuminating in many respects, but does not solve the problem entirely.

at a time of high political tension when Henry was at once furious with Becket for what he saw as turning his coat, but also needed to appear to make concessions to win the support of barons and bishops.[109] Clause 9 may have been such an apparent concession, in that it appeared to release alms property to ecclesiastical jurisdiction. Royal clerks seem to have adapted the common distinction between 'fee' and 'alms' ('Tenuras et elemosinas' or 'Feoda et elemosina', which were distinguished by the crucial question of secular service) to a jurisdictional one which had no previous warrant - and certainly no subsequent success.[110] For if the clause was drafted hurriedly in the heat of the moment, it was certainly also disingenuous. Henry's charters of that time and especially later include clauses which exempted religious houses from being impleaded for their lands, including that held in alms, except before the king: this was a flat contradiction of clause 9 and its 'Utrum' procedure.[111] Nor is there very much evidence of such a procedure ever being used in the way the clause described.[112] Clause nine merely illustrates the ability of Henry's lawyers to experiment and dream up different forms of action, and in particular to apply their two recurrent devices of using a jury in proof, and retaining royal supervision of all jurisdiction: for all that it appeared to offer jurisdiction to the church, 'Utrum' was a preliminary procedure in the royal court.[113]

In any case, the work of distinguishing between lay and ecclesiastical jurisdiction soon came to be done by the writ of prohibition to court christian, which a defendant brought there could purchase to forbid a case going any further in that forum.[114] Most prohibitions in the 1220s were for lay fee, which suggests that churches did continue to use ecclesiastical jurisdiction; and occasionally a house producing a charter in free alms was allowed to proceed in court christian.[115] But churches also used the royal remedies, and invoked their clauses forbidding pleading before any but the king.

Jurisdictional immunity was never a feature of free alms tenure, which was from the outset perceived in a seignorial context. Both the apparent Utrum of 1164, and the clergy's demands in the council of 1257 suggest that such an immunity was an aspiration amongst the rulers of the church.[116] But the ideal would have been difficult to realize in practice, in the first place because much land held in frankalmoin was liable, however vestigially, to secular burdens and could therefore be categorized as lay fee: jurisdiction over secular services clearly had to belong to the seignorial and royal courts. Perhaps where there were no services, as seems to have been envisaged in 1257, then the lay court willingly would release its jurisdiction: Henry II himself allowed this in the compromise terms of 1176, in which the criterion of secular services was the crux of his

---

[109] I follow Warren, *Henry II*, 447–90.
[110] Van Caenegem, *Royal Writs*, 279, no. 1; 'Hereford', no. 57.
[111] See above, note 72; Douglas, 'Tenure *in elemosina*', 124, esp. n. 102.
[112] A comprehensive examination is Alexandra Marr, 'The history of the assize *Utrum* to c.1260' (B.Litt. dissertation, Oxford), 1973; see pp. 84–6.
[113] Warren, *Henry II*, 317–61, for an account emphasizing experimentation.
[114] G.B. Flahiff, 'The writ of prohibition to court christian in the thirteenth century', *Medieval Studies* vi, 1944, 261–313, vii, 1945, 229–90.
[115] Flahiff, vi, 274–6, 310, vii, 259–60; *Curia Regis Rolls*, iv, 291 (1206).
[116] Kimball, 'Judicial aspects', 6–11.

jurisdictional distinction.[117] Nevertheless, the ideal was not shared either by donors, or by the clergy at large, who were of necessity more practical and less ideological in their approach to securing protection. Henry and Theobald co-operated in each others' spheres quite happily. It was only in the bitter struggle between Henry and Becket that off-the-shelf clarification was sought which in practice could not have worked: there was no problem with jurisdiction over the church's land – the problem was with politics. The same is true of clause three of the Constitutions, concerning criminous clerks, as well as others: Henry was interested not in excluding jurisdictions, but in getting the job done, and the court he most trusted to do that was his own. He was happy to let cases go to other courts, whether those of lords, bishops or popes, where justice and good judgement could be had in them; but he retained overall supervision and enforcement. Churches and donors shared these aims: they wanted the protection offered by their lords, and by the king, and by bishops and popes too. No theory of jurisdictional exclusivity could ever have suited them.

Royal supervision over the tenurial structure, both of the services and of title, produced a regularized tenure: we can at last speak of free alms tenure in which the ideas of perpetuity and freedom are inextricably embedded. Henry II created the classic free alms tenure of the textbook. This is witnessed by the standardization of the terms of charters, in which grants usually took the form 'in liberam, puram et perpetuam elemosinam'. Charters were now produced for a jurisdiction offering consistent treatment, so that they had to be cast in consistent form themselves. They were now addressed less to a future which could not be certainly controlled, only pleaded with, than to a higher jurisdiction which promised consistent enforcement of their terms. The clause 'Quare volo', expressing little more than hope, was replaced by 'Habendum et tenendum': definite tenurial terms were laid down, which would be recognized in the jurisdiction outside the relationship embodied in the grant. It is not therefore surprising that older charters were 'improved' to match modern terminology, and charters were produced where none had existed before.[118]

Frankalmoin tenure, however, contained elements of its origins within a more seignorial world, which are most obviously seen in the whole issue of freedom from secular exaction. From a world of flexibility, negotiation, and dispute over services, primarily in a seignorial context, we have moved to a fixed tenurial structure containing fixed burdens overseen from above. The imposition of central control on this older world, which used and thereby transformed the older concepts, both characterizes the common law, and accounts for the extraordinary tensions apparent in Bracton's account of free alms. On the one hand the author had to invent a distinction between 'free alms' and 'alms more free', and to explain that some lands were subject to church courts while others were not: but even his own account of which lay where is internally inconsistent. On the other hand, like Maitland and Kimball, he was unable to grasp the criteria which governed the liability of frankalmoin land to secular burdens; against his own earlier assertion to the contrary, he was finally forced to admit that pure alms

---

[117] Warren, *Henry II*, 538.
[118] Hyams, 'Charter as a source', 179–85; M.T. Clanchy, *From Memory to Written Record: England, 1066–1307*, 248–57.

might still have to bear services.[119] These awkwardnesses were the deposits of history left in free alms tenure as it was transformed by royal control. Royal judges had to examine documents which had been drawn up in a different world and addressed to a wider purpose than merely satisfying the conveyancing niceties which the imposition of consistent customs soon came to demand. These deposits argue, therefore, not only that the world which Henry II found on his accession was different from the one he left, but also that the change in the second half of the twelfth century was fairly rapid. Wherever the truth lies in the debate between Milsom and his critics, it is hard to doubt that the reign of Henry II was hugely important.

Three layers of questions demand three tiers of answers. In the first place (to take the last first), the nature of free alms can only be understood in a historical perspective going back at least to the eleventh century, rather than by analysing thirteenth-century common law. At root, 'alms' terminology originally articulated the nature of a gift, based on its spiritual intention; alms were 'lands given to churches'. Gradually this was transformed into 'lands held by churches': the 'alms of churches' could be contrasted with the 'fees of knights'.[120] Glanvill's statement that the baronies of ecclesiastical tenants-in-chief (the pre-conquest abbeys and churches) were 'of the alms of the lord king', although it implies the original idea of the gift, illustrates the extension of the meaning even to those lands most spectacularly burdened with military services.[121] Secondarily, donors wanted to realize two expectations which became customary: the immunity from secular services and exactions, as far as this was possible, and the perpetual tenure of the church. Benefactors and their churches tried to do this by any means at their disposal; jurisdictional exclusivity was irrelevant to those who wanted protection and security. Royal control transformed this nexus into a tenure, whose features the royal courts would enforce consistently. It was therefore a secular jurisdiction which succeeded in securing the churches' desire for perpetuity; but it also made it increasingly difficult to exempt churches from secular burdens in a tenurial structure which had inextricably embedded services in the land. This transformation did not so much produce a neat 'tenure', as freeze the deposits of a hundred years of a changing seignorial society into a coherent but awkward system.

Secondly, therefore, frankalmoin offers a paradigm of what happened under Henry II. Early-twelfth-century society was characterized by custom and flexibility (indeed sometimes by turbulence), and by a devolved and diffuse distribution of power. This was transformed into a polity which was in principle more explicitly ordered from the centre (although practice followed theory at some distance). Such a rapid re-ordering produced its own anomalies, and required further change, particularly in the form of further deliberate legal development such as was seen in Magna Carta and Edward I's legislation.[122]

Thirdly, and most generally, free alms tenure encapsulates the tension between the papacy's desire to separate the clergy from lay control, and its need to

[119] *Bracton*, ii, 59, 93–4, iii, 40, 127–8, 329–31, iv, 265–6.
[120] See above, note 110.
[121] *Glanvill*, vii, 1 (p. 74).
[122] Hyams, 'Charter as a source', 183. Ecclesiastical tenure featured in both: Magna Carta, 1217, cc. 39, 43; Thompson, 'From "alms" to "spiritual services" ', 252–60.

implement that separation through the possession of property. The result was the failure, in absolute terms, of the papal programme. Perhaps the acceptance by the Cistercians, of all orders, of land burdened with knight service is a touchstone of the impossibility of the ideal.[123] The church did not in fact try very hard to remove even that land given explicitly for spiritual purposes from the secular tenurial system: canon law did not offer support for freedom from secular services or jurisdiction for 'temporal' property. Churches were subject to their lords and could not avoid the seignorial context: nor did they want to, since they needed their lords' protection. Nor too, therefore, did they reject royal protection when it was offered and proved to be effective. But such secular protection brought with it a price, that the demands of the world – the structures of secular lordship – could not easily be avoided. The church could not have its cake and eat it, as Anselm tried to when, confronted by the irate William Rufus insistent that royal abbeys were his own, he asserted that they were his to protect and preserve, not to exploit and destroy.[124] Immunity from one set of laity, the reformed papacy found out, generally brought dependence on another; churches wanted royal protection against lords just as the papacy sought alliances against the empire.

The final twist in this story was that even the *spiritual* services in ecclesiastical tenure had become subject to royal law by the end of the thirteenth century. Perhaps this was a natural extension of the developments recounted here. In the thirteenth century frankalmoin must have begun to represent a rather old-fashioned relationship. Lay lords and tenants ceased to have much use for each other, in part because their services had become fixed and had been eroded; but patrons and their monasteries continued to value each other for the protection and support which they could mutually offer; the cycle of reciprocal benefits continued down the centuries. Nevertheless, grantors increasingly gave form to their assumption that their monks performed services, by specifying that their ecclesiastical grantees perform particular works, most obviously chantry obligations; precisely because they had been specified, these could be enforced in the lay forum. The later middle ages was therefore characterized not by indefinite spiritual services under ecclesiastical jurisdiction, but chantries and other specified benefits controlled by laity and subject to royal courts. The laity, it seemed, even took control of the church's spiritual function: hardly a more vivid demonstration of the failure of ecclesiastical separation from the world could be needed.[125]

This is to take the story too far into the future. We must end not in the shadow of the Dissolution of Battle Abbey, that sudden suppression of the perpetual good works whose origins and consequences for ecclesiastical tenure it has been my purpose to investigate. Rather, we should remember the reasons for its foundation, motives which lay at the heart of that tenure: it was made (in the words of the twelfth-century chronicler) for the souls of the slain, and to 'pay back for the blood shed there an unending chain of good works'.[126]

---

[123] Postles, 'Tenure in frankalmoign', 22–3.
[124] Frank Barlow, *The English Church, 1066–1154*, London and New York 1979, 288.
[125] Thompson, 'From "alms" to "spiritual services" ', 250–61.
[126] *Battle Chronicle*, 66–7; 'quatinus iugi bonorum operum instantia commissa illic effusi cruoris redimerentur'.

ANSELM IN ITALY, 1097–1100[1]

Sally N. Vaughn

In November 1097, King William Rufus drove his primate Archbishop Anselm of Canterbury into exile, where he remained mostly in Italy until the king's death by an arrow in the New Forest on 2 August 1100. The new king, Henry I, immediately recalled the beloved archbishop, promising him all that Rufus had denied him. The years 1097–1100 were, of course, crucial to Anselm; but during these years far more was at stake than just Anselm's archiepiscopate. For these years were also crucial for the survival of the reform papacy, and its daring project the first armed pilgrimage to recover the Holy Land. By the end of 1100, both seemed secure and successful.

But the way things *did* happen was not necessarily the way they *had to* happen. In just these years the reform papacy was at its most precarious, and could have been overthrown by the counterefforts of emperor, kings, or indeed clergy. The success of the first crusade, too, was never a foregone conclusion. And in 1097, it appeared most unlikely that Anselm would ever return to England.

It must be remembered that at the time Urban called the first crusade, he was in a very precarious position, with imperial and anti-pope forces occupying Rome itself. Urban's counterforce was the military support of the entrepreneurial and opportunistic Normans in southern Italy and Sicily, and the even less stable moral support of churchmen, largely in France. In Germany and parts of Italy, especially in the North, imperial sentiments prevailed. And Urban's hold on England and its king depended largely on the force of Anselm's personality and prestige. The weakness of reform papal influence in England is amply demonstrated by the refusal of nearly all the bishops and barons in England to support Anselm in his claim to the right to visit and consult the papal court in autumn 1097, on the eve of his exile. Anselm stood virtually alone.[2] Urban's earlier hard bargains struck with Rufus – the awarding of Anselm's pallium and the pawning of Normandy[3] – would have shown Urban his English adversary's strength, and his dependence on Anselm's support almost alone to hold England in the reform camp. Historians often write as if, in this period, the success of the reform papacy was a foregone conclusion – yet Urban and his predecessor Gregory VII clearly survived by the skin of their teeth.

---

[1] The research for this paper was made possible by a Faculty Development Leave, spring 1992, granted to me by the College of Humanities, Fine Arts and Communications of the University of Houston, for which I am extremely grateful. Much of my interpretation of the sources, while built on my previous work was enhanced by the concepts articulated in Karl Morrisons's splendid book, *History as a Visual Art in the Twelfth Century Renaissance*, Princeton 1990.
[2] Eadmer *HN* 82–86; Vaughn, *Anselm of Bec*, 200–202.
[3] Vaughn, *Anselm of Bec*, 176–188, 198–199.

With the calling of the first crusade, Urban had electrified Europe and Europeans from the highest nobility to the lowest peasant – men, women, and children. But the forces he unleashed were often beyond his control – whether children, peasants or the army of God. As fervour to fight for God exploded everywhere, an ominous cry rang out: Deus vult! Deus vult!

As H.E.J. Cowdry has shown, Urban's call to take the cross marks a great watershed in European *mentalité*: knights, who had been regarded as filled with sin for the shedding of blood, no longer need abandon their careers and lifestyles for remission of sins. 'When the call to the Crusade was made, it fulfilled this desire [for the remission of sins] more acceptably than anything that had gone before . . . the Crusade offered the knight the remission of sins *in and through* the exercise of his martial skills.'[4] The *miles Christi* no longer had to lay down his arms to attain sainthood, as St Martin: 'I am Christ's soldier; I am not allowed to fight.'[5] Now he could shed blood for the glory of Christ. Cowdrey sees this revolution as beginning with Gregory VII, who

> began to recognize among his contemporaries soldier-saints who were saints *because* they were soldiers; like Erlembald of Milan, the fierce Patarene leader who perished in 1075 during the savage communal violence that he had provoked. In Gregory's eyes he was a true *miles Christi* – a soldier of Christ; in 1078 he made it clear that he regarded him as virtually a saint.[6]

Thus the shedding of pagan, infidel, antiChristian, or even antipapal blood had become meritorious in papal eyes.

The revolutionary mentality, created by popes inspired by a vision of a new 'right order',[7] essentially turned European values upside down. The shedding of blood, so long forbidden to good Christians, had become the means to a desireable end: the rescue of the Holy Land from infidels and schismatics.

Significantly, a somewhat parallel but less exuberant development had occurred in Anselm's abbey of Bec, where the emphasis was on the conversion of adults – usually knights, on the model of Bec's founder Herluin – to the monastic life.[8] Thus a quasi-saint's life had been written at Bec, possibly during Anselm's tenure (1079–1093), of the great warrior-hero William Crispin, whose bravery on the battlefield, it claimed, inspired an appearance to him of the Virgin herself.[9] William then entered Bec, joined by a fellow warrior Hugh of Gournay, father of the crusader Hugh of Gournay.[10] Anselm, too, at least once took the role of

---

[4] H.E.J. Cowdrey, 'The Genesis of the Crusades,' in H.E.J. Cowdrey, *Popes, Monks, and Crusaders*, London 1984, xiii 23.
[5] Cowdrey, quoted on xiii 20.
[6] Cowdrey, xiii 20.
[7] On 'Right Order' cf. Gerd Tellenbach, *Church, State and Christian Society at the Time of the Investiture Contest*, tr. R.F. Bennett, Oxford 1940. As John La Monte saw it, 'The Hildebrandine Papacy aimed at world domination.' *Feudal Monarchy in the Latin Kingdom of Jerusalem*, Cambridge 1932, 203.
[8] Vaughn, *Anselm of Bec* 19, 64; cf. Eadmer, *Vita Anselmi*, in R.W. Southern, *The Life of St Anselm*, London 1972, 40 (hereafter *VA*).
[9] 'De Nobile Crispinorum genere,' in *Patrologia Latina*, ed. J.P. Migne, Paris 1854, cols 735–744 (Hereafter *PL*).
[10] J. Armitage Robinson, *Gilbert Crispin, Abbot of Westminster*, Cambridge 1911, 15.

quasi-warrior, for in 1095 Anselm assumed the defense of Canterbury and Kent at Rufus's request against a threatened serious rebellion;[11] 1101, as Robert Curthose invaded England, Anselm camped on the battlefield with his knights, ready to defend Henry I against his brother.[12] Thus Bec and Anselm seem to have shared the new *mentalité* fostered by Gregory VII. As Anselm's student Guibert of Nogent[13] expressed it,

> In our own time, God has instituted a holy manner of warfare, so that knights and the common people who, after the ancient manner of paganism, were aforetime immersed in internecine slaughter, have found a new way of winning salvation. They no longer need, as they did formerly, entirely to abandon the world by entering a monastery or by some other like commitment. They can obtain God's grace in their accustomed manner and dress, and by their accustomed way of life.[14]

The ferocity of the slaughter during the consequent conquest of Jerusalem, when the streets ran rivers of non-Christian blood,[15] was a sad consequence.

Moreover, the new *mentalité* essentially suggested that ends justified means. As Jonathan Riley-Smith has suggested, Urban II began his pontificate in exile. Because he was opposed by powerful forces in Europe, he 'had every reason for trying to build up all over Europe a party of "knights of St Peter" '. Moreover, he turned to scholars such as Anselm of Lucca to 'build a convincing case for Christian violence as something which could be commanded by God, was at the disposal of the Church, and would, when properly used, be an expression of Christian love.'

That this mentality of ends justifying means was widespread in England in the late eleventh century is suggested by the king's chief advisor Robert of Meulan (according to Orderic) urging King Henry I in 1102 to promise even London or York for the good of the realm – to be taken back later, if necessary, after victory was won.[16] This seems to have been a mentality that also would permit Anselm's biographer Eadmer to write books which 'interpreted' facts toward the greater good of presenting events in accordance with his own vision of 'right order'[17] His *Vita Anselmi* emerged as a panegyric to Anselm's sanctity, a widely distributed kind of public relations project, glossing over any tarnish to Anselm's pristine image; while his *Historia Novorum* seems to have been written almost as a secret history for the political instruction of the Canterbury monks.[18] Eadmer himself states that both must be compared for a true image of Anselm's actions.[19] Because apparently Eadmer chose to model *Historia Novorum* on Bede's *History of the*

---

11 Epp. 191, 192; Frank Barlow, *William Rufus*, Berkeley and Los Angeles 1983, 349, says Anselm did so 'with relish'.

12 Eadmer, 126; cf. Vaughn, *Anselm of Bec*, 231.

13 Guibert of Nogent, *De vita sua*, PL clvi, col. 874 (ed. E-R Labande, Paris 1981, 138–41).

14 Quoted in Cowdrey, *Popes, Monks and Crusaders*, xiii 23.

15 Fulbert of Chartres, *Historia Hierosolymitana*, I.28.

16 Orderic v. 316; Sally N. Vaughn, *Anselm of Bec and Robert of Meulan: The Innocence of the Dove and the Wisdom of the Serpent*, Berkeley and Los Angeles 1987, 232 ff.

17 On Anselm's vision of 'Right Order', see Vaughn, *Anselm of Bec*, 149–153.

18 Sally N. Vaughn, 'Eadmer's *Historia Novorum*: A Reinterpretation', *ante* x (1988), 25919689.

19 Eadmer, *VA* 2: 'I give warning that readers of [*Historia Novorum*] cannot fully understand Anselm's actions without this work.'

English Church and People, as I have suggested,[20] he must portray Anselm's role as confined to England, on the model of Anselm's predecessors the founders of the Canterbury primacy. The result obscures Anselm's role in the great events surrounding the reform papal initiatives. But *Vita Anselmi* portrays Anselm as a saint of all Christendom, a model for humanity. These conflicting ends have obstructed our view of events concerning Anselm.

Such a *mentalité* would also permit St Anselm to edit his collected letters with a view toward the greater good of displaying the 'right order' of his abbatiate at Bec and later of his archiepiscopate at Canterbury.[21] Most of the letters from 1097–1100 are lost; nevertheless, by correlating the *Vita Anselmi* and *Historia Novorum* accounts with the current events of the day, we can reconstruct the events of Anselm's years of exile and his role in the larger movements surrounding them. It is only in this context that the tangled web Eadmer weaves can be unravelled.

Perhaps another aspect of the new *mentalité* infusing Europe was Eadmer's unusual – indeed almost shocking – characterization of Anselm as possessing something called 'holy guile'. Eadmer described it as a process of teaching – soothing the student with kindly blandishments (*piis blandimentis*), concessions made to his youth which Anselm then slowly withdrew as the pupil approached spiritual maturity. At this point, even blows could be applied.[22] This concept seems also to draw on a perception that unusual means could be justified by pious ends.

Eadmer's own application of 'holy guile' is never more apparent than in his *Vita Anselmi* account of Anselm's exile from England, 1097–1100 – three and one-half tumultuous years during which he portrays Anselm as indeed making an arduous journey to Rome. But its difficulty is overshadowed by a portrait of Anselm as peacefully writing philosophy on a mountaintop, teaching and preaching in Lyons, and waiting for God to bring him back to England. Eadmer presents Anselm as once having presented his case to Pope Urban, retiring from worldly events and waiting out God's purpose. In due time, Anselm's faith was rewarded with restoration to England and his stewardship of its church. But when correlated with *Historia Novorum,* a different story emerges.

Eadmer portrays the precipitating event of Anselm's first exile as King William Rufus's return from his 1097 Welsh campaign and the king's accusation that the knights Anselm sent were of poor quality. Because we have a list of most of these knights, which includes Norman magnates and curiales and important local men who held elsewhere as tenants-in-chief,[23] it is likely that this charge was untrue. Called to court to answer this legal accusation, Anselm stood his ground and demanded to consult his ecclesiastical superior in Rome, Pope Urban II. This

---

[20] Vaughn, 'Eadmer's *Historia Novorum*'.

[21] While nearly everyone concedes that Anselm collected his abbatial letters from Bec, there is much dispute over whether he similarly collected and edited his archiepiscopal letters. Cf. R.W. Southern, 'Sally Vaughn's Anselm', *Albion* x 1988; and my reply, 'Anselm: Saint and Statesman,' in the same issue. For a fuller presentation of both arguments see Vaughn, *Anselm of Bec*, 132ff; and R.W. Southern, *St Anselm: A Portrait in a Landscape*, Cambridge 1990, 394–404 and 459–482.

[22] Eadmer, *VA* 16; cf. Vaughn, *Anselm of Bec*, 10–12 for a discussion of Anselm's 'Holy Guile'.

[23] *Domesday Monachorum*, ed. David C. Douglas, London 1944, 105; cf. 36–63 for an analysis of the list. These men included Hamo *Dapifer*, sheriff of Kent (six knights); the royal constable Hugh de Montfort (four knights); Gilbert fitz Richard of Clare (four knights); the count of Eu (four knights), William Peverel (two knights); Hugh of Port (two knights); and William of Briouze.

incident, relatively minor and insignificant in the context of Anselm's earlier quarrels with Rufus over Anselm's right to recognize Urban as pope, hold reform councils, and fill episcopal vacancies,[24] seems quite puzzling. In the past, Anselm had glossed over Rufus's more grievous offenses – moral corruption at his court, for example.[25] Now,

> Anselm reflected that *this sort of thing* [the lawsuit] could crop up all the time about nothing, so that he would always be thus occupied and unable to carry out his episcopal duties. So he decided that he must go to Rome and seek advice *about these things* from the See of St Peter.[26]

Eadmer seems to be saying that Anselm went to Rome to consult Urban primarily about Rufus himself, not about the more major issues which he later (1098) listed to the pope.[27] For nearly five years Anselm had *tolerated* these abuses.[28] Why did he choose this moment to decide that the problem was insoluable?

Eadmer's account suggests that, as Anselm had taught his monks at Bec 'with a certain holy guile', so Anselm had tried to teach the king. Anselm's tolerance represented 'kindly blandishments', concessions to youth, as he strove to draw Rufus on to a more mature and upright way of life.[29] Anselm believed that the primate of Britain's primary duty was to teach – or rather, as two oxen draw a plough, to rule England side by side with the king *through his teaching*:

> You must think of the Church as a plough. . . . In England . . . drawn by two men outstanding above the rest . . . [who] . . . rule the land: the king and the archbishop of Canterbury. The former rules by secular justice and sovereignty (*imperio*), the latter by divine doctrine and teaching (*magisterio*).[30]

But Rufus had a different agenda. His idea of his kingship saw Anselm's 'two-oxen' theory as 'robbing the king of the jewel of his sovereignty' – an accusation Rufus and his barons made repeatedly at the Council of Rockingham (25–28 February 1095).[31] Clearly that 'jewel' was Rufus's right alone to choose between the two rival popes claiming the papal throne: the Gregorian Reformist Urban II, and the Imperial appointee Wibert bishop of Ravenna as the antiPope Clement III. Rufus also clarified his own expectations that Anselm, in accordance with his oath of homage, obey the king as his feudal vassal in all things, recognizing the king as his superior.[32] Anselm replied that indeed he had done homage to Rufus, but only 'rightly and according to God's will' – and thus with an unspoken reservation, an assumption that he would obey God and St Peter above Rufus.[33] The lines of battle were drawn.

---

[24] Eadmer *HN* 72–3; 52–73 for Eadmer's account. Cf. Vaughn, *Anselm of Bec*, 175–193.

[25] Eadmer *HN* 42, 49.

[26] Eadmer, *VA* 88; my italics.

[27] Cf. *Sancti Anselmi Cantuariensis opera omnia*, ed. F.S. Schmitt, 6 vols, Stuttgart-Bad-Canstatt 1963–68, Ep. 210 (hereafter, Ep.).

[28] Ep. 206

[29] Eadmer *VA* 16–17.

[30] Eadmer *HN* 37

[31] Eadmer *HN* 53–67; *VA* 85–87.

[32] Eadmer *HN* 79–85.

[33] Eadmer *HN* 84–85.

At stake was Rufus's theory of a kind of Divine Right kingship, which only later clearly emerged in the words attributed by Orderic to Robert of Meulan, chief counsellor to both Rufus and Henry I: 'We [the king and his barons] to whom the common utility has been entrusted by Divine Providence, ought to look out for the safety of the realm . . .'[34]

It is significant that from the first public calling of the Crusade at the Council of Clermont in April 1095, Rufus had been cooperating with Anselm by filling episcopal vacancies rather promptly, sometimes with Bec-related men: after first placing St Albans under Canterbury guardianship, he judged a lawsuit in its favor and filled its vacancy with Richard d'Aubigny, from the Bec-related abbey of Lessay. He had promptly filled the abbatial vacancy at Battle with the Bec monk Henry, Anselm's prior at Canterbury. He had filled Worcester with the brother of a Bec student, and Hereford with a royal chaplain.[35] Frank Barlow suspects that Anselm may have been functioning from Whitsun 1095 to Whitsun 1097 as royal justiciar.[36] But why was Rufus having a change of heart?

Perhaps because Anselm was cooperating in Rufus's venture to gain Normandy – long the king's heart's desire – through his brother Robert Curthose's need for money. To take the Cross, Curthose pawned Normandy to Rufus for 10,000 marks. When Rufus laid a large tax on his English landholders in 1096 to raise cash, Anselm concluded that 'both reason and honor' required him to contribute.[37] He gave all he could from his personal resources and added 200 marks from the sale of precious objects in the Christ Church treasury, assigning to his monks in return his own manor of Pecham for a period of seven years.[38] During these two years of peace, Anselm was able to finish his *De Incarnatione Verbi* and *Cur Deus Homo*, and to advance Canterbury's claim to dominence over the churches of Wales and Ireland.[39] Rufus's cooperation with Anselm and Anselm's cooperation with Rufus suggest that for two years the two indeed worked in tandem, as two oxen drawing the plough of the church through England.

Certain evidence suggests that Anselm had an interest in the first crusade beyond the immediate benefits he was reaping from Curthose's departure. First, Anselm's close companion Boso of Bec had been at Clermont.[40] Second, of the major leaders of the first crusade, over half were close, intimate friends of Anselm. Anselm had known Robert Curthose from the duke's boyhood, as a close friend and adviser to his father.[41] He had been instrumental in negotiations between father and son at Curthose's 1079 rebellion,[42] and had attended the ducal and royal courts in Normandy often in the 1080s.[43] He had sought successfully Curthose's protection for Bec in the 1080s;[44] and in 1093 he respectfully requested

---

[34] Orderic v. 316.
[35] Vaughn, *Anselm of Bec*, 194.
[36] Frank Barlow, *William Rufus*, 360.
[37] Eadmer *HN* 74–75.
[38] Eadmer *HN* 77.
[39] Vaughn, *Anselm of Bec*, 195–196.
[40] *Vita Bosoni*, in *PL* 150, col. 726.
[41] Eadmer *HN*, 23.
[42] Vaughn, *Anselm of Bec*, 54–55.
[43] Vaughn, *Anselm of Bec*, 60–63.
[44] *De Libertate Beccensis Monasterii*, in J. Mabillon, *Annales Ordines Sancti Benedicti*, v. Paris 1745, 601–605.

Curthose's permission to become archbishop of Canterbury, acknowledging the duke as his feudal lord.[45]

Hugh of Gournay's family was one of Bec's most important early patrons, with which Anselm had lifelong ties.[46] Anselm's intimate and friendly letters to Robert of Flanders and his wife Clemence,[47] probably written 1100–1105, after Robert's return from crusade in 1100, suggest a long acquaintance also. Anselm enjoyed a very close friendship with the Conqueror's daughter and Curthose's sister Adela of Blois-Chartres, wife of the ill-fated crusader Stephen of Blois, for he wrote often to Adela and visited her frequently throughout his archiepiscopal career.[48] One of her own closest colleagues was the Bec student[49] and Anselm's close friend Ivo bishop of Chartres. Anselm also apparently had some ties to the crusader Hugh of Vermandois, whose wife visited Bec on the eve of the crusade.[50]

Moreover, unlike Anselm's cold reception of the visit to England of papal legate Walter of Albano in 1095,[51] and his later insistence to Popes Urban II and Paschal II that by right the archbishop of Canterbury ought to serve as papal legate in England,[52] Anselm, in 1096, tolerated the papal legates who seem to have arranged the pawning of Normandy to Rufus.[53]

Thus the crusaders Robert Curthose, Hugh of Gournay, Robert of Flanders, Stephen of Blois and Hugh of Vermandois all enjoyed close connection to Anselm. And the call to crusade had generated a new cooperation between England's king and archbishop. But the most closely tied to Anselm of all were the most illustrious of the first crusaders, Godfrey of Bouillon and Baldwin of Boulogne, the sons of Count Eustace and Countess Ida of Boulogne. Ida, of all Anselm's multiplicity of friends, was probably his closest and most intimate confidante, student, spiritual daughter and political ally.[54] Anselm corresponded with Ida from his earliest days at Bec and throughout his abbatial and episcopal careers to his death. Of the letters that he wrote as prior and abbot of Bec, only eight addressed to women have been preserved.[55] Three of the four abbatial letters to women are to Ida.[56] The first of these thanks her for her largess to Bec and for her long friendship and support, indicating a long-standing relationship.[57]

Ida's husband Count Eustace had died in 1082, shortly after Anselm became abbot of Bec, leaving her to rule for her three sons. They would mature to become Count Godfrey of Bouillon, Count Eustace II of Boulogne, and King Baldwin I of Jerusalem.

Ida was also the only one of the women to whom Anselm wrote while abbot

[45] Epp. 464, 153.
[46] Vaughn, *Anselm of Bec*, 64, 67; cf. Epp. 118, 420; and Sally N. Vaughn, 'St Anselm and Women', in *The Haskins Society Journal* ii 1990, 87–88.
[47] Epp. 180, 248, 249.
[48] Epp. 286, 340, 388, 448.
[49] Cf. Vaughn, *Anselm of Bec*, 32–33.
[50] Ep. 151; cf. Vaughn, *Anselm of Bec*, 144 for date.
[51] Epp. 191, 192; cf. Vaughn, *Anselm of Bec*, 187–193.
[52] Ep. 214; cf. Sally N. Vaughn, 'St Anselm and the English Investiture Controversy Reconsidered,' in *Journal of Medieval History* vi 1980, 61–86.
[53] Hugh of Flavigny, *MGH SS*, 8:474; cf. Vaughn, *Anselm of Bec*, 198–199.
[54] Vaughn, 'St Anselm and Women', 86–87.
[55] Epp. 10, 22, 45, 68, 82, 114, 131, 134.
[56] Epp. 82, 114, 131.
[57] Ep. 82.

with whom he continued to correspond after his translation to Canterbury. During the turbulent months of the archiepiscopal election in 1093, Anselm visited Boulogne to seek Ida's advice on his way to England.[58] Eadmer's account suggests that Ida was one of the few friends in whom Anselm could confide. And indeed, immediately after his election Anselm seems to have shared with Ida what he could tell few others – perhaps only Bec student Gundulf bishop of Rochester. She knows him inside and out, he states, so that she will understand that he hopes to tell her the details of his election in person himself soon.[59] As Anselm repeatedly wrote to and visited Ida,[60] her sons, too, must have benefitted from his presence and his teaching in a more direct way, much as Guibert of Nogent described Anselm's visits to him and the teaching he received from the great *magister* during Anselm's abbatiate.[61]

In passing, Stephen Runciman expressed mild surprise that the great vassal of the Emperor Henry V, Godfrey of Bouillon, Duke of Lower Lorraine, should have joined the Crusade, lumping together with Godfrey as Imperial supporters all his brothers.[62] In light of the Emperor's deep enmity toward Urban and that his own minion the anti-pope Wibert occupied Rome at the Crusader's arrival,[63] Godfrey of Bouillon's participation indeed seems remarkable. But Godfrey seems to have been raised in Boulogne, and inherited the estates and titles in the imperial realm only on the death of his childless uncle, Countess Ida's brother Godfrey – and then only very shortly before Urban's call to Crusade.[64] Ida had lived most of her life in Boulogne, returning to Germany only on the eve of the First Crusade to help Godfrey sell off some estates to finance his participation in the rescue of Jerusalem.[65]

Moreover, Countess Ida was the step-sister of Countess Matilda of Tuscany, who, with her mother Beatrice, was Pope Gregory VII's and Pope Urban II's most ardent supporter. The forces of the Pope and the anti-pope were at that moment engaged in open warfare.[66] Thus Urban preached the Crusade in France partly because in 1095 Imperial forces occupied Rome. Thus it may be incorrect to see Godfrey of Bouillon and his brothers as representing imperial support or even approval of the Crusade. Rather, they might be seen as French-Norman participants in support of Pope Urban and in defiance of imperial might – and as part of Anselm's friendship network, possibly educated in Anselm's style and imbued with Anselm's beliefs.

---

[58] Eadmer *HN* 28–29.

[59] Ep. 167.

[60] He visited her on his way to his election in England in 1093, on his way to Italy in 1097, on his way to Rome in 1103; She visited him at least once in England. Messengers flowed back and forth between them regularly, and her monks were often with him both at Bec and at Canterbury. cf. Eadmer *HN* 28–29; Epp. 82, 114, 131, 167, 208, 235, 244, 247; *VA* 100–101.

[61] Guibert of Nogent, *De Vita Sua*, col. 874 (ed. Labande 138–41); cf. 853–4 for a mention of Hugh of Lyon.

[62] Steven Runciman, *The First Crusade*, Abridged edition, Cambridge 1980, 64.

[63] Fulcher of Chartres, Book I Ch. V, VII.

[64] John Andressohn, *The Ancestry and Life of Godfrey of Bouillon*, Hallandal, Florida 1972, 25–26.

[65] *Vita B. Idae, Comitissa Viduae*, by a monk of St Vaast, in *Acta Sanctorum, Aprillus*, ii, ed. Godefrido Henschenio and Daniele Papebrochio, Antwerp 1675, 139–45. No surviving records I have found indicate any journeys to Germany other than her one journey home to help her son.

[66] Fulcher of Chartres, I. vii.

Attributed to Godfrey, who actually refused the crown, was this view of his role as 'Advocate of the Holy Sepulchre':[67]

> There are in the kingdom of Jerusalmem two chief lords, one spiritual and the other temporal: The Patriarch of Jerusalem is the spiritual lord, and the king rules the realm of Jerusalem as a temperal kingdom. [68]

The statement, although probably apocryphal, resembles Anselm's 'two oxen' theory for England more than the papal view that kings and emperors owe submission to St Peter. Even more significant is the letter Anselm wrote, after the Advocate's sudden and unexpected death, to Godfrey's successor, his brother Baldwin of Boulogne, former Count of Edessa and now, in 1100, King of Jerusalem. Anselm first spoke to Baldwin with great familiarity and affection, reminding him of the archbishop's friendship with his parents. Then Anselm outlined to the new king the qualities of a just ruler – who should, in Jerusalem, imitate the example of King David, and be an *advocatus* of God, as Godfrey had considered himself, not a king.[69] Thus, on the eve of his exile, Anselm had refined a political theory for England, and tried to teach it to the king, who countered with a rival royal theory over which the two clashed violently; he had important ties to many leaders who chose to take the Cross; and he supported the reform papacy by choosing to recognize Urban over Clement III.

With this background, we can now assess Anselm's actions as he set out for Italy on 8 November 1097, leaving King William Rufus in complete control of England – its barons and its ecclesiastics. According to Eadmer, not one soul at court had spoken up for Anselm as he was ejected from the realm and subjected to a humiliating search of his baggage on the dock as he boarded his ship.[70] Rufus had his heart's desire, complete control of Normandy, expecting Curthose never to return – and if he did, Rufus would never redeem the duchy to him.[71] In a campaign of clear imperial expansion, Rufus, having secured Normandy and struck out against Wales in Britain, would in the next two years (1098–1100) launch campaigns to conquer Maine, the French Vexin and Brittany on the borders of Normandy.[72] By 1100 he had conceived an elaborate plan to annex Aquitaine.[73] Curthose and the rest of Anselm's most powerful and influential friends among the Northern European nobility had just departed Italy the preceding spring for the

---

[67] Cf. I.S. Robinson, *The Papacy 1073–1198: Continuity and Innovation*, Cambridge 1990, 353.

[68] Ibelin, *Chronologie*, no. 455: 'Il y a ou reiaume de Jerusalem deus chiefs seignors, l'un esperituel, et l'autre temporel: le patriarche de Jerusalem est le seignor esperituel, et le rei dou reiaume de Jerusalem le seignor temporel doudit reiaume.' as quoted in La Monte, *Feudal Monarchy*, 204; and the sources cited there.

[69] Ep. 235.

[70] Eadmer *HN* 83: the bishops had said to Anselm: 'We owe allegiance to the King and from that allegiance we will not depart.' 86: Rufus and Robert of Meulan had just said Anselm's words should not be listened to by men of good sense. 'At this, all the nobles shouted approval and sought to drown the Father's voice with their clamour. . . .'; 88 for the searching of his baggage. *VA* 92: 'the king and all the members of the court were moved to anger against Anselm.' 98 for William Warelwasts's searching of Anselm's baggage.

[71] Vaughn, *Anselm of Bec*, 210.

[72] Barlow, *William Rufus*, 376–408.

[73] C. Warren Hollister, 'The Strange Death of William Rufus', in *Monarchy, Magnates and Institutions in the Anglo-Norman World*, London 1986, 67 and nn.

Holy Land and would be engaged in fierce fighting against the infidels in these same two years.

In the context of the European political world, with Anselm expelled from England, should Rufus succeed with his imperialistic military campaigns, the reform papacy would face the enmity of two empires in Europe – that centered in Germany and Northern Italy around the Emperor Henry V, and the empire William Rufus was attempting to create including England, Wales, Scotland, Normandy, Maine, Brittany, and the French Vexin. On the eve of his death, Rufus had arranged an elaborate plan to receive Aquitaine in pawn from Duke William IX, and Orderic reported that he was readying an army of 300,000 men and planned to extend his empire all the way to the Garonne.[74] Rumors flew that Rufus sought Paris itself.[75] The only remaining territories in Europe that would retain loyalty to the reform papacy would then have been southern Italy, a fragment of southern France, and perhaps Spain (respectively represented on the Crusade by the leaders Bohemond and Raymonde of St Gilles).

When Anselm left England, he took a pilgrim's staff from the Canterbury altar[76] – and thus publicly began a great pilgrimage himself.[77] The most detailed account is in *Historia Novorum*. Rufus immediately seized all the archbishopric's property and declared null and void every official act that Anselm had promulgated during his term of office.[78] Thus Anselm's whole archiepiscopate was now null and void in England. But although many of his friends had departed to crusade, Anselm still had many friends on the Continent, mostly women. He landed at Wissant, 'as Anselm desired,'[79] and proceeded immediately to St Bertin, Countess Ida's abbey, where he stayed more than five days amid a joyous welcome and great honors.[80] It is very likely that he consulted with Countess Ida, mother of the crusaders Baldwin and Godfrey, as he had in the earlier crises of his archiepiscopal election.[81]

Eadmer claims that Anselm's exile caused a great uproar throughout Europe: 'many different rumours reached the populace.'[82] While he describes a joyous tumult of welcome and jubilation everywhere Anselm went, he also, in passing, remarks that 'on the other hand there were some actuated by quite a different spirit who strove to waylay and rob him.' But at this point Anselm was 'hastening' on his journey.[83] Unmentioned by Eadmer, Anselm then may well have proceeded to Chartres, where Countess Adela of Blois, wife of the crusader Stephen, welcomed him with great joy in his similar journey during his second exile, 1103–1106. In 1103 she warned him of the 'great dangers from robbers and highwaymen', and the rigors of winter, if he crossed the Alps that November.[84] Eadmer does not

---

[74] Orderic v. 280–285.

[75] Suger, *Vie de Louis VI le Gross*, ed. Henri Waquet, Paris 1964, 11.

[76] Eadmer *HN* 87–88

[77] On the implications of this symbolic gesture, suggesting either the remission of sins or the waiving of penance, cf. Robinson, *The Papacy*, 342–345.

[78] Eadmer *HN* 87–88.

[79] Eadmer *VA* 99.

[80] Eadmer *HN* 89, *VA* 100–102.

[81] Eadmer *HN* 28–29.

[82] Eadmer *HN* 89.

[83] Eadmer *VA* 102.

[84] Epp. 286, 287; On Adela's friendship with Anselm, see Eadmer, *HN* 164–166; cf. S. Vaughn, *Anselm of Bec*, 288–291.

mention such a visit, but describes Anselm's welcome 'everywhere' by armies of monks and crowds of people. But Anselm's second visit in many ways recapitulates the rough outlines of the first – and such a warning was equally appropriate to the first exile.

Anselm then hastened to Burgundy, where he encountered a very hostile duke of Burgundy, who, according to Eadmer, attacked the party, asking for the archbishop specifically, set on robbing him of his treasure. Anselm, Eadmer reports, won over the duke's complete support with his holiness.[85] Somehow Anselm had 'shamed' the duke. Granting his blessing as the duke ordered his men to welcome Anselm as they would himself throughout the duchy, Anselm 'invoked the hatred of God upon *all of those who had incited* [the duke] to set upon the man of God.'[86] Adela's warning of 'robbers and outlaws' in 1103 may have been inspired by this incident – but one would hardly catagorize the duke of Burgundy as a robber and an outlaw – unless his attack had been incited by those Anselm cursed who opposed the 'law' of the reform papacy by siding with the emperor and the anti-pope.

On 23 December 1097 Anselm reached Cluny. Apparently the Duke of Burgundy's attack had alarmed him, and he immediately sent a message to his fellow primate Archbishop Hugh of Lyons, whom 'Anselm had known for many years past' and who loved Anselm for his holiness; Anselm 'so loved Archbishop Hugh and thought so highly of his *wisdom and the weight of his advice* that he determined to submit his whole case to his consideration and judgment and to that of the Reverend Hugh, Abbot of Cluny.'[87] Thus these three men – Anselm, Hugh of Lyons and Abbot Hugh of Cluny would discuss the future of England, now threatening to become a significant empire under the hostile Rufus – surely in the context of the prospects of the reform papacy now launched on the great gamble of the crusade and faced with the enmity of the German Empire. An alliance between these two hostile powers – England and Germany – would surely doom the incipient reform movement, possibly before the crusade could succeed, and was of the utmost consequence to these three reform papal supporters.

But at Lyons, Anselm learned through 'rumors' that 'to proceed further was little likely to advance his cause.'[88] He had been dashing pell-mell across Europe, intent on presenting his case to Urban. Now he stopped. Archbishop Hugh had earlier been at odds with Urban, regarding the pope as too compromising toward Europe's kings. Consequently, Urban had deprived him of his legatine powers in France.[89] After consulting with Hugh of Cluny and Hugh of Lyons, he wrote a very cautious letter to the Pope, quoted in full by Eadmer. Ignoring his earlier impassioned letter to Bec stressing his early committment to follow God's will and serve God as England's primate,[90] Anselm proclaimed his personal, but very

---

[85] Eadmer *HN* 89–90.

[86] Eadmer *HN* 90.

[87] Eadmer *HN* 91; cf. Epp. 176, in which Anselm confided to Hugh the troubles connected to his election to the archbishopric, and reporting the progress of events.

[88] Eadmer *HN* 91.

[89] Norman Cantor, *Church, Kingship, and Lay Investiture in England, 1089–1135*, New York 1958, 88–89; Cantor notes that Ivo of Chartres complained that Urban was 'a weak head' of the church.

[90] Ep. 148.

public, unwillingness to serve in the arena of worldly strife.[91] Glossing over Rufus's cooperation with him in episcopal appointments in the two years from 1095 to 1097 (and his with Rufus), Anselm painted a black picture of the king's 'lawless' behavior:

> The Law of God and the canonical and apostolic authorities I saw overlaid by arbitrary usages. When I spoke of all these evils I effected nothing [sic] and simple right was not so much regarded as were such arbitrary usages. So, knowing that if I tolerated these things to the end, I should to the damnation of my soul establish so vicious a usage for my successors.[92]

Thus, categorizing Rufus's attempts to establish royal power as granted by God and the subordination of the primate in his realm as 'arbitrary', ignoring Rufus's argument for the 'jewel of his sovereignty', Anselm warned that such 'arbitrary usages' were about to become the custom, and thus law, in England: 'If I tolerated these things to the end, I should . . . establish so vicious a usage for my successors.' Anselm himself believed that his own actions constituted precedents that would become firmly established law. As he stated later, 'If I were to return to England now, I would establish evil customs for both myself and my successors.'[93] Stressing the danger of Rufus's stance, Anselm hammered home the consequences of his actions:

> . . . the king was angry and claimed that for asking [permission to go to Rome], as though it were a grave offence, I should make him reparation and should assure him that I would not in future under any circumstances have recourse to the Pope, no matter what the need, would not even speak of such a thing.[94]

The gravity of the situation was eminently clear to Anselm: the reform papacy was about to lose the support of England. He had made it as clear as he could to Urban. For Anselm ended his letter with a request to be relieved of his duties as primate. 'After that I would have you consider in exercise of your wisdom and apostolic authority what is best for the Church of the English people. – '[95] not mentioning what was best for the Church of Rome, which was Urban's business, not Anselm's,[96] but implicit in the letter. But apparently Anselm, Hugh of Lyons and Hugh of Cluny – the latter two of whom were very close to papal events – feared that Urban would not recognize the urgency of the situation and would not act to curb Rufus. It may have been for this reason that Anselm stopped his headlong rush to Rome so abruptly at Lyons.

   'Meanwhile,' Eadmer continues,

> a report reached Rome [sic] that the Archbishop of Canterbury, Primate of Britain, had crossed the sea loaded with much gold and silver and was

---

[91] Ep. 206; Eadmer *HN* 91–3.
[92] Ep. 206.
[93] Ep. 355.
[94] Eadmer *HN* 93.
[95] Eadmer *HN* 93.
[96] Cf. the later case where Anselm carefully distinguished his own sphere of action from the pope's: Vaughn, *Anselm of Bec,* 289–294.

making for Rome. So from motives of greed quite a number of people kept watch upon his route, set spies and prepared traps to catch him. Foremost in so doing were the King of Germany's men on account of a quarrel which in those days had arisen between him and the Pope.[97]

Despite Eadmer's deliberate obfuscation, clearly the Emperor and the anti-pope and their supporters were setting ambushes to catch everyone of the monastic order on his way to Rome; a number of bishops, monks and clergy were captured, robbed, and even put to death. Eadmer calls these forces of the Emperor and the antipope 'brigands', not acknowledging that they represented the other side of a political power struggle for control of the papacy – and perhaps all Europe, just as throughout his account of Rufus's quarrels with Anselm Eadmer only hinted that Rufus's party was countering Anselm's 'two oxen' theory with legitimate counter arguments of royal divine right sovereignty. Eadmer's ambiguous use of 'Rome' to represent first the papal court, and then the opposition antipapal forces, shows how he glossed over conditions that did not suit his ideals. Moreover, all of these details were omitted from Eadmer's popular account meant to be circulated widely, *Vita Anselmi*.

Vita Anselmi merely states that Anselm waited at Lyons after sending the letter to Pope Urban until summoned by pontifical commands 'to put aside every objection and to make haste to come to' Pope Urban.[98] But *Historia Novorum* then reveals that Anselm proceeded cautiously. He sent 'pilgrims' ahead of him on the route to Rome who spread rumors that Anselm was held back by serious illness, and was not fit to journey on from Lyons any further. 'This report of the pilgrims,' Eadmer states, 'was not wholly void of truth. In fact [Anselm] had been so exhausted that we almost lost hope of his recovery.'[99] These rumours, clearly deliberately spread, outwitted the 'band of brigands', the imperial-antipapal forces: 'On hearing this report of the pilgrims they lost heart and abandoned all hope of waylaying Anselm.' Only after these rumours had been spread that Anselm was too ill and was not coming had lulled the anti-papal forces into security did Anselm, now having received the papal command, set out for Rome.

He did so incognito and in disguise. Accompanied by only Eadmer and Baldwin of Tournai, Anselm journeyed first to Aspres-sur-Buech, arriving on Saturday 20 March, where the three represented themselves as monks from France, pretending no knowledge of Archbishop Anselm, about whom they specifically held a conversation with the monks at Aspres-sur-Buech, according to *Historia Novorum*.[100] Then they proceeded via Gap to Susa, where the three identified themselves as monks of Bec, withholding the information that one of them was Anselm himself, even after the inquiry of the abbot of Susa as to Anselm's health.[101] Anselm then celebrated Easter at St. Michael's abbey in Chiusa, probably because his nephew Anselm was there.[102] Although in both *Vita Anselmi* and *Historia Novorum* Eadmer says the rest of the journey in disguise was safe and uneventful, Anselm's letters reveal that in at least two instances, just north of Rome, he was

---

[97] Eadmer *HN* 93–94.
[98] Eadmer *VA* 103.
[99] Eadmer *HN* 94.
[100] Eadmer *HN* 95.
[101] Eadmer *VA* 103.
[102] Eadmer *VA* 104 and note 3.

endangered. He received assistance from Count Humbert of Savoy, whom he later thanked for extending largess to him and conducting him;[103] and he thanked Ida of Boulogne's stepsister and the aunt of crusaders Godfrey of Bouillon and Baldwin of Boulogne, Matilda countess of Tuscany, whose army, he stated, had saved him.[104]

At Rome, Anselm encountered a tangled web of controversy. According to Eadmer, Urban welcomed him almost as an equal – as 'the apostolic patriarch of that other world,'[105] and heard his case, which Anselm explained, Eadmer says, 'in a manner which met the demands of both truth and discretion.'[106] Urban then sent a letter to Rufus advising, urging, commanding Rufus to restore Anselm's property and possessions. Anselm wrote an accompanying letter (both letters are lost).[107]

At the invitation of the Bec monk John abbot of Telese, and with Urban's encouragement, Anselm retired to the mountain village of Liberi to write *Cur Deus Homo*[108] and to await Rufus's reply; but he didn't stay there very long. For at that time Capua was 'in revolt',[109] and Roger duke of Apulia and Count of Sicily summoned Anselm to the battlefield (June, 1098). Pope Urban joined him shortly thereafter. In *Vita Anselmi*, Eadmer portrays Anselm as enjoying peace and monastic withdrawal throughout this summer, barely mentioning his stay at the siege of Capua. But in *Historia Novorum* Eadmer gives rather full details. He reveals that William Rufus was bombarding his fellow Normans in Italy and Sicily, particularly the count-duke Roger, with letters (now lost). Rufus also, Eadmer says, sent Roger and other Normans large gifts. While Eadmer states that these letters and gifts only served to make Roger more firmly committed to Anselm, and to honor and love him more, the evidence Eadmer presents suggests otherwise. For Eadmer states that Pope Urban shortly joined Anselm on the battlefield at Capua, bringing a large retinue with much rich display and pomp.[110] This conclave suggests a grave crisis. It seems to have been that Rufus was close to winning Roger – and perhaps other Normans – over to his side – for Roger, Eadmer says,

> tried by repeated requests to induce Anselm to do him the favour of staying on with him and accepting as a gift the best of his lands both in his manors and in his cities, whether fortified or open. Of these he was to take his choice and then to treat them as being his in his own right *for the rest of his life* for the use of himself and his friends.[111]

While Eadmer says this offer proves that Roger supported Anselm against Rufus, a more realistic assessment would be that William had won over Roger to an

---

[103] Ep. 262.
[104] Ep. 256.
[105] Eadmer *VA* 165.
[106] Eadmer *VA* 106.
[107] Eadmer *HN* 98.
[108] Eadmer *HN* 96–97; *VA* 107–108.
[109] But see Robinson, *The Papacy*, 369–374. The situation was very complicated. Capua was in fact held by another Norman lord who had been tempted to place himself under the Emperor – as had other Normans in Italy. See also G.A. Loud, *Church and Society in the Norman Principality of Capua, 1058–1197*, Oxford 1985, 91–2, 101.
[110] Eadmer *HN* 97–98.
[111] Eadmer *HN* 98, my italics.

Anglo-Norman Italo-Sicilian-Norman alliance that would have spelled the doom of the reform papal ambitions for Europe should it be combined with an imperial alliance – or even if the two Norman empires alone united against Urban. Roger's offer can perhaps be seen as a bribe, clear and simple, to induce Anselm to abandon England to Rufus forever, living out his days in luxury and honor in sunny Sicily.[112]

If so, it suggests Roger was acting to aid Rufus – as virulently anti-reform papacy as the German Emperor. The apparent alliance boded ill for Urban. And just at this moment, the crusade was going badly. The crusaders, far from sweeping into the Holy Land with glorious chivalric victories, found themselves bogged down in horrendous bloody battles which subjected them to disease, starvation, and repeated defeats.[113] This situation suggests that the reform papacy – and Anselm's archiepiscopate – were in truly dire straits in that summer of 1098.

They became even more dire when Roger ended the siege of Capua in victory. Significantly, Anselm retreated from Roger's camp and sought refuge at the abbey of St Lawrence, where in despair he 'was filled with a burning desire to give up the spiritual cure of England and with it the Archiepiscopate; to disclaim them absolutely and forever.'[114] As the greatest and most revered intellect of his day, Anselm's apparent defection from the papal cause, not to the other side but to retire from everything, would have been an additional grievous blow to the prestige of reform papacy at that point. But Eadmer's further account suggests that perhaps Anselm, Urban, or both had devised a plan to rescue the situation despite its apparent hopelessness.

Anselm had accompanied the Pope towards Salerno as far as Averso, but then left him to retreat to St. Lawrence. Nevertheless, the two may well have had ample opportunity to talk. At Salerno, Urban made very significant grants to Count Roger. According to Geoffrey Malaterra, Urban had to chase after the count, who was about to return to Sicily. When he caught up with him, on 5 July Urban granted to Roger *and to his successors* the astonishing privilege of serving as papal legate in Sicily.[115]

With this right, Roger would have almost complete control over the churches in his island realm, with the power to oversee himself the reorganization of the whole episcopal and monastic structure – and to control and direct his ecclesiastics, only retaining the obligation to consult Rome.

This extraordinary privilege, never granted to any other king in Europe, represents a major concession to the forces at work for sacerdotal kingship – including William Rufus. It succeeded in retaining Roger's alliance with the papacy against Rufus. It may have been a last, desperate move on the part of Urban to keep his last and most faithful ally in his camp when Roger appears to have been leaning

---

112 In just this way, Duke William and Lanfranc seem to have gotten rid of the rebellious Abbot Robert of St Evroul, deposed and replaced by a monk of Lessay, Bec's dependency. Robert ended up retiring to rich properties in Italy, granted by Robert Guiscard and his brothers. Orderic ii. 90, 94–96.

113 See, for example, Fulcher of Chartres, I.16, describing the conditions under which Stephen of Blois deserted; and *Gesta Francorum et aliorum Hierosolimitanorum*, in *Histoire Anonyme de la Première Croisade*, ed. Louis Bréhier, Paris 1964, 53–161 on the siege of Antioch.

114 Eadmer *HN* 98–99.

115 Eadmer *VA* 111 n. 1; cf. Robinson, *The Papacy* 174–176; and Cantor, *Church, Kingship, and Lay Investiture*, 118.

toward alliance with Rufus. The king of France, too, confronted with the twin threats of the smooth promises of his new brother-in-law, Rufus's chief advisor Robert of Meulan;[116] and invasion by Rufus, would have been vulnerable to Rufus's anti-papal campaign. The concession itself, in view of the crisis Urban faced, was a shrewd political move, a compromise that saved the day for Urban while he hoped for success in the Crusade or other events to rescue him from his precarious position.

When Anselm left England to seek papal aid, Rufus had remarked that 'He is better able to advise the pope than the pope to advise him',[117] a tribute to the intelligence and ability of the royal adversary that rings true. In his conversations with Pope Urban on the way to Salerno, Anselm may have helped to formulate the compromise. It is significant that the resulting configuration of the royal-ecclesiastical power structure in Sicily almost exactly parallels that claimed from Pope Gregory VII by the Conqueror and Lanfranc, Anselm's predecessor, in England.[118] This parallel might suggest that Anselm contributed some ideas to the compromise Urban offered Roger – and indeed, the compromise resembles somewhat Anselm's 'two oxen' theory. For not only did Anselm seek co-rule with the king, but the papal legatine privilege for himself as co-ruler of England.[119]

Interestingly, Eadmer reports in *Vita Anselmi* that Anselm acquiesced in Count Roger's orders that the Saracens among his troops at Capua were not to be converted, even though Anselm inspired them to convert, winning their love with his kindness and gifts of food.[120] This tactic succeeded so well that when Anselm passed through the Saracen camp huge crowds raised their hands to heaven and called down blessings on his head, kissing their hands and doing him reverence on bended knees in thanks for his kindness and generosity.[121] Eadmer glosses this over thus: 'With what policy – if one can use that word – he did this, is no concern of mine: that is between God and himself.'[122] Nevertheless, the spectacle of his Saracens bowing down to Anselm cannot have been lost on Count Roger. Eadmer reported this incident in *Vita Anselmi*, illustrating Amselm's holiness, and not in *Historia Novorum*, which presents the political context in which it occurred, thereby obscuring the possibility that Anselm cultivated the Saracen troops to influence Count Roger's political decision for or against papal support.

It is also significant that Anselm also later sought the same papal legatine privilege for himself that Urban had granted Roger from Urban's successor Paschal II, which Anselm said Urban had granted to him.[123] Summer 1098 would have been the most likely occasion, with Urban about to lose all his allies, including Anselm. The compromises were judicious. Comital, and later royal, power in Sicily was strengthened, but papal authority was maintained. In Anselm's case, archiepiscopal power, and thus papal power, over the common royal enemy was strengthened. At any rate, Urban would have had little to lose in

[116] For Robert, see Vaughn, *Anselm of Bec*, passim.
[117] Eadmer *HN* 80.
[118] Cf. Vaughn, *Anselm of Bec*, 157–171.
[119] Ep. 214.
[120] Eadmer *VA* 111–112.
[121] Eadmer *VA* 112.
[122] Eadmer *VA* 112.
[123] Ep. 214.

Anselm's case at that time, unless some plan was under discussion for restoring the archbishop to England.

Now, as the crusaders progressed toward their victory over Jerusalem in 1099, Anselm's party seems to have begun to spread virulent rumors abroad that Rufus was forbidding the conversion of his Jews – and worse, forcing converted Jews to recant. These tactics Eadmer reported in *Historia Novorum*, but not *Vita Anselmi*, where Roger's similar but less viciously reported treatment of his Saracens appears. For after the compromise with Urban, Roger remained a loyal follower of the reform papacy, and thus must be presented positively. To put the incidents side by side might reveal too much similarity between the now-papal hero Roger, and Eadmer's major villain Rufus. Eadmer admits that he is reporting these stories of Rufus and the Jews 'without asserting or denying their truth or otherwise,'[124] suggesting something of a propaganda campaign to malign the English king.

Moreover, added to them were reports that Rufus was denying the power of God and the saints to influence human affairs, capped by this royal quotation: 'What is this? God a just judge? Perish the man who after this believes so. For the future, by this and that I swear it, answer shall be made to my judgment, not to God's, which inclines to one side or the other in answer to each man's prayer.'[125] Let us note that we only have Eadmer's word for these slanderous statements – for none of the relevant letters concerning this great crisis and dispute survive. Indeed, from this point to Rufus's death, Eadmer builds his portrait of Rufus to a crescendo of blasphemy and madness – a portrait that can hardly accord with the competent and successful conqueror overrunning all the realms around his own at that very time.[126]

From these stories, according to Eadmer, Anselm once more concluded that he must 'renounce the office of primate of England, knowing as he did that his ways and the king's could not by any possibility be reconciled anymore.'[127] Paschal then forcefully and publicly called Anselm back to his duty: 'by the law of the Christian Church you must always be [England's] archbishop, having over it so long as you live *the power of binding and loosing*.'[128] Thus, once more, Urban reaffirmed Anselm's almost papal power over that other world of England, as Anselm desired.

When Anselm replied that to do so, he had to cope with the fact that 'all those [in England] with one accord kept on trying to make me under pretext of doing right do what is not right, to renounce obedience to St Peter in order not to violate the allegiance which I owed to an earthly sovereign,'[129] Urban responded that he was willing 'to avenge them with the sword of St Peter. I charge you to present yourself at the Council which I have arranged to hold at Bari . . . on 1 October next, that you may hear and see for yourself how, as just judgment demands, I have determined to deal with the King of England himself and his men and others like him who set themselves up against the liberty of the Church of God.'[130] With

---

124 Eadmer *HN* 99.
125 Eadmer *HN* 99–102.
126 Cf. Vaughn, *Anselm of Bec*, 211–213.
127 Eadmer *HN* 102.
128 Eadmer *HN* 103.
129 Eadmer *HN* 104.
130 Eadmer *HN* 104.

this apparent compromise between Urban and Anselm, granting Anselm quasi-papal authority in England if only he could return, Anselm seemed satisfied to await the forthcoming Council of Bari in October 1098.

If one read only *Vita Anselmi*, one would conclude that the Council of Bari lacked any significance except for Anselm's disputation of the errors of the Greeks. Even *Historia Novorum* is so garbled that although Anselm's cause seems to have been the focus of discussion, issues discussed and decisions reached are obscured. In a very showmanlike presentation, Urban summoned Father Anselm before the Council to dispute the Greeks, with these dramatic words: 'Father and teacher, Anselm, Archbishop of Canterbury, where are you?' Anselm replied, 'My Lord and Father, what is your command? Here I am.' Urban responded: 'Pray, . . . why do you remain silent . . .? Come, I beseech you, . . . and give us your help in battling for your Mother and ours, whom as you see these Greeks are trying to rob of her integrity. . . . Therefore help us, as though you had been sent here by God, as in truth you have been for this very purpose.'[131] Interestingly, Eadmer says that the men of the Council did not know who Anselm was, 'asking who this man was and where he came from,'[132] This statement seems to imply that Anselm and Urban had been conferring much in private in the preceding crisis of the siege of Capua, working closely together, but without the knowledge and participation of the papal *curia*.

Having introduced Anselm with such great drama, Urban then dismissed the Council until the next morning, when, he said, their minds would be clearer for the discussion. Psychologically this move would have great impact. For the next morning, at a session called 'earlier than usual,' Anselm began a brilliant intellectual tour-de-force: 'standing on high before all the assembled company, the Holy Spirit directing his heart and tongue, he so treated the question, discoursed upon it, and brought it to a conclusion, that there was not a single person in that whole assembly who did not agree that he was satisfied upon the point.'[133]

Immediately thereafter, with the scene set and the council aglow with Anselm's spiritual defense of the Church, Urban presented in full Anselm's cause against England's king. 'Besides all else,' Urban concluded,

> this King has exiled Anselm from his kingdom because he could not break [Anselm] of his loyal obedience to St Peter. I can assure you that reports of the kind of life that tyrant leads have been brought again and again to the apostolic See. . . . The judgment is plain and the judgment admits of no doubt. If once, twice, three times you have called and he has refused to listen, refused to accept discipline, it only remains that, *pierced by the sword of St Peter*, laid low under the stroke of his curse, he be made to feel the punishment which he deserves until he turn from his wickedness.[134]

At the end of this dramatic speech, a sentence of excommunication was unanimously pronounced. But this is buried in Eadmer's account of how Anselm

---

[131] Eadmer *HN* 105.
[132] Eadmer *HN* 105.
[133] Eadmer *HN* 106.
[134] Eadmer *HN* 106–107.

immediately arose and interceded for his persecutor, prevailing upon Pope Urban to rescind sentence.[135]

What happened next we cannot know for sure, because Eadmer turned to a maddening and lengthy digression discussing the cope of the Bishop of Benevento. We are left in the dark about subsequent deliberations. Nevertheless, Anselm's subsequent letter to Urban may lift the veil somewhat. At that moment, Anselm stated, excommunication would be ignored and even ridiculed in England.[136] Clearly Anselm judged that Rufus was now so powerful and successful that the king could ignore Papal sanctions with impunity.

Anselm and Urban then journeyed together to Rome. On their arrival, Urban's messenger to Rufus returned, stating that 'while the king had in some sort accepted the pope's letter, he had altogether refused to accept Anselm's [both letters are now lost]; so far from that, the king had sworn by the Face of God that as . . . was common knowledge, Anselm was the king's man.'[137] This reply suggests that Anselm had written to Rufus once more pressing his 'two oxen' theory; Rufus's response seems belligerant, to say the least. What Pope Urban offered Rufus we cannot know, but Anselm's letter enraged Rufus: he threatened to tear out the messenger's eyes.[138] And right on the heels of the papal messenger came Rufus's spokesmen, led by William Warelwast. Urban received them at his 1098 Christmas council, and told them in unequivocal terms that the king must restore Anselm or face certain excommunication at his Council scheduled for three weeks after Easter. But William requested a private meeting with Urban. Thereafter he remained in Rome for

> many weeks . . . distributing and promising gifts to those whom he judged would be inclined to receive them. In this way the pope was induced to reconsider his sentence and at William's entreaty granted the king a postponement until the feast of St Michael.[139]

Eadmer emphasizes that this statement was made at Christmas, implying that, with Michelmas nearly a year away, the pope was abandoning Anselm. At that, Anselm wanted to leave Rome, realizing 'that it was quite useless to wait in Rome for advice or help;'[140] but Urban forbade his departure, ordering Anselm to remain until the forthcoming Council. Incredibly, in *Historia Novorum* Eadmer insists that Urban now began treating Anselm as an equal, that 'it was as if there were not two separate courts but rather one joint court of both the pope and Anselm.' He describes Urban as 'paying [Anselm] court.'[141] Significantly, Urban does not refer to 'the other world' of which he treated Anselm as 'almost a pope' when the archbishop first arrived in Rome.[142]

In *Vita Anselmi* Eadmer describes Englishmen coming to Rome and prostrating themselves at Anselm's feet, 'as at the feet of a Roman pontiff.'[143] Moreover,

---

135 Eadmer *HN* 107.
136 Ep. 210.
137 Eadmer *HN* 110.
138 Eadmer *HN* 110.
139 Eadmer *HN* 111.
140 Eadmer *HN* 111.
141 Eadmer *HN* 112.
142 Eadmer *VA* 105
143 Eadmer *VA* 114.

when Anselm fled these prostrations, Urban commanded him to accept them.[144] The scenario Eadmer sketches suggests that perhaps Urban's grant of equal status to – or rather enforcment upon – Anselm, and Urban's apparent public display of it, may be Eadmer's way of communicating to the informed reader that an offer had been made to placate Anselm by designating him as Urban's successor as pope – and certain Englishmen supported it. Indeed, this plan would represent a shrewd political settlement. Anselm could be promised promotion and honored, Rufus would be free of his infuriating archbishop, and, presumably, Urban would gain the support he desperately needed for the reform papacy. Urban was old, and in fact died shortly thereafter on 29 July 1099. Paschal II was elected pope two weeks later, on 13 August, and consecrated the next day. But Anselm appears to have wanted no part of whatever offer was made to him.

Meanwhile, it seems, a great number of 'the citizens of Rome' who were 'hostile to the pope because of their loyalty to the Emperor' banded together and tried to capture Anselm, but 'as soon as they saw his face, they were filled with fear and, throwing down their arms, they prostrated themselves on the ground and asked him to favour them with his blessing.'[145] Were imperial and anti-papal forces also wooing Anselm in the struggle for control of the papacy – and of Christendom?

Urban's political position was somewhat stronger by spring 1099; he had managed through his compromise to retain the loyalty and support of Count Roger of Sicily, and had averted Roger's defection to an alliance with Rufus. By now the Crusaders had captured Antioch and Edessa, where they had set up feudal states with allegiance at least nominally to the reform papacy, and were on the march to Jerusalem.

The Vatican Council convened in the third week after Easter, probably 24–25 April 1099. 'Bishops who had come from Italy and France'[146] gathered for the great conclave must have included the important primate Archbishop Hugh of Lyons, Anselm's good friend and supporter. It was remarked that never before had an Archbishop of Canterbury attended a papal council, (which was untrue: Anselm was at Bari) so that there was some discussion of the protocol required in the seating of the participants. Urban chose the apse for Anselm, a seat of distinction,[147] so Eadmer reports. Thus Anselm's presence aroused some anxiety about whether or how to honor him.

The Council had a huge agenda. The crusade, Friday feasting, the Greek schism, and clerical concubines were among the issues for discussion, but Eadmer ignores them all to discuss only those items relevant to Anselm. And what becomes clear from his account is that Urban intended to ignore Anselm's case. Only at the end of the Council, when Urban requested Reingar bishop of Lucca to read out all the conciliar decrees passed did anyone mention Anselm. Reingar himself, interrupting his recitation of the decrees, broke out in a long speech decrying the neglect of Anselm's case. It appears that Urban had been prepared to end the Council with neither Anselm nor Rufus mentioned. Anselm had remained silent throughout, and this time Urban ignored him. Perhaps if he had been offered

---

[144] Eadmer *VA* 114.
[145] Eadmer *VA* 115.
[146] Eadmer *HN* 112.
[147] Eadmer *HN* 112.

the papacy, he had declined it, or matters still remained unsettled. But the contrast to the Council of Bari is striking. Clearly Urban's attitude toward Anselm had changed significantly.

Reingar now protested that 'It is only right [that Anselm's case should be heard]; for, if not, it will not escape the notice of the Judge who judges justly.'[148] So, at the very end of the Council, and only when forced to do so, Urban tacked on a cool and distant recognition of the problem: a reaffirmation of the sentence he had originally pronounced at Clermont in 1095 against lay investiture of churches and clerical homage to laymen on penalty of excommunication.[149] The repetition of these decrees may have been meant to appear as somewhat a sop to Anselm's cause. It implied a threat to excommunicate all the clergy of England, from whom Rufus had demanded vows of homage, as he had from Anselm. But it also focused on the very issue Rufus had stressed: Anselm had done homage to Rufus,[150] was thus his man, and thus his subject and not his equal. Thus there is some sense in which it could be taken as a criticism – even a condemnation – of Anselm. Or it could be taken as suggesting a shift of papal support to Rufus, by striking a blow at Anselm.

Anselm's response was to leave Rome the next day, concluding that 'we had received at the hands of the pope no judgment or help beyond what we have already mentioned.'[151] Eadmer implies that Anselm's party left disappointed, suggesting that Urban's choice to reissue the papal ban against clerical homage, while a barb that may have appeared to have been aimed at England's king, had also struck England's primate. This possibility suggests that Urban was somewhat equivocal about Anselm's cause.

Anselm headed for Lyons, probably in company with his good friend Archbishop Hugh. In *Historia Novorum* Eadmer says that 'as we had now given up all expectation of returning to England in King William's lifetime, we decided to make a permanent stay at Lyons.' In *Vita Anselmi* he states: 'so we fixed our abode [in Lyons], having lost all hope of returning to England while king William was alive.'[152] And William was still a young man, in his thirties, with a long life expectancy. Anselm's cause now appeared truly hopeless.

In Lyons, Eadmer states, Archbishop Hugh treated Anselm 'like a native and lord of the place. . . . [Hugh himself performing] the offices of an inferior, and almost of a suffragan.'[153] Hugh had now been restored as papal legate in France, but his promotion of Anselm's prestige immediately after Urban had humiliated Anselm at the Vatican Council suggests that he once more viewed with alarm Urben's propensity to placate kings at the expense of reform. According to Eadmer, Anselm began performing all the functions of a bishop at the behest of Archbishop Hugh, despite Anselm's protests that it was not right for a bishop to perform episcopal services in another's diocese. But vast crowds flocked to him for these services, and Anselm performed them, always carefully asking permission first of the recipient's rightful bishop.[154] These included the bishop of

148 Eadmer *HN* 112–113.
149 Eadmer *HN* 114.
150 Eadmer *HN* 41.
151 Eadmer *HN* 114.
152 Eadmer *VA* 116.
153 Eadmer *VA* 116; *HN* 114–115.
154 Eadmer *HN* 115.

Macon and Guy, Archbishop of Vienne, who, Eadmer states, explicitly invited him to Vienne.[155] Eadmer implies that there were others, as well. Anselm's actions, and the deference given him throughout France, as earlier in Rome, was almost that of a pope, who alone (except God) would outrank bishops and archbishops. The deference seems to have been given from the foremost bishops and archbishops in Northern France to a man just publicly humiliated at a great papal council. Was there a movement afoot to form yet a third papal party, perhaps masterminded by Hugh of Lyons and promoting Anselm, to rival the Gregorian papacy and the imperial papacy? The actions of the French bishops in so honoring and elevating Anselm suggest defiance of Urban. Meanwhile, Anselm continued to exercise his archiepiscopal functions throughout France, apparently for the next year – summer 1099–summer 1100.[156]

Meanwhile, the Crusaders had succeeded in conquering Jerusalem at last, entering the city in triumph on 15 July 1099. On 22 July – and thus before Urban's death on 29 July, – 'the people of God's army' elected Godfrey of Bouillon as "princeps regni", because of the 'nobility of his character',[157] over the objections of the clergy, who seem to have favored Raymond of St Gilles.[158] At that time, the military commanders present were Godfrey, Robert Curthose, Robert of Flanders, Tancred, and Raymond of St Gilles. The first three were friends of Anselm. Shortly after the election Tancred appears allied to Godfrey's brother Eustace.[159] Thus it appears that Anselm's friends held the majority in the election. That they elected Godfrey of Bouillon not as king but as 'Advocate of the Holy Sepulchre', a title which recalls Anselm's theories of kingship, is somewhat strange. For the logical candidate would have been the hero of the siege of Jerusalm, Robert Curthose of Normandy.

Also over the objection of the clergy, who thought the pope should appoint the patriarch, the military commanders elected as patriarch of Jerusalem Arnulf of Chocques, chaplain of Robert Curthose,[160] Anselm's longtime friend and still potential ally against William Rufus. Interestingly, the election occurred on 1 August, the feast day of St Peter in Chains.[161] The *Gesta Francorum* describes Arnulf as 'a wise and honorable man', and describes Godfrey as 'elected by God'[162]

Whether or not the Gregorian papal party viewed this situation as threatening in light of Anselm's concurrent activities – or had even heard the news of it yet – remains a mystery. But the candidate of 'the clergy' was Raymond of St Gilles, whom Urban had initially chosen to lead the Crusade. And before his death Urban had dispatched Daimbert archbishop of Pisa to replace the papal legate Adhelmar de Puy, who had died in 1098.[163] On his arrival, Daimbert held a great council, which judged the patriarchal election invalid, deposed Arnulf, and then elected

---

[155] Eadmer *VA* 117.
[156] For Macon, see Eadmer *HN* 121.
[157] Fulcher of Chartres, I.30
[158] *Gesta Francorum*, 207.
[159] *Gesta Francorum*, 209.
[160] *Gesta Francorum*, 208; Cf. Robinson, *The Papacy*, 352–355.
[161] *Gesta Francorum*, 208.
[162] *Gesta Francorum*, 207, and nn.: Albert d'Aix, 5.33, and Raynmond d' Aguilar, 300–301, corroborates this statement.
[163] Robinson, *The Papacy*, 48.

Daimbert himself patriarch. Roger of Sicily's nephew Bohemond, not present at the earlier elections, assisted Daimbert in taking control.[164] It appears that two factions struggled for control of Jerusalem – both reform parties, only one of which represented Urban;'s reform papacy. The other consisted of men with close ties of friendship to Anselm – an 'Anselmian party'.

Strangely, Eadmer barely mentions the death of Pope Urban and not at all the accession of Pope Paschal, saying it was of no concern to Anselm. What did concern Anselm was the death of William Rufus – the event which allowed Anselm's return to England. During this time Anselm was travelling around, visiting at least Vienne, Macon and Cluny, in each of which he held great public celebrations of the mass.[165]

Eadmer reports that Rufus responded to Urban's death, and the news that the new Pope 'resembled Anselm', with these words: 'By the face of God, if he is like that, he is no good. But let him keep strictly to himself, for his popedom shall not get the upper hand of me this time; to that I take my oath; meantime, I have gained my freedom and shall do freely as I like.' Eadmer states that 'He had the idea that not even the pope of the whole world could have any jurisdiction in his realm unless it were by his permission.'[166]

Paschal was elected to replace Urban on 13 August 1099. Although Eadmer's words suggest that some were promoting the candidacy of Anselm, no accounts mention him as a candidate, suggesting his promoters were estranged from the papal court at Urban's death. Perhaps significantly, Hugh of Lyons had just resigned his office as papal legate to take the Cross.[167]

Rufus's reported pronouncement clearly spelled Anselm's doom. Rufus could refuse to recognize the new pope, could threaten or even carry out the recognition of Clement III, the antipope – or perhaps no pope at all. Rufus, then and through the following year, was at the apex of his power, now in control of England, Normandy, Maine, and Brittany. He had negotiated with William of Aquitaine to take that county in pawn, and on the eve of his death was awaiting the completion of the outfitting of ships to carry out his plan to extend his realm to the Garonne.[168] He had been attacking the French Vexin for some time, and rumors flew that he coveted even Paris. These feats of conquest and diplomacy led the chroniclers to compare him to Alexander the Great and Julius Caesar. Indeed, Rufus's triumphal entry into Le Mans resembled the pomp and ceremony of an Imperial triumph. And Geoffrey Gaimar envisioned Rufus conquering all the way to Rome.[169]

If Rufus were successful in his grand design, both the reform papacy and the 'Anselmian party' would be in deep trouble. Rufus could ally himself with Germany, and doom the Reform Papacy. Even alone, the empire he envisioned would change the course of European history. Much was at stake. No reaction

---

[164] Jonathan Riley-Smith, *The Crusades*, New Haven 1987, 48. Cf. Robinson, *The Papacy*, 352–3, for a close discussion of these elections.

[165] Eadmer *VA* 117–120.

[166] Eadmer *HN* 116.

[167] Norman Cantor, *Church, Kingship and Lay Investiture*, 124.

[168] Orderic v. 280–285.

[169] For the comparison to Alexander, see M.T. Clanchy, *England and its Rulers, 1066–1272*, Totowa 1983, 69; For references to Julius Caesar and the statement of Gaimar, see Barlow, *William Rufus*, 379.

from Paschal is recorded. But Hugh of Lyon wrote to Rufus a diplomatic and persuasive letter urging him to please God, reinstate Anselm, and govern England rightly.[170] Rufus may have responded by sending a messenger to Lyon to confer with Hugh,[171] but nothing came of it.

Meanwhile, after August 1199, Robert Curthouse departed Jerusalem for home, stopping in southern Italy to arrange what must have been a hasty marriage, but a brilliant one, to Sybil of Conversano. He doubtless planned to use the huge dowry to redeem Normandy. Robert could now return to Normandy a conquering hero. If indeed an Anselmian party had dominated the foundation of the kingdom of Jerusalem, Curthose's action now would explain the election of the relatively obscure Godfrey over Robert as prince. For Robert's role would have been seen to return to Normandy to fight for God against the menacing Rufus. For while Curthose moved toward home, stopping only to aarrange the marriage that would allow him to redeem Normandy, strange events occurred in Jerusalem. Daimbert was annointed Patriarch on Christmas Day 1099. Thus the papal party had imposed its will on the 'Anselmian party'. By Easter 1100 Godfrey had agreed to swear homage to the Patriarch and grant him the city, reserving his own use of it only until he conquered his own lands. But by 18 July 1100 Godfrey was dead – Fulcher says of natural causes, but all the sources are vague.[172] Strangely Godfrey died almost exactly a year to the day from his coronation, and while Daimbert was away besieging Haifa.[173] Godfrey's friends immediately seized the city, proclaiming Baldwin the heir, claiming Godfrey had designated him.[174] This claim is strange also – for Godfrey was a young man and could not have expected to die. Baldwin apparently experienced some difficulty travelling the short distance from Edessa to Jerusalem. Daimbert is said to have made strenuous attempts to prevent Baldwin's accession, involving other Crusaders. In fact, Baldwin did not reach the city until November. But between July and November, Baldwin met the papal legate Maurice at Laodocia. It was Maurice who enabled Baldwin to enter Jerusalem and receive the oaths and homages of his vassals. Daimbert was conspicuously absent.[175] Unlike Godfrey, Baldwin proclaimed himself king. Anselm wrote to him immediately, suggesting that he might better serve as God's *advocatus*, but nevertheless instructing him on his proper rule of Jerusalem, on the model of King David.[176] Relations between Jerusalem's king and patriarch remained turbulent for the next twelve years.

But apparently the stormy relations between the reform papacy and the 'Anselmian party, were resolved, and by November Paschal could support Anselm's friend against his own protégé Daimbert. The crucial intervening event was the death of William Rufus.

In July, when Godfrey died, Robert Curthose's progress toward Normandy was delayed by his crucial marriage, but Rufus was moving swiftly toward annexation of Aquitaine and beyond. Meanwhile, rumours were spreading through France –

[170] G.P. Gilson, 'Two Letters addressed to William Rufus,' EHR xii, 1897, 290.
[171] Ep. 210.
[172] Fulcher of Chartres, I.36.
[173] La Monte, *Feudal Kingdom*, 6.
[174] La Monte, *Feudal Kingdom*, 5n, assembles the sources.
[175] La Monte, *Feudal Kingdom*, 6.
[176] Ep. 235.

'many things were prophesied by many people about the king's death, and it was said . . . because of strange and unusual signs . . . and the visions of many religious persons . . . – that the divine vengeance was soon going to fall on him for his persecution of Anselm.'[177] Eadmer reports them as centering largely around Anselm's closest friends, confidantes, allies and fellow political planners in France, Hugh of Cluny and Hugh of Lyons.[178] But Orderic says, more generally, that the visions of these monks and prelates were being revealed in great public convocations.[179] It is almost as if there were a great swell of public feeling that the tyrant must die. Ominously, it was around 1 August, the day of the Feast of St Peter in chains, that the majority of the visions foretelling the king's death occurred.[180] On that day Fulchered abbot of Shrewsbury, a former monk of Sées, preached to a crowd at Gloucester Abbey, announcing that God was about to punish the enemies of his church: 'the bow of divine wrath is drawn . . . the arrow has been taken from the quiver. The wise man will correct his life to avoid the blow.'[181] Immediately Serlo abbot of Gloucester, whose church Rufus had patronized well, sent a messenger to warn the king. He arrived before dawn the following morning.[182] Rufus, after a morning of indigestion, was about to go hunting. Significantly, William of Malmesbury's account seems to describe three warnings in the form of dreams – suggesting the customery warnings before sentence of excommunication was passed.[183]

King William Rufus died in the New Forest on the day after the Feast of St Peter, 2 August 1100.[184] Eadmer is circumspect about the means of the king's death. 'An arrow pierced his heart and killed him instantly.'[185] 'Whether, as some say, that arrow struck him in its flight or, as the majority declare, he stumbled and falling violently upon it met his death, is a question we think in unnecessary to go into.'[186] The means, Eadmer implies, were less important than the justice of the end. But it was common knowledge that Rufus was shot with an arrow by Walter Tirel – a vassal of and allied by marriage to Anselm's and Bec's long-time patrons and supporters the Clares and the Giffards.[187] Later, Walter would deny the accusation, claiming that Rufus was struck down by the hand of God.[188] Anselm's close coterie of ecclesiastical supporters received the news almost instantly – by

---

[177] Eadmer *VA* 122.
[178] Cf. R.W. Southern, *The Life of St Anselm*, pp. 122–123 notes, for a summation of these visions; and Hollister, 'The Strange Death of William Rufus, 59–76.
[179] Quoted in Southern, *The Life of St Anselm*, 122n. Southern believes Orderic's reports are independent of those of Malmesbury, Florence of Worcester, and Eadmer, *VA* 122 n. 3.
[180] Hollister, 'The Strange Death of William Rufus', discusses all the prophesies in great detail, 62–63; Southern, *The Life of St Anselm*, 122–123nn, reprints some of them together.
[181] Orderic v. 286–288.
[182] Orderic v. 288–290.
[183] GR 2:377–379.
[184] Eadmer *VA* 124.
[185] Eadmer *VA* 126.
[186] Eadmer *HN* 116.
[187] Hollister, 'Strange Death of William Rufus, 67–69 for the family connections to Tirel; Vaughn, *Anselm of Bec*, 19–77 and 367–371 for the Clare patronage to Bec, founded by a vassal of Gilbert of Brionne, whose children and grandchildren became the Clares.
[188] Barlow, *William Rufus*, 424. Barlow reports that Suger and John of Salisbury agreed with that concept.

messengers as well as visions.[189] But, as the affair was Anselm's, England's and Normandy's, no mention is made anywhere of Paschal in the reports.

Modern historians who have studied the strange death of William Rufus have assumed with Eadmer that his demise only affected England, and that only his brother and successor Henry I benefited from the king's death, and thus, if the death were murder, the finger would point to Henry. I have endeavored to show here that many others benefited more than Henry. The new king urged Anselm to return to England to resume his rightful place, expecting to be a co-ruler with the king without rendering homage. But more importantly for the future of the reform papacy, and perhaps for the rest of Europe, Rufus's budding empire dissolved on his death. Robert Curthose was on his way home to reclaim Normandy, and even had a claim to England,[190] grabbed at once by his quick-thinking brother Henry. With the Anglo-Norman state thus threatened with civil war, Maine and Brittany reverted to their comital lines; Aquitaine remained independent; Wales, Scotland and France were safe from invasion; and the incipient movement toward a third faction to claim the papal throne apparently died on the vine.

Eadmer and many of the prophesies state that 'by the just judgment of God [the king] was stricken down and slain.'[191] On the eve of Rufus's assassination, Hugh of Cluny had matter of factly stated in a conversation with Anselm that 'during the previous night (July 31) the king had been accused before the throne of God, judged, and had sentence of damnation passed upon him.'[192] Eadmer, with his usual obfuscation, chose to be 'content to trust his words alone, and omitted to ask him how he knew this.' Hugh of Cluny uttered these words on 1 August, the Feast Day of St Peter in Chains. And the throne of God on earth was the throne of St Peter, now claiming sovereignty over emperors and kings alike, exultant over its conquest and rule over the Holy Land, and filled with a new vision of the *militia Christi* justly slaying infidels, antiChristians, and even antipapists with the sword of God; and the new Christian, papal hero, the *miles Christi*, remitting his sins with the just shedding of blood. One wonders if, at the end of that court so cryptically reported by Hugh of Cluny – if it took place – the participants – whoever they were – may have murmured: Deus vult, Deus vult.

---

[189] Eadmer *VA* 124, 126.
[190] Later, when Henry failed to cooperate with his archbishop, Anselm seems obliquely to have threaten to support Curthose against him. Cf. S. Vaughn, *Anselm of Bec*, 298.
[191] Eadmer *HN* 116.
[192] Eadmer *VA* 123.

JUDHAEL OF TOTNES: THE LIFE AND TIMES OF A POST-CONQUEST BARON[1]

John Bryan Williams

Below the level of the great magnates who played central roles in early Anglo-Norman political history were a number of powerful regional lords, whom F.M. Stenton called 'second-rank' barons. These lay landholders must have been influential figures in their own regions, but, unless their families later became prominent, they have left few traces in Anglo-Norman political narratives. Their obscurity is often more apparent than real. In many cases we can reconstruct with great success their careers and their roles in the early years of the Conquest. The result of this kind of research is a richer and more detailed knowledge of the Anglo-Norman baronial class.

This paper attempts to follow the career of one such second-rank baron named by tradition and by Domesday Book as Judhael 'of Totnes'.[2] The sources available for this project are sporadic charters, a passage in a miracle account, a small bit of archeological evidence and the data available in the Exeter and Exchequer Domesdays. Although these documents leave many questions unanswered, they can, when combined, give us a fairly detailed account of Judhael's movements, his holdings, and his moments of success and failure. This baron seems to have had a very long life. He was a young man in the reign of William I and lived well into the 1120s. He lived through a period of great political fluidity and social transformation. His career shows how a successful second-rank baron took part in and responded to these changes.

I

Judhael of Totnes held a group of 107 manors concentrated in the river basins of the eastern Devon coast in 1086, the earliest date at which his whereabouts can be certainly known.[3] It is less certain where he came from and how he acquired his Domesday lands. In a charter from the early twelfth century Judhael calls himself the son of *Aluredus* and he himself has a son named *Aluredus*. Based on these two

---

[1] Research for this paper was begun for a seminar on Domesday England at the University of Chicago conducted by Professor Robert Bartlett. The author wishes to thank Professor Bartlett, Elisabeth Gooch Austin and Jon Lehrich for their suggestions and comments. Peter Kapper drew the maps.
[2] It should be noted that the subject of this paper is called *Judhaelus* only in Exchequer Domesday; Exeter Domesday and charters use *Iuhellus* or *Ioelus*. This paper follows the usage of modern scholarship and calls him Judhael.
[3] My quantitative analysis of Judhael's lands (see below) does not include his one manor in Cornwall. For the sake of comparison, I have confined my analysis to Devon. The Cornwall estate is Froxton. Judhael sublet it to Thurstan; it was worth 11s.

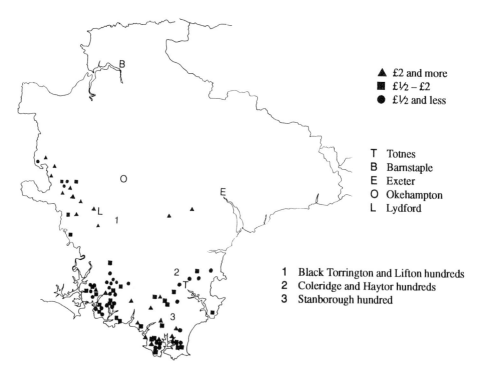

Map 1. Value distribution of the holdings of the honour of Totnes in 1086

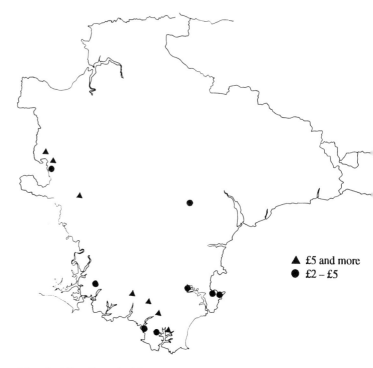

Map 2. The direct holdings of Judhael in the honour of Totnes

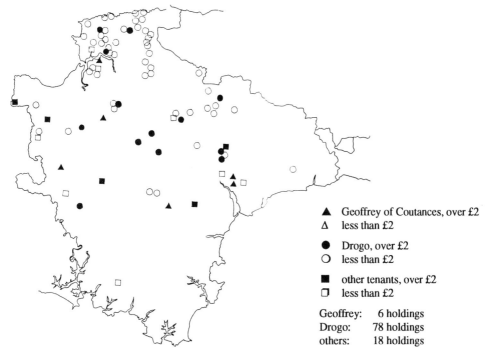

Map 3. The honour of Barnstaple in 1086 with tenants

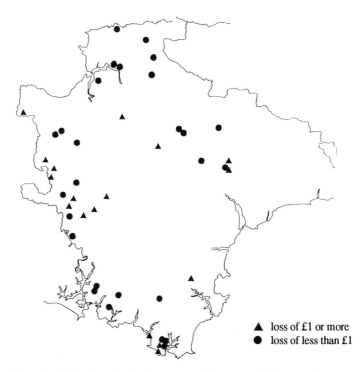

Map 4. Value loss in the honours of Totnes and Barnstaple between olim and 1086

names, it has been assumed by many scholars that Judhael was a Breton. However, it has proved impossible to identify positively this Judhael with any of the other Judhaels or Alfreds found in Breton documents.[4] Conflicting with the Breton theory is what might be called a 'Norman theory,'based on the 'Joel son of Alfred the Giant' mentioned by Orderic Vitalis in connection with the 1079 rebellion of Robert Curthose.[5] According to Orderic, Robert left Normandy accompanied by a group of landless, high-spirited young nobles and wandered around France and Flanders for the next five years. Since we know that Judhael had a substantial and well subinfeudated estate in England six years later and held at least one manor from Queen Matilda, it is very unlikely that he was landless in 1079 or that he spent the next five years away from England.[6] However, a sympathy with Robert Curthose would help explain some of the later events in his life. It is likely that Judhael of Totnes is Orderic's Joel son of Alfred the Giant, but more documentation would be necessary to eliminate all doubts.[7]

The passage from Orderic implies that Judhael received his lands at a date close to 1086, but other kinds of evidence suggest that he received them very soon after the Conquest. Judhael's lands were in a strategically important and militarily vulnerable area in the earliest period of the Conquest. In 1068 William I put down a large regional uprising centered in the city of Exeter. After an eighteen-day siege he captured the city and left Baldwin of Meules, the brother of Richard fitz Gilbert, to fortify the town.[8] William then marched all the way into Cornwall to suppress the rebellion.[9] Two years later the West Saxons of Somerset, Devon and Cornwall rebelled again and were put down, this time by Geoffrey of Coutances (a major Domesday Devon landholder), William fitz Osbern and Brian of Brittany.[10]

Accompanying the internal unrest was the seemingly constant threat of maritime attacks on the region. Orderic says of the coast near Exeter, 'it is reached by the shortest passage from Ireland or Brittany.'[11] Danish marauders in the ninth and tenth centuries regularly raided the Devon coast from their bases in Ireland and this pattern continued in the years after the Conquest.[12] In 1068, Orderic reports

---

[4] See J.H. Round, *Feudal England*, London, reset edition 1964, p. 254.

[5] Orderic, iii, 100–2. This theory was proposed already in 1850 by Mr. R.J. King in *Antiquities of Totnes*, but was discarded because this *Iohel Aluredi gigantis filius* was not in the Le Prévost edition of Orderic. See Hugh R. Watkin, *The History of Totnes Priory and Medieval Town*, Torquay 1917, ii, 656–8.

[6] The manor held from the queen was Ashprington *DB*, 1,71 (101c). All Domesday citations (*DB*) are from the new John Morris edition. *Devon* is edited in two volumes by C. and F. Thorne, Chichester 1985. This edition incorporates Exeter Domesday information into its entries and notes. Unless otherwise cited, Exeter citations come from these volumes.

[7] Alfred the Giant is a well-known Norman noble of the mid-eleventh century. He attested in a charter of William of Bellême in 1025, fought with Nigel I of the Cotentin in 1029, and appears with Dukes Robert and William in four other charters (Fauroux, nos. 33, 69, 99 and 195). If Alfred was from the Cotentin he could very well have been of Breton origin, which would explain the family naming pattern. I would like to thank Dr K.S.B. Keats-Rohan for her helpful suggestions and hope her work will further clarify this point.

[8] Orderic, ii, 214; *The Anglo-Saxon Chronicle* (*ASC*), trans. S. I. Tucker, published in *English Historical Documents: 1042–1189*, eds D.C. Douglas and G.W. Greenaway, London 1968, 1067, D version, 147.

[9] Orderic, ii, 214.

[10] Orderic, ii, 228.

[11] Orderic, ii, 210.

[12] See chapter one of M.M. Oppenheim, *The Maritime History of Devon*, Exeter 1968. The canons

that two sons of King Harold, who had sought the protection of King Dermot of Leinster, appeared off the coast of Exeter with 66 ships. On this occasion, they were beaten by Brian of Brittany and William Gualdi.[13] The Anglo-Saxon Chronicle records two more attacks by the sons of Harold in the region, one going up the Avon to Bristol and another up the Taw river into the lands of the honour of Barnstaple.[14] Florence of Worcester reports an attack on Somerset in 1068 by three sons of King Harold. He says that Harold's sons returned to Ireland with a large amount of plunder from Devon and Cornwall.[15] Although the chroniclers may be giving divergent accounts of the same expeditions, it is clear that the region was repeatedly subjected to sea attacks. Exeter Domesday records that nine manors on the Devon coast were devastated *per Irlandinos homines*.[16]

As he had done a year earlier in the coastal areas of Sussex, it would make sense that William established trusted collaborators as castellans in vulnerable river basin areas of the Southwest in the wake of the rebellion and the invasions from Ireland. It is quite possible that Judhael was made a castellan in Totnes at the same time Baldwin of Meules was made castellan of Exeter.[17] Baldwin was the first sheriff of Devon and the only lay tenant-in-chief to hold more land than Judhael in Domesday Devon. Evidence from Domesday Book lends more support to this theory.

II

In his foundation charter for the Priory of St Mary, Totnes, Judhael said he was making his donation *pro Willielmo rege Anglorum, de quo illum honorem habebat*. Although it is probably too early to take this use of honour to mean the technical twelfth-century 'honour,' the shape of Judhael's Domesday lands seems to suggest something very similar to it.[18] His holdings were unusually compact and organized. They were concentrated in the South Hams area of Devon, on the fertile, coastal lowlands between the Tavy and the Dart rivers and along the border with Cornwall, in the hillier regions of what is called the 'Culm Measures Belt,' a region of heavier clay.[19] (Map 1) In plough-team and population density, Judhael's South Devon lands were second only to those of the fertile red sandstone area

of Laon who were traveling in the region in 1113 (see below) report that it was common for Irish boats to abduct people from Bristol and sell them elsewhere as slaves. See *PL* clvi, col. 986. William of Malmesbury discusses this trade in the *Vita Wulfstani*, ed. R.R. Darlington, London 1928, 43–4. Depletion of human resources is one way the productivity of these regions could have been reduced. (See below, pp. 281–2).

[13] Orderic, ii, 224.

[14] *ASC*, 1067, D version, p. 149 and 1069, D version, p. 150.

[15] *Florentii Wigorniensis monachi chronicon ex chronicis*, ed. B. Thorpe, London 1849, ii, 3–4.

[16] See R. Weldon Finn, 'Devonshire', in *The Domesday Geography of South-West England*, eds H.C. Darby and R. Weldon Finn, Cambridge 1967, pp. 273–4, where there is a small map of these devastated estates.

[17] This suggestion has been made recently in Marjorie Chibnall, *Anglo-Norman England: 1066–1166*, Oxford 1986, p.16.

[18] I am following Stenton's definition of the honour as described in the second chapter of *The First Century*. A very concise version of it is, 'a fief of a great lord, charged with a definite amount of military service to the King' (p. 55).

[19] For a geological and climatological description, see Finn, 291.

surrounding Exeter. The river basins were the center of the Domesday Devon fish and salt industries.[20]

As the Domesday toponymic implies, Totnes was the *caput* of Judhael's lands. Until that time Totnes had been a royal holding. It was the site of an Anglo-Saxon *burh* and had a mint which had operated continually from the tenth century.[21] Like the *burh* at Barnstaple and the earlier Roman fortifications at Exeter, Totnes was situated several miles inland in a river system vulnerable to maritime invasions from the south and east. Domesday records that Totnes had 110 burgesses, which Finn converts into a population of 550, a figure greater than for those of the other Devon towns of Barnstaple (350), Lydford (350) and Okehampton, and about one-quarter the population of Exeter (2000).[22] According to the Domesday customs for Devon, in cases of special war taxation Barnstaple, Lydford, and Totnes together paid a fee equal to that of Exeter.[23]

Totnes, however, was the only established town in Devon held directly by a tenant-in-chief. Although Geoffrey of Coutances possessed the honour of Barnstaple, the King still held the town itself. Lydford too was held by the King. The only other town held by a magnate was Okehampton, which Baldwin of Meules had created *ex nihilo* with the King's permission and which in Domesday Book is nothing more than a large fortified manor with a population of less than a hundred people.[24]

Although Domesday Book mentions no devastated houses, interpreted often as evidence for castle-building, it makes sense that, like Baldwin of Meules in Exeter and like every other Norman baron interested in securing his new territory, Judhael would have immediately fortified Totnes. The earliest documentation of the existence of Totnes castle is from 1113, by which time Judhael no longer controlled the honour, but a formal observation concerning the castle's location suggests that he built it. The castle of Totnes was a regular motte-and-bailey type, but was one of the rare instances in which the axis of the castle did not run parallel to the river by which the town stands. Instead, the axis projected into the town and was surrounded by populated areas on three sides. Only three other castles from the early Anglo-Norman period shared this configuration. One of these was Barnstaple, where Judhael was lord by 1113.[25]

III

A glance at a map of Judhael's holdings (Map 1) would suggest that his wealth was concentrated in the river areas in Plympton, Stanborough and Coleridge hundreds, but a hundred-by-hundred breakdown demonstrates that the wealth of his lands was more evenly distributed. Lifton and Black Torrington hundreds, which were off the coast and tended to have larger and fewer manors, were two of

---

[20] See the maps in Finn, 242–3, 248–9.
[21] See Watkin, ii, 619–53 for the pre-Conquest history of Totnes.
[22] Finn, 279–85.
[23] *DB* C,6 (100a).
[24] Finn, 284–5.
[25] The write-up of the excavations is found in S.E. Rigold, 'Totnes Castle: Recent Excavations by the Ancient Monuments Department, Ministry of Works', in *Transactions of the Devonshire Association*, lxxxi, 1954, 228–56. A recent summary is found in Robert Higham, 'Early Castles in Devon (1068–1201)', in *Château Gaillard: Etudes de Castellologie médiévale*, ix, 1978, 101–17.

the top three most valuable hundreds. Stanborough Hundred, which included the coastal areas devastated by the Irish, was the second most valuable area, remarkable for its high number of sheep and pigs. All of the hundreds demonstrated a plough-team to plough-land deficiency. Finn has found that for Devon as a whole 71% of all manors had a plough-team deficiency, while only 6% had excess ploughs.[26] For Judhael's lands the percentages were 59% and 9%, respectively.

According to the *valebat* figures, the lands of the future honour of Totnes were worth £163[27] around the time Judhael acquired the lands.[28] It is clear that Judhael's claims to these manors were not based on a single antecessor. Thirty-seven different names are mentioned as tenants or subtenants of Judhael's lands in 1066; the average number of holdings per name was 2.9. The number of holdings a tenant possessed did not reflect his overall wealth. Alfred, who we can safely assume was one person, was the wealthiest tenant in 1066. (Table 1) He held only two large estates in Black Torrington hundred. Grim's two manors in Lifton hundred made him the fourth wealthiest. Other holders, like Alwin and Aubrey (even if there were, as is likely, several Alwins and Aubreys) held larger numbers of small manors in localized clusters. An Aubrey's holdings in Plympton dominated the hundred's northern section. Below these top names were tenants holding very modest estates, including fifteen names which are mentioned in connection with only one place. As Table 1 shows, no one name is predominant in the listing of the ten most valuable estates.

Table 1 Ten most valuable holdings in the future honour of Totnes with the names of their holders

Place	Holder	Olim value
Pyworthy	Alfred	220s
Thrushelton	Grim	200s
Clawton	Alfred	200s
Raddon	Oswulf	150s
Broadwoodwidger	Cynestan	120s
Worthele	Alwin	120s
Leigh	Alwin	120s
Tellcott	Aldred	100s
Loddiswell	Heca	100s
Charleston	Heca	100s

[26] Finn, p. 240. These percentages have been noted solely for the purpose of comparison, while accepting Sally Harvey's thesis that the plough-land records something more complex than just arable land. See 'Taxation and the Ploughland in Domesday Book', in *Domesday Book: A Reassessment*, ed. P. Sawyer, Worcester 1985, 86–103.

[27] This would make Judhael's a 'class D' barony, according to the scheme set out by W.J. Corbett, in 'England 1087–1154', in *The Cambridge Medieval History*, Cambridge 1929, v, 510–11.

[28] This paper does not assume that *valebat* indicates value in 1066, because the Exeter Domesday formula is *quando eam recepit*. I will call these values '*olim* value'.

Between this time and 1086 the pool of tenants' names decreased from thirty-seven to twelve (with a corresponding increase from 2.9 to 8.2 holdings per name) and the valuable lands had been consolidated. (Table 2) Judhael of Totnes seems to have organized his honour according to the principle which Lennard noticed in the estates of other lay tenants-in-chief: the lord maintains direct control over his most valuable manors.[29] In clear contrast to the 1066 situation, Judhael held 14 of the top twenty most valuable estates, including the five largest.

Table 2   Ten most valuable holdings in the honour of Totnes in 1086 with the names of their holders.

Place	Holder	1086 value
Thrushelton	Judhael	200s
Clawton	Judhael	160s
Pyworthy	Judhael	160s
Worthele	Judhael	120s
Leigh	Judhael	120s
Raddon	Nigel	100s
Loddiswell	Judhael	100s
Charleton	Judhael	100s
Broadwoodwidger	Nigel	80s
Tetcott	Judhael	80s

A map of his direct holdings shows no geographic pattern. They were united only by their high value. (Map 2) The holdings, either direct or indirect, of the entire honour, including his proceeds from Totnes, amounted to £162.5. In land holdings alone (the 107 manors) he possessed £152 in Devon. Of this he held £71 directly, or 47% of the total land value, leaving 53% of his lands to his tenants. This percentage of subinfeudation is comparable to those of the estates of first-rank barons who have been studied and suggests a long period of tenure.[30] Richard Mortimer contends that enfeoffment proceeded slowly between 1066 and 1086, and therefore the direct/enfeoffed ratio depends on the length of the lord's tenure.[31] The data available for Judhael's holdings only allow us to test this theory in one case. According to Exeter book, the manor of Follaton, valued at 10s., was granted by Judhael to the Priory of St Mary's in Totnes *pro anima regine*.[32] This means that Judhael had held Follaton directly until at least November 1083, the time of Queen Matilda's death.[33]

A consequence of Judhael's principle of keeping the most valuable lands for himself was that when he wanted to reward his tenants with valuable estates, he

[29] R. Lennard, *Rural England: 1086–1135*, Oxford 1959, pp. 50–1.
[30] For enfeoffment percentages of first-rank barons, see J.F.A. Mason, 'Roger de Montgomery and His Sons', in *TRHS*, ser. 5, xiii, 1963, 4–7; and Richard Mortimer, 'The Beginnings of the Honour of Clare', *ante*, iii, 1981, 134.
[31] Mortimer, p. 134.
[32] *Liber Exoniensis*, in *Domesday Book. Additamenta*, ed. H. Ellis, London 1816, 305.
[33] Follaton, *DB* 17,58 (109c).

had to give them a larger number of smaller manors. Moreover, because he had a smaller pool of tenants, individual holders were likely to have a larger number of estates than their Anglo-Saxon predecessors. The shape this phenomenon assumed on the map of the honour of Totnes was that of large clusters of holdings under one name, created out of many 1066 holdings that had been under many different names. This phenomenon has been noticed in other tenants-in-chief's holdings by Le Patourel and Mortimer.[34] The more dispersed and heterogeneous kinds of Anglo-Saxon estates tended to be reshaped into more coherent land units. A Nigel (Table 2) who we can assume is one person, held a valuable group of manors concentrated in Lifton hundred, one Ralph had a block of manors in central Plympton hundred and another Ralph in Haytor hundred. A very dense group of small manors in south Plympton belonged to a holder named William. The composition of these blocks indicates that there was no attempt to maintain the integrity of the 1066 blocks when the lands were redistributed. The estate blocks of the Anglo-Saxon holders were broken up and put back together in new forms. Nigel's 1086 estate in North Lifton hundred, for example, was put together from the lands of Cynestan, Oswulf, Aldred, Saewin, Brictry, Aelfric, Alwin and four unnamed thanes. The sub-tenant Aiulf is the only person who appears in both the *olim* and 1086 lists, as the holder of the manor of Lidemore, worth 25s.[35]

Exeter Domesday provides us with elusive, but potentially very interesting information about Judhael's land management. In many of the Exeter Domesday entries, numbers are given for virgates-in-demesne and tenant virgates. Little or nothing has been written about these figures. What can be known about them empirically is that they are given for all the large 1066 estates and that, when added together, they almost always equal the total hidage given for the manors. The smaller manors usually only give one number for hides. It can be assumed that in these cases the resources were so limited that a division was not feasible. Without any secondary literature to inform my opinion, I have assumed that the sub-hidage figures represent 1066 methods of land utilization and can tell us the kind of things that the 1086 figures for ploughs in demesne and tenant ploughs can tell us. (Table 3) Making this assumption, it seems that the larger Anglo-Saxon holders tended to have about as many resources in demesne as their Anglo-Norman counterparts, although some hundred figures show local differences. Most of the hundreds had hides-in-demesne percentages between 30–40%; the honour-wide distribution percentage was 32%, slightly higher than, but close to the figure of 26% for the 1086 plough-teams in demesne.

---

[34] Mortimer, 123; John Le Patourel, 'The Norman Colonization of Britain', in *I Normanni e la loro espansione in Europa nell' alto medioevo*, Spoleto xvi, 1969, 425.
[35] *DB* 17,8 (109a).

Table 3

(a) Demesne-tenant utilization in Totnes and Barnstaple hidage, 1066

	Hides	Hides in demesne	% of total hides
Totnes	70.4	22.7	32%
Barnstaple	56.2	14.1	25%

(b) Demesne-tenant utilization of plough teams in 1086[36]

	Pl. teams	Pl. teams in demesne	% of total pl. teams
Totnes	314.25	82.5	26%
Barnstaple	326.49	96.5	30%

If we assume there is an analogy between the Exeter Domesday hidage numbers and the Exchequer Domesday plough-team distribution, it should be concluded that there was continuity between Anglo-Saxon and Anglo-Norman manorial resource distribution.[37]

IV

The data discussed above suggest an interpretation of the way the Conquest occurred in the lands of Judhael's honour of Totnes. It seems likely that Judhael received the raw material for his honour in the coastal areas of Devon at an early point in the Conquest, perhaps as a castellan, as part of an ongoing security arrangement with the King. He built a castle and began distributing his lands as he saw fit, without regard to pre-existing estate arrangements. He gradually dispersed the smaller, less valuable manors to his followers, and kept the most valuable for himself. But at the manorial level, there was little change. Distribution of resources between demesne and tenants remained similar to that of the Anglo-Saxon holders before Judhael.[38]

Judhael's management of the honour did not make it more valuable. It has already been noted that the *olim* value of his holdings was £166, while the 1086 value of Judhael's holdings, excluding the fees due from the town of Totnes, was £152. Another £6 should be subtracted from this figure because two entries give only 1086 values. For the estates with which we can make a comparison,

---

[36] The Totnes plough-team figures show the typical small number of ploughs in demesne on large estates. Only one manor violates this rule: Judhael's manor of Pyworthy divided up 10 ploughs evenly between the lord and tenants.

[37] For a very interesting recent addition to the debate between manorial 'reorganization' versus 'continuity', see Robin Fleming, *Kings and Lords in Conquest England*, Cambridge 1991, 107–26.

[38] Based on the shape of analogous honours in the West Country, Professor Fleming concludes that Judhael's honour of Totnes was a later 'territorial' holding, established on the lands of five small Anglo-Saxon landholders and supplemented by 'self-interested and aggressive private enterprise, based on theft, intimidation and the extension of protection' (p. 210).

Judhael's lands dropped £20 (about 12%) in value between *olim* and 1086; the honour of Totnes was the only large lay holding in Devon that lost value.[39]

A map of the areas of loss of value shows that they are somewhat localized. (Map 4) A map of value loss in Geoffrey of Coutances's honour of Barnstaple (which as a whole gained in value between *olim* and 1086) shows that Barnstaple value loss was fairly evenly distributed throughout the honour. In the case of Judhael's lands, however, it is clear that one focus of land loss was the peninsula southeast of the Tavy river, the area which Exeter Domesday says was devastated *per Irlandinos homines*. The best explanation for this pattern seems to be that the devastated areas had partially recovered their productivity in 1086, but were still producing less than they had before the attacks.[40] The other area of concentration of value loss was in the large estates in Lifton hundred, an area where Geoffrey of Coutances's holdings also lost value. For this value loss there are no clues in the sources.

Value loss in the coastal areas of the honour of Totnes recalls the earlier speculations about the events of 1066–86. In a time when less disturbed areas in other parts of Devon and the Southwest were becoming more productive and growing in value, a loss of value, corroborated by sources describing naval attacks from Ireland, suggests that Judhael's lands were experiencing or had experienced the effects of military activity. These findings support the argument that the area was contested and militarily vulnerable. If this were true, then Judhael's rather unusual arrangement could be explainable as a special security precaution taken by the King, analogous to the measure William had earlier taken on the Sussex coast.

Exeter Domesday offers valuable information in support of this theory. When the Exchequer scribe wrote *olim* to describe past values of Judhael's estates, he was shortening the Exeter Domesday formula, *quando Iuhellus eam recepit*. There is no reason to suspect that the formula, 'when he acquired it,' is especially artificial. It seems to indicate straightforwardly the condition of the land when Judhael obtained it. The manor of Coleridge records as its *olim* value, *quando Iuhellus recepit erat vastata*.[41] If a manor was devastated, it was recorded as such. Therefore, the devastation and value loss reflected in Domesday seem to have happened after Judhael acquired the lands. For example, we can conclude that Judhael was controlling the manors in Stanborough Hundred when they were devastated by the Irish. If this 'when he acquired it' formula can be trusted, it

---

[39] Professor Fleming's correlation between 'redistribution of resources' and value loss in Circuit Three counties does not work as well in Devon. The holdings of Geoffrey of Coutances and Baldwin the Sheriff, which were based on a large number of small 1066 holdings, both gained about 20% in value in the same period, while the value of Robert of Mortain's Devon holdings, clearly built around the lands of the king's thegn Ordulf II of Devon, showed no change. For Robert and Ordulf, see H.P.R. Finberg, 'Childe's Tomb', in *Transactions of the Devonshire Association*, lxxviii, 1946, 265–80 and *Tavistock Abbey: A Study in the Social and Economic History of Devon*, Cambridge 1951, 3–7.

[40] For a general discussion of value loss due to military activity, see pp. 238–9 of H.C. Darby, *Domesday England*, Cambridge 1977. For a critique of reading value loss as the effect of military activity, see Fleming, 123. The well-documented capture and enslavement by Irish raiders of people in the southwestern coastal regions (who were likely to be young agricultural workers) would reduce the area's production potential and therefore its value. See above, note 12.

[41] *Liber Exoniensis*, p. 308.

suggests that Judhael acquired his lands soon after the Conquest and that he received a territory which suffered damage from military campaigns during his tenure.

V

The only extant documentary source for Judhael's activities at Totnes is his undated foundation of St Mary's Priory as a house dependent on the Benedictine monastery of St Serge in Angers. This deed has survived in two places, in a copy held at St Mary's and in a French copy, which contains clearly post-foundation interpolations.[42] The latter, although less accurate as an original charter, is very important for another reason. Added to the text of the charter is an annotation. It says:

> When King William died, his son William succeeded to the kingdom and, after Judhael of Totnes had been expelled, he gave the estate to Roger of Nonant. This Roger at first brought a great many troubles to the monks, but afterwards through the intervention of the King, Roger conceded all the same things and in the same words as had Judhael, and he accepted twenty pounds of coin from the monks and his wife accepted a half mark of gold. It happened however that the King came to Normandy and that Roger came with him. Abbot Acchardus came to the King and, with Roger present, asked him to confirm the donation. The King devoutly asked for a benefice of the place and, accepting it from the abbot, happily gave his seal and promised him even better things. Witnesses to this matter were count Hugo and Robert fitz Haimon.[43]

Using the royal itinerary and a necrology reference to the Abbot Acchardus, it can be concluded that the time of this event was February 1091. Roger of Nonant, the baron who replaced Judhael as lord of Totnes, appears in a charter issued in January 1091, as the king was preparing to cross the Channel and therefore it is likely that he accompanied the king to Normandy.[44] The witnesses Count Hugh and Robert fitz Haimon both fit the story as well. All of this evidence suggests that Judhael of Totnes had been stripped of his honour by early 1091.

He must have lost his honour shortly after William Rufus came to power. Frank Barlow has remarked how unusual such an act of disenfranchisement was during the reign of William II.[45] The sources give us no clues as to what Judhael did to receive such an extreme punishment. If he was the son of Alfred the Giant and was

---

[42] The English copy was found at the beginning of this century by Robert Kitson in Bovey Tracey, Devon, and reproduced in a plate in the beginning of the second volume of Watkin's history. It can be found today in the Devon Record Office under the collocation 312M/TY1. The French copy can be found in Paris BN, 3/MS lat. 5476, fo. 268. It has been published in Dugdale, *Monasticon Anglicanum*, 2nd edn, eds Calley, Ellis and Bandinel, London 1846, v, 360; also in Oliver, *Monasticon Diocesis Exoniensis*, London 1846, p. 241. The conclusion that the French document has later interpolations is based on differences in the dispositions of the two documents. Except for small problems in chronology, the reconstruction of Watkin, i, 7–10, is correct.

[43] For Latin text see Dugdale, v, 360.

[44] For Abbot Acchardus, see Watkin, ii, 1003–6; *Regesta*, i, no. 319.

[45] Frank Barlow, *William Rufus*, Los Angeles and London 1983, p. 171.

involved in Robert Curthose's rebellion of 1079, he could have been allied with Robert again in 1088 and left England.[46] It is also conceivable that Judhael participated in the rebellion of Geoffrey of Coutances and Robert fitz Baldwin in the Southwest on William II's accession. Like Geoffrey and other faithful servants of Rufus' father, Judhael might have been forgiven and immediately reinstated in some other lands, the record of which does not survive. On the other hand, as the historian of Totnes Hugh Watkin fantasized, Judhael could have had a period of 'exile,' and even have participated in the First Crusade.[47] He does not appear again until after 1107 and then as lord of Barnstaple. Whatever happened to Judhael in this period, it is clear that in the first years of the twelfth century the Nonant family possessed and was disposing freely of the lands that belonged to Judhael in Domesday Book. Thanks to the discovery early in this century of a box of charters of Totnes Priory, the Nonant donations to St Mary's in the early twelfth century can be reconstructed quite accurately.[48] The Nonants considered themselves the founders of the monastery and appropriated the donations that had been made by Judhael in his earlier foundation charter. A royal charter from 1104–7 confirming Roger's gifts to Totnes Priory[49] and a reconfirmation of the Nonant gifts to the monastery made by Roger II of Nonant in the 1130s clearly show that the Nonants were controlling the same lands that Judhael had controlled in 1086.[50] The Nonant 'tenement' of Totnes, as it was called in the *cartae baronum* in 1166, must have looked substantially like Judhael's 1086 honour.

VI

Judhael's return to favor, like Roger of Nonant's acquisition of the Totnes lands, depended on another person's demise. In the final years of Rufus' reign or in the early years of Henry I's reign Judhael was granted the honour of Barnstaple. In Domesday Book the Barnstaple lands were held by one of William's most important magnates, Geoffrey of Mowbray, Bishop of Coutances. Although Geoffrey had participated in the rebellions at the beginning of Rufus' reign, he had been allowed to retain his lands.[51] His nephew Robert of Mowbray, Earl of Northumberland, inherited the honour along with about 180 other manors on Geoffrey's death in 1093. Robert forfeited these lands after he refused to appear at William's Easter court of 1095 and a few months later was captured and imprisoned for life.[52] Presumably, the honour was forfeited to the Crown and at some later time it was granted to Judhael. Because witnesses visited Judhael at Barnstaple in 1113, he must have been granted the lands in the period 1095–1113.

The main source of information for Judhael's Barnstaple activities is the

---

[46] See above p. 274.
[47] Watkin, ii, 663.
[48] Watkin has translated these documents in the first volume of his history. Transcriptions and the documents themselves are available in the Devon Record Office. Watkin's order of the documents has been slightly revised.
[49] This document was part of the Bovey Tracey collection and is now Devon Record Office 312M/TY2. It is accepted by the *Regesta* editors. It is 735, in vol. ii, eds H.A. Cronne and C. Johnson, Oxford, 1965.
[50] Devon Record Office, 312M/TY5.
[51] Orderic, ii, 266; Barlow, 86–92.
[52] Orderic, ii, 266 and iv, 278–82; Barlow, 346–8.

documentation of St Mary Magdalene's in Barnstaple, a Cluniac house dependent
on St Martin des Champs in Paris. Although it is certain that Judhael founded this
house, it is not clear when. There are two documentary traditions for Judhael's
foundation: one would place it in the reign of William II (1095–1100), the other in
the early years of the reign of Henry I. Several scholars have tried to explain the
first tradition without success.[53]

The second tradition is better documented and more feasible. This foundation
charter[54] carries the approval of the Bishop of Exeter, William Warelwast, and
therefore could only have been written after 1107, the year of Willam's appointment.[55] In this charter Judhael generously provided for the needs of his new
Cluniac house, which he said stood *extra castellum meum*, and expressed a desire
to retire to it at the appropriate time of his life. In founding a Cluniac house,
Judhael was following Henry's new ecclesiastical orientation, especially important after the settlement of the Investiture Controversy in 1107. Henry's reign saw
the establishment of fifteen new Cluniac houses, four of which were founded in
1107.[56]

The clear *ante quem* of these events is 1113 because in this year a group of
canons from Laon who travelled through the English countryside performing
miracles with relics of the Virgin noted seeing Judhael in Barnstaple. The monk
Herman, when he later wrote up the travel account into a proper narrative, described it thus:

> After these occurrences we came to a castle which is called Barnstaple,
> where lived a lord named Judhael of Totnes, whose wife was the sister of
> Guermundus of Picquigny. This lord, partly for the influence of his wife,
> who was from the diocese of Amiens and our province, but more import-
> antly for the miracles which had been done by Our Lady, most graciously

[53] The charter is a confirmation of Judhael's donation by *Willelmus Dei gratia rex Anglorum*. It
has been published in Marrier, *S. Martini de Campis Historia*, p. 48; Dugdale, v, 198; Oliver, 198;
J. Depoin, *Recueil de chartes et documents de Saint-Martin-des-Champs monastère parisien*
(Paris, 1914), ii, no. 231. See also *Regesta*, i, no. 486, where it is rightly judged spurious but for the
wrong reasons. Watkin's explanation is that this 'William' really ought to read 'Henry' (ii, 661–2)
while Depoin thinks this 'William' is Prince William who drowned on the White Ship in 1120 (ii,
77, note 125). Far more reasonable than these explanations is that the document is false, considering that the papal confirmations of St Martin's privileges do not mention English holdings before
1119 (Depoin, i, no. 157).

[54] Several different copies of this charter have been discovered and published. One is in the
cartulary of St Martin (BN, Trésor des Chartes L. 1440). It was calendared by Round *(Calendar of
Documents in France*, no. 1268) and published by Depoin (ii, no. 230). Another copy in the
possession of the monks of Barnstaple was inspected by Edward II *(Charter Rolls* 10 Edward II, n.
39) and published by Dugdale (v, 197). The Bishop of Exeter's copy was part of the Cottonian
collection and now may be in the British Library. A photostatic copy of a thirteenth-century copy
of the English version was recently found in the North Devon Record Office in the collection of
the North Devon Athenaeum. This photostat has no collocation. Based on internal evidence (the
insertion of the church of Tawstock which could not have been part of Judhael's original grant), the
copy inspected by Edward II is considered the most dependable.

[55] William's confirmation of Judhael's donations is an important document for the insitutional
history of the see of Exeter. See D.W. Blake, 'Bishop William Warelwast', in *Transactions of the
Devonshire Association*, civ, 1972, 15–33.

[56] See D. Knowles and R.N. Hadcock, *Medieval Religious Houses: England and Wales*, New York
1974, 96–8. Judhael's endowment and Henry I's contemporary donation of 9 houses in London
were the two earliest English grants to the Parisian house. (Depoin, nos. 228–9).

accepted us, and kept us there for three days and gave us a silver goblet and a valuable chalice, and not only vessels and other ornaments which are now in the church of Laon, but also a horse to carry the gifts, not to mention many other things; in addition he added coins which valued 15 livres in the currency of Laon.[57]

This passage tells us that in 1113 Judhael of Totnes was well established in the honour. Within a few years of this date he founded a monastery which connected him with Cluny and which had been encouraged and approved by one of the most prominent prelates in England. He was married to the sister of Guermundus of Picquigny, who would later gain prominence as the Patriarch of Jerusalem.[58] Judhael emerges from the obscurity surrounding the years following his expulsion from Totnes as a wealthy, prosperous and pious second-rank baron.

VII

Judhael's new honour was similar in many ways to his old one. After the royal lands and the lands of Baldwin the Sheriff, Totnes and Barnstaple were the largest estates in Devon. When Henry I decided to reinstate Judhael in Devon lands, he restored him to a wealth and status comparable to what he had previously enjoyed.[59] The manors mentioned in Judhael's foundation of Barnstaple Priory were all held by Geoffrey of Coutances in 1086, so it is safe to assume that Judhael received essentially the same honour of Barnstaple that Geoffrey and his nephew Robert held until 1095.

Map 3, of Domesday Barnstaple holdings, shows an honour with a concentration of manors in the area of the *caput* greater than that around Totnes, but with a wider distribution of holdings throughout northern and central Devon. Geoffrey held two valuable manors in the vicinity of Exeter and several more in Black Torrington and Lifton hundreds, where his honour would have overlapped with Judhael's. Following the same logic as Judhael, Geoffrey held only six manors directly, but these were six of the ten most valuable manors in the honour. He seems to have left most of the honour under the direction of a certain Drogo, who held directly 78 of the 101 manors and had subtenants on three more. Because of his arrangement with Drogo, Geoffrey's percentage of enfeoffment was 70%, much higher than that of Judhael in Totnes and that of other lay tenants-in-chief who have been studied.[60] Geoffrey did not seem to be interested in playing a large part in the administration of his Devon lands, even at the risk of losing some of their revenues.

As in the case of 1066 Totnes, the lands of the future honour of Barnstaple had

---

[57] *Hermani monachi De Miraculis S. Mariae Laudunensis de gestis venerabilis Bartholomei episcopi et S. Norberti Libri Tres*, in *PL*, clvi, cols 983–4. The date of 1113 for the journey was supported by J.S. Tatlock in 'The English Journey of the Laon Canons', *Speculum*, viii, 1933, 454–65. The account was probably written in the 1140s from notes taken by the canons during the voyage. The Judael of Totnes passages are discussed on p. 462 and note 6 of the same page. See also chapter 8 of Benedicta Ward, *Miracles and the Medieval Mind*, Philadelphia 1982.
[58] See Robert Fossier, *La terre et les hommes en Picardie jusqu' a la fine du XIII siècle*, Louvain 1960, ii, 611, note 91.
[59] See Barlow's comment about the equality of the trade, p. 171.
[60] See above, pp. 276–80.

a much larger pool of Anglo-Saxon names, none of which dominated the map like the later Anglo-Norman holders.[61] The honour was not based on the large holdings of a single antecessor. Geoffrey's honour was very similar to Totnes in its resource distribution. (Table 3) Its 1066 percentage of hides in demesne was 25% and its 1086 demesne plough-teams percentage was 30%, compared to the 32% and 25% distributions in the honour of Totnes. In the light of the very different ways these honours were administered, the similarity of resource distribution percentages seems significant.

The area in which the two honours differ is in value trends. In contrast to Totnes' value loss between *olim* and 1086, Barnstaple showed a 20% increase in value. Its total value increased from £138 to £174.[62] The manors for which a direct comparison between 1066 and 1086 is possible show an increase of £17; £7.5 of the £20 loss in Barnstaple was in Black Torrington and Lifton hundreds, the areas where the manors of the honour of Totnes also showed significant value loss. (Map 4)

VIII

While Judhael's mark on Totnes seems to have been ephemeral, his presence at Barnstaple had greater durability. In the early thirteenth century the burgesses of Barnstaple unanimously confirmed Judhael's foundation and agreed to mill all their grain with the monks of St Mary Magdalene.[63] In 1233 William Brewer, Bishop of Exeter inspected Judhael's charter and approved it as legitimate and binding.[64] Unlike the fate of his donation at Totnes, which was never mentioned by the Nonant family, Judhael's Barnstaple gift was always cited as the original one, despite the fact that his son Alfred lost the honour for supporting the rebellion of Baldwin of Redvers in 1136.[65]

By the 1120s Judhael of Totnes must have been a very old man. When he witnessed Henry I's restoration of several churches in Devon and Cornwall at Exeter in 1123 he must have been at the very least in his middle or late 60s.[66] The few references to him suggest that by that time he commanded a degree of respect. Henry I referred to him posthumously as 'Judhael of venerable memory,' and the *Gesta Stephani* author calls him 'that very illustrious man.' At the time he made his donation of Barnstaple Priory, Judhael was already talking as if he were near end of his active life. He had taken a vow to establish a monastery for the well-being of his soul and he was anticipating retiring to the monastic life.

According to the necrology of St Martin des Champs, Judhael shed 'the weight

---

[61] In 1066 there were 2.9 holdings per name while in 1086 this rate was 6.4.

[62] Value increase was characteristic of the county of Devon as a whole. Baldwin the Sheriff''s estate (the largest lay holding in the county) also increased in value by 17%, from £255 to £306.

[63] In Trésor des Chartes, L. 1440. *Cal. Docs. France*, no. 1275.

[64] Dugdale, v, 198.

[65] See *Gesta Stephani*, ed. and trans. R.K. Potter, revised R.H.C. Davis, Oxford 1976, 32–47. Under the tutelage of the Braose and Tracy families, the monastery continued to grow and receive royal charters through the twelfth and thirteenth centuries. See the succession of confirmations of Henry I (*Regesta*, ii, no. 1292, no. 1667, no. 1912), an 1146 confirmation by Henry de Tracy (Dugdale, v, 198), and a charter of William of Braose issued in 1157–60 (*Cal. Docs. France*, no. 1272).

[66] *Regesta*, ii, no. 1391 and Round, *Feudal England*, 482.

of his flesh' and entered the monastery of St Martin sometime between 1123 and 1129 and died on the 14th of August of one of these years. The necrology has this entry for 14 August, 'Judhael. Let a mass be said, *capa*, in the choir. He gave us Barnstaple. The Prior owes refection of twenty silver shillings.'[67] Judhael must have been dead by 1130 because in the Pipe Roll 31 Henry I his son Alfred paid £110 in relief.[68]

IX

Although it is certain that the Nonant family controlled the lands that had made up Judhael's 1086 honour of Totnes and that Judhael possessed the honour of Barnstaple after 1113, a variety of sources indicates a lingering connection between Judhael and his Domesday honour. Evidence suggests that Judhael or one of his vassals retained control of the castle of Totnes after he had been expelled from the honour of Totnes. Moreover, it seems likely that he paid the farm of the castle of Totnes to the monks of St Mary's Priory of Totnes, the house which Judhael had created and endowed a few years before.

The account of the journey of the canons of Laon in 1113 offers the first clue. After stopping in Barnstaple, and making the report cited above, the canons proceeded south to Totnes.

> After this we came to the castle of the previously mentioned lord Judhael, which is called Totnes; certain of his men escorted us there, where we were received honorably by some monks and where we stayed for three days. An old man who had been lame since birth lived there; everybody knew him because he was the brother of the *praepositus* of the castle. This man, when he heard about the miracles which had been done, came to the bier with great faith and devotion, and, drinking water washed in the relics, right there stood erect in front of all the people. This miracle was received with such veneration that quickly the brother of this man, the *praepositus* of the castle, offered 40 English shillings to the bier; many other people after him added gifts too.[69]

According to this passage, Judhael could come and go as he pleased with armed men to the castle of Totnes in 1113, almost twenty years after he had been thrown out of the honour of Totnes by William Rufus. It also describes friendly monks and a generous *praepositus* of the castle of Totnes. Coming with the protection of

---

[67] Depoin, iii, 12, n. 342.

[68] *Pipe Roll 31 Henry I*, 153. Since the amount of relief payments was not yet fixed, Alfred's payment can tell us nothing of the value of Judhael's estate at his death. In the 1130 Devon Pipe Roll a knight named *Johelus de Meduana* (Judhael of Mayenne) appears. He had earlier appeared as a witness in a royal charter redacted betweeen 1123 and 1128. The *Regesta* editors assume that Judhael of Mayenne is Judhael of Totnes and Barnstaple. Their theory is proven wrong by, among other things, several charters from the reign of Stephen which mention Judhael of Mayenne. In two charters issued by the Empress Matilda in July 1141 Judhael of Mayenne is mentioned as a hostage against the good faith of the Empress in agreements with her magnates. See *Regesta*, iii, no. 275 and no. 634.

[69] *PL*, clvi, cols 984–5. This passage first came to my attention in a footnote in Round's *Feudal England* on p. 486. Round, unlike several later historians, acknowledged that there is a problem in chronology.

Judhael of Totnes, the canons of Laon were welcomed warmly. They seemed to think that the castle of Totnes still belonged to Judhael.

Several other sources suggest a lingering connection between Judhael and Totnes. Although in the important royal charter issued at Exeter in 1123, the witness list records *Johel de Berdestaple* and *Guy de Totness* (the son of Roger I of Nonant), Henry I called Judhael's son Alfred *Aluredus de Totnes* in a charter concerning Barnstaple in the 1130s.[70] An archeological find also connects Alfred to Totnes. The excavations of Totnes castle conducted in the 1950s recovered only one seal from all the excavations on the site. In a twelfth-century script it reads *sigillum Alfredi*.[71] Since no member of the Nonant family had this name, it seems likely that this Alfred is Alfred the son of Judhael. In 1206 the barony of Totnes was divided between Henry de Nonant and William de Braose. William based his claim partly on the fact that his ancestor Aanor was the daughter of Judhael of Totnes.[72]

If Judhael somehow held the castle of Totnes in the early twelfth century he and his descendants must have paid the *firma castelli* that appears in several twelfth-century charters issued by the Nonant family. In the earliest royal confirmation of the foundation of Totnes Priory of 1104–07, Henry I affirmed among other things, 20s. of income to be paid to the monks *de firma iam dicta castelli*.[73] Upon his succession, Roger II of Nonant, the grandson of the first Roger, issued a very detailed reconfirmation of his gifts to the monastery. Among these gifts was the 20s *de firma de Totenes*[74] and several years later, as he prepared to depart on a pilgrimage to Compostella, Roger II noted that the income of the *firma castelli* had increased to 24s and that it was paid by the *praepositi* of the town. He granted to the monks in perpetuity the entire payment, however much it would increase.[75]

This documentation suggests that, although Judhael had been expelled from Totnes and never appeared in the extant documents of the Nonant family, he and his descendants remained in some meaningful way 'of Totnes'; that is, they maintained ties with Totnes, either through direct control or through a relationship with the *praepositi* of the castle and town.[76] It suggests a rather unusual tenancy arrangement in which an expelled tenant-in chief, with the apparent consent of his successor, maintains control of the most important military fortification in the

---

[70] *Regesta*, ii, no. 1391 and no. 1912, respectively. It should also be noted that in two charters issued by Bishop William Warelwast in favor of Plympton Priory in 1133 Alfred is called *Aluredus de Barnastapula*. These documents are Devon Record Office ED/PP/1 and ED/PP/2.

[71] Sigold, 'Totnes Castle', 252.

[72] Aanor was the wife of Philip of Braose, who received half of the honour of Barnstaple after the expulsion of Alfred of Barnstaple/Totnes in 1136. See 'Barnstaple' and 'Totnes' in Ivor J. Sanders, *English Baronies: A Study of Their Origin and Descent*, Oxford 1960, and Oswald J. Reichel, 'Some Notes on Devonshire Domesday Identifications', in *Transactions of the Devonshire Association*, xxxiv, 1902, 728–30.

[73] Devon Record Office 312M/TY1; *Regesta*, ii, no. 735; Watkin, I, document 1.

[74] Devon Record Office 312M/TY5; Watkin, I, document 5.

[75] Devon Record Office 312M/TY14; Watkin, I, document 14.

[76] *Praepositus* is a very vague term and is used in the documents cited above to describe both the person keeping the castle and the burgesses of Totnes. One possibility is that the *praepositus* mentioned by the canons of Laon is a castellan involved in a relationship of double homage with Judhael and the Nonant family. I would like to thank Dr Marjorie Chibnall for her comments on this point.

caput of the honour. Whatever the exact nature of this arrangement was, it demonstrates that the behavior of local lords often diverged from what modern scholars might expect.

X

This reconstruction of the life of Judhael of Totnes from 1086 to the 1120s tells us something about the resources and opportunities available to second-rank barons of the early Anglo-Norman period. With good timing and correct political choices, a young baron could succeed in securing a large and valuable honour in south-western England. It should probably be assumed that Judhael received the strategically important honour of Totnes (along with direct control of its *caput*) as a reward for past military services and as part of an ongoing security arrangement. The evidence for naval raids, devastation and value loss in the time of Judhael's tenure suggests that the security problems and Judhael's obligations were very real.

As a manager of his manorial resources, Judhael acted for the most part like the 'first-rank' Domesday landlords who have been studied. He took over the most valuable estates of the honour of Totnes and rewarded his followers with the ones that remained. In 1086 he held about half of his honour's resources in his direct control, but beyond this he did little to change the manorial structure of his lands. In behavior very typical of Anglo-Norman lords, Judhael built a castle and founded a monastery in his new lands.

The picture of the honour of Totnes found in Domesday Book quickly changed. By 1091 Judhael had been dispossessed of his Domesday holdings. Just as a good political choice had brought him the honour of Totnes, a poor choice probably took it away. His influence as lord of Totnes would be erased by his successors, the Nonant family. Although Judhael and his family probably maintained a presence in the town and castle of Totnes, the Nonants controlled the estates that Judhael had controlled in 1086 and considered themselves the founders of the monastery that Judhael had founded a few years before.

His fortunes began to swing upward again in the early years of the reign of Henry I. By 1113 he held another Devon estate, the honour of Barnstaple, and was once again a respectable English baron. He built a castle, at least one church, and founded a new monastery with connections to the powerful and fashionable Cluny. The comparability of his new honour to his old one suggests that care was taken to restore Judhael to his former status and wealth. He died at the Cluniac house of St Martin des Champs in Paris sometime in the 1120s. Unlike his tenure of the honour of Totnes, Judhael's legacy in the honour of Barnstaple was lasting. His descendants controlled the honour well into the thirteenth century and cited him as their most distinguished predecessor. Although Judhael's career is not the story of the meteoric rise of a family into the uppermost ranks of Anglo-Norman magnates, it does help explain how the experiences of an Anglo-Norman baron could have long-lasting effects on the region in which he obtained lands and settled.